Health Studies

Health Studies

A CRITICAL AND CROSS-CULTURAL READER

EDITED BY COLIN SAMSON

BLACKWELL
Publishers

Copyright © Blackwell Publishers Ltd 1999
Editorial selection, arrangement and apparatus copyright © Colin Samson 1999

First published 1999

2 4 6 8 10 9 7 5 3 1

Blackwell Publishers Ltd
108 Cowley Road
Oxford OX4 1JF
UK

Blackwell Publishers Inc.
350 Main Street
Malden, Massachusetts 02148
USA

British Library Cataloguing in Publication Data

A CIP catalogue record for this book is available from the
British Library.

Library of Congress Cataloging-in-Publication Data

Health studies : a critical and cross-cultural reader / edited by Colin Samson.
p. cm.
Includes bibliographical references and index.
ISBN 0–631–20189–0 (hbk; alk. paper)
ISBN 0–631–20190–4 (pbk; alk. paper)
1. Health – Social aspects Cross-cultural studies.   2. Social
medicine Cross-cultural studies.   3. Medical anthropology Cross-
cultural studies.   I. Samson, Colin.
RA418.H3945   1999
306.4′61 – dc21   99–25165   CIP

Typeset in Book Antique 10/12 pt
by Graphicraft Limited, Hong Kong
Printed in Great Britain by TJ International, Padstow, Cornwall

This book is printed on acid-free paper.

CONTENTS

PREFACE

In compiling this book, I have been concerned with the need to bring together diverse forms of knowledge related to fundamental issues of health and illness. One of the most important assumptions I make is that these issues cannot be understood adequately from the point of view of only one academic discipline or profession. This is reflected in the growing popularity of interdisciplinary fields of study such as Cultural Studies, Area Studies and Health Studies. My own training has been in the field of sociology, and I have taught and researched in medical sociology and medical anthropology. I have found the social sciences useful for understanding the ideologies that govern perceptions of health and illness, and they have contributed greatly to documenting the social bases of the distributions of diseases and the organization of health services. However, the social sciences take us only so far.

The primary methods of the social sciences – relying on a prescribed range of techniques – obscure as much as they illuminate. In my research and teaching, I have realized that other disciplines, such as psychology, philosophy and social history, are indispensable for understanding the 'big picture'. In these disciplines, different sorts of assumptions are made and the method of study varies. More-over, the humanities, literature, popular culture and biographical works often contribute insights that would be incapable of emerging from the social science paradigms. The freedom from any accepted method enables a writer such as John Berger, in *A Fortunate Man*, to use his imagination to tell us about the meaning a particular doctor attaches to his work.

This book aims to convey a cross-disciplinary 'Health Studies' for the many students who wish to understand health in the broadest terms. I do not make any effort to summarize the contributions of the various disciplines, partly because any summary would be both inadequate and a caricature. My introductions to the four parts of the book extract what I believe to be meaningful contributions from a variety of different sources. They are not tied together by any academic affinity but rather by their common ability to clearly – and often dramatically –

articulate the subtleties and complexities of health and illness. The reader will find, for example, mentions of writers such as Henry Miller alongside sociologists and health psychologists, and representatives of indigenous communities alongside anthropologists.

The selections are wide and varied. I begin with a difficult reading, Michel Foucault's 'Spaces and Classes'. This comes first not because I wish the book to be a hard slog, but because Foucault's influence on our understandings of health has been so great. Rarely do students receive any introduction to his writing, except through secondary sources. In this book, I affirm the primary text as essential to understanding. One will learn more by grappling with one chapter of Foucault than through a dozen commentaries on his work. To soften the blow, I provide a short synopsis of my understanding of the reading in the introduction to Part I.

In the selections and in my own introductions, I have attempted to convey a *critical* understanding of medicine, especially Western biomedicine. While it is undeniable that biomedicine has had many beneficial effects on individuals, groups and whole societies, I will leave the plaudits to the very effective self-publicity of the medical profession and the mass media. Instead, I concentrate on other implications of medicine and other ways of understanding the body and illness.

Foucault's framing of medicine as a particularly *social* form of scientific perception sets the tone for Part I. This is followed by social historian Ludmilla Jordanova's analysis of medical perception, not merely as a 'clinical gaze', but as a particularly masculine apprehension of the body and illness. We end Part I with anthropologist Paul Rabinow's essay on the Human Genome Initiative. This draws out a logical extension of Foucault's theory, as well as the Cartesian emphasis on the body as primarily a mechanical entity. Part II switches attention to the relationship between the self and illness. Here we look at evidence from the field of social psychology, presented in James Lynch's essay, on the important effect of emotions and human contact on health problems. We then move on to Roger Levin's detailed rendering of the self and cancer, which can be contrasted with Susan Sontag's important essays 'Illness as Metaphor' and 'AIDS and Its Metaphors', which highlight the crucial role of language and social stereotypes in the understanding of both cancer and AIDS. Political scientist Fred Frohock rounds off Part II with his discussion of the role of paranormal and spiritual understandings of illness. As with many other selections in the rest of the book, these dwell on *individual* cases of sufferers and healers.

Part III looks in some detail at the roles of the physician or healer and the doctor–patient relationship. This section presents an empathic portrait of a patient by the neurologist and essayist Oliver Sacks, an account of being a patient by sociologist Arthur Frank, a sociological study of ME sufferers by Lesley Cooper and a portrait of a country doctor by the art critic and essayist John Berger. Part IV examines more global health concerns. It begins with Friedrich Engels' famous exposition of the effects of industrialization on the health of the English working class. We then move to anthropologist Megan Vaughan's study of the colonial role of medicine in Africa. The Alaskan Native writer Harold Napoleon provides an account of the colonial roots of the health problems, especially alcoholism, that the Yup'ik and other native people have been so afflicted with in the twentieth century. We end with a selection from anthropologist Nancy Scheper-Hughes's award-winning book *Death without Weeping* which examines the social and political causes of health problems among shantytown-dwellers in the northeast of Brazil.

Several people have helped in the preparation of this book. I owe a debt to my students at the University of Essex and the University of California at Berkeley, on whom many of the ideas and selections in the book were 'tested out'. Pauline Lane of the University of East London worked with me on the initial concept of the book as well as on the introductory essay in Part I. Rampaul Chamba of the University of California at San Diego read through all of my essays and provided excellent feedback. I am grateful to the Sociology Department at the University of Essex for permitting me a year's study leave in 1997/8. I spent the year as a Visiting Scholar at the Institute for the Study of Social Change at the University of California at Berkeley. While there, Janice Tanegawa, David Minkus, David Wellman and Troy Duster made my stay convivial and memorable and enabled the writing and preparation of this book. I have benefited from Jason Pearce's detailed editing, and I am grateful to him for his hard work. I would also like to thank Connie Hallam and Ann Dean for taking charge of permissions requests and indexing respectively, and Jill Landeryou, Leanda Shrimpton, Lorna Berrett, Joanna Pyke, Sarah Falkus and Rhonda Pearce at Blackwell Publishers for their contributions to the end result.

Colin Samson

ACKNOWLEDGEMENTS

We gratefully acknowledge permission to reproduce copyright material:

John Berger: extract from *A Fortunate Man*, text Copyright © 1967 by John Berger, reprinted by permission of Pantheon Books, a division of Random House, Inc. The reading reproduces the text from pages 62–109, omitting the numerous photographs by Jean Mohr;

Lesley Cooper: 'Myalgic Encephalomyelitis and the Medical Encounter' from *Sociology of Health and Illness*, 19 (1997), Copyright © 1997 Blackwell Publishers/Editorial Board, reprinted by permission of Blackwell Publishers. The reading omits the abstract and 'key words' from the article;

Friedrich Engels: extract from 'The Results of Industrialisation' from *The Condition of the Working Class in England*, translated and edited by W. O. Henderson and W. H. Chaloner, Copyright © 1958 by Basil Blackwell, reprinted by permission of the publishers, Blackwell Publishers and Stanford University Press. The notes in square brackets are editorial notes from the 1958 edition;

Michel Foucault: 'Spaces and Classes' from *The Birth of the Clinic*, translated by A. M. Sheridan-Smith (Tavistock Publications, 1973), reprinted by permission of Routledge;

Arthur W. Frank: 'The Body as Territory and as Wonder' from *At the Will of the Body*, Copyright © 1991 by Arthur W. Frank and Catherine E. Foote, reprinted by permission of Houghton Mifflin Company. All rights reserved;

Fred Frohock: extract from 'Holistic Medicine' from *Healing Powers* (1992), reprinted by permission of the author and the University of Chicago Press;

L. J. Jordanova: extract from 'Natural Facts' in C. MacCormack and M. Strathern (eds), *Nature, Culture and Gender* (1989), reprinted by permission of Cambridge University Press and the author. The reading omits a long acknowledgement note and two plates of an eighteenth-century French wax figure. The References have been edited down to include only those cited in the extract;

Roger Levin: 'Cancer and the Self' from D. M. Levin, *Pathologies of the Modern Self* (1987), reprinted by permission of the publishers, New York University Press;

James J. Lynch: 'Human Contact in Life-Threatening Environments' from *The Broken Heart* (1977), Copyright © 1977 by James J. Lynch, reprinted by permission of BasicBooks, a division of HarperCollins Publishers, Inc. The notes combine the bibliographic endnotes and relevant explanatory footnotes from the original publication;

Harold Napoleon: extract from *Yuuyaraq: The Way of the Human Being* (ANKN, 1991), reprinted by permission of Alaska Native Knowledge Network, University of Alaska Fairbanks;

Paul Rabinow: extract from 'Artificiality and Enlightenment' in Zone 6: *Incorporations*, edited by Jonathan Crary and Sanford Kwinter (New York: Zone Books, 1992), Copyright © 1992 Urzone, Inc, reprinted by permission of Zone Books;

Oliver Sacks: 'The Last Hippie' from the *New York Review of Books*, 22 March 1992, reprinted by permission of The Wylie Agency on behalf of the author;

Nancy Scheper-Hughes: extract from 'Nervoso' from *Death without Weeping: Mother Love and Child Death in Northeast Brazil*, Copyright © 1992 The Regents of the University of California, reprinted by permission of the author, the Regents of the University of California, and the University of California Press. The References have been edited down to include only those cited in the extract;

Susan Sontag: extract from *Aids and Its Metaphors* (Penguin Books, 1989), Copyright © Susan Sontag, 1988, 1989, reprinted by permission of Penguin Books Ltd and Farrar Straus & Giroux; extracts from *Illness as Metaphor* (Penguin Books, 1979), Copyright © Susan Sontag, 1977, 1978, reprinted by permission of Penguin Books Ltd, and The Wylie Agency on behalf of the author;

Megan Vaughan: extract from 'Rats' Tails and Trypanosomes' from *Curing Their Ills: Colonial Power and African Illness*, Copyright © 1991 by Megan Vaughan, reprinted by permission of the publishers, Blackwell Publishers and Stanford University Press. The References have been edited down to include only those cited in the extract;

William Carlos Williams: lines from 'The Injury', Copyright © 1953 by William Carlos Williams, from *Collected Poems Vol. II: 1939–1962* edited by Christopher McGowan (New Directions, 1988), reprinted by permission of New Directions Publishing Corp. and Carcanet Press Ltd.

Despite every effort to trace and contact copyright owners prior to publication this has not always been possible. We apologize for any apparent infringement of copyright and, if notified, we will be pleased to rectify any errors or omissions at the earliest opportunity.

PART I

Biomedicine and the Body

CHAPTER 1

Biomedicine and the Body

> The body of a living person lost all respect and dignity and
> became exactly like a dead body under my gaze and searching
> fingers, and disintegrated in my mind into a jumble of organs
> and dismembered limbs.
> **Nawal El Sadaawi,** *Memoirs of a Woman Doctor*

THE ORIGINS OF THE BIOMEDICAL VIEW OF THE BODY

Biological medicine as it is currently practised, researched and conceived owes much to the radical reformulations of the world that were made during the seventeenth and eighteenth centuries in Europe, during the Enlightenment. The twentieth-century French social philosopher Michel Foucault has helped us understand medicine as a product of specific ideas about the body, the person and illness. Such fundamental medical ideas as the localization of disease in particular organs and of the human body as essentially a material entity became 'objective' knowledge and a basis for medical power. In Foucault's terms, medicine is indebted to new conceptions of 'truth' and methods for ascertaining it that surfaced at this time.

The world-view associated with the Enlightenment was engaged with overturning the culture of the 'Dark Ages' or Middle Ages, thought to be suffused with superstition, primitivism and unreason. In contrast, the scientists, medics and philosophers of the Enlightenment initiated a new search for knowledge and truth, promoting the values of rationalism, empiricism, secularism, liberal tolerance and progress.[1] The scientific apprehension and representation of the world through the newly acquired logical, rational and mathematical techniques lent itself to the development of physical medicine, which emerged at this time as part of the pursuit to define both nature and human life itself in cause-and-effect terms. Broadly, Enlightenment medicine reflected a confidence in scientific methods of observation and experimentation to *control* nature and *intervene* to correct the ailments that seemed to cut life short. Since then the basic scientific assumptions embodied in medicine have proliferated, becoming the bases for a 'profession'. The approach to sickness advocated by the medical profession has now become almost a monopoly by virtue of its legitimization by the state in all Western countries as well as other societies.

By contrast with biological medicine, the medical system operating in Europe from Ancient Greece to the Enlightenment was founded on a belief in the similarity between the bodily order and the cosmic order (see Canguilhem, 1988: 52). Like other, non-European medical systems, the 'old' medical system resisted the idea that humans could substantially intervene to control nature. Greek medicine and much of that practised in the Middle Ages under the influence of Galen (AD *c*.130–*c*.200) assumed a theory of equilibrium, based around four bodily humours, each corresponding to a natural element. Phlegm corresponded to water, blood to air, yellow bile to fire and black bile to earth (see Lowe, 1982: 85). A unity was assumed to connect the humours of the person – the microcosm – with the elements of the world – the cosmos or macrocosm.

The French philosopher René Descartes (1596–1650) is often credited with founding a basic set of principles that overturned the more 'holistic' views of the Middle Ages and in so doing established a model which subsequent medical scientists and doctors have closely followed. In Christian doctrine, and in what would be considered the doctrine of the 'Dark Ages' by advocates of the world-view of the Enlightenment, the soul was an other-worldly essence which was not entirely separate from the body. But it was the soul, not the body, that contained our humanly essence. The soul would either flourish in heaven or roast in hell. The body was merely the mundane, physical representative of the soul on earth. As such it was a transitory phenomenon. The soul was sacred, the body profane; thus, a corrupted body, either diseased, criminal or prone to weaknesses such as adultery, could reflect upon the status of the soul.

Descartes' innovation was to alter the relationship between the soul and the body through putting forward the theory of mind–body dualism.[2] The soul, which was not discarded by Descartes, came to be equated with the mind. The mind/soul entity resided in the body, but Descartes was not certain that it could be located in any particular physical area – at some points he suggested the pineal gland, at other times the brain. From its perch within the body, the mind, through thinking, could direct the body to act. Descartes then established the notion, crucial to modern medicine as we shall see, that the mind, as the repository of our essence or soul, was a separate entity from the body. The mind, as a soul in the body, retained its sacred status as the essence of human existence. Descartes' well-known phrase 'I think, therefore I am' established the mind as the basis of individual identity. Thus, whereas the mind as the new soul was sacred, the body, having severed its spiritual links with the soul, not only continued to be profane but, with developments in scientific method, became a spiritually free-floating physical object, mere matter, operating according to the laws of mechanics. With the body constituted as both separate from what we would call our human essence and purely material, the way was cleared for the medical – what contemporary sociologists call 'biomedical'[3] – understanding of illness and disease as primarily physical in nature.

Some time ago, the philosopher Gilbert Ryle (1949) drew attention to the immense chasm between body and mind that Descartes opened up. Bodies are external and can be freely inspected; bodies occupy space; bodies are public; bodies are physical objects. Minds, on the other hand, are not in public space; they are inner; only the individual truly has access to the workings of his or her own mind and thinking, although inferences as to what people are thinking were later postulated by psychology, psychiatry and psychoanalysis. 'Only our bodies can meet,' stated Ryle (1949: 16), summing up the Cartesian dualism of mind and body. With the mind operating as a metaphysical 'ghost', the body became a 'machine'. As a machine, it became incumbent upon philosophers and medical scientists of the Enlightenment to know the mechanics of the body.[4] The key to the identification, treatment and cure of disease was held to lie in understanding how the body 'worked'.

THE ANATOMY LESSON

By means of physical examination, hospital (rather than home) treatment and anatomical dissections, the body became a material object that could be worked on by the emerging professional class of physicians in Europe. The anatomical dissection was perhaps the most crucial innovation in the development of bio-medical ideas concerning the body. In 1543 the anatomist, doctor and artist Andreas Vesalius of Brussels (1514–64) produced what could be seen as the founding document of Enlightenment medicine, *De Humani Corporis fabrica*, literally 'On the fabric of the human body'. The book consisted of a large number of systematic and detailed anatomical drawings, revealing what had hitherto been unknown to physicians and scientists because of the medieval strictures against surgery which emanated from the theological doctrine of the sanctity of the body. As contemporary sociologist Bryan Turner (1992: 50) paraphrased this doctrine, '[w]hat God had closed within the body should not be opened for secular purposes by the surgeon.' The effect of Vesalius's work was to bring to light new 'facts' about the internal structure and functioning of the body which differed from accepted Christian principles. Importantly, Vesalius also differed from the primary authority in physiology and anatomy, Galen, whose work was based on animal anatomy. In breaking with both the dominant scientific and religious convictions of the time, Vesalius, through the methods of dissection and experiment, became *the* source for obtaining facts of human anatomy (Hall, 1954: 50).

Anatomical dissections began in Europe in the sixteenth century in the form of anatomy lessons performed by surgeons for students. These lessons were held in amphitheatres and were open to the public, becoming spectacles of scientific wonder, testaments to the skill and knowledge of the surgeon, and mass enter-tainment. Anatomy lessons were institutionalized in Holland, and it is from these lessons that Rembrandt's famous painting *The Anatomy Lesson of Dr. Nicholaes Tulp* (*c*.1632) is taken. The group portrait of Tulp with members of the Guild of Surgeons depicts the surgeon dissecting the arm and hand of a corpse on a slab.[5] Sociologically, the anatomy lesson was a critical stage in the development of biomedicine. The open and public display of the corpse signified the triumph of scientific investigation and rationalism over theological conceptions of the sanctity and dignity of the body and the intimate correspondences between body and soul.

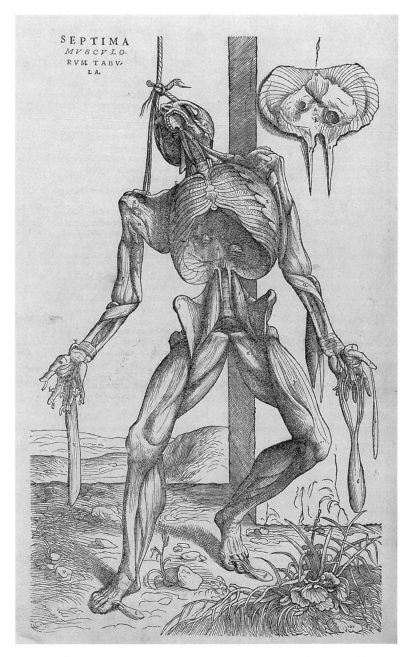

Figure 1.1 Illustration from Andreas Vesalius, *De Humani Corporis fabrica*, 1543
By permission of the British Library, C.54.k.12.

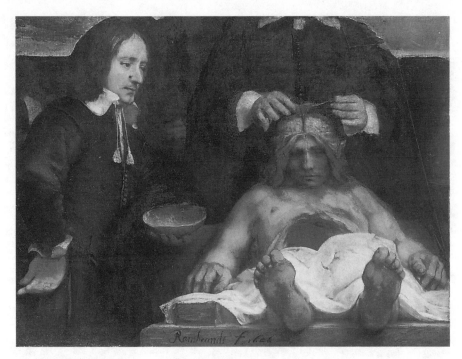

Figure 1.2   Rembrandt, *The Anatomy Lesson of Dr. Joan Deyman*, 1656
Amsterdams Historisch Museum.

Another important aspect of anatomical dissections is the close link between the development of the science of anatomy and capital punishment. In England, many of the subjects of dissections were executed prisoners whose bodies were either purchased by the surgeons from executioners or obtained by illegal means such as grave-robbing. The dissection was a further act of defilement and vengeance against the person. The fear of the dissecting table was as great as the fear of the gallows. In eighteenth-century London there were several riots against the surgeons who came to Tyburn, the primary site in the capital for public executions, to procure bodies. Over time, the usefulness of corpses declined, but the practice of dissecting criminals continued. According to Linebaugh (1975: 76), '[e]xcept for a minority of surgeons and sympathetic observers, dissection was considered less as a necessary method for enlarging the understanding of *homo corpus* than as a mutilation of the dead person, a form of aggravating capital punishment.'

The connections between medical science and this 'aggravating capital punishment' are clearly represented in some of the art of the seventeenth and eighteenth centuries. Rembrandt's *The Anatomy Lesson of Dr. Joan Deyman* (figure 1.2), painted in 1656, shows the dissection of the stomach and skull of a prisoner who had been hanged for theft. Because of the slightness of his crime, he was given a

Figure 1.3   Hogarth, *The Reward of Cruelty*, engraving, 1751
From *Engravings by Hogarth*, edited by S. Shesgreen, New York: Dover Publications Inc., 1973.

Christian burial. Emphasizing not the cruelty of the surgeons but the moral lesson
that those who live as criminals and degenerates will end up on the surgeon's
slab is William Hogarth's anatomy lesson engraving of 1751 *The Reward of
Cruelty* (figure 1.3). The engraving is accompanied by a poem by the Reverend
James Townley which states that this hideous fate – the dead man still has the

noose around his neck, a rope and pulley attached to a bolt fastened into his skull hold his head aloft, and his stomach, slit open with a surgeon's knife, spills out entrails which are being sniffed by a mongrel – is the consequence of a life of rape and murder.

Our first reading, 'Spaces and Classes', is the first chapter of **Michel Foucault**'s influential work *The Birth of the Clinic*. We begin with Foucault because it is his approach – which he defines elsewhere as the genealogical or archaeological method – which so clearly informs any critical understanding of health and illness. In particular, *The Birth of the Clinic* establishes medicine as a form of perception, the history of which is chronicled by Foucault in the remainder of his book. 'Spaces and Classes' represents merely a first phase in his history of medical perception. For Foucault, the medical understanding of illness was bound up with the identification of body parts and functions through a form of 'mapping' on the anatomical atlas (see also Armstrong, 1983). Anatomical drawings clearly followed from the idea of the body as a transparent object. They were a means of rendering the cells, tissues, organs and flesh into patterns. These patterns could provide clues to bodily functions and relationships, as well as to shades of normality and abnormality. As represented in anatomical drawings, the body became something that was defined as separate from the person. The goal of medicine, in Foucault's view, is to 'subtract' and 'abstract' the patient, who becomes 'an external fact to the disease'. In medical encounters, the persons of the doctor and the patient are simply 'disturbances' that must be brushed aside in order that the complexities of the disease entity can be apprehended. Most of what Foucault elaborates is a rich description of the various social conventions which comprise this 'gaze' in terms of the configuration and localization of disease.

It is very much in this spirit that Foucault refers to the 'clinical gaze', which is a pervasive mode of perception deployed inside the medical institution, the clinic or hospital. It is in these clinical settings that the theory and practice of medicine come together (see also Komesaroff, 1995: 76). Foucault suggests not only that the way that physicians 'look' (gaze) upon the body is a representation of the subjectivities of the perception of the physician, but also that such gazes manufacture and perpetuate distinctive power relations. Medical knowledge that is the product of the clinical gaze establishes an authoritative 'truth' about the body and the person. And, as such, definitions and identifications that emerge from observations of the physical body and its movements and behaviour produce power. Such observations, which eventually form the basis for the medical categorization of illness, ignore the individual patient as a person. As soon as definitions, categories and taxonomies are formalized in texts and taken to be sources of authority, medical power is expressed in the routines, rituals and bureaucracies of hospitals and clinics.

Although we popularly think of the hospital as an institution for the healing of the sick, as Foucault tells us several times in the reading it also *produces* sickness. At least until twentieth-century procedures to ensure hygiene and asepsis, the collection of all the sick in one place led to cross-infection of patients. Indeed, cross-infection is still a peril of hospitalization in Western countries. A recent medical report in Britain (Office of Health Economics, 1997) stated that one in ten British hospital patients suffers from an infection contracted after admission, and that 5,000 patients die each year as a result of such infections. In 1997 a leading sports-injury clinic in Paris infected hundreds of patients with a tuberculosis bacterium (Henley, 1997).

THE BODY AS MACHINE

With the anatomy lesson and other developments in physiology such as William Harvey's notable finding of the circulation of blood, and hence the 'pumping' action of the heart (presented in his *Anatomical Essay on the Motion of the Heart and Blood in Animals*, 1628), the mind–body dualism articulated by Descartes in his *Meditations on First Philosophy* (1641) could be grafted on to seventeenth-century medico-scientific ideas to provide a solid turn towards the notion of the body as a machine. Descartes himself compared the body to a clock, which could operate mechanically without a mind. The laws of nature, Descartes suggested, became heavily bound up with the mechanical structure and behaviour of matter (see Sorrell, 1987: 35–7).

Although Descartes actually argued that divine arrangement – and not mechanics – explained the connection between the mind's experiences and the body's actions (Sorrell, 1987: 91), gradually more secular machine analogies appeared in the writings of European philosophers, medical practitioners and scientists. Giorgio Baglivi (1668–1706), a Professor of Anatomy at Rome, illustrates this tendency:

> Whoever examines the bodily organism will certainly not fail to discern pincers in the jaws and teeth; a container in the stomach; watermains in the veins, the arteries and other ducts; a piston in the heart; sieves or filters in the bowels; in the lungs, bellows; in the muscles, the force of the lever; in the corner of the eye a pulley, and so on . . . It remains unquestionable that all these phenomena must be seen in the forces of the wedge, of equilibrium, of the lever, of the spring, and of all the other principles of mechanics. (quoted by Synnott, 1992: 93)

Over time, the medical concentration on the machine-like nature of the body proceeded by shedding the Cartesian emphasis on the metaphysical nature of the mind or soul. As science became increasingly secularized and scientists felt less obliged to refer to the existence of other-worldly and non-material phenomena, the mind or soul also came to be considered in mechanical terms, analogous to those for the body. In 1748 Julien Offroy de La Mettrie published *L'Homme Machine*, a work of medicine and philosophy which attacked the Cartesian metaphysical soul by proposing a material or bodily soul, scorning the 'speculation' of physicians and praising the empirical demonstrations of surgeons. In the treatment of the sick, La Mettrie viewed the mind as dependent on the body (see Wellman, 1992).

By dispensing with the presence of a nebulous soul, the purely rational and materialist approach to the body has proceeded to the present. From the twentieth

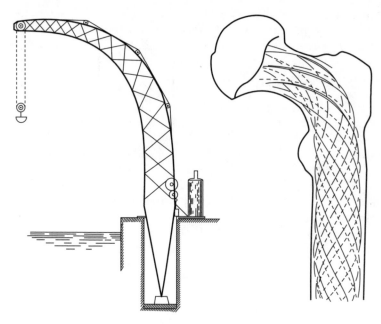

Figure 1.4(a)   The construction of the upper end of the thigh-bone, as depicted by Professor F. Dixon, compared with a drawing of Fairbairn's crane (W. Finerty)
Source: Keith (1919).

century we can find articulations of the body as machine which differ only in detail from those of Baglivi three centuries earlier. *The Engines of the Human Body*, a book by Arthur Keith, Professor of the Royal College of Surgeons, published in 1919, offered the view that the body in all of its *parts* – and this segmentation of the body is critical to the machine analogy – can be seen as a superior internal-combustion engine. According to Keith, the body, like the machine, maintains a constant temperature through cooling mechanisms. The main combustion chamber, the heart, is cooled by sweating in the summer and shivering in winter. The muscles of the leg are like the sprocket and chain of a motorcycle (Keith, 1919). Several decades later the same trope appears in almost identical fashion: 'It is impossible to imagine how anyone could have made sense of the heart before we knew what a pump was,' declared Jonathan Miller (1978: 10), a popular British doctor, in the book that followed from his BBC television series 'The Body in Question'. For Miller, 'before the invention of automatic gun-turrets, there was no model to explain the finesse of voluntary muscular movement.' Miller implies that the invention of certain types of mechanical device was *required* for medical knowledge. Because machines supplied the essential metaphors and language, it is as if we could not even speak of the body before their invention.

Because they are always being created, improved and recreated, machines constantly supply new sources of analogy. While the imagery used to describe

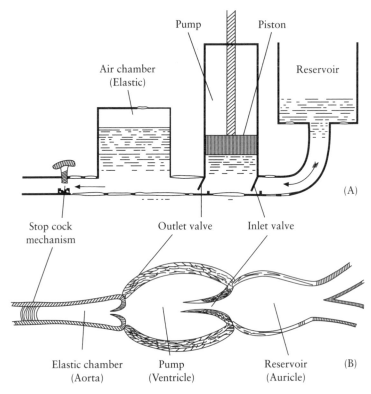

Pump   Piston

Air chamber   Reservoir
(Elastic)

(A)

Stop cock   Outlet valve   Inlet valve
mechanism

Elastic chamber   Pump   Reservoir   (B)
(Aorta)   (Ventricle)   (Auricle)

Figure 1.4(b)   The various parts of a force-pump (A) compared with the parts of the left ventricular pump (B)

Source: Keith (1919).

and understand the body and disease in contemporary scientific medicine is now diverse and nuanced (using, for example, the jargon of computing in recent times), the machine analogy persists and has not been displaced by other metaphors. Not only is there an obduracy to the machine analogy, but the pervasive use of computer technology in medicine and elsewhere has rendered the distinction between humans and machines more difficult to sustain. Humans are not just apprehended and represented by the computer and the descriptive language which accompanies it; machines, often computer-driven or -designed, have now become 'spare parts' for humans. This has led Donna Haraway (1991, 1997: 126–7) to refer to a new type of human/machine being as a 'cyborg', a hybrid composed of both organic matter and machinery.

THE GENDERED BODY

Following from an analysis of medicine as a social and cultural form of perception, the body can be understood as 'discursive' and 'socially constructed' rather than as an anatomical given. The notion of medicine as a form of discourse, a language which actually creates a subject, is taken up quite explicitly by our other two authors in this part.

The second reading, 'Natural Facts' by the social historian **Ludmilla Jordanova,** examines the role of gender in the development of science and medicine, emphasizing that women's bodies have consistently been associated with 'nature' as a consequence of their having a child-bearing capacity. Jordanova suggests that women's bodies have always been conceived of in opposition to men as well as in relation to nature. The differentiation between nature and culture as different ontological spheres in Enlightenment thought has been important to the perception of women's bodies as primarily natural, fertile, child-bearing entities. Many European philosophers and scientists associated women with nature and emotion, while men were viewed as operating in the spheres of culture and rationality. This sexual polarization became even more defined in the nineteenth century as capitalism fully displaced feudalism, removing many women from craft and other work in its wake. The occupational and professional world of work became sharply counterposed to the domestic sphere of the home. The former symbolized the public, rational and masculine domain, the latter, the private, emotive and feminine zone. It was given manifold expression in Britain by physicians, scientists, philosophers and politicians. Lowe (1982: 103) cites the 1842 *Encyclopaedia Britannica* to illustrate this dichotomy:

> The man, bold and vigorous, is qualified for being a protector; the woman, delicate and timid, requires protection. Hence it is that man never admires a woman for possessing bodily strength or personal courage; and women always despise men who are totally destitute of these qualities. The man, as protector, is directed by nature to govern; the woman, conscious of inferiority, is disposed to obey. Their intellectual powers correspond to the destination of nature . . .

Although Foucault did not consider gender in 'Spaces and Classes', it is important to understand the clinical gaze as a masculine gaze, informed by the belief that observed social differences between the sexes are themselves rooted in nature. The *de facto* exclusion of women from the practice of professional medicine meant that medical discourse was formulated almost entirely by men. This same discourse – one of differential sexual, physical and psychological health – infused the arguments used to exclude women from the profession and to promulgate sexist ideas within medicine.

The exclusion of women from the medical profession was predicated on a number of observations. In nineteenth-century Europe and North America, women were viewed as less suited for educational and scientific pursuits such as medicine because of their biological constitutions – their weaknesses, emotions, smaller brains and reproductive roles (see Sayers, 1982; Bonner, 1992: 6–12). However, the 1858 Medical Act establishing the basis for the registration of doctors in Britain did not exclude women. Although the law was very clear, universities did not admit women for medical education and examination and hence entry onto the medical register. Only a few British women were able to practise medicine in the nineteenth century, and these were mostly those who had already trained abroad. Not until the turn of the twentieth century was it that these practices were (reluctantly) rescinded. Eventually, in 1975, the quota system operating in medical schools was abolished by an Act of Parliament (the Sex Discrimination Act), enabling women to enter the profession on an equal basis with men. Even though today nearly half of all newly qualified doctors in Britain are female, the top echelons of the medical profession are still disproportionately male. In 1989 only 15 per cent of hospital consultants were female. In the high-prestige field of surgery, women accounted for just 3 per cent of consultants, while they represented 20 per cent of anaesthetists and 26 per cent of psychiatrists, both low-prestige specialities (Department of Health, 1991: 21).

Until recently, then, physicians were primarily men. However, before the association of healing with modern science, women figured prominently as medical authorities and healers. As Blake (1990: 15) argued, '[e]vidence suggests that, from the Middle Ages on, women constituted the majority of health carers, fulfilling the role of doctor, in diagnosing and prescribing treatment, and the role of nurse, in tending the sick.' One of the best known cases in point is midwifery, an exclusively female province until the seventeenth century. With the emergence of scientific medicine and the sharp attacks on the methods of midwives by medical men – including William Harvey, who championed the use of forceps in child-delivery (see Merchant, 1980: 149–63) – women were gradually displaced. Over the centuries, medicine has reflected the ideologies and modes of perception of such men as much as it has the various classificatory conventions that Foucault so richly elaborated. The male bias towards technological solutions for bodily ailments and functions has become part of the inheritance of medical science.

Importantly, Jordanova argues that it was not just the visible aspects of the body that the physicians sought to unveil, but also the elusive quality that made a woman, especially in terms of aesthetic beauty. The mapping of women's bodies, like the medical use of executed prisoners, represented an extension of the clinical gaze. Having an affinity with broader social and political attitudes, medicine provided support for the patriarchal control of women's sexuality and social rights. The medical construction of the female body, Jordanova suggests, played a vital role in the subordination of women in Western societies. It gathered legitimacy and power from being founded on purportedly 'objective' understandings of the anatomy and physiology of womanhood, and of the relationship between the body and public life. Thus, women were frequently portrayed as weak, emotional and in need of male protection, with masculine power being legitimated through alleged biological superiority.

TECHNO-ANATOMY

Not only has medicine constructed a similarity between the human body and the machine, but it has used machines as means to understand, observe and enter the body. All manner of mechanical devices have been employed in the service of

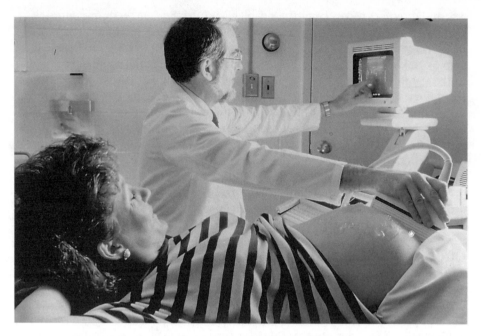

Figure 1.5   Pregnant woman undergoing ultrasound examination
Science Photo Library/Will and Deni McIntyre.

apprehending and treating disease. Mechanical technology has served as a crucial determinant of the directions pursued in the development of biomedicine. While historically physicians diagnosed through the outward appearance of disease, perceiving the clinical manifestations with their own senses, disease is increasingly apprehended and mediated through machines (see Reisner, 1978; Khushf 1977: 151). Not only are these apparatuses used as means to represent disease, they are increasingly becoming the treatments for disorders of the body – limbs can be simulated by prostheses, organs can be artificially produced and life-support machines can keep diseased or comatose bodies 'alive'.

In contemporary medical practice, a synchronicity between the human as machine and the machine as a healer presents itself. A 1993 special issue of *Scientific American* celebrating the achievements of medicine began by illustrating the current state of the field with glossy photographs of a child in an oxygen balloon, a team of surgeons doing open-heart surgery, a colour scan photograph of the head, an ultrasound of a pregnant woman, a CAT scan, a man with artificial limbs playing basketball and the AIDS quilt. With the exception of the quilt, all of the pictures depicted machines as solving problems of the body. What was celebrated was the health of the machine-like humans, who owed their recovery to the powers of the machines, and of the doctors manipulating them.

The image of the human body as a machine facilitates the development of the machine as healer. This is especially prominent in the arena of reproductive health, where the recent discovery of the problem of infertility in Western countries, in particular, has lent itself to an almost exclusive focus on mechanical solutions.[6] *In vitro* fertilization, embryo transfer techniques and surrogate motherhood all employ mechanical means to achieve conception, relegating women (and men) to the status of passive objects. As Oakley (1987: 39) has remarked, 'it is now technologically possible to ignore the status of pregnant women as human beings'. In its emphasis on artificially induced mechanical conception, biomedicine continually breaks through new barriers to motherhood, making conception and childbirth attainable for an ever growing range of women. The implications of these technologies are profound. What was historically a 'natural' process of reproduction, involving heterosexual copulation, has now become something that can achieve its aims without this kind of intimacy. Babies can be born without their parents ever having sex. They can be born to homosexual parents. The possibilities of parenthood are now limitless. Instead of devoting scientific energy to the factors which predispose women and men to infertility or to the problems surrounding the raising of the world's millions of parentless children, the important medical puzzles, and those which are accorded prestige within the community of medical scientists, are those connected with the expansion of conception. A mother, in this process, is little more than a vessel, and a father is a test-tube sperm. The resultant baby, who must be looked after, is seen as an end in itself, with, as Oakley (1987) again observed, little attention paid to what happens after the delivery.

With the emergence of ever more sophisticated imaging technology such as ultra-scans and magnetic resonance imaging, the patient's body has become removed not only from the person – this was Foucault's point – but from the diagnostic process. Viewing the body through imaging, the physician or 'technician' can further abstract or subtract the physical, corporeal body itself. Bodies become reconfigured into landscapes, graphs, maps and colour resonates. The way that technology 'frames' and gives meaning to the body is drawn from medicine as well as the creators of the technology. These 'creators' are computer graphic designers who recreate the visual representation of the body. As the body parts are depicted on a flat computer screen, they can be enhanced, replicated, enlarged, reduced, recorded and recreated. This new techno-anatomy presents the human body as if it were a new geography, an unmapped landscape, almost as if it were a new territory to be colonized, named and controlled.

As technological medicine expands, it manufactures new ways of understanding and displaying the body. One recent expression of this is the Visible Human Project set up by the National Library of Medicine (NLM) in the United States. In 1991 the NLM created a digital transverse cross-section of the cadaver of a 39-year-old male. This was done by embedding the corpse in gelatine, then freezing it and slicing it from head to toe, cut across at one millimetre intervals. Each layer was exposed and a colour photograph taken (Lorensen, 1996: 2). Out of this, a three-dimensional dataset has been created. Over 1,800 images of the sliced and recreated three-dimensional body are available for global display via the Internet, where a techno-anatomy lesson is unveiled before the eyes of all who log on. Fittingly, the first cadaver used for this project was that of a convicted murderer who had donated his body to science. This *global* display of a convicted prisoner's body begs comparison with the close association historically between anatomy lessons and punishment. The 'lesson' which was a dreaded humiliation of the offender is now a mawkish donation of death-row convicts finding redemption in global digital examination.

Imaging technology fragments the human body into cell-lines, graphs and colour codes. The patient is rendered as a universalized datum, disconnected from both any tangible, corporeal body and the sentient human being, becoming an image that can be moved through computer networks anywhere around the world. Understanding such a patient does not require human touch.

The final reading in the section is taken from the work of the American anthropologist **Paul Rabinow**. In analysing the impact of one of the biggest genetic projects undertaken, the Human Genome Project, Rabinow suggests that the project extends processes of dissection and fragmentation of the body to the limit. It moves medicine into concerns that transcend immediate visibility. One implication of genetic mapping, according to Rabinow, is the possibility of individual identity becoming an imposed genetic identity. He envisages that, just as the early maps of the body defined power relations between doctors and lay people, as well as between men and women, genetic mapping creates new hierarchies and forms of social order. With the heightening of concern over the economic costs of health care, identity could be conferred in relation to the genetic risk of disease.

This would accord with the growing proliferation of knowledge from the field of medical genetics, which is being widely generalized and universalized as definitive of individual and group health. Even though most genetic tests can reveal only a probability of or predisposition to a disease, the various kinds of screening procedure are used as an axis of social, as well as medical, inclusion and exclusion. For example, in the United States people with sickle-cell conditions were subject to screening under the 1972 National Sickle Cell Anaemia Control Act. Even though this and other carrier-screening procedures only define a *probability* for disease, they could have serious social and political implications for African-Americans, who, along with people of Mediterranean descent, are known to suffer disproportionately from sickle-cell anaemia. Screening can result in exclusion from health insurance and certain professions; and, in some states of the USA, 'at risk' citizens are not allowed to apply for a marriage licence, or schooling for their children, without a sickle-cell test. Genetic screening information is of particular interest to insurers and health care providers because it gives them an estimate of the probable future costs of patients and even unborn children. There is already evidence that many employers in the United States are using genetic tests to eliminate workers who may be susceptible to particular toxins instead of making the workplace cleaner and safer (see Draper, 1991).

As Troy Duster (1990) has argued in his *Backdoor to Eugenics*, medical genetics now raises the strong possibility that technology will be used for eugenic purposes. Eugenics, which literally means 'noble in heredity', is the practice of promoting the reproduction of those deemed most biologically and intellectually 'fit' (positive eugenics) and preventing that of the 'unfit' (negative eugenics). While there were no specific positive eugenics policies, negative eugenics was carried out on a widespread scale in the United States and Germany. In the United States, eugenics dominated discussions of the concept of mental defect or feeble-mindedness from 1900 to 1920. While segregation in institutions or 'colonies' and sterilization were the two major ways of treating 'defective stock' in the USA, in Nazi Germany eugenic science informed genocidal acts carried out against Jews, gypsies and the mentally ill (see Kevles, 1985, 1992).

Once again, there is a prospect of using genetics as a means of filtering out not only individuals, but whole groups who are deemed not to be 'healthy' or to contain excessive risks of pathology. This, Duster believes, is politically motivated. Thus, it is no accident that in the United States screening for Tay–Sachs disease and for sickle-cell anaemia were carried out in completely different ways. Tay–Sachs disease is a fatal degenerative disease that primarily affects Ashkenazi Jews. Screening for it between 1965 and 1985 was carried out on a voluntary basis and elicited the support of the Jewish community. Screening for sickle-cell anaemia, a much less fatal disease principally affecting African-Americans, on the other hand, was made compulsory and undertaken with little consultation with African-American communities. In 1968 the Nobel laureate Linus Pauling, recalling Nazi rituals, suggested that carriers of sickle-cell genes ought to be tattooed on the forehead so that they would refrain from falling in love with one another. The difference between the two approaches to screening, according to Duster (1990: 46–7), lies in the fact that Jews, as a group, are more likely to be wealthy, successful and influential, while African-Americans are heavily concentrated in the poorest sectors of American society.

If Rabinow's vision proves correct, the experiences of African-Americans could represent merely one unfortunate facet of an overall geneticization of life. People could be allocated new identities through their genes, creating new biosocial and chromosomatic groups. At the time of writing, Rabinow could not have foreseen that the cloning of a sheep in Scotland, ironically called 'Dolly', was to raise the stakes for human genetics research. As health researchers and biotechnology companies have begun to concentrate their efforts on identifying ever more genetic markers for disease and techniques of altering human DNA have developed, individuals and their environments have become subordinated to more abstractly material factors.

What has been described in this introduction, and what is traced in the three readings, is a brief history of the role of the body in Western biomedicine. It begins with a chronology of medical perception, which has been characterized as materialist in its focus on the corporeal body, yet at the same time abstract in its removal of the body from the soul and from the person. This form of perception is heavily influenced by social biases and prejudices, such as those around the role of punishment and the place of women in society. Currently, the Human Genome Project presents a logical extension of the medical obsession with the body as a machine. It, too, is materialist and abstract in the ways indicated, and it incorporates social and political prejudices surrounding the definitions of diseases and the kinds of people deemed susceptible to them. Yet it is virtually a quantum leap in abstraction, in that genes can be manufactured and implanted completely independently of the person as a human being. While this might be characterized as a move from the modern to the postmodern condition, it is certainly the case that the kinds of practices described by Rabinow and made policy and science through eugenics were only possible through a prior scientific and medical conception of the body as machine, separate from the person.

Notes

1. Useful introductions to the ideas of the Enlightenment are provided by Cassirer (1964), Lively (1966) and Brown (1979).
2. Descartes' ideas are complex and subtle. For more detailed information the non-specialist reader should consult Williams (1978) and Sorrell (1987) among the many introductions to Descartes.
3. It is important to make this terminological distinction. 'Medical' technically may refer to a very wide range of approaches to illness and healing that are outside of the medical tradition which we identify as emanating from the European Enlightenment. Because this tradition, as opposed to, say, Chinese, Ayurvedic, Native American, African, homeopathic and even Ancient Greek medical systems, has been predicated on a materialist and biological conception of the human body, it is referred to as 'biomedicine'. A clear explication of the use of the term 'biomedicine' is provided by O'Connor (1994: 5).
4. This should not be taken to mean that this was the *only* philosophy underpinning medicine. As Porter (1990: 49) has pointed out, somatic ideas still persisted after Descartes.
5. A detailed account of this painting and its relationship to the culture and practice of anatomy lessons is provided by Heckscher (1958).
6. The use of the word 'discovery' is intentional. Farquhar (1996: 83) has noted that infertility is the only medical condition in which the patient must articulate a 'desire' in order that the condition be recognized. The diagnosis is merely a recognition of that desire.

References

Armstrong, David (1983), *The Political Anatomy of the Body: Medical Knowledge in Britain in the Twentieth Century*, Cambridge: Cambridge University Press.
Blake, Catriona (1990), *The Charge of the Parasols: Women's Entry to the Medical Profession*, London: The Women's Press.
Bonner, Thomas Neville (1992), *To the Ends of the Earth: Women's Search for Education in Medicine*, Cambridge, MA: Harvard University Press.
Brown, S. C. (1979) (ed.), *Philosophers of the Enlightenment*, Brighton: Harvester.
Canguilhem, Georges (1988), *Ideology and Rationality in the History of the Life Sciences*, translated by Arthur Goldhammer, Cambridge, MA: MIT Press.
Cassirer, Ernst (1964), *The Philosophy of the Enlightenment*, Boston, MA: Beacon.

Department of Health (1991), *Women Doctors and Their Careers: Report of the Joint Working Party*, London: Department of Health.

Draper, Elaine (1991), *Risky Business: Genetic Testing and Exclusionary Practices in the Hazardous Workplace*, Cambridge: Cambridge University Press.

Duster, Troy (1990), *Backdoor to Eugenics*, New York: Routledge.

Farquhar, Dion (1996), *The Other Machine: Discourse and Reproductive Technologies*, New York: Routledge.

Foucault, Michel (1980), *Power/Knowledge: Selected Interviews and Other Writings 1972–1977*, translated by Colin Gordon, Brighton: Harvester.

Hall, A. R. (1954), *The Scientific Revolution 1500–1800: The Formation of the Modern Scientific Attitude*, Boston, MA: Beacon.

Haraway, Donna (1991), *Simians, Cyborgs and Women: The Reinvention of Nature*, New York: Routledge.

—— (1997), *Modest_Witness@Second_Millennium.FemaleMan_Meets_OncoMouse: Feminism and Technoscience*, New York: Routledge.

Heckscher, William (1958), *Rembrandt's Anatomy of Dr. Nicholaes Tulp*, New York: New York University Press.

Henley, John (1997), 'Threat of TB Kept from Patients of Paris Clinic', *The Guardian*, 16 September, p. 10.

Keith, Arthur (1919), *The Engines of the Human Body: Being the Substance of Christmas Lectures Given at the Royal Institution of Great Britain, Christmas 1916–1917*, London: Williams and Norgate.

Kevles, Daniel (1985), *In the Name of Eugenics: Genetics and the Uses of Human Heredity*, Berkeley: University of California Press.

—— (1992), 'Out of Eugenics: The Historical Politics of the Human Genome', in Daniel Kevles and Leroy Hood (eds), *The Code of Codes: Scientific and Social Issues in the Human Genome Project*, Cambridge, MA: Harvard University Press, 3–36.

Khushf, George (1997), 'Why Bioethics Need the Philosophy of Medicine: Some Implications of Reflection on Concepts of Health and Disease', *Theoretical Medicine*, 18(2): 145–63.

Komesaroff, Paul (1995), 'From Bioethics to Microethics: Ethical Debate and Clinical Medicine', in Paul Komesaroff (ed.), *Troubled Bodies: Critical Perspectives on Postmodernism, Medical Ethics and the Body*, Durham, NC: Duke University Press, 62–86.

Linebaugh, Peter (1975), 'The Tyburn Riot against the Surgeons', in Douglas Hay et al. (eds), *Albion's Fatal Tree: Crime and Society in Eighteenth Century England*, New York: Pantheon, 65–118.

Lively, J. F. (1966), *The Enlightenment*, London: Longmans.

Lorensen, B. (1996), *Marching through the Visible Man*, Internet web site, http://www.crd.ge.com/esl/egsp/projects/vm/.

Lowe, Donald (1982), *History of Bourgeois Perception*, Chicago, IL: University of Chicago Press.

Martin, Emily (1992), *The Woman in the Body: A Cultural Analysis of Reproduction*, 2nd edn, Boston, MA: Beacon.

Merchant, Carolyn (1980), *The Death of Nature: Women, Ecology and the Scientific Revolution*, New York: Harper and Row.

Miller, Jonathan (1978), *The Body in Question*, New York: Random House.

Nelkin, Dorothy (1992), 'The Social Power of Genetic Information', in Daniel Kevles and Leroy Hood (eds), *The Code of Codes: Scientific and Social Issues in the Human Genome Project*, Cambridge, MA: Harvard University Press, 177–90.

Oakley, Ann (1987), 'From Walking Wombs to Test Tube Babies', in Michelle Stanworth (ed.), *Reproductive Technologies: Gender, Motherhood and Medicine*, Oxford: Polity, 36–56.

O'Connor, Bonnie Blair (1994), *Healing Traditions: Alternative Medicine and the Health Professions*, Philadelphia, PA: University of Pennsylvania Press.

Office of Health Economics (1997), *Acquired Hospital Infections*, London: OHE.

Porter, Roy (1990), 'Barely Touching: A Social Perspective on Mind and Body', in G. S. Rousseau (ed.), *Languages of Psyche: Mind and Body in Enlightenment Thought*, Clark Library Lectures 1985–1986, Berkeley, CA: University of California Press, 45–80.

Reiser, Stanley Joel (1978), *Medicine and the Reign of Technology*, Cambridge: Cambridge University Press.

Ryle, Gilbert (1949), *The Concept of Mind*, Harmondsworth: Penguin.

El Sadaawi, Nawal (1989), *Memoirs of a Woman Doctor*, San Francisco: City Lights Books.

Sayers, Janet (1982), *Biological Politics*, London: Tavistock.

Sorrell, Tom (1987), *Descartes*, Oxford: Oxford University Press.

Synnott, Anthony (1992), 'Tomb, Temple, Machine and Self: The Social Construction of the Body', *British Journal of Sociology*, 43(1): 79–110.

Turner, Bryan (1992), *Regulating Bodies: Essays in Medical Sociology*, London: Routledge.

Wellman, Kathleen (1992), *La Mettrie: Medicine, Philosophy and Enlightenment*, Durham, NC: Duke University Press.

Williams, Bernard (1978), *Descartes: The Project of Pure Enquiry*, Harmondsworth: Penguin.

CHAPTER 2

Spaces and Classes

Michel Foucault

For us, the human body defines, by natural right, the space of origin and of distribution of disease: a space whose lines, volumes, surfaces, and routes are laid down, in accordance with a now familiar geometry, by the anatomical atlas. But this order of the solid, visible body is only one way—in all likelihood neither the first, nor the most fundamental—in which one spatializes disease. There have been, and will be, other distributions of illness.

When will we be able to define the structures that determine, in the secret volume of the body, the course of allergic reactions? Has anyone ever drawn up the specific geometry of a virus diffusion in the thin layer of a segment of tissue? Is the law governing the spatialization of these phenomena to be found in a Euclidean anatomy? After all, one only has to remember that the old theory of sympathies spoke a vocabulary of correspondences, vicinities, and homologies, terms for which the perceived space of anatomy hardly offers a coherent lexicon. Every great thought in the field of pathology lays down a configuration for disease whose spatial requisites are not necessarily those of classical geometry.

The exact superposition of the 'body' of the disease and the body of the sick man is no more than a historical, temporary datum. Their encounter is self-evident only for us, or, rather, we are only just beginning to detach ourselves from it. The space of *configuration* of the disease and the space of *localization* of the illness in the body have been superimposed, in medical experience, for only a relatively short period of time—the period that coincides with nineteenth-century medicine and the privileges accorded to pathological anatomy. This is the period that marks the suzerainty of the gaze, since in the same perceptual field, following the same continuities or the same breaks, experience reads at a glance the visible lesions of the organism and the coherence of pathological forms; the illness is articulated exactly on the body, and its logical distribution is carried out at once in terms of anatomical masses. The 'glance' has simply to exercise its right of origin over truth.

But how did this supposedly natural, immemorial right come about? How was this locus, in which disease indicated its presence, able to determine in so sovereign a way the figure that groups its elements together? Paradoxically, never was the space of configuration of disease more free, more independent of its space of localization than in classificatory medicine, that is to say, in that form of medical thought that, historically, just preceded the anatomo-clinical method, and made it structurally possible.

'Never treat a disease without first being sure of its species,' said Gilibert.[1] From the *Nosologie* of Sauvages (1761) to the *Nosographie* of Pinel (1798), the classificatory rule dominates medical theory and practice: it appears as the immanent logic of morbid forms, the principle of their decipherment, and the semantic rule of their definition: 'Pay no heed to those envious men who would cast the shadow of contempt over the writings of the celebrated Sauvages. . . . Remember that of all the doctors who have ever lived he is perhaps the only one to have subjected all our dogmas to the infallible rules of healthy logic. Observe with what care he defines his words, with what scrupulousness he circumscribes the definitions of each malady.' Before it is removed from the density of the body, disease is given an organization, hierarchized into families, genera, and species. Apparently, this is no more than a 'picture' that helps us to learn and to remember the proliferating domain of the diseases. But at a deeper level than this spatial 'metaphor', and in order to make it possible, classificatory medicine presupposes a certain 'configuration' of disease: it has never been formulated for itself, but one can define its essential requisites after the event. Just as the genealogical tree, at a lower level than the comparison that it involves and all its imaginary themes, presupposes a space in which kinship is formalizable, the nosological picture involves a figure of the diseases that is neither the chain of causes and effects nor the chronological series of events nor its visible trajectory in the human body.

This organization treats localization in the organism as a subsidiary problem, but defines a fundamental system of relations involving envelopments, subordinations, divisions, resemblances. This space involves: a 'vertical', in which the implications are drawn up—fever, 'a successive struggle between cold and heat', may occur in a single episode, or in several; these may follow without interruption or after an interval; this respite may not exceed twelve hours, attain a whole day, last two whole days, or have a poorly defined rhythm;[2] and a 'horizontal', in which the homologies are transferred—in the two great subdivisions of the spasms are to be found, in perfect symmetry, the 'partial tonics', the 'general tonics', the 'partial clonics', and the 'general clonics';[3] or again, in the order of the discharges, what catarrh is to the throat, dysentery is to the intestines;[4] a deep space, anterior to all perceptions, and governing them from afar; it is on the basis of this space, the lines that it intersects, the masses that it distributes or hierarchizes, that disease, emerging beneath our gaze, becomes embodied in a living organism.

What are the principles of this primary configuration of disease?

1. The doctors of the eighteenth century identified it with 'historical', as opposed to philosophical, 'knowledge'. Knowledge is historical that circumscribes

pleurisy by its four phenomena: fever, difficulty in breathing, coughing, and pains
in the side. Knowledge would be philosophical that called into question the origin,
the principle, the causes of the disease: cold, serous discharge, inflammation of
the pleura. The distinction between the historical and the philosophical is not the
distinction between cause and effect: Cullen based his classificatory system on the
attribution of related causes;[5] nor is the distinction between principle and consequences, since Sydenham thought he was engaged in historical research when
studying 'the way in which nature produces and sustains the different forms of
disease';[6] nor even is it exactly the difference between the visible and the hidden
or conjectural, for one sometimes has to track down a 'history' that is enclosed
upon itself and develops invisibly, like hectic fever in certain phthisics: 'reefs
caught under water'.[7] The historical embraces whatever, *de facto* or *de jure*,
sooner or later, directly or indirectly, may be offered to the gaze. A cause that
can be seen, a symptom that is gradually discovered, a principle that can be
deciphered from its root do not belong to the order of 'philosophical' knowledge,
but to a 'very simple' knowledge, which 'must precede all others', and which
situates the original form of medical experience. It is a question of defining a sort
of fundamental area in which perspectives are levelled off, and in which shifts
of level are aligned: an effect has the same status as its cause, the antecedent
coincides with what follows it. In this homogeneous space series are broken and
time abolished: a local inflammation is merely the ideal juxtaposition of its historical elements (redness, tumour, heat, pain) without their network of reciprocal
determinations or their temporal intersection being involved.

Disease is perceived fundamentally in a space of projection without depth, of
coincidence without development. There is only one plane and one moment. The
form in which truth is originally shown is the surface in which relief is both
manifested and abolished—the portrait: 'He who writes the history of diseases
must . . . observe attentively the clear and natural phenomena of diseases, however uninteresting they may seem. In this he must imitate the painters who when
they paint a portrait are careful to mark the smallest signs and natural things that
are to be found on the face of the person they are painting.'[8] The first structure
provided by classificatory medicine is the flat surface of perpetual simultaneity.
Table and picture.

2. It is a space in which analogies define essences. The pictures resemble things,
but they also resemble one another. The *distance* that separates one disease from
another can be measured only by the *degree* of their *resemblance*, without reference to the logico-temporal divergence of genealogy. The disappearance of voluntary movements and reduced activity in the internal or external sense organs
form the general outline that emerges beneath such particular forms as apoplexy,
syncope, or paralysis. Within this great kinship, minor divergences are established:
apoplexy robs one of the use of all the senses, and of all voluntary motility, but
it spares the breathing and the functioning of the heart; paralysis affects only
a locally assignable sector of the nervous system and motility; like apoplexy,
syncope has a general effect, but it also interrupts respiratory movements.[9] The
perspective distribution, which enables us to see in paralysis a symptom, in

syncope an episode, and in apoplexy an organic and functional attack, does not exist for the classificatory gaze, which is sensitive only to surface divisions, in which vicinity is not defined by measurable distances but by formal similarities. When they become dense enough, these similarities cross the threshold of mere kinship and accede to unity of essence. There is no fundamental difference between an apoplexy that suddenly suspends motility, and the chronic, evolutive forms that gradually invade the whole motor system: in that simultaneous space in which forms distributed by time come together and are superimposed, kinship folds back into identity. In a flat, homogeneous, non-measurable world, there is essential disease where there is a plethora of similarities.

3. The form of the similarity uncovers the rational order of the diseases. When one perceives a resemblance, one does not simply lay down a system of convenient, relative 'mappings'; one begins to read off the intelligible ordering of the diseases. The veil is lifted from the principle of their creation; this is the general order of nature. As in the case of plants or animals, the action of disease is fundamentally specific: 'The supreme being is not subjected to less certain laws in producing diseases or in maturing morbific humours, than in growing plants and animals. . . . He who observes attentively the order, the time, the hour at which the attack of quart fever begins, the phenomena of shivering, of heat, in a word all the symptoms proper to it, will have as many reasons to believe that this disease is a species as he has to believe that a plant constitutes a species because it grows, flowers, and dies always in the same way.'[10]

This botanical model has a double importance for medical thought. First, it made it possible to turn the principle of the analogy of forms into the law of the production of essences; and, secondly, it allowed the perceptual attention of the doctor—which, here and there, discovers and relates—to communicate with the ontological order—which organizes from the inside, prior to all manifestation—the world of disease. The order of disease is simply a 'carbon copy' of the world of life; the same structures govern each, the same forms of division, the same ordering. The rationality of life is identical with the rationality of that which threatens it. Their relationship is not one of nature and counter-nature; but, in a natural order common to both, they fit into one another, one superimposed upon the other. In disease, one *recognizes (reconnaît)* life because it is on the law of life that *knowledge (connaissance)* of the disease is also based.

4. We are dealing with species that are both natural and ideal. Natural, because it is in them that diseases state their essential truths; ideal insofar as they are never experienced unchanged and undisturbed.

The first disturbance is introduced with and by disease itself. To the pure nosological essence, which fixes and exhausts its place in the order of the species without residue, the patient adds, in the form of so many disturbances, his predispositions, his age, his way of life, and a whole series of events that, in relation to the essential nucleus, appear as accidents. In order to know the truth of the pathological fact, the doctor must abstract the patient: 'He who describes a disease must take care to distinguish the symptoms that necessarily accompany it, and which are proper to it, from those that are only accidental and fortuitous,

such as those that depend on the temperament and age of the patient.'[11] Paradoxically, in relation to that which he is suffering from, the patient is only an
external fact; the medical reading must take him into account only to place him
in parentheses. Of course, the doctor must know 'the internal structure of our
bodies'; but only in order to subtract it, and to free to the doctor's gaze 'the
nature and combination of symptoms, crises, and other circumstances that
accompany diseases'.[12] It is not the pathological that functions, in relation to life,
as a *counter-nature*, but the patient in relation to the disease itself.

And not only the patient; the doctor, too. His intervention is an act of violence
if it is not subjected strictly to the ideal ordering of nosology: 'The knowledge of
diseases is the doctor's compass; the success of the cure depends on an exact
knowledge of the disease'; the doctor's gaze is directed initially not towards that
concrete body, that visible whole, that positive plenitude that faces him—the
patient—but towards intervals in nature, lacunae, distances, in which there appear,
like negatives, 'the signs that differentiate one disease from another, the true
from the false, the legitimate from the bastard, the malign from the benign'.[13] It
is a grid that catches the real patient and holds back any therapeutic indiscretion.
If, for polemical reasons, the remedy is administered too early, it contradicts and
blurs the essence of the disease; it prevents the disease from acceding to its true
nature, and, by making it irregular, makes it untreatable. In the period of invasion, the doctor must hold his breath, for 'the beginnings of disease reveal its
class, its genus, and its species'; when the symptoms increase and become more
marked, it is enough 'to diminish their violence and reduce the pains'; when the
disease has settled in, one must 'follow step by step the paths followed by nature',
strengthening it if it is too weak, diminishing it if it strives too vigorously to
destroy what resists it.[14]

In the rational space of disease, doctors and patients do not occupy a place as
of right; they are tolerated as disturbances that can hardly be avoided: the paradoxical role of medicine consists, above all, in neutralizing them, in maintaining
the maximum difference between them, so that, in the void that appears between
them, the ideal configuration of the disease becomes a concrete, free form, totalized
at last in a motionless, simultaneous picture, lacking both density and secrecy,
where recognition opens of itself onto the order of essences.

Classificatory thought gives itself an essential space, which it proceeds to efface
at each moment. Disease exists only in that space, since that space constitutes it
as nature; and yet it always appears rather out of phase in relation to that space,
because it is manifested in a real patient, beneath the observing eye of a forearmed
doctor. The fine two-dimensional space of the portrait is both the origin and the
final result: that which makes possible, at the outset, a rational, well-founded
body of medical knowledge, and that towards which it must constantly proceed
through that which conceals it. One of the tasks of medicine, therefore, is to
rejoin its own condition, but by a path in which it must efface each of its steps,
because it attains its aim in a gradual neutralization of itself. The condition of its
truth is the necessity that blurs its outlines. Hence the strange character of the
medical gaze; it is caught up in an endless reciprocity. It is directed upon that

which is visible in the disease—but on the basis of the patient, who hides this visible element even as he shows it; consequently, in order to know, he must recognize, while already being in possession of the knowledge that will lend support to his recognition. And, as it moves forward, this gaze is really retreating, since it reaches the truth of the disease only by allowing it to win the struggle and to fulfill, in all its phenomena, its true nature.

Disease, which can be mapped out on the picture, becomes apparent in the body. There it meets a space with a quite different configuration: the concrete space of perception. Its laws define the visible forms assumed by disease in a sick organism: the way in which disease is distributed in the organism, manifests its presence there, progresses by altering solids, movements, or functions, causes lesions that become visible under autopsy, triggers off, at one point or another, the interplay of symptoms, causes reactions, and thus moves towards a fatal, and for it favourable, outcome. We are dealing here with those complex, derived figures by means of which the essence of the disease, with its structure of a picture, is articulated upon the thick, dense volume of the organism and becomes *embodied* within it.

How can the flat, homogeneous, homological space of classes become visible in a geographical system of masses differentiated by their volume and distance? How can a disease, defined by its *place* in a family, be characterized by its *seat* in an organism? This is the problem that might be called the *secondary spatialization* of the pathological.

For classificatory medicine, presence in an organ is never absolutely necessary to define a disease: this disease may travel from one point of localization to another, reach other bodily surfaces, while remaining identical in nature. The space of the body and the space of the disease possess enough latitude to slide away from one another. The same, single spasmodic malady may move from the lower part of the abdomen, where it may cause dyspepsia, visceral congestion, interruption of the menstrual or haemorrhoidal flow, towards the chest, with breathlessness, palpitations, the feeling of a lump in the throat, coughing, and finally reach the head, causing epileptic convulsions, syncopes, or sleepiness.[15] These movements, which are accompanied by symptomatic changes, may occur in time in a single individual; they may also be found by examining a series of individuals with different link points: in its visceral form, spasm is encountered, above all, in lymphatic subjects, while in its cerebral form it is encountered more among sanguine temperaments. But in any case, the essential pathological configuration is not altered. The organs are the concrete supports of the disease; they never constitute its indispensable conditions. The system of points that defines the relation of the disease to the organism is neither constant nor necessary. They do not possess a common, previously defined space.

In this corporal space in which it circulates freely, disease undergoes metastases and metamorphoses. Nothing confines it to a particular course. A nosebleed may become haemoptysis (spitting of blood) or cerebral haemorrhage; the only thing that must remain is the specific form of blood discharge. This is why the medicine of spaces has, throughout its history, been linked to the doctrine of sympathies—

each notion being compelled to reinforce the other for the correct balance of the system. Sympathetic communication through the organism is sometimes carried out by a locally assignable relay (the diaphragm for spasms, the stomach for the discharge of humour); sometimes by a whole system of diffusion that radiates through the body (the nervous system for pains and convulsions, the vascular system for inflammations); in other cases, by means of a simple functional correspondence (a suppression of the excretions is communicated from the intestines to the kidneys, and from these to the skin); lastly, by means of an adjustment of the nervous system from one region to another (lumbar pains in the hydrocele). But the anatomical redistribution of the disease, whether through correspondence, diffusion, or relay, does not alter its essential structure; sympathy operates the interplay between the space of localization and the space of configuration; it defines their reciprocal freedom and the boundaries of that freedom.

Or, rather, threshold, not boundary. For beyond the sympathetic transference of the structural homology that it authorizes, a relation may be set up between one disease and another that is a relation of causality, but not of kinship. By virtue of its own creative force, one pathological form may engender another that is very far removed in the nosological picture. Hence the complications; hence the mixed forms; hence certain regular, or at least frequent, successions, as that between mania and paralysis. Haslam knew of delirious patients whose 'speech is disturbed, whose mouths are twisted, whose arms and legs are deprived of voluntary movement, whose memory is weakened', and who, generally speaking, 'have no awareness of their position'.[16] Overlapping of the symptoms or simultaneity of their extreme forms are not enough to constitute a single disease; the distance between verbal excitation and motor paralysis in the table of morbid kinships prevents a chronological proximity from deciding on a unity. Hence the idea of a causality that moves by virtue of a slight time-lag; sometimes the onset of mania appears first, sometimes the motor signs introduce the whole set of symptoms. 'The paralytic affections are a much more frequent cause of madness than is thought; and they are also a very common effect of mania.' No sympathetic translation can cross this gap between the species; and the solidarity of the symptoms in the organism are not enough to constitute a unity that clashes with the essences. There is, therefore, an inter-nosological causality, whose role is the contrary of sympathy: sympathy preserves the fundamental form by ranging over time and space; causality dissociates the simultaneities and intersections in order to maintain the essential purities.

In this pathology, time plays a limited role. It is admitted that a disease may last, and that its various episodes may appear in turn; ever since Hippocrates doctors have calculated the critical days of a disease, and known the significant values of the arterial pulsations: 'When the rebounding pulse appears at each thirtieth pulsation, or thereabouts, the haemorrhage occurs four days later, more or less; when it occurs at every sixteenth pulsation, the haemorrhage will occur in three days' time. . . . Lastly, when it recurs every fourth, third, second pulsation, or when it is continual, one must expect the haemorrhage within twenty-four hours.'[17] But this numerically fixed duration is part of the essential structure of disease, just as chronic catarrh becomes, after a period of time, phthisic fever. There is no process of evolution in which duration introduces new events of itself and at its own insistence; time is integrated as a nosological constant, not as an organic variable. The time of the body does not affect, and still less determines, the time of the disease.

What communicates the essential 'body' of the disease to the real body of the patient are not, therefore, the points of localization, nor the effects of duration, but, rather, the quality. In one of the experiments described before the Prussian Royal Academy in 1764, Meckel explains how he observed the alteration in the brain during different diseases. When he carried out an autopsy, he removed from the brain small cubes of equal volume ('6 lines in each direction') in different places in the cerebral mass: he compared these extractions with each other, and with similar cubes taken from other corpses. The instruments used for this comparison were weighing scales; in phthisis, a disease involving exhaustion, the specific weight of the brain was found to be relatively lower than in the case of apoplexy, a disease involving discharge (1 dr 3¾ gr as against 1 dr 6 or 7 gr); whereas in the case of a normal subject who had died naturally the average weight was 1 dr 5 gr. These weights may vary according to the part of the brain from which the samples have been extracted: in phthisis it is, above all, the cerebellum that is light; in apoplexy the central areas are heavy.[18] Between the disease and the organism, then, there are connexion points that are situated according to a regional principle; but these are only sectors in which the disease secretes or transposes its specific qualities: the brains of maniacs are light, dry, and friable because mania is a lively, hot, explosive disease; those of phthisics are exhausted and languishing, inert, anaemic, because phthisis belongs to the general class of the haemorrhages. The set of qualities characterizing a disease is laid down in an organ, which then serves as a support for the symptoms. The disease and the body communicate only through the non-spatial element of quality.

It is understandable, then, that medicine should turn away from what Sauvages called a 'mathematical' form of knowledge: 'Knowing quantities and being able to measure them, being able, for example, to determine the force and speed of the pulse, the degree of heat, the intensity of pain, the violence of the cough, and other such symptoms.'[19] Meckel measured, not to obtain knowledge of mathematical form, but to gauge the intensity of the pathological quality that constituted the disease. No measurable mechanics of the body can, in its physical or mathematical particularities, account for a pathological phenomenon; convulsions may be due to a dehydration and contraction of the nervous system—and this is certainly a phenomenon of a mechanical order; but it is a mechanics of interlinked qualities, articulated movements, upheavals that are triggered off in series, not a mechanics of quantifiable segments. It may involve a mechanism, but it cannot belong to the order of Mechanics as such. 'Physicians must confine themselves to knowing the forces of medicines and diseases by means of their operations; they must observe them with care and strive to know their laws, and be tireless in the search for physical causes.'[20] A true mathematization of disease would imply a common, homogeneous space, with organic figures and a nosological ordering.

On the contrary, their shift implies a qualitative gaze; in order to grasp the disease, one must look at those parts where there is dryness, ardour, excitation, and where there is humidity, discharge, debility. How can one distinguish, beneath the same fever, the same coughing, the same tiredness, pleurisy of the phthisis, if one does not recognize here a dry inflammation of the lungs, and there a serous discharge? How can one distinguish, if not by their quality, the convulsions of an epileptic suffering from cerebral inflammation, and those of a hypochondriac suffering from congestion of the viscera? A subtle perception of qualities, a perception of the differences between one case and another, a delicate perception of variants—a whole hermeneutics of the pathological fact, based on modulated, coloured experience, is required; one should measure variations, balances, excesses, and defects.

> The human body is made up of vessels and fluids; . . . when the vessels and fibres have neither too much nor too little tone, when the fluids have just the right consistency, when they have neither too much nor too little movement, man is in a state of health; if the movement . . . is too strong, the solids harden and the fluids thicken; if it is too weak, the fibre slackens and the blood becomes thinner.[21]

And the medical gaze, open to these fine qualities, necessarily becomes attentive to all their modulations; the decipherment of disease in its specific characteristics is based on a subtle form of perception that must take account of each particular equilibrium. But in what does this particularity consist? It is not that of an organism in which pathological process and reactions are linked together in a unique way to form a 'case'. We are dealing, rather, with qualitative varieties of the illness, to which are added the varieties that may be presented by the temperaments, thus modulating the qualitative varieties in the second stage. What classificatory medicine calls 'particular histories' are the effects of multiplication caused by the qualitative variations (owing to the temperaments) of the essential qualities that characterize illnesses. The individual patient finds himself at the point at which the result of this multiplication appears.

Hence his paradoxical position. If one wishes to know the illness from which he is suffering, one must subtract the individual, with his particular qualities: 'The author of nature,' said Zimmermann, 'has fixed the course of most diseases through immutable laws that one soon discovers if the course of the disease is not interrupted or disturbed by the patient';[22] at this level the individual was merely a negative element, the accident of the disease, which, for it and in it, is most alien to its essence. But the individual now reappears as the positive, ineffaceable support of all these qualitative phenomena, which articulate upon the organism the fundamental ordering of the disease; it is the local, sensible presence of this order—a segment of enigmatic space that unites the nosological plane of kinships to the anatomic volume of vicinities. The patient is a geometrically impossible spatial synthesis, but for that very reason unique, central, and irreplaceable: an order that has become density in a set of qualifying modulations. And the same Zimmermann, who recognized in the patient only the negative of the disease, is 'sometimes tempted', contrary to Sydenham's general descriptions, 'to admit only of particular histories. However simple nature may be as a whole, it is nevertheless varied in its parts; consequently, we must try to know it both as a whole and in its parts.'[23] The medicine of species becomes engaged in a renewed attention to the individual—an ever-more impatient attention, ever less able to tolerate the general forms of perception and the hasty inspection of essences.

'Every morning a certain Aesculapius has fifty or sixty patients in his waiting room; he listens to the complaints of each, arranges them into four lines, pre-scribes a bleeding for the first, a purge for the second, a clyster for the third, and a change of air for the fourth.'[24] This is not medicine; the same is true of hospital practice, which kills the capacity for observation and stifles the talents of the observer by the sheer number of things to observe. Medical perception must be directed neither to series nor to groups; it must be structured as a look through 'a magnifying glass, which, when applied to different parts of an object, makes one notice other parts that one would not otherwise perceive',[25] thus initiating the endless task of understanding the individual. At this point, one is brought back to the theme of the portrait referred to above, but this time treated in reverse. The patient is the rediscovered portrait of the disease; he is the disease itself, with shadow and relief, modulations, nuances, depth; and when describing the disease the doctor must strive to restore this living density: 'One must render the patient's own infirmities, his own pains, his own gestures, his own posture, his own terms, and his own complaints.'[26]

Through the play of primary spatialization, the medicine of species situated the disease in an area of homologies in which the individual could receive no positive status; in secondary spatialization, on the other hand, it required an acute per-ception of the individual, freed from collective medical structures, free of any group gaze and of hospital experience itself. Doctor and patient are caught up in an ever-greater proximity, bound together, the doctor by an ever-more attentive, more insistent, more penetrating gaze, the patient by all the silent, irreplaceable qualities that, in him, betray—that is, reveal and conceal—the clearly ordered forms of the disease. Between the nosological characters and terminal features to be read on the patient's face, the qualities have roamed freely over the body. The medical gaze need hardly dwell on this body for long, at least in its densities and functioning.

Let us call tertiary spatialization all the gestures by which, in a given society, a disease is circumscribed, medically invested, isolated, divided up into closed, privileged regions, or distributed throughout cure centres, arranged in the most favorable way. Tertiary is not intended to imply a derivative, less essential struc-ture than the preceding ones; it brings into play a system of options that reveals the way in which a group, in order to protect itself, practises exclusions, estab-lishes the forms of assistance, and reacts to poverty and to the fear of death. But to a greater extent than the other forms of spatialization, it is the locus of various dialectics: heterogeneous figures, time-lags, political struggles, demands and uto-pias, economic constraints, social confrontations. In it, a whole corpus of medical practices and institutions confronts the primary and secondary spatializations with forms of a social space whose genesis, structure, and laws are of a different nature. And yet, or, rather, for this very reason, it is the point of origin of the most radical questionings. It so happened that it was on the basis of this tertiary spatialization that the whole of medical experience was overturned and defined for its most concrete perceptions, new dimensions, and a new foundation.

In the medicine of species, disease has, as a birthright, forms and seasons that are alien to the space of societies. There is a 'savage' nature of disease that is both its true nature and its most obedient course: alone, free of intervention, without medical artifice, it reveals the ordered, almost vegetal nervure of its essence. But the more complex the social space in which it is situated becomes, the more *de-natured* it becomes. Before the advent of civilization, people had only the simplest, most necessary diseases. Peasants and workers still remain close to the basic noso-logical table; the simplicity of their lives allows it to show through in its reasonable order: they have none of those variable, complex, intermingled nervous ills, but down-to-earth apoplexies, or uncomplicated attacks of mania.[27] As one improves one's conditions of life, and as the social network tightens its grip around indi-viduals, 'health seems to diminish by degrees'; diseases become diversified, and combine with one another; 'their number is already great in the superior order of the bourgeois; . . . it is as great as possible in people of quality'.[28]

Like civilization, the hospital is an artificial locus in which the transplanted disease runs the risk of losing its essential identity. It comes up against a form of complication that doctors call prison or hospital fever: muscular asthenia, dry or coated tongue, livid face, sticky skin, diarrhoea, pale urine, difficulty in breath-ing, death on the eighth or eleventh day, or on the thirteenth at the latest.[29] More generally, contact with other diseases, in this unkempt garden where the species cross-breed, alters the proper nature of the disease and makes it more difficult to decipher; and how in this necessary proximity can one 'correct the malign effluvium that exudes from the bodies of the sick, from gangrenous limbs, decayed bones, contagious ulcers, and putrid fevers'?[30] And, in any case, can one efface the unfortunate impression that the sight of these places, which for many are nothing more than 'temples of death', will have on a sick man or woman, removed from the familiar surroundings of his home and family? This loneliness in a crowd, this despair disturb, with the healthy reactions of the organism, the natural course of the disease; it would require a very skilful hospital doctor 'to avoid the danger of the false experience that seems to result from the artificial diseases to which he devotes himself in the hospitals. In fact, no hospital disease is a pure disease'.[31]

The natural locus of disease is the natural locus of life—the family: gentle, spontaneous care, expressive of love and a common desire for a cure, assists nature in its struggle against the illness, and allows the illness itself to attain its own truth. The hospital doctor sees only distorted, altered diseases, a whole teratology of the pathological; the family doctor 'soon acquires true experience based on the natural phenomena of all species of disease'.[32] This family medicine must necessarily be respectful: 'Observe the sick, assist nature without violating it, and wait, admitting in all modesty that much knowledge is still lacking.'[33] Thus, on the subject of the pathology of species, there is a revival of the old dispute between active medicine and expectant medicine.[34] The nosologists of necessity favoured the latter, and one of these, Vitet, in a classification containing over two thousand species, and bearing the title *Médecine expectante*, invariably prescribes quina to help nature follow its natural course.[35]

The medicine of species implies, therefore, a free spatialization for the disease, with no privileged region, no constraint imposed by hospital conditions—a sort of spontaneous division in the setting of its birth and development that must function as the paradoxical and natural locus of its own abolition. At the place in which it appears, it is obliged, by the same movement, to disappear. It must not be fixed in a medically prepared domain, but be allowed, in the positive sense of the term, to 'vegetate' in its original soil: the family, a social space conceived in its most natural, most primitive, most morally secure form, both enclosed upon itself and entirely transparent, where the illness is left to itself. Now, this structure coincides exactly with the way in which, in political thought, the problem of assistance is reflected.

The criticism levelled at hospital foundations was a commonplace of eighteenth-century economic analysis. The funds on which they are based are, of course, inalienable: they are the perpetual due of the poor. But poverty is not perpetual; needs change, and assistance must be given to those provinces and towns that need it. To do so would not be to contravene the wishes of the donors, but on the contrary to give them back their true form; their 'principal aim was to serve the public, to relieve the State; without departing from the intention of the founders, and even in conformity with their views, one must regard as a common mass all the funds donated to the hospitals'.[36] The single, sacrosanct foundation must be dissolved in favor of a generalized system of assistance, of which society is both the sole administrator and the undifferentiated beneficiary. Moreover, it is an error in economics to base assistance on an immobilization of capital—that is to say, on an impoverishment of the nation, which, in turn, brings with it the need for new foundations; hence, at worst, a stifling of activity. Assistance should be related neither to productive wealth (capital), nor to the wealth produced (profits, which are always capitalizable), but to the very principle that produces wealth: work. It is by giving the poor work that one will help the poor without impoverishing the nation.[37]

The sick man is no doubt incapable of working, but if he is placed in a hospital he becomes a double burden for society: the assistance that he is given relates only to himself, and his family is, in turn, left exposed to poverty and disease. The hospital, which creates disease by means of the enclosed, pestilential domain that it constitutes, creates further disease in the social space in which it is placed. This separation, intended to protect, communicates disease and multiplies it to infinity. Inversely, if it is left in the free field of its birth and development, it will never be more than itself—as it appeared, so will it be extinguished—and the assistance that is given in the home will make up for the poverty that the disease has caused. The care spontaneously given by family and friends will cost nobody anything; and the financial assistance given to the sick man will be to the advantage of the family: 'someone will have to eat the meat from which his broth is made; and in heating his tisane, it costs no more to warm his children as well'.[38] The chain of one disease engendering another, and that of the perpetual impoverishment of poverty, is thus broken when one gives up trying to create for the sick a differentiated, distinct space, which results, in an ambiguous but clumsy way, in both the protection and the preservation of disease.

Independently of their justifications, the thought structure of the economists and that of the classificatory doctors coincide in broad terms: the space in which disease is isolated and reaches fulfilment is an absolutely open space, without either division or a privileged, fixed figure, reduced solely to the plane of visible manifestations; a homogeneous space in which no intervention is authorized except that of a gaze which is effaced as it alights, and of assistance whose sole value is its transitory compensation—a space with no other morphology than that of the resemblances perceived from one individual to another, and of the treatment administered by private medicine to a private patient.

But, by being carried to its conclusion in this way, the structure is inverted. Is a medical experience, diluted in the free space of a society reduced to the single, nodal, and necessary figure of the family, not bound up with the very structure of society? Does it not involve, because of the special attention that it pays to the individual, a generalized vigilance that by extension applies to the group as a whole? It would be necessary to conceive of a medicine sufficiently bound up with the state for it to be able, with the cooperation of the state, to carry out a constant, general, but differentiated policy of assistance; medicine becomes a task for the nation. (Menuret in the early days of the French Revolution dreamt of a system of free medical care administered by doctors who would be paid by the government out of the income from former church property.[39]) In this way a certain supervision would be exercised over the doctors themselves; abuses would be prevented and quacks forbidden to practise, and, by means of an organized, healthy, rational medicine, home care would prevent the patient's becoming a victim of medicine and avoid exposure to contagion of the patient's family. Good medicine would be given status and legal protection by the state; and it would be the task of the state 'to make sure that a true art of curing does exist'.[40] The medicine of individual perception, of family assistance, of home care can be based only on a collectively controlled structure, or on one that is integrated into the social space in its entirety. At this point, a quite new form, virtually unknown in the eighteenth century, of institutional spatialization of disease, makes its appearance. The medicine of spaces disappears.

Notes

1. Gilibert, *L'anarchie médicinale* (Neuchâtel, 1772, vol. I, p. 198).
2. F. Boissier de Sauvages, *Nosologie méthodique* (Lyons, 1772, vol. II).
3. *Ibid.*, vol. III.

4. W. Cullen, *Institutions de médecine pratique* (Fr. trans., Paris 1785, vol. II, pp. 39–60).
5. W. Cullen, *Institutions de médecine pratique* (Fr. trans., Paris, 1785, 2 vols.).
6. Th. Sydenham, *Médecine pratique* (Fr. trans. Jault, Paris, 1784, p. 390).
7. *Ibid.*
8. Th. Sydenham, quoted by Sauvages, *op. cit.*, vol. I, p. 88.
9. W. Cullen, *op. cit.*, vol. II, p. 86.
10. Sydenham, quoted by Sauvages, *op. cit.*, vol. I, pp. 124–5.
11. *Ibid.*
12. Clifton, *État de la médecine ancienne et moderne* (Fr. trans., Paris, 1742, p. 213).
13. Frier, *Guide pour la conservation de l'homme* (Grenoble, 1789, p. 113).
14. T. Guindant, *La nature opprimée par la médecine moderne* (Paris, 1768, pp. 10–11).
15. *L'Encyclopédie*, article 'Spasme'.
16. J. Haslam, *Observations on Madness* (London, 1798, p. 259).
17. Fr. Solano de Luques, *Observations nouvelles et extraordinaires sur la prédiction des crises*, enlarged by several new cases by Nihell (Fr. trans., Paris, 1748, p. 2).
18. Account in *Gazette salutaire*, vol. XXI, 2 August 1764.
19. Sauvages, *op. cit.*, vol. I, pp. 91–2.
20. Tissot, *Avis aux gens de lettres sur leur santé* (Lausanne, 1767, p. 28).
21. *Ibid.*, p. 28.
22. Zimmermann, *Traité de l'expérience* (Fr. trans., Paris, 1800, vol. I, p. 122).
23. *Ibid.*, p. 184.
24. *Ibid.*, p. 187.
25. *Ibid.*, p. 127.
26. *Ibid.*, p. 178.
27. Tissot, *Traité des nerfs et de leurs maladies* (Paris, 1778–1780, vol. II, pp. 432–44).
28. Tissot, *Essai sur la santé des gens du monde* (Lausanne, 1770, pp. 8–12).
29. Tenon, *Mémoires sur les hôpitaux* (Paris, 1788, p. 451).
30. Percival, 'Lettre à M. Aikin', in J. Aikin, *Observations sur les hôpitaux* (Fr. trans., Paris, 1777, p. 113).
31. Dupont de Nemours, *Idées sur les secours à donner* (Paris, 1786, pp. 24–5).
32. *Ibid.*
33. Moscati, *De l'emploi des systèmes dans la médecine pratique* (Fr. trans., Strasbourg, Year VII, pp. 26–7).
34. Cf. Vicq d'Azyr, *Remarques sur la médecine agissante* (Paris, 1786).
35. Vitet, *La médecine expectante* (Paris, 1806, 6 vols.).
36. Chamousset (C.H.P.), 'Plan général pour l'administration des hôpitaux', *Vues d'un citoyen* (Paris, 1757, vol. II).
37. Turgot, article 'Fondation', in *L'Encyclopédie*.
38. Dupont de Nemours, *op. cit.*, pp. 14–30.
39. J.-J. Menuret, *Essai sur les moyens de former de bons médecins* (Paris, 1791).
40. Jadelot, *Adresse à Nos Seigneurs de l'Assemblée Nationale sur la nécessité et le moyen de perfectionner l'enseignement de la médecine* (Nancy, 1790, p. 7).

CHAPTER 3

Natural Facts: A Historical Perspective on Science and Sexuality

L. J. Jordanova

INTRODUCTION

The distinction between women as natural and men as cultural appeals to a set of ideas about the biological foundations of womanhood. Understanding the historical dimensions of these two inter-related pairs of dichotomies in European thought entails revealing the connections between science and sexuality. Sex roles were constituted in a scientific and medical language, and, conversely, the natural sciences and medicine were suffused with sexual imagery. This paper explores the links between nature/culture, woman/man through a historical study of the biomedical sciences and the metaphors and symbols they employed. I draw my examples principally from eighteenth- and nineteenth-century France and Britain.

Since the eighteenth century the polarities seem to have hardened, yet the lived experience to which they supposedly relate was extremely complex. Recent feminist history has shown the diversity of women's social and occupational roles despite the inflexibility of contemporary ideas about them.[1] The lack of fit between ideas and experience clearly points to the ideological function of the nature/culture dichotomy as applied to gender. This ideological message was increasingly conveyed in the language of medicine.

As there seems no easy way to reconcile material conditions with ideas of sex roles, some feminist scholars have been tempted to turn for help to another dichotomy, that of oppressor/oppressed. Dichotomies such as man/woman illustrate the simplistic model of oppression which is useful because it seems to imply a clear power relationship:

nature	:	culture
woman	:	man
oppressed	:	oppressor
(because powerless)		(because powerful)

This approach takes a simple social relationship and finds a natural basis for it, so that, for example, women become the bearers of ignorance and men of knowledge. We then construct this as a form of oppression. But in doing so, we abstract from the dichotomy only one of its dimensions. Historically, the notion of women as natural contained not just women as superstitious but also women as the carriers of a new morality through which the artificiality of civilization could be transcended. In the same way, men as culture implied not just the progressive light of reason but also the corruption and exploitation of civil society. Next to what is presented as the desirable domination of superstition by reason, and women by men, in Mozart's opera *The Magic Flute*, one must put repugnance for the exploitation and inequality generated by masculine domination expressed in the eighteenth-century French novel *Paul et Virginie*. And in the end, it is not the possibility of finding texts with these extreme views clearly expressed which is most interesting, but rather the extent to which they were inseparably intertwined, as, for example, in the popular books on women published in the mid nineteenth century by the French historian Jules Michelet.

In our attempts to understand the deployment of symbols and metaphors, we must recognize the fact that one of the most powerful ways of using them in our culture has been in the form of these dichotomies, where the two opposed terms mutually define each other. It is not just male and female, masculine and feminine, or nature and culture, but also town and country, matter and spirit, body and mind, capitalist and worker – our entire philosophical set describes natural and social phenomena in terms of oppositional characteristics. Each polarity has its own history, but it also develops related meanings to other dichotomies. For instance, the pairs church and state, town and country also contain allusions to gender differences, and to nature and culture. Transformations between sets of dichotomies are performed all the time. Thus, man/woman is only one couple in a common matrix, and this reinforces the point that it cannot be seen as isolated or autonomous.

The power of dichotomies such as man/woman, nature/culture, city/country does not just consist in the apparent clarity of definition by contrast. More important is the possibility of a dialectical relationship between the members of each pair which is an essential part of their social value. The fact that there are a number of related pairs, and that the terms of each one have a complex relationship to one another further reinforces the point that we are not speaking here of simple linear hierarchies. Debates about sex and sex roles, especially during the nineteenth century, hinged precisely on the ways in which sexual boundaries might become blurred. It is as if the social order depended on clarity with respect to certain key distinctions whose symbolic meanings spread far beyond their explicit context. At certain times (perhaps times of perceived rapid change), physicians were deeply concerned about the feminization of men, for which homosexuality could be adduced as evidence, and the masculinization of women, which they believed could result from excessive physical or mental work. Raymond Williams has suggested that oppositional pairs provided a way to explore the parameters of change without upsetting the social order. He takes a case which is analogous and closely related to the one this book addresses – the long established Western dichotomy between the city and the country:

> On the country has gathered the idea of a natural way of life: of peace, innocence, and simple virtue. On the city has gathered the idea of an achieved centre: of learning, communication, light. Powerful hostile associations have also developed: on the city as a place of noise, worldliness and ambition; on the country as a place of backwardness, ignorance, limitation [Williams 1975: 9].

This quotation illustrates the point that more complexity can be held within dichotomies than at first sight appears. It also suggests that the city/country opposition has a sexual dimension. The innocence and simple virtues of country people were typically expressed through the unworldly sentiment of women. The negative image of the country, pervasive in Enlightenment writings, portrayed the superstitious and credulous behaviour of peasant women. The 'light' and civilization of city culture were symbols of male capacity for abstract thought and intellectual genius. The negative side of urban life was best expressed in exploitative domination and economic competition, clear metaphors of masculinity. Despite the superficial clarity of the city/country polarity, Williams stresses that it is the relationship between the two which has posed fundamental questions. Cities arise out of the countryside, urban and rural life are inescapably linked, while between cities and the country lie a whole host of intermediate forms of human settlements: villages, towns, suburbs, garden cities. The dichotomy seems to deny historical reality, which suggests that there must be a reason for the persistence of these archetypes; possibly it lies in the way they provide coherence in the face of threatened social disorganization.

The oppositions between women as nature and men as culture were expressed concretely through distinctions commonly made such as that between women's work and men's work. The ideological dimension to these oppositions is discernible in the dichotomy constructed by the elite of the medical profession between male strength and female vulnerability. Social and conceptual changes take place slowly and in piecemeal and fragmented ways. Our project is not to search for neat consistent ideological structures, but through the contradictions, tensions and paradoxes to find patterns we can understand.

There are strong reasons for beginning with the Enlightenment. In this period the shifts in meaning and usage of words such as culture, civil, civilize, nature and life provide indicators of deep changes in the way human society and its relations with the natural world were conceived. Ultimately, the Enlightenment is no easier to define than notions of nature and culture are, but, in the term itself, we can see an appeal to light as a symbol of a certain form of knowledge which had the potential for improving human existence. Rational knowledge based on empirical information derived from the senses was deemed the best foundation for secure knowledge. Starting with a sensualist epistemology, and a number of assumptions about the potential social application of an understanding of natural laws, many Enlightenment writers critically examined forms of social organization. In so doing, they employed a language fraught with sexual metaphor, and systematically examined the natural facts of sexuality.

Science and medicine were fundamental to this endeavour in three different ways. First, natural philosophers and medical writers addressed themselves to phenomena in the natural world such as reproduction and generation, sexual behaviour, and sex-related diseases. Second, science and medicine held a privileged position because their methods appeared to be the only ones which would lead away from religious orthodoxy and towards a secular, empirically based knowledge of the natural and social worlds. Finally, as I hope to show, science and medicine as activities were associated with sexual metaphors which were clearly expressed in designating nature as a woman to be unveiled, unclothed and penetrated by masculine science. The relationship between women and nature, and men and culture must therefore be examined through the mediations of science and medicine.

ENLIGHTENED ENVIRONMENTALISM

In the self-conscious scientism of the Enlightenment, the capacity of the human mind to delve into the secrets of nature was celebrated. Increasingly this capacity for scientific prowess was conceptualized as a male gift, just as nature was the fertile woman, and sometimes the archetypal mother (Kolodny 1975). People had explored their capacity to master and manipulate nature for many centuries (Glacken 1967), but the powerful analytical tools of the natural sciences and the techniques of engineering and technology enormously enhanced their confidence that human power over the environment was boundless. As Bacon expressed it in the early seventeenth century, 'My only earthly wish is . . . to stretch the deplorably narrow limits of man's dominion over the universe to their promised bounds' (Farrington 1964: 62). And the process by which Bacon thought this would be achieved was a casting off of 'the darkness of antiquity' in favour of the detailed study of nature (Farrington 1964: 69). 'I am come in very truth leading to you Nature with all her children to bind her to your service and make her your slave' (Farrington 1964: 62).

In discussions of human domination over nature, the concept of environment comes to hold an important, and complex, place from the late eighteenth century onwards (Jordanova 1979). Above all, the environment was that cluster of variables which acted upon organisms and were responsible for many of their characteristics. An understanding of human beings in sickness and in health was to be based on a large number of powerful environmental factors; climate, diet, housing, work, family situation, geography and atmosphere. This notion of environment could be split into two. First, there were variables such as custom and government which were human creations and were, at least in principle, amenable to change. Second, there were parameters such as climate, meteorology in general, geographical features such as rivers and mountains, which were in the province of immutable natural laws and proved more challenging to human power. In the first case environment denoted culture, in the second, nature.

Taking environment in the sense of culture, it was clear to people at the end of the eighteenth century that living things and their environment were continually interacting and changing each other in the process. This was also true of sexuality, for, although sex roles were seen as being in some sense 'in nature' because of their relationship to physical characteristics, it was also acknowledged that they were mutable, just as physiology and anatomy in general were taken to be. The customs and habits of day-to-day life such as diet, exercise and occupation, and more general social forces such as modes of government were taken to have profound effects on all aspects of people's lives; their sexuality was no exception. The foundation for these beliefs was a complex conceptual framework which spoke naturalistically about the physiological, mental and social aspects of human beings. An understanding of this framework is therefore an essential background for any account of the relations between nature, culture and gender in the period.

In the bio-medical sciences of the late eighteenth century, mind and body were not seen as incommensurable, absolutely distinct categories. Mental events, such as anger, fear or grief, were known to have physical effects, while illnesses such as fevers produced emotional and intellectual changes. I would argue that at the end of the eighteenth century a model of health and illness became dominant in which lifestyle and social roles were closely related to health. This model was applied to both men and women, but with different implications. A tight linkage was assumed between jobs performed in the social arena (for women, the production, suckling and care of children, the creation of a natural morality through family life) and health and disease. Women thus became a distinct class of persons, not by virtue of their reproductive organs, but through their social lives. The total physiology of women could, it was argued, only be understood in terms of lifestyle and the social roles they ought to fulfil, if they were not doing so already.

I want to stress that the model applied to both sexes. For example, people who lived in certain climates, such as men who worked in mines or factories, were known to be susceptible to particular diseases. Physicians therefore advocated that they take precautions to preserve their health: appropriate diet, exercise, housing, clothing, behaviour, regimen. The same argument applied to women, and in fact each way of life held its own particular dangers for the health of men and women which could be held at bay by the appropriate preventive measures. In the case of women, permissible occupation was tightly defined according to putatively natural criteria. There was thus a reflexive relationship between physiology and lifestyle; each affected the other. Through habit and custom, physiological changes took place which had been socially induced.

The emphasis on occupation and lifestyle as determinants of health, which led to a radical boundary being drawn between the sexes, had as its explicit theoretical basis a physiology which recognized few basic boundaries. It conflated moral and physical, mind and body; it created a language capable of containing biological, psychological and social considerations. This is clearly revealed in the use of bridging concepts such as 'temperament', 'habit', 'constitution' and 'sensibility' as technical terms in medicine. These concepts alluded to aspects of human physiology which were not just physical or mental, but contained something of both while being also closely bound to social change. As a result, the temperament and constitution of an individual were seen as products of biological, psychological and social interactions.

Because health was determined to a large extent by variables outside the human body, each person had a distinct physiological make-up which corresponded to his or her unique experience. Groups of people living under the same environmental conditions displayed similar biological and social characteristics. The systematic understanding of these conditions, on which appropriate therapy could be based, was derived from the analysis of a number of distinct variables. The factors affecting groups and individuals had to be clearly delineated. Yet although it was seldom made explicit, there were considered to be limits to the extent to which people could be changed. It was widely acknowledged that there was much variation among women which derived from different climates, patterns of work and so on, but that, nevertheless, all women had in common certain physiological features, not directly a matter of their reproductive organs. For it was a basic premise of physicians in late-eighteenth-century France that women were quite distinct from men by virtue of their whole anatomy and physiology. As Cabanis put it at the end of the eighteenth century: 'Nature has not simply distinguished the sexes by a single set of organs, the direct instruments of reproduction: between men and women there exist other differences of structure which relate more to the role which has been assigned to them' (1956, I: 275). The teleological argument was made more explicit by his contemporary Roussel: 'The soft parts which are part of the female constitution . . . also manifest differences which enable one to catch a glimpse of the functions to which a woman is called, and of the passive state to which nature has destined her' (1803: 11–12).

The ways in which gender differences were conceptualized can be illustrated by referring to the medical notion of sensibility. This was a physiological property which, although present in all parts of the body, was most clearly expressed through the state of the nervous system (Figlio 1975). The nervous system was taken by many to be that physiological system which, because it brought together physical and mental dimensions of human beings, expressed most precisely the total state of the individual, especially with respect to the impact of social changes. Thus it was said that increases in hysterical illnesses in women during the eighteenth century were evidence of the growing use of luxuries such as tea and coffee, and of other changes (Pomme 1782: 578–82). By virtue of their sex, women had a distinct sensibility which could be further modified during their lifetimes. Women, it was said, are highly *sensible* (in the sense of sensitive, or even sensitized) like children, and more passionate than men. This is because of 'the great mobility of their fibres, especially those in the uterus; hence their irritability, and suffering from vapours' (Macquart 1799, II: 511). The peculiar sensibility of women could also be used to explain their greater life expectancy in a way which associated lifestyle with the physical consistency of the constituent fibres of their bodies. Barthez, a prominent eighteenth-century French physician, explained:

Probably women enjoy this increase in their average age because of the softness and flexibility of the tissue of their fibres, and particularly because of their periodic evacuations which rejuvenate them, so to speak, each month, renew their blood, and re-establish their usual freshness . . . Another important cause of women living longer than men is that they are usually more accustomed to suffering infirmities, or to experiencing miseries in life. This habit gives their vital sensibility more moderation, and can only render them less susceptible to illness [1806, II: 298].

However, he went on to say that because of their 'delicate and feeble constitution', women feel things more deeply than men. This aptly portrays the ambivalence which we have already noted in the association of woman and nature. Women are tougher *and* softer, more vulnerable *and* more tenacious of life than men. However, more often than not, the softness of women was returned to again and again, and it was a metaphor that was imaginatively built on to construct a whole image of the dependent nature of woman:

This muscular feebleness inspires in women an instinctive disgust of strenuous exercise; it draws them towards amusements and sedentary occupations. One could add that the separation of their hips makes walking more painful for women . . . This habitual feeling of weakness inspires less confidence . . . and as a woman finds herself less able to exist on her own, the more she needs to attract the attention of others, to strengthen herself using those around her whom she judges most capable of protecting her [Cabanis 1956, I: 278].

Eighteenth-century physiology was based upon necessary links between biological, psychological and social phenomena, not on the anatomical organs of reproduction alone. Although the physiological presuppositions on which Cabanis' views were based applied to both sexes, there was an important asymmetry in that women's occupations were taken to be rooted in and a necessary consequence of their reproductive functions, whereas men's jobs were unrestricted. Women's destiny to bear and suckle children was taken to define their whole body and mind, and therefore their psychological capacities and social tasks. Men were thereby potential members of the broadest social and cultural groups, while women's sphere of action, it was constantly insisted, was the private arena of home and family. As a result, women became a central part of contemporary social debates which focussed on the family as the natural, i.e. biological, element in the social fabric, and on women, who through motherhood were the central figures in the family.

The links between women, motherhood, the family and natural morality may help to explain the emphasis on the breast in much medical literature. There is a danger in our seeing the uterus as the constant object of attention in the search for the biological roots of womanhood. It seems likely that different parts of the body were emphasized at different periods, and from different points of view. While the uterus and ovaries interested nineteenth-century gynaecologists, the breast caught the attention of eighteenth-century medical practitioners who were concerned with moral philosophy and ethics. The breast symbolized women's role in the family through its association with the suckling of babies. It appeared to define the occupational status of females in private work in the family, not in public life. The breast was visible – it was the sign of femininity that men recognized. It could thus be said to be a social law that sexual attraction was founded on the breast, and a natural law that women should breast feed their own children. Based on the natural goodness of the breast it was easy to create a moral injunction on women to feed their own children. It was, it was claimed, an undeniable law which, if thwarted, resulted in suffering for the child and in punishment for the rest of the mother's life, including the miscarriage of subsequent children. 'It is thus that one exposes oneself to cries of pain, for having been unfeeling about those of nature' (Macquart 1799, I: 77). The breasts of women not only symbolized the most fundamental social bond, that between mother and child, but they were also the means by which families were made since their beauty elicited the desires of the male for the female. An excellent example of this fusion of aesthetic, medical and social arguments is Roussel's book on women, *Système Physique et Moral de la Femme* (A Physical and Moral System of Woman) which was an instant success when it first appeared in 1775 and at once became part of literary culture (Alibert 1803: 7). It is significant that in praising Roussel, Alibert employed the metaphor of science unclothing woman: 'I would like to see the author . . . portrayed receiving . . . homage from the enchanting sex whose organism he has unveiled with so much delicacy and so much insight [pénétration]' (Alibert 1803: 7).

There was a strong aesthetic component in medical writings on women in this period. Discussing the beauty of the breast in the same breath as its vital nutritive function was not undisciplined confusion but indicative of the conflation of social and physiological functions. The breast was good, both morally and biologically, hence its attractiveness and the resultant sociability between the sexes. Indeed the family and thus society were predicated on natural sociability, a quality which Roussel characterized as a major universal law. In these ways the physiological, the social and the aesthetic aspects of human existence were brought together.

So far we have noted a number of overlapping sets of dichotomies and the extent to which the two members of each pair were blurred:

nature	:	culture
woman	:	man
physical	:	mental
mothering	:	thinking
feeling and superstition	:	abstract knowledge and thought
country	:	city
darkness	:	light
nature	:	science and civilization

I have also stressed that these associations worked in two ways so that the association of women with nature had a positive and a negative side. Their sentiment and simple, pure morality constituted the first side, their ignorance and lack of intellectual powers, the second. It was common in the eighteenth century to emphasize the second, negative aspects of female naturalness in attacks on superstition and credulity. *Philosophes* in the vanguard of the Enlightenment believed that they had to fight against the superstition and ignorance of the mass of the people because these were impediments to social progress, and one of the vehicles for their polemic was a form of sex-role stereotyping. The classic example of the problem was the uneducated women under the thumb of her priest who fed her a diet of religious dogma, urging her to believe things which served his interests alone. This situation was the antithesis of that the savants were trying to promote, where people, free from the influence of the entrenched powers of the aristocracy and clergy, lived according to simple moral precepts derived from the direct study of nature. Women were seen as a major impediment in this process of enlightenment, because they repeated hearsay and tittle tattle and were more prone than men to religious enthusiasm. It was therefore in the interests of savants to polarize women and men, reaction and progress.

The opposition between superstition and tradition on the one hand, and enlightenment and progress on the other, functioned not just in the passionate anti-clericalism of eighteenth- and nineteenth-century France, but in debates about the care of children and about midwifery. The theme of the irrationality and irresponsibility of women's ways with small children was articulated in Britain by William Codogan in his *Essay on Nursing*, first published in 1748. He argued that 'the Preservation of Children should become the Care of Men of Sense' because 'this Business has been too long fatally left to the Management of Women' (1753: 3). He justified the charge of female irresponsibility by invoking the 'superstitious Practices and Ceremonies' which they had inherited from 'their Great Grandmothers' (1753: 4). He recommended a transfer from female to male authority regarding infant care. He was not simply co-opting a new field for male medical practitioners for he also wished fathers to take a more active role: 'I . . . earnestly recommend it to every Father to have his Child nursed under his own Eye, to make use of his own Reason and Sense' (1753: 29). Cadogan thought that women perpetuated ancient practices such as swaddling which should be abolished in favour of the forms of care advised by physicians. He never suggested that men should take over the care of children, but that women should perform their alloted tasks under the advice of men, both their husbands and their doctors. So, it was not that female functions had been abolished or co-opted, but that a hierarchy had been established where women acted under the supervision of men. Men such as Cadogan did not argue for a changed division of labour but for an altered division of power.

The same image of female irresponsibility was implied in attitudes to mid-wives. The relationship between midwives and other medical practitioners was a complex one (Donnison 1977). There was the element of competition for patients and the related issue of fees for services. It was commonly implied that midwives were dangerous and ignorant in comparison with physicians and surgeons. This claim must be seen in the context of the great concern about quacks, i.e. unlicensed practitioners, in the second half of the eighteenth century. Among the most common complaints against them was that they sold specific remedies and tried to keep the recipes secret. According to the medical establishment, such charlatans clearly traded on the ignorance and blind faith of the simple people who bought their potions rather than employing the skilled eye and brain of a better educated practitioner. Midwives appeared especially suspicious to enlightened savants. Their territory was the intimate and tightly knit circle of women, at least in the imagination of their detractors. Midwives being women with children themselves, and being associated with birth, were at the centre of stereotypes about women and their world.

The treatment of midwives in Britain and France provides an excellent example of the ways in which women were subject to social regulation in a manner which suggests that they were feared as polluting, morally and sexually. It is well known that the midwife was frequently the butt of caricatures and bawdy humour and that she was castigated for drunkenness and uncleanliness (Donnison 1977: 33–4). This suspicion was made explicit in the proofs of morality which were demanded of them. In eighteenth-century France this often took the form of a letter from their priest attesting to their good character.[2] At this time both males and females were trained to be *accoucheurs*, the former becoming surgeons, the latter midwives. The education of these two groups was done separately; in fact the idea of instructing them together was considered indecent. The young surgeons were apparently not subject to the moral restraints applied to midwives. They were typically much younger than the pupil midwives, the boys were mostly in their early teens while the women were rarely younger than 20 and mostly married. One decisive difference between the two groups might be the greater sexual experience of the women who had, in all probability, borne children themselves. We could argue that young boys were in principle just as potentially 'dangerous' in the childbirth situation as married women were, probably from our perspective more so. Yet there is no evidence that it was seen that way at the time by medical men. The reasons are partly sexual, and partly a question of class, since the midwives were certainly of humbler origins than the surgeons. The delivery of babies was performed by both men and women, although it would be hard to devise simple rules which determined whether a man or a woman delivered any particular mother. Here we have a situation where the actual division between the sexes was blurred in that, in addition to midwifery, women from all social strata practised a whole range of medical techniques. What we can detect is an unease about the demarcation between male and female medical practitioners resulting in recurrent attempts to control and clarify the sexual boundaries.

Unease about midwives in relation to their male competitors for custom was expressed quite explicitly in a poem by the medical practitioner turned parson and poet, George Crabbe.[3] In *The Parish Register* of 1807 he describes the battle between an established midwife and a young doctor newly arrived in the village (Crabbe 1823, I: 122–5). 'The young doctor . . . sneered at the midwife as "Nature's slave", who trusted only to luck, and in emergencies to prayer, while he, with his "skill" and "courage", took pleasure in bending Nature to his will' (Donnison 1977: 38).

The uncomfortable position of the midwife illustrates one of the ways in which beliefs in women as bearers of tradition and men as bearers of modernity worked. The fact that forceps were used by men may have further reinforced their image of modernity and power through new techniques. The professional struggle hinged on who should have charge of birth, the event which, more than any other, occupied the centre stage of many women's lives and of the symbolic structures associated with women.[4]

It was as mothers that women were archetypally seen, and, in the case of anatomical drawings, actually in the state of pregnancy itself. But of course there were other images too, especially those derived from classical mythology and used in engravings, oil paintings, statues, bas reliefs, and representations for ceremonial or official purposes. The classical traditions, and their eighteenth-century transformations are extremely complex from the point of view of sexual symbolism. One example may however be useful to illustrate the association of a female deity with natural health.

In his *Sermon on Exercise* of 1772, Benjamin Rush contrasted the natural therapy of exercise with the artificiality of specific remedies. To illustrate the superiority of the former approach to illness he constructed a parable. A wondrously beautiful woman appears to a group of chronically sick people who are suffering from the disastrous effects of quack concoctions. She addresses them with the words: 'Ye children of men, listen for a while to the voice of instruction . . . My name is Hygiaea. I preside over the health of mankind. Descard all your medicines, and seek relief from Temperance and Exercise alone' (Rush 1947: 371). They heed her advice and their natural vigour is restored.

I have argued that there was a complex language in medical writings in the second half of the eighteenth century which employed the nature/culture dichotomy in relation to gender. The attributes of women ranged from ignorance and superstition to true civilizing wisdom. Some of those attributes were visually represented in explicit models, statues, engravings and anatomical plates.

IMAGES OF WOMAN – NATURE DISROBES BEFORE REASON

An important eighteenth-century example of images of woman rendered visual is the wax anatomical models of human figures used for making anatomical drawings and for display in popular museums (Haviland and Parish 1970, Thompson 1925, Deer 1977). These were intended for teaching, both popular and technical, and for decoration. Although male and female anatomical organs, especially the female abdomen, were commonly depicted in anatomy texts from the sixteenth century onwards (Choulant 1962), these models are distinctly different. In the wax series, many of which were made in Florence at the end of the eighteenth century (Azzaroli 1975), the female figures are recumbent, frequently adorned with pearl necklaces. They have long hair, and occasionally they have hair in the public area also. These 'Venuses' as they were significantly called lie on velvet or silk cushions, in a passive, almost sexually inviting pose. Comparable male figures are usually upright, and often in a position of motion. The female models can be opened to display the removable viscera, and most often contain a foetus, while the male ones are made in a variety of forms to display the different physiological systems.[5] The figures of recumbent women seem to convey, for the first time, the sexual potential of medical anatomy. Until this time it was usual in engravings for the actual genitals to be covered by a cloth but in the waxes, as in some contemporaneous medical illustrations, they are not just present, but drawn to the attention. Not only is the literal naturalness of women portrayed, in their total nakedness and by the presence of a foetus, but their symbolic naturalness is implied in the whole conception of such figures. Female nature had been unclothed by male science, making her understandable under general scrutiny. The image was made explicit in the statue in the Paris medical faculty of a young woman, her breasts bare, her head slightly bowed beneath the veil she is taking off, which bears the inscription 'Nature unveils herself before Science'.

Women's bodies as objects of medical enquiry as well as of sexual desire became the focus for a physiological literature which expressed a refined aesthetic of women's natural beauty, and found in their bodies an expression of their social condition. To understand women was thus a scientific and medical task which involved revealing the manner of physiological functioning, both normal and pathological, that was peculiar to women. It was for this reason that when Jules Michelet wished to comprehend the condition of women in mid-nineteenth-century France, his first port of call was the dissecting room, and his reading was anatomy texts. In the cadavers of women, Michelet saw their lives revealed and explained before his very eyes. Once again a dual meaning of woman as natural was evoked: she was taken as a creature defined by her biology and as the feminine natural object of masculine science. But perhaps we should add a new third sense. In her pregnant state woman evoked nature yet again through her capacity to reproduce the species, to pass on life. With the definition of life as a new guiding concept at the end of the eighteenth century (Figlio 1976: 25ff.), the mechanism whereby life was transmitted took on fresh significance. The capacity to engender life seemed a special elusive force, made concrete through the female reproductive system. This sacred function went hand in hand with female anatomy. One expression of this was the concern among anatomists to discover ideal female beauty. During the eighteenth century medical writers placed great emphasis on the aesthetics of the human body, and on the natural beauty of women which, they argued, should remain undeformed by clothing, and especially by corsets (Choulant 1962: 304).

The peak of the sexualized female anatomy was a German painting and lithograph of a beautiful young woman, who had been drowned, being dissected by an anatomist, Professor Lucae, who was interested in the physical basis of female attractiveness. A group of men stand around the table on which a female corpse is lying. She has long hair and well-defined breasts. One of the men has begun the dissection and is working on her thorax. He is holding up a sheet of skin, the part which covers her breast, as if it were a thin article of clothing so delicate and fine is its texture. The corpse is being undressed scientifically, the constituent parts of the body are being displayed for scrutiny and analysis. The powerful sexual image is integral to the whole pictorial effect.[6]

By the 1860s when this engraving was produced, the image it contained might be associated with others which were relatively new to the general public. I am thinking in particular of the fierce public debates about vivisection, which in Britain was opposed, interestingly enough, by a number of women's groups and early feminists (French 1975: 239–50). In vivisectional experiments, pictures of which were prominently displayed in the propaganda put out by critics, there was the same contrast between the utter passivity of the living material used and the active intrusion and manipulation of the experimenters. Despite the long history of anatomical dissections, and the fact that the victim was dead, the anatomizing of the corpse, especially as portrayed in Hasselhorst's picture of Lucae, seems to have similar qualities to the vivisectional experiment. And the exaggerated femininity of the corpse reinforced its passivity. It is almost as if women in their sexually stereotyped roles were made kin to all living objects brought under the penetrating enquiry of male reason.

Notes

1. See for example, Hufton (1971, 1975–6).
2. This account is based on my archival work in Lille using departmental and municipal collections. See also Gélis (1977) and Morel (1977).
3. For a very brief introductory account of Crabbe see Brett (1968).
4. In fiction, Sterne's *Tristram Shandy*, first published 1759–67, provides an illustration of this point.
5. Here I have alluded briefly to what is in fact a very complex issue. There were many different traditions of anatomical models but little has been written about them. See however Thompson (1925), on early ivory manikins, and on anatomical illustration in general, Wolf-Heidegger and Cetto (1967: especially pp. 434, 438, 504, 505, 546–7). Collections which include these or similar figures are: Wellcome Collections, Science Museum, London; Institut für Geschichte der Medizin der Universität, Vienna; Museo 'La Specola', Florence.
6. The original painting is in the Historisches Museum, Frankfurt, the lithograph is in the Wellcome Institute for the History of Medicine, London. An illustration of the former is in Wolf-Heidegger and Cetto (1967: 546).

References

Alibert, J. L. 1803. 'Eloge historique de Pierre Roussel', in *Système Physique et Moral de la Femme*, P. Roussel, pp. 1–52. Paris: Crapart, Caille et Ravier.

Azzaroli, M. L. 1975. 'La Specola. The Zoological Museum of Florence University', *Atti del 1° Congresso Internazionale sulla Ceroplastica nella Scienza e Nell'Arte*, pp. 5–31 + 9 plates.

Barthez, P. J. 1806. *Nouveaux Elémens de la Science de l'Homme*. 2 vols. Paris: Goujor et Brunot.

Brett, R. L. 1968. *George Crabbe*, revised edition. London: Longmans.

Cabanis, P. J. G. 1956. *Oeuvres Philosophiques*, 2 vols. Paris: Presses Universitaires de France.

Cadogan, W. 1753. *An Essay upon Nursing and the Management of Children from their Birth to Three Years of Age*. 6th edition. London: The Foundling Hospital.

Choulant, J. L. 1962. *History and Bibliography of Anatomic Illustration*. New York and London: Hafner.

Crabbe, G. 1823. *The Works of the Rev. George Crabbe*. 8 vols. London: John Murray.

Deer, L. 1977. 'Italian anatomical waxes in the Wellcome Collection: the missing link', *Rivista di Storia delle Scienze mediche e naturali*, 20, pp. 281–98.

Donnison, J. 1977. *Midwives and Medical Men. A History of Inter-Professional Rivalries and Women's Rights*. London: Heinemann.

Farrington, B. 1964. *The Philosophy of Francis Bacon. An Essay on its Development from 1603 to 1609 with new Translations of Fundamental Texts*. Liverpool: Liverpool University Press.

Figlio, K. 1975. 'Theories of perception and the physiology of mind in the late eighteenth century', *History of Science*, 12, pp. 177–212.

—— 1976. 'The metaphor of organisation: a historiographical perspective on the bio-medical sciences of the early nineteenth century', *History of Science*, 14, pp. 17–53.

French, R. D. 1975. *Antivivisection and Medical Science in Victorian Society*. Princeton and London: Princeton University Press.

Gélis, J. 1977. 'Sages-femmes et accoucheurs: l'obstétrique populaire aux XVIIe et XVIIIe siècles', *Annales: Économies, Sociétés, Civilisations*, 32, part 5, pp. 927–57.

Glacken, C. 1967. *Traces on the Rhodian Shore. Nature and Culture in Western Thought from ancient times to the end of the eighteenth century*. Berkeley, Los Angeles and London: University of California Press.

Haviland, T. N., Parish, L. C. 1970. 'A brief account of the use of wax models in the study of medicine', *Journal of the History of Medicine*, 25, pp. 52–75.

Hufton, O. 1971. 'Women in revolution 1789–1796', *Past and Present*, 53, pp. 90–108.

—— 1975–6. 'Women and the family economy in eighteenth-century France', *French Historical Studies*, 9, pp. 1–22.

Jordanova, L. J. 1979. 'Earth science and environmental medicine: the synthesis of the late Enlightenment', in *Images of the Earth: Essays in the History of the Environmental Sciences*, ed. L. J. Jordanova and R. Porter, pp. 119–46. Chalfont St Giles: British Society for the History of Science.

Kolodny, A. 1975. *The Lay of the Land*. Chapel Hill: University of North Carolina Press.

Macquart, L. C. H. 1799. *Dictionnaire de la Conservation de l'Homme*, 2 vols. Paris: Bidault.

Morel, M.-F. 1977. 'Ville et compagne dans le discours medical sur la petite enfance au XVIIIe siècle', *Annales: Économies, Sociétés, Civilisations*, 32, part 5, pp. 1,007–24.

Pomme, P. 1782. *Traité des Affections Vaporeuses des Deux Sexes*. Paris: L'Imprimerie Royale.

Roussel, P. 1803. *Système Physique et Moral de la Femme*, 2nd edition. Paris: Crapart, Caille et Ravier.

Rush, B. 1947. *The Selected Writings of Benjamin Rush*. New York: Philosophical Library.

Thompson, C. J. S. 1925. 'Anatomical manikins', *Journal of Anatomy*, 59, part 4, pp. 442–5 + 2 plates.

Williams, R. 1975. *The Country and the City*. St Albans: Paladin.

Wolf-Heidegger, G. and Cetto, A. M. 1967. *Die Anatomische Sektion in Bildlicher Darstellung*. Basle and New York: S. Karger.

CHAPTER 4

Artificiality and Enlightenment: From Sociobiology to Biosociality

Paul Rabinow

WORLDLY GENETICS: ARTIFICIALITY AND ENLIGHTENMENT

Michel Foucault identified the distinctively modern form of power as "bio-technico-power." Biopower, he writes, designates "what brought life and its mechanism into the realm of explicit calculations and made knowledge-power an agent of transformation of human life." Historically, practices and discourses of biopower have clustered around two distinct poles: the "anatomopolitics of the human body," the anchor point and target of disciplinary technologies, on the one hand, and a regulatory pole centered on population, with a panoply of strategies concentrating on knowledge, control and welfare, on the other.[1] My current work turns on a new articulation of the discourses and practices of biopower, currently symbolized by, but not restricted to, the Human Genome Initiative.[2] In this paper, I shall sketch some of the ways in which I believe the two poles of the body and the population are being rearticulated into what could be called a postdisciplinary rationality.[3]

In the annex to his book on Michel Foucault – entitled "On the Death of Man and Superman" – Gilles Deleuze presents a schema of three "force-forms," to use his terminology, which are roughly equivalent to Michel Foucault's three epistemes. In the classical form, *infinity* and *perfection* are the forces shaping beings; beings have a form toward which they strive, and the task of science is to represent correctly the table of those forms in an encyclopedic fashion. In the modern form, *finitude* establishes a field of life, labor and language within which Man appears as a distinctive being, who is both the subject and object of his own understanding, but an understanding that is never complete because of its very structure. Finally, here in the present day, a field of the *surhomme* – which I prefer to call the "afterman" – in which finitude, as empiricity, gives way to a play of forces and forms that Deleuze labels *"fini-illimité."*[4] In this new constellation, beings have neither a perfected form nor an essential opacity. The best example of this "unlimited-finite" is DNA: an infinity of beings can and has arisen from the four bases out of which DNA is constituted. François Jacob, the Nobel Prize–winning biologist, makes a similiar point when he writes, "a limited amount of genetic information in the germ line, produces an enormous number of protein structures . . . in the soma. . . . [N]ature operates to create diversity by endlessly combining bits and pieces."[5] Whether Deleuze has seized the significance of Jacob's facts remains an open question. Still, it is intriguing when something as cryptic as Rimbaud's formula that "the man of the future will be filled with animals" takes on a perfectly material meaning – as we shall see when we turn to the concept of model organism in the new genetics.[6]

Deleuze convincingly claims that Foucault lost his wager that it would be the language of the anthropological triad – life, labor, language – that would open the way for a new episteme, washing the figure of Man away like a wave crashing over a drawing in the sand. Foucault himself acknowledged that his prediction had been wrong when, a decade after the publication of *The Order of Things*, he mocked the "relentless theorization of writing," not as the dawning of the new age but as the death rattle of an old one.[7] Deleuze's claim is not that language is irrelevant but rather that the new epochal practices are emerging in the domains of labor and life. Again, whether Deleuze has correctly grasped the significance of these new practices remains to be seen; regardless, they are clearly important. It seems prudent to approach these terms heuristically, taking them singly and as a series of bonded base pairs – labor and life, life and language, language and labor – to see where they lead.

My research strategy focuses on the practices of life as the most potent present site of new knowledges and powers. The logical place to examine these changes is the Human Genome Initiative (sponsored by the National Institutes of Health and the Department of Energy), whose mandate is to produce a map of our DNA. The Initiative is very much a technoscience project in two senses. Like most modern science, it is deeply imbricated with technological advances in the most literal way, in this case the confidence that qualitatively more rapid, accurate and efficient machinery will be invented if the money is made available (this is already happening). The second sense of technological is the more important and interesting one: the object to be known – the human genome – will be known in such a way that it can be *changed*. This dimension is thoroughly modern; one could even say that it instantiates the definition of modern rationality. Representing and intervening, knowledge and power, understanding and reform, are built in, from the start, as simultaneous goals and means.

My initial stance toward the Initiative and its associated institutions and practices is rather traditionally ethnographic: neither committed nor opposed, I seek to describe what is going on. I follow Foucault when he asks, "Shall we try reason? To my mind nothing would be more sterile. First, because the field has nothing to do with guilt or innocence. What we have to do is analyze specific rationalities rather than always invoking the progress of rationalization in general."[8] My ethnographic question is: How will our social and ethical practices change as this project advances? I intend to approach this question on a number of levels and in a variety of sites. First, there is the Initiative itself. Second, there are adjacent enterprises and institutions in which and through which new understandings, new practices and new technologies of life and labor will certainly be articulated – prime among them the biotechnology industry. Finally, the emergence of bioethics and environmental ethics lodged in a number of different institutions will bear scrutiny as a key locus of discursive reform.

THE HUMAN GENOME INITIATIVE

What is the Human Genome Initiative? A genome is "the entire complement of genetic material in the set of chromosomes of a particular organism."[9] DNA is composed of four bases that bond into two kinds of pairs wound in the famous double helix. The current estimate is that we have about three billion base pairs in our DNA; the mouse has about the same number, while corn or salamanders have more than thirty times as many base pairs in their DNA as we do. No one knows why. Most of the DNA has no known function. It is currently held, not without a certain uneasiness, that 90 percent of human DNA is "junk." The renowned Cambridge molecular biologist, Sydney Brenner, makes a helpful distinction between "junk" and "garbage." Garbage is something used up and worthless, which one throws away; junk, though, is something one stores for some unspecified future use. It seems highly unlikely that 90 percent of our DNA is evolutionarily irrelevant – but what its precise relevance could be remains unknown.

Our genes, therefore, constitute the remaining 10 percent of the DNA. What are genes? They are segments of the DNA that code for proteins. Genes apparently vary in size from about ten thousand base pairs up to two million base pairs. Genes, or at any rate most human genes known today (1 percent of the presumed total), are not simply spatial units in the sense of a continuous sequence of base pairs; rather, they are regions of DNA made up of spans called "exons," interspersed by regions called "introns." When a gene is activated – and little is known about this process – the segment of DNA is transcribed to a type of RNA. The introns are spliced out, and the exons are joined together to form messenger RNA. This segment is then translated to code for a protein.

We don't know how many genes we have. It is estimated that Homo sapiens has between fifty thousand and one hundred thousand genes – with a rather large margin of error. We also don't know where most of these genes are – neither which chromosome they are found on nor where they are located on that chromosome. The Initiative is designed to change all this: literally to map our genes. This poses two obvious questions: What is a map? And who is the "we" of "our" genes?

For the first question, then: At present there are three different kinds of maps – linkage, physical and sequence. Linkage maps are the most familiar to us from the Mendelian genetics we learned in high school. They are based on extensive studies of family genealogies (the Mormon historical archives provide the most complete historical documentation, and the French have a similar project) and show how linked traits are inherited. Linkage maps show which genes are reinherited and roughly where they are on the chromosomes. This provides a helpful first step for identifying the probable location of disease genes in gross terms – but only a first step. In the hunt for the cystic fibrosis gene, for example, linkage maps narrowed down the area to be explored before other types of mapping completed the task.

There are several types of physical maps: "a physical map is a representation of the location of identifiable landmarks on the DNA."[10] The discovery of "restriction enzymes" provided a major advance in mapping capabilities. These proteins serve to cut DNA into chunks at specific sites. The chunk of DNA can then be cloned and its makeup chemically analyzed and then reconstructed in its original order in the genome. These maps are physical in the literal sense that one has a chunk of DNA and one identifies the gene's location on it (these have been assembled into "libraries"). The problem is to locate these physical chunks on a larger chromosomal map. Cloning techniques involving bacteria were used for a number of years, but new techniques, such as "in situ hybridization techniques," are replacing the more time-consuming cloning techniques.

Polymerase chain reaction reduces the need for cloning and physical libraries. It is necessary to clone segments of DNA in order to get enough identical copies to analyze, but this multiplication can now be done more rapidly and efficiently by having the DNA do the work itself, as follows: first, one constructs a small piece of DNA, perhaps twenty base pairs long, called a "primer" or oligonucleotide, which is then commercially made to specification. The raw material from which one takes the base pairs (to be assembled like Lego blocks) is either salmon sperm or the biomass left over from fermentation processes. A particularly rich source are the by-products of soy sauce (hence the Japanese have an edge in this market). This DNA is refined into single bases, or nucleosides, and recombined according to the desired specifications at a cost of about one dollar per coupling in a DNA synthesizer. The nucleosides could all be made synthetically, but it is currently cheaper given the small quantities needed – most primers are about twenty bases long – to stick to salmon sperm and soy sauce biomass. The current world production of DNA for a year is perhaps several grams, but as demand grows there will be a growing market for the oligonucleotides, custom-made strips of DNA. As Gerald Zon, a biochemist at Applied Biosystems, Inc., put it: The company's dream is to be the world's supplier of synthetic DNA.[11]

Two primers are targeted to attach themselves to the DNA at specific sites called "sequence-tagged sites" (STS's). These primers then simply "instruct" the single strand of DNA to reproduce itself without having to be inserted into another organism – this is the polymerase chain reaction (PCR). So, instead of having physically to clone a gene, one can simply tell one's friends in Osaka or Omaha which primers to build and where to apply them, and they can do the job themselves (eventually including the DNA preparation, which will be automated). The major advantage of the PCR–STS technique is that it yields information that can be described as "information in a database": "No access to the biological materials that led to the definition or mapping of an STS is required by a scientist wishing to assay a DNA sample for its presence."[12] The computer would tell any laboratory where to look and which primer to construct, and within twenty-four hours, one would have the bit of DNA one is interested in. These segments could then be sequenced by laboratories anywhere in the world and entered into a data base. Such developments have opened the door to what promises to be "a common language for physical mapping of the human genome."[13]

Sequencing means actually identifying the series of base pairs on the physical map. There is ongoing controversy about whether it is necessary to have the complete sequence of the genome (after all, there are vast regions of junk whose role is currently unknown), the complete set of genes (what most genes do is unknown) or merely the sequence of "expressed" genes (that is, those genes whose protein products are known). While there are formidable technological problems involved in all this, and formidable technological solutions appearing with the predicted rapidity, the principles and the goal are clear enough. "The technical means have become available to root the physical map of the human genome firmly in the DNA sequence itself. Sequence information is the natural language of physical mapping."[14] Of course, the database is not a language but a computer code, and by "natural" our scientist probably means "currently most useful."

Still, even when the whole human genome is mapped and even when it is sequenced, as Charles Cantor, senior scientist at the Department of Energy, has said, we will know nothing about how it works.[15] We will have a kind of structure without function. Much more work remains to be done, and currently is being done, on the hard scientific problems: protein structure, emergent levels of complexity and the rest. (Remember, the entire genetic makeup of a human being is found in most of our cells, but *how* a cell becomes – and remains – a brain cell instead of a toe cell is not known.) What we will have a decade from now is the material sequence of the *unlimited-finite*, a sequence map of three billion base pairs and between fifty thousand and one hundred thousand genes.

As to the second question: Whose genome is it? Obviously, not everyone has exactly the same genes or, for that matter, junk DNA – if we did, we would presumably be identical (and probably extinct). There was some debate early on in the project as to exactly whose genome was being mapped; there was a half-serious proposal to have a very rich individual finance the analysis of his own genome.[16] The problem is now shelved – literally – in the clone libraries. The collective standard consists of different physical pieces mapped at centers around the world. Cantor has pointed out that given the way genes are currently located on chromosomes (linkage maps), the easiest genome to map and sequence would necessarily be composed of the largest number of abnormal genes. In other words, *the pathological would be the path to the normal.*

Interestingly, all of the sequenced genes need not come from human beings. Genomes of other organisms are also being mapped. Several of these organisms, about which a great deal is already known, have been designated as model systems. Many genes work in the same way, regardless of the living being in which they are found. Thus, in principle, wherever we find a specific protein we can know what DNA sequence produced it. This "genetic code" has not changed during evolution and, therefore, many genes of simpler organisms are basically the same as human genes. Since, for ethical reasons, many simpler organisms are easier to study, much of what we know about human genetics derives from the model genetic systems such as yeast and mice. Fruit flies have proved to be an extremely useful model system. "One DNA sequence, called the 'homeobox', was first identified in the genes of fruit flies and later in those of higher organisms, including human beings."[17] This short stretch of nucleotides (in a nearly regular sequence) appears to play a role in turning genes on and off.

Comparisons with even simpler organisms are useful in the identification of genes encoding proteins essential to life. The elaboration of protein sequences and their differences has led to new classifications and a new understanding of evolutionary relationships and processes. An Office of Technology Assessment report laconically asserts the utility of comparisons of human and mouse DNA sequences for the "identification of genes unique to higher organisms because mice genes are more homologous to human genes than are the genes of any other well characterized organism."[18] Rimbaud's mysterious claim that "the man of the future will be filled with animals" indeed seems sound – if we interpret it to mean that we would know in some detail how we have evolved and what we have retained and added in the process.

FROM STIGMA TO RISK: NORMAL HANDICAPS

My educated guess is that the new genetics will prove to be an infinitely greater force for reshaping society and life than was the revolution in physics, because it will be embedded throughout the social fabric at the microlevel by medical practices and a variety of other discourses. The new genetics will carry with it its own distinctive promises and dangers.[19] Previous eugenics projects have been modern social projects cast in biological metaphors. Although their social effects have ranged from public hygiene to the Holocaust, none had much to do with the serious speech acts of biology, even if they were all pervaded with discourses of truth.[20] Sociobiology, as Marshall Sahlins and others have shown, is a social project: from liberal, philanthropic interventions designated to moralize and discipline the poor and degenerate, to *Rassenhygien* and its social extirpations, to entrepreneurial sociobiology and its supply-side social sadism, the construction of society has been at stake.[21] Eugenics was frequently professed by reputable, extremely well placed scientists, but – I want to assert here, and I argue the point elsewhere – the specific projects themselves did not emerge from within scientific practice: they were never *dans le vrai*, to use Georges Canguilhem's telling phrase.

In the future, the new genetics will cease to be a biological metaphor for modern society and will become instead a circulation network of identity terms and restriction loci, around which and through which a truly new type of autoproduction will emerge, which I call "biosociality." If sociobiology is culture constructed on the basis of a metaphor of nature, then in biosociality, nature will be modeled on culture understood as practice. Nature will be known and remade through technique and will finally become artificial, just as culture becomes natural. Were such a project to be brought to fruition, it would stand as the basis for overcoming the nature/culture split.

A crucial step in overcoming the nature/culture split will be the dissolution of the category of "the social." By "society" I don't mean some naturalized universal, which is found everywhere and studied by sociologists and anthropologists simply because it is an object waiting to be described; rather, I mean something more specific. In my recent book, *French Modern: Norms and Forms of the Social Environment*, I argue that if our definition is something like Raymond Williams's usage in the first edition of his book of modern commonplaces, *Keywords* – that is, the whole way of life of a people (hence open to empirical analysis and planned change) – then society and the social sciences are the ground plan for modernity.[22]

We can see the beginnings of the dissolution of modernist society happening in recent transformations of the concept of risk. Robert Castel, in his 1981 book, *La Gestion des risques*, presents a grid of analysis whose insights extend far beyond his specific concerns with psychiatry, shedding particular light on current trends in the biosciences.[23] Castel's book is an interrogation of postdisciplinary society, which he characterizes thus: first, a mutation of social technologies that minimize direct therapeutic intervention, supplanted by an increasing emphasis on a preventive administrative management of populations at risk; and second, the promotion of working on oneself in a continuous fashion so as to produce an efficient and adaptable subject. These trends lead away from holistic approaches to the subject or social contextualism and move instead toward an instrumentalized approach to both environment and individual as a sum of diverse factors amenable to analysis by specialists. The most salient aspect of this trend for the present discussion is an increasing institutional gap between diagnostics and therapeutics. Although this gap is not a new one, to be sure, the potential for its widening nonetheless poses a new range of social, ethical and cultural problems, which will become more prominent as biosociality progresses.

Modern prevention is, above all, the tracking down of risks – not in the sense of the result of specific dangers posed by the immediate presence of a person or a group, but rather, the composition of impersonal "factors" that make a risk probable. Prevention, then, is surveillance not of the individual but of likely occurrences of diseases, anomalies, deviant behavior to be minimized and healthy behavior to be maximized. We are partially moving away from the older face-to-face surveillance of individuals and groups known to be dangerous or ill (for disciplinary or therapeutic purposes), toward projecting risk factors that deconstruct and reconstruct the individual or group subject. This new mode anticipates possible loci of dangerous irruptions through the identification of sites statistically locatable in relation to norms and means. Through the use of computers, individuals sharing certain traits or sets of traits can be grouped together in a way that not only decontextualizes them from their social environment but also is nonsubjective in a double sense: it is objectively arrived at, and does not apply to a subject in anything like the older sense of the word (that is, the suffering, meaningfully situated integrator of social, historical and bodily experiences). Castel names this trend "the technocratic administration of differences." Computerized series dissolve the traditional subject and retain only abstract givens as part of factors in a series. The target is not a person but a population at risk. As an AIDS-advocacy group in France put it: It is not who one is but what one does that puts one at risk. One's practices are not totalizing, although they may be mortal.[24]

Although epidemiological social-tracking methods were first implemented comprehensively in the tuberculosis campaign, they came to their contemporary maturity elsewhere. The distinction that Castel underscores as symptomatic of this change is that between *disease* and *handicap*. A "handicap," according to a French government report authored by the highly respected technocrat François Bloch-Laine, is "any physical, mental or situational condition that produces a weakness or trouble in relation to what is considered normal; normal is defined as the mean of capacities and chances of most individuals in the same society."[25] The concept of handicap was first used officially in England during World War II as a means of evaluating the available workforce in a way that included as many people as possible. Handicaps were deficits to be compensated for socially, psychologically and spatially, not illnesses to be treated – orthopedics not therapeutics. "The concept of handicap naturalizes the subject's history as well as assimilating expected performance levels at a particular historical moment to a naturalized normality."[26] True, this particular individual is blind or deaf or mute or short or tall or paralyzed, but can he or she operate the lathe, answer the telephone, guard the door? If not, what can we do to him or her, to the work or to the environment, that would make this possible? Performance is a relative term. Practices make the person; or rather, they don't – they just make practitioners.[27]

There is a large historical step indeed from the rich web of social and personal significations Western culture inscribed in tuberculosis to the inclusive grid of the welfare state, which has yet to inspire much poetry or yield a celebrated *Bildungsroman*. It has, however, increased life expectancy and produced millions of documents, many of them inscribed in silicon. The objectivism of social factors is now giving way to a new genetics and the beginnings of a redefinition and eventual operationalization of nature.

In a chapter entitled "What Is (Going) To Be Done?" in his book *Proceed with Caution: Predicting Genetic Risks in the Recombinant DNA Era*, Neil Holtzman documents the ways that genetic screening will be used in the coming years when its scope and sensitivity is increased dramatically by such technological advances as PCR, which will reduce cost, time and resistance. There are already tests for such conditions as sickle-cell anemia, and diagnostics for cystic fibrosis and Alzheimer's are on the horizon. These diseases are among the estimated four thousand single-gene disorders. There is a much larger number of diseases, disorders and discomforts that are polygenetic. Genetic testing will soon be moving into areas in which presymptomatic testing will be at a premium. Thus, Holtzman suggests that once a test is available for identifying a "susceptibility-conferring genotype" for breast cancer, earlier and more frequent mammograms would be recommended or even required (for insurance purposes).[28] He adds:

> Monitoring those with genetic predispositions to insulin-dependent diabetes mellitus, colorectal cancer, neurofibromatosis, retinoblastoma, or Wilms tumor for the purpose of detecting early manifestations of the disease might prove beneficial. Discovering those with genetic predispositions could be accomplished either by population-wide screening or, less completely, by testing families in which disease has already occurred.[29]

This remark involves a large number of issues, but the only one I shall underline here is the certain formation of new group and individual identities and practices arising out of these new truths. There will be, for example, neurofibromatosis groups who will meet to share their experiences, lobby for their disease, educate their children, redo their home environment, and so on – and that is what I mean by "biosociality." I am not discussing some hypothetical gene for aggression or altruism. Rather there will be groups formed around the chromosome 17, locus 16,256, site 654,376 allele variant with a guanine substitution. These groups will have medical specialists, laboratories, narratives, traditions and a heavy panoply of pastoral keepers to help them experience, share, intervene in, and "understand" their fate.

Fate it will be. It will carry with it no depth. It makes absolutely no sense to seek the meaning of the lack of a guanine base because it has no meaning. One's relation to one's father or mother is not shrouded in the depths of discourse here, the relationship is material even when it is environmental: Did your father smoke? Did your mother take DES? Rest assured they didn't know what they were doing. It follows that other forms of pastoral care will become more prominent, in order to overcome the handicap and to prepare for the risks. These therapies for the normal will be diverse, ranging from behavior modifications, to stress management, to interactional therapies of all sorts.[30] We might even see a return of tragedy in postmodernist form, although we will likely not simply rail against the gods, but rather be driven to overcome our fates through more technoscience. The nineties will be the decade of genetics, immunology and environmentalism – for, clearly, these are the leading vehicles for the infiltration of technoscience, capitalism and culture into what the moderns called "nature."

Donna Haraway labels these changes "the death of the clinic": "The clinic's methods required bodies and works: we have texts and surfaces. Our domina-tions don't work by medicalization and normalization any more; they work by networking, communication redesign, stress management."[31] I only partially agree; a multiplication and complex imbrication of rationalities continue to exist. Obvi-ously, older forms of cultural classification of bio-identity such as race, gender and age have no more disappeared than medicalization and normalization have – although the meanings and the practices that constitute them certainly are changing. Postdisciplinary practices will coexist with disciplinary technologies; post–social-biological classifications will only gradually colonize older cultural grids. Thus, Troy Duster has shown how testing for sickle-cell anemia has reinforced preexistent racial and social categories, even though the distribution of the gene is far wider than the African-American community.[32] In complicated and often insidious ways, the older categories may even take on a renewed force as the new genetics begins to spread not only in the obvious racism so rampant today but more subtly in studies of blacks' alleged higher susceptibility to tuberculosis. My argument is simply that these older cultural classifications will be joined by a vast array of new ones, which will cross-cut, partially supersede and eventually redefine the older categories in ways that are well worth monitoring.

Notes

1. Michel Foucault, *The History of Sexuality*, vol. 1: *An Introduction*, trans. Robert Hurley (New York: Pantheon, 1978), p. 139.
2. *Mapping Our Genes, Genome Projects: How Big, How Fast?* (Washington, D.C.: Office of Technology Assessment, 1988).
3. For what it's worth, I don't think "postdisciplinary" can be equated with "postmodern."
4. Gilles Deleuze, *Foucault* (Paris: Minuit, 1986): "L'homme tend à libérer en lui la vie, le travail et le language" (p. 140). Foucault's version is found in *The Order of Things: An Archaeology of the Human Sciences* (New York: Vintage, 1966). On natural history in the Classical age, see Henri Daudin, *Cuvier et Lamarck: Les Classes zoologiques et l'idée de série animale* (Paris: Alcan, 1926). On the philosophical understanding of Man, see Jules Vuillemin, *L'Héritage kantien et la révolution copernicienne: Fichte, Cohen, Heidegger* (Paris: P.U.F., 1954).
5. François Jacob, *The Possible and the Actual* (New York: Pantheon, 1982), p. 39.
6. Deleuze, *Foucault*: "L'homme de l'avenir est chargé des animaux" (p. 141).
7. Michel Foucault, "Truth and Power," in Paul Rabinow, ed., *The Foucault Reader* (New York: Pantheon, 1984), p. 127; idem, *The Order of Things*, p. 387.
8. Michel Foucault, "The Subject and Power," in Hubert Dreyfus and Paul Rabinow, *Michel Foucault: Beyond Structuralism and Hermeneutics* (2d ed., Chicago: University of Chicago Press, 1983), p. 210.
9. *Mapping Our Genes*, p. 21.
10. Ibid., p. 30.
11. Interview with author, March 19, 1990.
12. *Mapping Our Genes*, p. 1434.
13. Maynard Olson, Leroy Hood, Charles Cantor and David Botstein, "A Common Language for Physical Mapping of the Human Genome," *Science* 245 (Sept. 29, 1989).
14. *Mapping Our Genes*, 1435. Natural languages exist in a context of culture and background practices. Codes are representational but only in the representation degree zero sense of transparency and definitional arbitrariness. I intend to deal with "language" and its relations with "labor" and "life" in another paper.
15. Charles Cantor, Opening Remarks, *Human Genome: I* (San Diego, Oct. 1, 1989).
16. If, as Allan Wilson and his team convincingly argue, there was an "original Eve," the mother of us all, in Africa about 200,000 years ago, there would be an argument to take an African genome as the standard from which other groups have varied: A. C.

Wilson, E. A. Zimmer, E. M. Prager and T. D. Kocher, "Restriction Mapping in the Molecular Systematics of Mammals: A Retrospective Salute," in B. Fernholm, K. Bremer and H. Jornvall, eds., *The Hierarchy of Life* (Amsterdam: Elsevier, 1989), pp. 407–19.

17. *Mapping Our Genes*, p. 67.

18. Ibid., p. 68.

19. Both Daniel J. Kevles and John Heilbron agreed with the importance of the social impact of the Initiative. Heilbron: "Oh, a thousand times more important" (Feb. 14, 1990).

20. For this distinction, see Dreyfus and Rabinow, *Michel Foucault*, ch. 3.

21. Marshall Sahlins, *The Use and Abuse of Biology: An Anthropological Critique of Sociobiology* (Ann Arbor: University of Michigan Press, 1976); Robert N. Proctor, *Racial Hygiene: Medicine under the Nazis* (Cambridge, Mass.: Harvard University Press, 1988): Daniel J. Kevles, *In the Name of Eugenics: Genetics and the Uses of Human Heredity* (Berkeley: University of California Press, 1985); and Benno Muller-Hill, *Murderous Science: Elimination by Scientific Selection of Jews, Gypsies, and Others, Germany 1933–45* (Oxford: Oxford University Press, 1988).

22. Paul Rabinow, *French Modern: Norms and Forms of the Social Environment* (Cambridge, Mass.: MIT Press, 1989); Raymond Williams, *Keywords: A Vocabulary of Culture and Society* (New York: Oxford University Press, 1976).

23. Robert Castel, *La Gestion des risques, de l'anti-psychiatrie à l'après-psychanalyse* (Paris: Minuit, 1981).

24. The third term here is genetics. If, as is hinted at, there were a genetic component to AIDS susceptibility, then the equation would be more complex.

25. François Bloch-Laine, *Etude du problème général de l'inadaptation des personnes handicapées, la Documentation française* (1969), p. 111 (cited in Castel, *La Gestion des risques*, p. 117).

26. Bloch-Laine, *Etude*, p. 122.

27. Credit is due to James Faubion for clarity on this point.

28. Tom White rightly underlines that all of these developments could be and most likely will be contested.

29. Neil A. Holtzman, *Proceed with Caution: Predicting Genetic Risks in the Recombinant DNA Era* (Baltimore and London: Johns Hopkins University Press, 1989), pp. 235–6.

30. Robert Castel, *Advanced Psychiatric Society* (Berkeley: University of California Press, 1986).

31. Donna Haraway, "A Manifesto for Cyborgs," *Socialist Review* 15.2 (March–April 1985), p. 69.

32. Troy Duster, *Backdoor to Eugenics* (London: Routledge, 1990).

PART II

Disease and the Self

CHAPTER 5

Disease and the Self

Life is 440 horsepower in a 2 cylinder engine.
Henry Miller, *Tropic of Cancer*

THE INDIVIDUAL AND THE COSMOS

While the mechanical aspects of biomedicine deserve to be emphasized, as they were in the first part of this book, it is equally important to understand what the variations and alternatives are. Practitioners inside and outside the official profession of medicine have been moved by a plethora of influences, ranging from the radical materialism of the machine metaphor to the metaphysics of spiritual approaches. This does not mean that the body has not been *predominantly* understood in physical, engineering or computing terms, only that the 'machine' is somewhat more supple and that the things which can affect it are sometimes less directly physical than would be expected from a purely Cartesian model.

We need only look to Hippocrates of Cos (*fl.*400 BC) and the Hippocratic Corpus for evidence of this.[1] Hippocrates is perhaps the figure who most popularly represents the self-image of the medical profession. Physicians in Western countries must recite the Hippocratic oath when graduating from medical school or joining professional societies. His image is emblazoned on the logo of the American Medical Association. Although the practices of medicine have been modified in important ways over the centuries, the Hippocratic philosophy of health has proven robust in the face of potentially antagonistic and powerful competitors, such as Christianity. It represents the persistent autonomy of medicine as a distinct social institution in Western societies (Temkin, 1991: 256).

In Hippocratic medicine, health is viewed as being influenced by environmental factors such as the quality of the air, water and food, the winds, the topography of the land and general living practices. Understanding the effects of environmental forces is a primary duty of the Hippocratic physician. Health in Hippocratic medicine is an expression of harmony in the environment, ways of living and human nature. The four humours – blood, phlegm, yellow bile and black bile – are thought to control all human activities. Contra Descartes, the mind and body mutually influence each other. Although distinct and tangible entities – Hippocrates was always a naturalist – they cannot be understood separately from one another and are part of a larger equilibrium that, if upset, would indicate illness. Whenever this equilibrium is disrupted, rational therapeutic procedures, dietary prescriptions, regimens and other interventions are called for. Importantly, Hippocrates sanctioned an ethical as well as a philosophical system, urging physicians to adopt an attitude of reverence towards patients. Respect for the patient is essential to healing in the Hippocratic Corpus.[2]

From the Hippocratic Corpus we can envision a medical system that is both environmental and psychosomatic. It is open to the possibility that the state of the body is influenced by natural phenomena, external and internal to the person. Even dreams feature in the Hippocratic Corpus, and the relationship of the content of dreams to the state of the body is the subject of several commentaries. Thus, for example, 'a rough sea indicates disease of the bowels. Light and gentle laxatives should be used to effect thorough purgation' (Chadwick and Mann, 1950: 199). The Hippocratic Corpus also suggests that frames of mind and psychological states profoundly affect the body.

Similar presuppositions about health and illness – especially the idea of health as a state of balance, the importance of environmental influences and the interdependence of mind and body – were developed in ancient China.[3] Although many of the ideas date from the first millennium BC, the major concepts were shaped by Confucianism and Taoism and appeared in the Han period (206 BC–AD 220). Deriving from the ancient doctrine of systematic correspondences, which holds that the visible and invisible worlds such as day and night and the alternation of the tides stand in mutual dependence through certain lines of correspondence, the concepts of *yin* and *yang* are central to Chinese ideas about health and illness. All parts of the human body, as a microcosm of the universe, are assigned *yin* and *yang* qualities, which imply a balance of different life-forces (*ch'i*). Illness arises from a pattern of causes leading to disharmony and imbalance. The healthy individual and the healthy society are part of a great patterned order.

The Chinese idea of the body, as it developed from the concept of systematic correspondences, concerned itself with interrelations between parts of a whole, indivisible system. Although the importing of Western science into China in the twentieth century had a corrosive effect on the practice and philosophy of Chinese medicine, the ideologists of the Communist Revolution of 1949 promoted a synthesis between traditional Chinese medicine and Maoist–Marxist thought. In particular, both systems coalesced around notions of holism, seeing the individual in terms of larger, psychological, social and economic structures. An individual organ, for example, is part of a whole functioning system which can only be grasped in terms of its totality. Therefore, the understanding of the lungs would include the whole respiratory tract, the nose, the skin and the secretions associated with those organs. Similarly, if a patient has a headache, it is not appropriate to treat only the head (Unschuld, 1985: 256). Like Hippocratic principles, whereby 'the patient must oppose the illness together with the physician' (Temkin, 1991: 206), the patient plays an active role in treatment. The individual is responsible for the maintenance of his or her own health and to a large extent for the restoration of health when the organism is out of balance. The doctor takes part, but recovery is to a large degree dependent on the patient. The ideal doctor in Chinese medicine, also similar to Hippocratic ideals, is a sage who has knowledge of the social, psychological, environmental and spiritual worlds. In marked contrast to Western biomedicine, treatment emphasizes the mildest possible therapy using herbal potions, massage, acupuncture and moxibustion (burning small cones of the powdered herb moxa on the body at pressure points).

PSYCHOSOMATICS AND SOCIAL CHANGE

One important route into considerations of the possible linkages between cosmos, mind and health has been through the numerous and diverse attempts over the last century, especially, to link social and psychological factors with health and illness. Rather than looking for pathology within a mechanical body, it is held by advocates of 'psychosomatics' that bodily illnesses may originate in the mind, or more specifically in some given psychological or emotional state. Psychosomatic theories differ among themselves as to what exactly the relationship between mind and body consists of and even as to how these two entities should be defined. For the most part, however, psychosomatic research assumes an autonomy of the mind or psyche that is subject to influence by social circumstances. The mind may work positively or negatively upon the body to produce health or illness. In psychosomatic theories developed within the academic disciplines of psychology and medicine, this occurs via biological processes connected with the various organ systems of the body and the immune system, as well as through identifiable pathogens.

There is, however, no fundamental contradiction between psychosomatics and the idea of the mechanical body. Psychosomatic accounts take it for granted that the body is a 'machine', operating according to the materialist principles of scientific medicine. Research in the field borrows its methodology from the natural sciences, assuming that mental and bodily states can be objectively delineated, catalogued, measured and statistically correlated. Most psychosomatic health research is conducted through controlled experiments. 'Variables', such as mood, stress and emotions within the person, are identified and correlated with a wide spectrum of health indicators, usually in an artificial laboratory situation. The only modification from the purely physical accounts of illness examined in part I is the opening up of the possibility of non-physical impacts on the physical body.

A stimulus to the turn to psychosomatics and a reason for its broad popularity has been the increasing realization that rapid and drastic changes in the ways and pace of life – sometimes described as 'modernization', 'urbanization', and outside Europe as 'Westernization' or 'globalization' – have had a pronounced, often negative effect on the health of individuals and whole populations. Social change seems to have occurred so quickly that established patterns of social organization and psychological orientation have not been able to defend people against the effects of new forms of technology, work rhythms, and spatial and temporal arrangements. Even though psychosomatic theories may dwell on the internal and individual interpretation of external situations, it is these large-scale social transformations that have made it possible for us to think about health and illness as being radically affected by disruptions to established ways of life. Following this logic, a chain of causation can be established linking social change, mental states, physiological states and illness. Social change can be seen as precipitating unbalanced or disturbed mental states, which in turn adversely affect bodily functions, resulting in illness.

Much of the significant social change thought to be pertinent to questions of health has occurred relatively recently. In Britain, oral historians such as Ronald Blythe and George Ewart Evans have carefully chronicled the rapid social upheavals that have occurred over the last century in people's lives. Addressing the changes in the English countryside brought about by technologies such as the internal-combustion engine and mechanized farming, G. Evans (1993: 1) remarks, 'It was not simply that a mode of life had greatly changed but a whole culture that had preserved its continuity from earliest times had now received its quietus, and was swept aside in less than a couple of generations.' The English countryside before this time was not, of course, an idyllic disease-free paradise. Occasional harvest failures and pestilences such as the bubonic plague wiped out swathes of the pre-industrial population, but it was the development of trade and industry that became most associated with epidemics. Speaking of seventeenth-century England, Laslett (1984: 147) remarks,

> it was not the distant upland 'undeveloped' areas which suffered . . . sudden mortalities to the greatest extent. It was the centres of wealth and activity, which were also the centres of infection, whose vulnerability remained . . . Accordingly, the further a place was from a market town and the greater its altitude, the less, not the more, was it likely to suffer mortality crises.

However, despite the long reign of industry and, when combined with colonialism, the immense wealth it generated, it has recently been realized that greater profits can be achieved through financial manipulation and the provision of services which operate on high-turnover, low-wage, non-skilled and non-unionized labour. This 'deindustrialization' in Western countries has created new patterns of work and unemployment. While the disastrous health effects of industrialization in the nineteenth century have been well documented (and are discussed in Friedrich Engels' contribution to part IV of this book), the consequences for the health of workers and their communities in the wake of plant closures, the phasing out of heavy industries, privatizations and 'down-sizing' are only just beginning to become apparent. Job loss, de-skilling and the reduction of family income are associated with a wide range of health problems. Bluestone and Harrison (1982: 63–6) cite a variety of studies which indicate that workers who have lost their jobs as a result of deindustrialization suffer, among other things, more hypertension, heart disease, ulcers and mental-health-related problems such as depression and suicide than those who are still in the workforce.

Increasingly, conditions of work in the new service economy emphasize pro-ductivity and speed. The introduction of computers and information technology (IT) reduces the time in which tasks can be done and thus demands both more and continuous mental activity within the working day. In contemporary Western societies, according to Michael Young in *The Metronomic Society* (1988), we must fill our time productively and possess a command of increasingly more information not only in order to function competently, but to survive in the world. Our time is 'taken up' in that it is occupied with demands throughout the day, and, as each demand imposes itself upon us, we must possess technical knowledge in order to satisfy it. As time is continually consumed with demands, mental space is filled to capacity, so that individuals have little autonomy of thought or action. Electronic technology enforces a direct and 'objective' (in the sense that it is separate from the opinions and biases of people) check on the nature, quality and productivity of work. This characteristic of the 'information age' has lead Zuboff (1988) to associate IT in the workplace with the nineteenth-century panopticon designed by the utilitarian philosopher Jeremy Bentham. The panopticon was an industrial blueprint for prisons and other institutions which permitted supervisors and authority figures to constantly monitor the activities of subordinates and inmates.

Henry Miller's remark that 'life is 440 horsepower in a 2 cylinder engine', expresses the overburdening of the body/machine with 'life' in the twentieth century. Life has become more onerous, cumbersome and occupied with more and higher expectations of the individual. Michael Young (1988) suggests that many individuals in Western societies experience time in such a way that circadian rhythms which operate in a 24-hour cycle – heart rate, metabolism, breathing, body temperature and the like – are violated. Humans require a certain amount of activity, inactivity and sleep. If time is not made available for these alterna-tions, Young believes, various health disorders will result. He supports this in part by citing various studies of workers on unusual hours and night shifts which require a reorientation of sleep and metabolism. These studies indicate a greater incidence of digestive and gastrointestinal disorders and increased impairment of judgement. It is no accident, according to Young, that the Three Mile Island, Chernobyl', and Bhopāl disasters all occurred at night, when night-shift workers were in charge of operations.

These drastic social transformations – sweeping away established cultural, spatial and temporal patterns and with them whole ways of life and world-views – alter the contours of health and illness. Especially important are the changing patterns of diseases that have manifested in the last century. Bryan Turner (1995: 8) has argued that in the nineteenth century the majority of mortality was caused by infectious diseases such as smallpox, tuberculosis, typhoid, pneumonia and rubella. To a large degree, these could be, and eventually were, controlled by inoculations. On the other hand, in the last century it was long-term chronic dis-eases such as cancer, heart disease and strokes that claimed most lives. Since they are long term and, according to psychosomatic research, thought to vary accord-ing to the psychological and social characteristics of sufferers, it is not clear that strict biomedical knowledge is required. That is, the Cartesian tradition, hiving off mind from body and viewing the body as one would an internal-combustion engine, is only ever going to be partial and could even be detrimental. Psychological and sociological knowledge is therefore necessary to deal with both the possible origins of the disease and the emotional antecedents of illness in the patient. Over the long term, nursing and psychological care are perhaps more important to a sufferer of chronic illness than biomedical interventions.

HEALTH IN AN AGE OF INDIVIDUALISM AND STRESS

As numerous social scientists including, most famously, Marx and his followers have asserted, the advent and take-off of industrial capitalism established a radical individualism in Western societies. This individualism, manifest in concerns for the sanctity of private property, capital accumulation, labour productivity and the pursuit of profit, displaced the earlier feudal bonds of paternalism which had held people together in the agrarian social order. The move of populations from the country to the city in industrializing nations was accompanied by a destabilization of institutions such as the family and the Church. Social relationships between people were drastically altered. Differences based on inherited social status diminished, but so did the sense of order and community which feudalism had fostered. The new capitalist order was based quite squarely on utilitarian ethics, which placed the individual above all else in what Charles Darwin was to describe as 'the struggle for existence'.

The French diplomat Alexis de Tocqueville (1945: 104), writing in the 1830s, coined the term 'individualism'. For him, individualism was a distinguishing mark of the American way of life. It was 'a mature and calm feeling which disposes each member of the community to sever himself from the mass of his fellows and to draw apart with his family and friends, so that after he has formed a little circle of his own, he willingly leaves society at large to itself'. The psychological consequence of this were that 'it throws him back forever upon himself alone and threatens in the end to confine him entirely within the solitude of his own heart.' Into the twentieth century, individualism, especially in the form of the pursuit of one's own goals and ambitions at all costs, seems to have steadily grown, so that it is now considered the major characteristic of many Western cultures, especially the United States (see, for example, Bellah et al., 1985). People are constantly thrown back into the solitude of their own hearts.

James Lynch, in *The Broken Heart*, a chapter of which is our first reading in this section, clearly demonstrates how a lack of social support, the emotional climate that accompanies individualism, may determine the extent and character of symptoms experienced in illness. Lynch argues that contemporary social conditions have resulted in increased levels of divorce, infidelity, unrequited love and simulated love and that these have had disastrous health consequences. Love, a possible antidote to rampant individualism, has increasingly become fraught with difficulties connected with the instability of long-term relationships (see Beck and

Beck-Gernsheim, 1995: 181). Focusing on the human need for love, Lynch views loneliness as a major cause of physical illness.

To support this theory, Lynch conducted research in a trauma unit and a coronary care unit in the United States. As part of the study as a whole, he attempted to measure the impact that contact – visits from relatives, the presence of people in the room, the nurse taking a pulse, someone holding the patient's hand – had on the vital indicators of the patient. Lynch found extensive evidence that heart rates come closer to normal among very ill people when human contact is present. The simple procedure of pulse-taking on a 72-year-old woman with a 2:1 heart blockage resulted in a change from the pattern of the 2:1 block to an accelerated, more normal heart rate during the period of human contact.

The extensive body of research in psychosomatics along the lines suggested by Lynch's experiment points to the importance of social support as a factor in the maintenance of health. Almost all of the research on the topic suggests that being integrated into supportive social networks correlates with good health, while a diminution or absence of these bonds has a negative effect on health. There are a great variety of theories as to why this should be the case. In their review of the relationship between health and social support, Pilisuk and Parks (1986: 55) argue that social support is a positive psychological buffer in that it protects the self-concept. By doing so, it reduces psychic strain and can guard against the damaging effects of stress on the immune system. They also note that social support reinforces a sense of control over well-being.

Similar implications can be drawn from foundational theories in both psycho-analysis and sociology. John Bowlby (1988) posited that childhood attachments to parents, especially the mother and the provision of a 'secure base' – a home from which the infant can explore and to which it can retreat to security – are necessary to long-term physical and psychological health. Conversely, separation, especially from the mother, was seen by Bowlby as having life-long negative con-sequences. This was linked to universal biological propensities related to species survival. Although he disavowed biological theories, Emile Durkheim's classic study *Suicide* (1951 [1897]) demonstrates a similar point – that is, integration into group and communal life is necessary for psychosocial well-being. Suicide, in Durkheim's study, was shown to be much more prevalent among people belonging to groups that did not encourage communal attachments and had low levels of social integration. Significantly, both Durkheim and, to a lesser extent, Bowlby have pioneered schools of thought within their respective disciplines.

Recent research has shown that those people with the most supportive social networks seem both to be healthier generally and, when ill, to recover faster, and this occurs across types of illness, age and gender variables. For example, Totman (1990) reports a study of first-time mothers who were divided into two groups. One group was unsupported and the other received support from an untrained woman in the form of friendly conversation and touch (when asked for). Totman (1990: 147) summarizes the findings as follows: 'Complications in the unsup-ported group were much more common than those in the supported group. Three-quarters of the mothers without support had complications – induction, foetal distress, stillbirth or Caesarian section – against only 12 percent of those in the supported group.'[4]

An important concept which links particular situations and life events to the psyche and to illness is 'stress'. Stress has been conceived of as the personal experience that results from 'stressors' – events and circumstances, ranging from the most mundane to the cataclysmic, which make exacting demands on the individual. Stressors may be psychological (an identity crisis), physical (violence) or social (loss of job or spouse) in nature and may be the product of an unpleasant life situation or a single life event such as divorce or the death of a loved one. What is involved in stress theories is the notion that discomforting life situations cause anxiety and tension within the individual, and these in turn contribute to bodily disequilibrium and eventually to the onset of illness. Although a number of different possibilities are presented by this concept, the most common formulation tends to follow the behaviouristic stimulus–response model. That is, a toxic external stimulus acts upon the individual and this elicits a pathological reaction in the body.

The original prompt for the interest in the influence of stress was the work of physician Hans Selye, who in 1956 published *The Stress of Life*. On the basis of experiments with laboratory animals, Selye argued that there were particular physiological responses to external stress involving the autonomic nervous system and the pituitary gland.[5] He posited three stages in the reaction to stress: (1) *alarm* – the body is first attacked and its resistance lowered; (2) it then mobilizes against the stress through *resistance*; but if the stress persists, (3) *exhaustion* sets in, resistance is lowered and illness ensues. More recent research has concentrated on how psychological abilities are crucial intermediaries between stress and illness.

As in Hippocratic and Chinese medicine, writers and researchers who focus on stress often explicitly invoke notions of equilibrium, balance and harmony. Accordingly, stress may involve an imbalance between the perception of demands being made on a person and his or her ability to meet these demands. In contemporary Western societies, the common competing demands of work, career, children, education and personal health make such a 'balance' difficult. Sometimes stress is framed in terms of an imbalance in the individual between aspirations and achievements or the capability of the individual in his or her environment to meet these aspirations. Strong desires and wishes – for material possessions, money, family, children, love – which are unfulfilled, it is held, may cause illness.[6]

In the context of stress, it has been argued that external threats to the person may trigger auto-aggression – the body turning against itself. The normal processes by which cancer cells, for example, are destroyed and healthy tissue protected are reversed. The crucial determinant tipping the balance as to whether a given person becomes ill, according to Totman (1990: 126), lies in the psychology of the person. Physiological pathways between psychological and bodily states, such as the immune deficiencies commonly found among clinically depressed people, support the auto-aggression thesis. Totman (1990: 128) cites studies comparing people in marriages that had broken down with those who reported marital satisfaction. Both women and men whose relationships had failed showed signs of depression as well as evidence of impoverished immune response, while the maritally satisfied group showed less depression and better immune response.[7] A more recent study by the same research team found that marital conflict in couples, wives more than husbands, was associated with endocrine and immunological changes (Kiecolt-Glaser et al., 1997). Psychosomatic research suggests that there may be both tangible benefits to health and less severe symptoms of illness as a result of physical support, social support and human love and concern. In this section, James Lynch vividly demonstrates how human concern can improve health, even for hospitalized chronic patients. In contrast to much psychosomatic research, his study is undertaken in the context of the lived experience of patients in a hospital and does not suffer from artificiality and contrivance, criticisms that could be lodged against the experimental research method so pervasive in psychosomatics.

METAPHORS OF ILLNESS

A major implication of the psychosomatic approach is that the sick bear some degree of responsibility for their condition. No longer is the body purely an impersonal object ruled by the 'objective' laws of mechanics – or at least, it is not governed *only* by these laws. The 'personality' of the sufferer shapes how sickness occurs, develops and ends. Under this kind of thinking, people with particular kinds of psychological profiles are thought to be predisposed to specific illnesses. The character of the sufferer, in Susan Sontag's terms, is a metaphor for the disease they acquire.

There are many variants of these ideas. One which has been developed quite extensively in the field of health psychology derives from the long-standing view that more ambitious and aggressive people are more likely to suffer heart attacks than those who are more at peace with themselves and the world. In 1892 the medical educator and physician Sir William Osler described the coronary patient as a 'keen and ambitious man, who has his engine set at full speed ahead' (quoted by Chesney et al., 1995: 130). It is a commonplace observation made by Europeans that the various native people they encountered on their conquests seemed to suffer less from 'diseases of civilization', that their lives seemed less stressful and hurried. They were less concerned with betterment and achievement. Their appearance was often of healthy, muscular and handsome people.[8] In the first reading of this book, Foucault remarked on the contrast between the psychosomatic conditions of 'civilized' and 'uncivilized' people: '[b]efore the advent of civilization, people had only the simplest, most necessary diseases. Peasants and workers . . . have none of those variable, complex, intermingled nervous ills, but down-to-earth apoplexies, or uncomplicated attacks of mania.'

In order to examine such notions, at least within the framework and epistemological assumptions of Western culture, psychologists in the 1950s devised constructs of two ideal type personalities. Type 'A' describes a cluster of personality traits such as intense striving for achievement, competitiveness, easily provoked impatience, abruptness of gesture and speech, overcommitment to vocation, profession or work, excessive drive and hostility. Totman (1990: 93) notes that, even before the spate of Type 'A' research, coronary-prone people were often described as 'having a strong sense of duty, as being more than normally concerned with social correctness and nicety, as being rigid and unscrupulous, as over-controlling their emotions and as possessing obsessional traits'. A sense of time urgency is also sometimes included, and some reports suggest that even facial grimaces and less spontaneity of emotions are characteristic of the Type 'A' personality. Most Type 'A' personalities are involved in professional or office work which is organized according to the job, not the hour. For such people, work itself often consists of a series of time-consuming, almost endless tasks. Increasingly there is little to separate the spheres of leisure, home, vacation and entertainment on the one hand and work on the other. There are a substantial number of studies, though these are by no means unanimous, pointing to Type 'A' personality as a 'predictor' of chronic heart disease (Wright, 1988; Totman, 1990: 85–94; P. Evans, 1991b: 193; Sheridan and Radmacher, 1992: 263–9).

The Type 'B' personality, not implicated in heart disease, is the opposite – relaxed, unmotivated, sometimes to the point of lethargy. Such a personality is characteristic of blue-collar and manual workers whose tasks are more discrete and for whom work is clearly a separate sphere of activity from the rest of life. The toxicity of stress is believed to be burned off by exercise and the more frequent use of the muscles. For office workers, sedentary for most of the day, stress cannot be 'vented' in the same way. By implication, the shift into a service economy, a Westernized global order and the displacement of more relaxing rhythms of life mean that it is becoming more difficult to be a Type 'B' person.

One of the main problems with these studies, however, is that they are profoundly un-naturalistic. Virtually all of them rely on objectivist techniques, especially questionnaires. These claim to 'measure' personality characteristics such as hostility, competitiveness, speed, impatience and job involvement on the basis of answers which volunteer subjects provide. While one would not dismiss these out of hand, it is important to recognize that numerous methodological problems are raised by techniques which objectify what are highly subjective and context-bound personal and emotional traits. The pleas by some health psychologists to devise 'standardized measures of hostility' (Sheridan and Radmacher, 1992: 267) appear only to further avoid the difficult and prior questions such as what 'hostility' is, how it is understood in various social and cultural contexts and how it relates to lived experience.

A long-term chronic illness in which psychological factors have been heavily implicated, and for which metaphors abound, is cancer. The second reading in this section, written by **Roger Levin**, demonstrates how an account of a metaphored illness can be presented without objectifying the patient or the disease. Levin's subtle and empathic description of cancer and cancer patients emerges from his own therapeutic engagements with such patients. Terming it an 'epistemic challenge to our culture', he presents us with a deadly disease that is mystifying –

it often inexplicably regresses, some patients uncannily predict the moment of their own death – and personal without resorting to 'personality' constructs.

As with Type 'A' personality and coronary disease, the idea that there may be a cancer personality is not simply a recent development of academic psychology, but can be traced to an older notion – from nineteenth-century physicians, who often attributed cancer to the emotional character or life experiences of their patients (LeShan, 1989: 7–11). Again, the review of studies produced by Totman (1990) is instructive in illustrating the psychosomatic research pointing to the correlations between a wide range of emotional styles and the development of cancer. In this context, Totman (1990: 80–1) notes that:

> a . . . theme to emerge with some consistency, is a tendency among people at risk of developing certain forms of cancer to show an abnormal pattern in the expression of their emotions. The observation that cancer patients suppress, repress and deny negative feelings such as anger, depression and guilt, has been made by numerous clinicians specialising in cancer . . .

The bottling up or 'repression' of particular emotions such as grief, anger and lust is often held up as a hallmark of the cancer personality. Because of the central place of sexual repression in Freudian thought, psychoanalytic theories have had much to say about the relationship between the inner emotional life and health in general. The psychoanalytic interpretation of cancer was made prominent in the work of Wilhelm Reich, an ardent advocate of psychosomatics, who associated cancer with repressed sexual desire. Writing in 1942, Reich (1942: 324–5) connected cancer and other diseases with disturbances of sexual activity, noting that 'cancer in women is predominantly localized in the sexual organs. The connection with frigidity is obvious and known to many gynecologists.' Elsewhere Reich defined cancer as 'a disease following emotional resignation – a bioenergetic shrinking – a giving up of hope' (quoted by Sontag, 1990: 23). Reich and other advocates of a psychoanalytic understanding of cancer attempted to identify various pathways, chiefly biological, to explain why such emotionally or sexually repressed people became victims of cancer.

In psychosomatic research the concern with cancer and repression has continually expanded, so that there are now volumes of studies linking emotional repression to a host of diseases. A recent study in the journal *Psychosomatic Medicine*, for example, found that HIV infection progressed more rapidly among gay men who concealed their homosexual identity than among those who did not (Cole et al., 1996). Summing up their conclusions, the authors state that their 'findings are consistent with previous research linking psychological inhibition to alterations in measures of sympathetic nervous system activation, immune function, and physical health' (Cole et al., 1996: 229).

Chronic illness is viewed as a metaphor for personality deficiencies not only in psychosomatic research and psychoanalytic thought; it is strongly represented in popular culture as well. In the 1960s the human potential movement focused on illness as a metaphor, partly in an attempt to break free of the mechanical model of illness and the body adopted by both psychology and medicine. Influenced by

European existentialist philosophy, Eastern religions and the contemplative branches of American intellectual thought (William James, Walt Whitman, Ralph Waldo Emerson), the movement concentrated on consciousness, the self and 'personal growth' and viewed health in very general psychosocial terms.

However, in its splicing together of Eastern and Western philosophies, it attempted to expand rather than reject scientific approaches to the self and the relationship between the self and health. Concentrating on a delineation of the role of 'consciousness', Abraham Maslow (1969: 54), for example, believed that 'being oneself, being natural or spontaneous, being authentic, expressing one's identity, all these are also biological statements since they imply the acceptance of one's constitutional, temperamental, anatomical, neurological, hormonal and instinctoid-motivational nature'. Maslow (1954) invented the well-known hierarchy of levels of human need from the most 'basic' – food, shelter, sex – to the 'higher' – wisdom and knowledge. Those who had acquired needs at the top of the hierarchy were dubbed 'self-actualizing' individuals. Maslow believed that self-actualizing people were capable of seeing the universe, their physical and social surroundings and their health as one whole. Maslow believed that such individuals had risen above mere primitive cravings and were a superior type of human being, enjoying better health. The ideas of Maslow were highly influential among the generation of middle-class people who came of age in the 1960s and 1970s, particularly in the United States.

With its emphasis on personal responsibility, equilibrium and holism, it is easy to see the influence of these ideas on the contemporary New Age movement, currently a diverse, predominantly middle-class social movement on both sides of the Atlantic. As for the human potential movement before it, health has become a major focus of the New Age movement. In understanding health, it is also eclectic, employing ideas that originate from many different cultures and historical periods. It has been influenced also by non-Western religion and philosophy, drawing freely on Chinese medicine, Zen Buddhism, Japanese *shiatsu* massage, Ayurvedic practices and Native American cosmologies. Allied to these borrowings in the New Age mix has been the 'New Physics', championed especially by Fritjof Capra (1982), the teachings and writings of psychologists such as Jung, Reich, Maslow and Perls, and more recently the popular writings of physicians in the United States such as Larry Dossey and Deepak Chopra.

In her study of New Age health practitioners in California, anthropologist J. A. English-Lueck (1990: 19–20) identified various New Age health beliefs. First, illness is no random event. It is a lesson. It indicates that body and mind are not being used properly. Consequently, illness should be seen as a learning experience, an opportunity for release and psychological growth. This notion was articulated clearly by Caroline Myss (1991: 83), writing in the British volume *The New Age*, when she stated that 'disease is unconscious change (or choice by default) manifesting in a person's body either because the person lacks the courage to look clearly at what is not working in their life, does not believe that stress affects the body or lacks the skills of introspection or self-analysis that allows the dissolution of stress through positive channels'. Secondly, according to English-Lueck, in the New Age the body is affected by energy pathways which the patient must tap into. Thus, illness is the result of non-material, including spiritual, forces. Higher energies (or spiritual powers) may affect the bodily organism. Energies can be used positively through the patient consciously connecting with them and recognizing their influence. This notion is sometimes supported by making a link to a health belief system in which energies have become well established (*ch'i* in Chinese medicine, *prana* in Ayurvedic medicine and Hinduism, *chakras* in Buddhist cosmology). Thirdly, energy can affect energy. Energy sources are introduced in healing techniques in order to affect bodily energy (homeopathy and acupuncture, for example). Fourthly, generalization is inappropriate. Each patient is different. Each person possesses a different level of consciousness, or spirituality, and all bodies are individually distinct. Finally, a basic epistemological assumption of New Age ideology is that spiritual, physical, emotional and mental realities are inseparably linked. Although there are similarities, the New Age vision of health represents a departure from psychosomatics in that the body is much less a material entity and is affected by less tangible pathways such as 'energies'.

To some extent, New Age notions of health and illness can be liberating for sufferers. The emphasis on personal responsibility can wrest back control that is often ceded to the doctor and technology in the biomedical setting. Through various popular New Age writings, lay people have been made aware of the possibility that they possess certain powers to attenuate or heal illnesses and to prevent more long-term conditions through their own activities, behaviour and frames of mind. Deepak Chopra's (1993) *Ageless Body, Timeless Mind* could be read as a manual of popular empowerment. Selling over a million copies and reaching number one on the *New York Times* bestseller list, the book, at times eloquently, sketches out a role for each individual person to play in maintaining his or her own health and controlling some of the worst effects of ageing. For Chopra, there is no 'objective' world 'out there' which is independent of human volition. Among the insights that Chopra imparts are that people can be trained to regulate their heart beats, thoughts and frames of mind and that mental processes affect the physical body in powerful ways. Our freedom to perceive events in different ways and sudden improvements in our social situations can transform our bodies, even down to the DNA, according to Chopra.

What is ironic about New Age and personal growth health philosophies is that they encourage the kinds of personal orientations that, when practised by large groups of people, reinforce an individualism that undercuts social support, a force that has been found to raise levels of healthiness. The focus on the pursuit of good *individual* health as an end in itself could lead to an obliviousness to the presence of others and a reduction of the complexities of the social world. In many of the writings of practitioners, the 'social' is hardly referred to at all, and other people appear only as objects to be manipulated for the benefit of the individual. Not only is individualism as a personal lifestyle encouraged, but the deep attachments to self which are assumed by many New Age and personal growth theorists foster hedonism and narcissism. In turn, hedonistic and narcissistic personalities

– perhaps now a dominant character in many parts of the United States – possess hardly any of the qualities necessary to support the well-being of communities or any population group exceeding one.

Another criticism of these views of health is that they underestimate the physiological power of disease and overestimate the role of the individual psyche. The use of psychological metaphors for cancer and other diseases and the targeting of the patient as a special type of emotional deviant in psychological, psychoanalytic and New Age discourse came under sharp attack from **Susan Sontag** in her famous essay *Illness as Metaphor*, an excerpt from which is our third reading. Sontag argues that the elaborate theories propounded by psychologists, psychoanalysts, human potential theorists and New Age writers amount to a blaming of cancer victims for their illness. These theories, she argues, are based only on contemporary fashions in emotional style and are similar to the moralizing of the nineteenth century regarding tuberculosis patients. The 'repression' notion, she contends, betrays a prejudice for certain kinds of emotional expression – an unbridling of feelings rather than discretion – and, for Sontag, this implies a cavalier morality. Such metaphors, according to Sontag, are symptomatic of how little is known about the physical terrain of the illness. *When* a biomedical remedy is found, she believes, such images will cease and become altogether meaningless.

Without subscribing to Sontag's views on the primacy of physical causes in relation to cancer, one could add that psychosomatic theories emphasizing the role of 'repression' in illness are deeply ethnocentric, in that they are based on a now popular Western idea of what constitutes healthy emotional demeanour. The indigenous people of the Far North, for example, are known to be sparing in their expression of emotions. For many indigenous North Americans – Indians and Inuit – committing oneself to a particular position, expressing feelings in a straightforward manner and being forthright is seen as foolhardy, because by doing so one cuts off options for action.[9] If those urging us to view psychological repression as a cause of cancer are correct, then we would expect very high rates of cancer among native North Americans compared to the general population, rather than the lower rates that have been reported (T. Young, 1994: 95–113). Ironically, the recent trend of increasing rates of cancer among native people coincides with their exposure to a dominating culture which, while retaining a good measure of repressive Puritanism from the Judaeo-Christian tradition, relies to a large degree on open conflict, free expression and individualism.

The early public discourse on AIDS presents a parallel case. Here we have a condition which has been subject to metaphor, primarily through imputations of shameful sexual conduct, which, it is alleged, caused the HIV virus to appear. In the reading, Sontag shows how the moral castigation of the AIDS patient, or simply of members of the 'at-risk group', has occurred through the biomedical framing of the disease as both wilful and inevitably fatal. There has been – and this is probably still the case after the time of Sontag's writing – a tendency to focus on the consequences of the syndrome in a Eurocentric manner. That is, the prevalence of heterosexuals among the sufferers in Africa provides very different contours and, if taken into account, would call for a very different set of meta-phors. These issues notwithstanding, Sontag's essay presents a serious challenge to the psychosomatic approach. If illnesses are metaphors for imputed personal and psychological faults, the patient bears a heavy burden for his or her condi-tion. When it comes to a positive suggestion, Sontag advocates biomedical therapy, ridiculing 'alternative medicine' for what she sees as its impotence in the face of chronic illness.

SPIRITUAL HEALING

It is another step, however, to suggest that less tangible, less immediately measur-able, even cosmic, phenomena may be implicated in illness. To do so is to face the vast gulf between knowledge as it is constituted in academic and scientific establishments and something considered distinctly non-rational. Our health, ac-cording to spiritual approaches, is deeply entwined with our feelings, thoughts, experiences and the ways in which we live our lives. How we think and live, in turn, is connected to a larger cosmos of which all humans are a part. The cosmos is always divided so that there is a realm of the sacred in which venerated objects and activities are set aside from the mundane life. Disturbances of the sacred realm or the violation of taboos may explain why sickness and other misfortunes occur. What is assumed, then, is that invisible forces, which are not capable of apprehension through the immediate senses, can act upon the body or cause misfortune to people. Whether they afflict certain individuals and groups rather than others is related, perhaps in complex ways, to this larger cosmic order. For example, people in hunting societies believe that their health is partly dependent on respect for the animal spirits that govern their lives. If they do not respect them in a certain prescribed manner, the animal spirits will not release any more game. People will then become ill, starve and eventually die, if the situation is not rectified. This belief system is evident among the Innu or Naskapi of the Labrador–Quebec peninsula in Canada (Henriksen, 1973: 35) and appears in slightly dif-ferent forms in other hunting societies.[10]

What this and other spiritual visions of human fate imply for healing is that purely rational and mechanical techniques are not the only ones which humans have been successful in deploying. A spiritual approach has the advantage of posing the possibility of non-mechanical methods – for example, those used by a shaman or priest – as treatment approaches. Shamans and priests do not claim expertise over the physiological workings of the body. Rather, their powers lie in an understanding, frequently intuitive, of the way in which the cosmos connects with individual people.

Until very recently, strictly spiritual or 'paranormal' notions of illness causation and healing were ignored in academic research. Even where they have been con-sidered, in the anthropology of E. E. Evans-Pritchard in the 1930s for example, they have often been explained in rational Western terms of cause and effect.[11] More recently, anthropologists have sought to depict indigenous beliefs as a kind

of parallel, 'not qualitatively different . . . from Western science' in the words of
Western anthropologist Colin Scott (1996: 84), describing Cree Indian philosophy.
Likewise, psychosomatic medicine, because of its association with academic and
biomedical institutions, claims legitimacy from science. This is most apparent in
its method. Scientific observational and statistical techniques of verification of
the effects of non-material forces are demanded in order that anything beyond
the purely physical can be accepted as relevant to health and illness. This is
clearly apparent in the studies of environmental and personality linkages to illness, which are hypothesized to operate through concrete, although often 'not-
proven', physiological pathways.

   However, as **Fred Frohock**, in the fourth of our readings, suggests in his vignettes of academically trained psychologists who have become what we might
call 'spiritual healers', the academic and scientific establishments have had great
difficulty coming to terms with the paranormal. Those trained in the canons of
scientific knowledge have doubted their own sanity in embracing what are frequently seen as 'superstitious' or 'unscientific' forms of healing. It is a kind of
intangible mental transference between individuals that Frohock's subjects seem
to be involved in. These mental powers transcend the individual healer and
patient. The healer is only a conduit for 'the healing forces of the larger natural
world'.

   There are undoubtedly numerous patients, like Frohock's example of the woman
who recovered from Lou Gehrig's disease, who have successfully recovered from
their ailments after receiving psychic healing. A recent observation of spirit healing in Zambia is here recounted by Edith Turner (1996: xxii):

> I saw the traditional doctors trying to pull an afflicting spirit out of the body of a
> sick woman. For the task they used cupping horns and worked their ritual to draw
> the spirit into a horn. At the climax of the drumming and singing, after many
> attempts, it suddenly became clear that the spirit was actually coming out. And at
> that point I saw with my own eyes a large gray ball, something between solid and
> smoke, a kind of globular ghost, emerge from her back. The doctors put whatever it
> was into a bag and later showed it; then it appeared to have taken the form of a
> tooth. They fed the tooth with blood and meal, and the woman recovered.

And, in Alaska, the same anthropologist observed and participated in many
healings with the Inupiat people:

> During Claire's [the healer's] treatment of Netta, four of us – Claire, Clem, Carrie,
> and to a certain extent, I – could perceive how Netta's spirit continually parted
> company with her tortured organs and wandered towards its outlet in her fontanel.
> Claire freed the blockage in the stomach again and again and brought the spirit
> back down into Netta's body. The activity of Claire's arms and head showed what
> she was doing (Turner, 1996: 32).

Occurrences such as these receive very little attention in most books and articles
in health studies, medicine, nursing, sociology or psychology. Other than in

relation to 'ancient' or 'primitive' healing systems, they are generally ignored. In Frohock's discussion of LeShan, he speculates that this may be a result of the lack of 'theory' in paranormal studies. Few practitioners have any concrete ideas as to exactly why their techniques work – or don't, as the case may be. While Western biomedicine can tap into established scientific principles of proof and verification that have been virtually unquestioned in Western culture, there are few sources of cultural validation for spiritual healing. There is no equivalent to the logical, rationalist experimentation that occurs with psychosomatic research. It is not appropriate in the mode of Hans Selye, to test spiritual healing on laboratory rats. Rather, spiritual healing is both highly individual and connected to the ways of life and experiences of particular groups of people such as the Zambians and Inupiat, cited above. Although some experimental studies have suggested that spiritual phenomena such as prayer correlate with beneficial results for hospitalized patients (Byrd, 1988; Oxman et al., 1995), for the most part spiritual healing operates intuitively and cannot be 'captured' by experiments and other scientific measurement devices used in academic psychology or clinical medicine.

Perhaps most fundamentally, as Frohock puts it, 'to believe in the paranormal would require abandoning conventional understandings of reality'. To enter into spiritual healing, or to take it seriously, as Frohock obviously does, requires us to draw out a much wider web of linkages that relate to our health and well-being. If some of these are beyond the tools that science has developed to picture 'reality', then it is easy to see how those who see science and reality as synonymous would take fright.

Notes

1. How much of the work in the Hippocratic Corpus, written between 420 and 350 BC, was actually written by, rather than derived from, Hippocrates is not known.
2. Good discussions of Hippocrates can be found in Dubos (1968: 82–4), Temkin (1991) and Nutton (1995: 19–31).
3. A good general introduction to Chinese medicine, on which this discussion in part relies, is Unschuld (1985).
4. The study which drew these conclusions is Sosa et al. (1980).
5. Among the clear and simple accounts of the stress hypothesis are Sarafino (1990: chs. 3–5), Totman (1990: chs. 4–5), P. Evans (1991a) and Sheridan and Radmacher (1992: ch. 7).
6. Extensive documentation of the various studies which purport to show such causal connections is presented in Totman (1990).
7. The studies in question were Kiecolt-Glaser et al. (1987, 1988).
8. Thus, in the 1830s the American painter George Catlin (1989) described the native peoples of North America as having 'long black hair, black eyes, tall, straight and elastic forms'.
9. Good expositions of this may be found in Briggs (1970) on the Inuit in the Canadian Arctic and Brody (1981) on northern Athapaskan people in British Columbia.
10. Referring to the Kalahari Bushmen, Guenther (1988: 199) calls this a 'sympathy bond' between hunters and the hunted.

11. The prototype for this kind of study is E. E. Evans-Pritchard's (1937) *Witchcraft, Oracles, and Magic among the Azande*. Evans-Pritchard characterizes the medical beliefs of the Azande as 'rational' in that they have 'chains of causation' which are parallel to Western science. Thus, an Azande may claim to have have fallen ill from a snakebite and that this was ultimately a result of being bewitched. According to Evans-Pritchard, the Azande would agree with the Westerner that the venom had 'caused' the pain, but this act of the snake would have been a result of another, 'magical' force. Otherwise, why would the snake bite one particular victim out of all the other possible victims? Thus, it is Western medicine, in the eyes of the Azande, that foreshortens the chain of causation.

References

Beck, Ulrich, and Elisabeth Beck-Gernsheim (1995), *The Normal Chaos of Love*, translated by Mark Ritter and Jane Wiebel, Oxford: Polity Press.

Bellah, Robert, et al. (1985), *Habits of the Heart: Individualism and Commitment in American Life*, Berkeley, CA: University of California Press.

Bluestone, Barry, and Bennett Harrison (1982), *The Deindustrialisation of America: Plant Closings, Community Abandonment, and the Dismantling of Basic Industry*, New York: Basic.

Bowlby, John (1988), *A Secure Base: Parent–Child Attachment and Healthy Human Development*, New York: Basic.

Briggs, Jean (1970), *Never in Anger*, Cambridge, MA: Harvard University Press.

Brody, Hugh (1981), *Maps and Dreams: Indians and the British Columbia Frontier*, Vancouver: Douglas and McIntyre.

Byrd, Randolph (1988), 'Positive Therapeutic Effects of Intercessory Prayer in a Coronary Care Unit Population', *Southern Medical Journal*, 81(7): 826–9.

Capra, Fritjof (1982), *The Turning Point*, London: Flamingo.

Catlin, George (1989), *North American Indians*, New York: Penguin.

Chadwick, John, and W. N. Mann (1950) (eds), *The Medical Works of Hippocrates*, Oxford: Blackwell.

Chesney, Margaret, et al. (1985), 'Modifying Type A Behavior', in James Rosen and Laura Solomon (eds), *Prevention in Health Psychology*, Hanover, NH: University Press of New England, 130–42.

Chopra, Deepak (1993), *Ageless Body, Timeless Mind: The Quantum Alternative to Growing Old*, New York: Harmony.

Cole, Steve, et al. (1996), 'Accelerated Course of Human Immunodeficiency Virus Infection in Gay Men Who Conceal Their Homosexual Identity', *Psychosomatic Medicine*, 58: 219–31.

Dubos, Rene (1968), *Man, Medicine and the Environment*, Harmondsworth: Penguin.

Durkheim, Emile (1951), *Suicide: A Study in Sociology*, New York: Free Press.

English-Lueck, J. A. (1990), *Health in the New Age: A Study of California Holistic Practices*, Albuquerque, NM: University of New Mexico Press.

Evans, George Ewart (1993), *The Crooked Scythe: An Anthology of Oral History*, London: Faber and Faber.

Evans, Philip (1991*a*), 'Stress and Coping', in Marian Pitts and Keith Phillips (eds), *The Psychology of Health: An Introduction*, London: Routledge, 30–48.

—— (1991*b*), 'Coronary Heart Disease', in Marian Pitts and Keith Phillips (eds), *The Psychology of Health: An Introduction*, London: Routledge, 187–98.

Evans-Pritchard, E. E. (1937), *Witchcraft, Oracles, and Magic among the Azande*, Oxford: Clarendon Press.

Guenther, Matthias (1988), 'Animals in Bushman Thought, Myth and Art', in Tim Ingold et al. (eds), *Hunters and Gatherers 2: Property, Power and Ideology*, Oxford: Berg, 192–202.

Henriksen, Georg (1973), *Hunters in the Barrens: The Naskapi on the Edge of the White Man's World*, St John's: Institute for Social and Economic Research.

Kiecolt-Glaser, Janice, et al. (1987), 'Marital Quality, Marital Disruption and Immune Function', *Psychosomatic Medicine*, 49: 13–33.

—— (1988), 'Marital Discord and Immunity in Males', *Psychosomatic Medicine*, 50: 213–29.

—— (1997), 'Marital Conflict in Older Adults: Endocrinological and Immunological Correlates', *Psychosomatic Medicine*, 59: 339–49.

Laslett, Peter (1984), *The World We Have Lost: Further Explored*, New York: Charles Scribner's.

LeShan, Lawrence (1989), *Cancer as a Turning Point*, Bath: Gateway Books.

Maslow, Abraham H. (1954), *Motivation and Personality*, New York: Harper and Row.

—— (1969), 'A Theory of Metamotivation: The Biological Rooting of the Value-Life', in Hung-Min Chiang and Abraham H. Maslow (eds), *The Healthy Personality*, New York: Van Nostrand Reinhold Company, 35–56.

Miller, Henry (1934), *Tropic of Cancer*, Paris: Obelisk Press.

Myss, Caroline (1991), 'Redefining the Healing Process', in William Bloom (ed.), *The New Age: An Anthology of Essential Writings*, London: Rider, 81–7.

Nutton, Vivian (1995), 'Medicine in the Greek World, 800–50 BC', in Lawrence I. Conrad et al. (eds), *The Western Medical Tradition: 800 BC to AD 1800*, Cambridge: Cambridge University Press, 11–38.

Oxman, Thomas, et al. (1995), 'Lack of Social Participation or Religious Strength and Comfort as Risk Factors for Death after Cardiac Surgery in the Elderly', *Psychosomatic Medicine*, 57: 5–15.

Pilisuk, Marc, and Susan Hillier Parks (1986), *The Healing Web: Social Networks and Human Survival*, Hanover, NH: University Press of New England.

Reich, Wilhelm (1942), *The Function of the Orgasm: Sex-Economic Problems of Biological Energy*, translated by Theodore P. Wolfe, New York: Noonday Press.

Sarafino, Edward (1990), *Health Psychology: Biopsychosocial Interactions*, New York: John Wiley and Sons.

Scott, Colin (1996), 'Science for the West, Myth for the Rest? The Case of James Bay Cree Knowledge Construction', in Laura Nader (ed.), *Naked Science: Anthropological Inquiry into Boundaries, Power and Knowledge*, New York: Routledge, 69–86.

Sheridan, Charles, and Sally Radmacher (1992), *Health Psychology: Challenging the Biomedical Model*, New York: John Wiley and Sons.

Sontag, Susan (1990), *Illness as Metaphor and AIDS and its Metaphors*, New York: Anchor.

Sosa, R., et al. (1980), 'The Effect of a Supportive Companion on Perinatal Problems, Length of Labor and Mother–Infant Interaction', *New England Journal of Medicine*, 303: 597–600.

Temkin, Owsei (1991), *Hippocrates in a World of Pagans and Christians*, Baltimore, MD: Johns Hopkins University Press.

Tocqueville, Alexis de (1945), *Democracy in America, vol. 2*, New York: Vintage.

Totman, Richard (1990), *Mind, Stress and Health*, London: Souvenir Press.

Turner, Bryan (1995), *Medical Power and Social Knowledge*, 2nd edn, London: Sage.

Turner, Edith (1996), *The Hands Feel It: Healing and Spirit Presence among a Northern Alaskan People*, DeKalb, IL: Northern Illinois University Press.

Unschuld, Paul (1985), *Medicine in China: A History of Ideas*, Berkeley, CA: University of California Press.

Wright, Logan (1988), 'The Type A Behavior Pattern and Coronary Artery Disease', *American Psychologist*, 43(1): 2–14.

Young, Michael (1988), *The Metronomic Society*, London: Thames and Hudson.

Young, T. Kue (1994), *The Health of Native Americans: Toward a Biocultural Epidemiology*, New York: Oxford University Press.

Zuboff, Shoshana (1988), *In the Age of the Smart Machine*, New York: Basic.

CHAPTER 6

Human Contact in Life-Threatening Environments

James J. Lynch

A man wholly solitary would be either a god or a brute.
Aristotle (384–322 B.C.)

When faced with danger or the threat of danger, human beings can derive an enormous sense of comfort from their fellow man. Whether the danger is artificially contrived in a laboratory or part of the infinite variety of real life stresses, human beings instinctively seek out each other's company in adverse circumstances. The child frightened by the darkness of night reflexively cries out to its parents for reassurance and comfort. Indeed, all of us seek human reassurance. The idea of being alone, all alone, in the face of danger terrifies children and adults alike.

History is filled with examples that demonstrate how human contact acts as one of nature's most powerful antidotes to stress. There is a quality about human companionship in life-threatening situations that helps accentuate its biological and psychological power. Throughout the first nightmarish winter of the siege of Leningrad in World War II, the city's radio station remained on the air to reassure the people that they were not alone. When the radio announcers were too weak or cold to play music or recite the news, they would turn on a metronome which monotonously clicked back and forth, echoing through loudspeakers on the streets to reassure the people they were not alone.

Apart from physical torture and death, solitary confinement has long been recognized as one of the most dreaded of human experiences. And those who endure unusually harsh prison environments frequently credit their survival to the strength they were able to derive from their fellow men. Dr. Joel Dimsdale, a psychiatrist, recently described his interviews with survivors of Nazi concentration camps during World War II. Many of the survivors listed the strength they were able to derive from their fellow prisoners as the most significant factor in their will to live. On the other hand, many victims who were suddenly torn away from their loved ones succumbed to a syndrome that was labeled "musselmann" by their fellow inmates. Unable to relate to others in the camps, they often gave way to profound despair, lost hope, and perished.[1]

But while almost everyone would agree that human relationships are critical to survival, it is not at all clear just what it is about the presence of another human being that is so important, especially in life-threatening environments. It is this lack of clarity about a phenomenon universally recognized as important that has led us to reexamine two environments in which sudden death is an ever-present danger: coronary care units and a hospital shock-trauma unit. We studied the effects of human contact in an especially intimate way by monitoring the hearts of patients whose lives were in mortal peril. Unlike other life-threatening environments, these units held patients who were totally helpless; they could not seek out other human beings, but were instead forced by their physical weakness to wait until someone came to their bedside. Our interest in studying these critically ill patients was prompted by evidence suggesting that human interactions could alter heart rhythm.[2]

Since cardiac arrhythmias in the wake of a heart attack are the primary cause of sudden death, understanding the effects of human contact in these environments seemed to us to be vitally important.

Human Contact in Coronary Care Units

Coronary care units are specialized hospital areas that have gradually evolved over the past two decades. These units were developed when it was recognized that many cardiac patients who might have been saved with appropriate medical care were needlessly dying after suffering heart attacks. Of special concern was the fact that many of these patients were already in hospitals and had appeared well on the road to recovery. Not infrequently it was noted that nurses would check on these patients, report that they looked quite healthy, and then return a few minutes later to find them dead. These sudden, unobserved hospital deaths led to the realization that these patients ought to be placed in special units and watched constantly for a few days after a heart attack. If recurrent cardiac complications did occur during this period, then the medical personnel could at least take immediate measures to aid the patient. One of the major sources of complications stemmed from the fact that there is a marked rise in the incidence of abnormal heartbeats in the first 24 to 72 hours after a heart attack. These abnormal beats have the potential for seriously disrupting the normal rhythm of the heart and can lead to ventricular fibrillation and sudden death.[3]

Among the major advances stimulated by the creation of these units was the development of an electronic system that could continuously monitor the heartbeats of all patients. With this device, physicians could constantly watch each patient's heartbeat and thus anticipate the development of cardiac problems, often long before such problems could become more serious. A procedure for maintaining a continuous intravenous drip in the patient's arm was also developed so that the medical staff could quickly give medications needed to help suppress the incidence of cardiac arrhythmias as well as promptly inject any other necessary medications. Special equipment for delivering emergency treatment should the patient's heart suddenly "arrest" (that is, stop beating) was also developed. But the single most important development was the introduction of specialized training courses—given not only to cardiologists but to all the medical staff, including resident physicians and nurses—enabling all coronary care personnel to recognize cardiac problems before they developed into major difficulties. All staff members were also trained to deliver emergency treatment in the event of cardiac arrest. This training was of special importance, since for long periods, especially at night in local hospitals, nurses are the only staff on immediate floor duty and are often the first to be confronted with sudden cardiac arrest. The medical effectiveness of these units was convincingly established when it was shown that the incidence of sudden death dropped by 35 to 40 percent in hospitals that were equipped with these facilities and had specially trained staff.

The continuous monitoring of each patient's heartbeat also enabled researchers to observe the effects of human interactions on the heart in a way that had previously been impossible. Before the development of such units, records on the effects of human companionship in times of distress depended either upon observations of how people behaved in such situations or upon their reports as to how they felt during these experiences. A person's reactions could not be directly linked to any physical changes because no means existed for continuously recording those changes.

Yet, beyond the objective benefit of viewing a person's heart in a way that was previously impossible, it is important to note that these clinical environments also generate impressions and feelings that are difficult to describe with words alone. This difficulty is felt not just by scientists conducting research in such units but by everyone involved in the drama—patients, loved ones, and medical staff. Certainly anyone who has ever visited a loved one or who has ever been a patient in such a unit will understand the problem. Such units generate powerful emotional reactions. These vary somewhat, depending on why the person is there, but in almost every case the impressions are long-lasting.

Because these units have evolved gradually over a long period of time, medical personnel have gradually been able to adapt to the new medical technology. But to heart patients, many of whom may not have been in a hospital since their birth decades earlier, such units are totally strange and overwhelming. The psychological impact of suddenly finding oneself a patient in such a unit can be devastating. Lying in bed with needles in one's arms, tubes in one's nose, sensors on one's chest recording every heartbeat on a television screen, being forced to use a bed-pan, threatened with imminent death, rendered totally helpless and dependent on others—the experience is shattering.

As his heart blips ominously on a television screen next to his bed, a patient's life is reduced to a few essentials. What does it all mean? Is he going to die? Would he have done anything differently? The world of the patient's wife or children or loved ones is also reduced to a few stark essentials, for the man or woman they visit in such a unit may not be alive the next time they come back.

What do you say in such circumstances—what can you say to help—what is important to communicate? For the medical staff the trauma is somewhat different, although deep down, usually buried from their own awareness, they know they are looking at their own ultimate fate. Yet they also know they must watch the television screens at the central desk, remain detached, but be kind and compassionate, competent, and prepared for emergencies. How do they communicate to a patient—what can they say to reassure them—how do they feel when their patients die?

The very existence of units that house people faced with the imminent possibility of death helps outline in stark simplicity certain elementary facts about life. One of these is our basic need to communicate. When someone's life is in mortal peril, this need is stripped of all its usual complexity and is expressed most directly through simple acts like holding hands. Having watched many people visit their loved ones in coronary care units, I have been struck by the way that most people finally say good-bye. They will speak to each other, if the patient is physically able, usually in subdued tones; they will try to make every effort to appear confident, and sometimes they will even joke But when they say good-bye, it is almost as if some deep, primitive, instinctive ritual takes over. Surprisingly, many wives do not kiss their husbands good-bye, as if they were afraid that such contact might hurt their ill mate. But just before leaving, they will stop speaking and silently hold the patient's hand or touch his body or even stand at the foot of the bed and hold the patient's foot. The contact is brief, yet deeply poignant. More often than not, the final good-bye does not involve words, almost as if words alone were insufficient to communicate their true feelings. The most simple and direct type of human communication does not need words.

Sitting in such units as observers, we could monitor this essential aspect of life . . . we could literally look into the very heart of human relationships. We could also monitor the physical effects of human interactions in a way that had never been possible before. And yet, this remarkable technical capacity also made it clear how limited a scientific view of human relationships really was. While we could objectively and precisely quantify how a patient's heart changed when his wife consoled him, it was also obvious that a heart rate increase or decrease of 20 beats per minute or a burst of arrhythmic heartbeats could not describe the essence of the interaction. We could measure the effects of human interactions and human experiences up to a point—but there was something beyond. And while this idea may seem obvious to the readers of this book, the very real gap between objective measurement and subjective experience must be emphasized. For in the love expressed between a wife and her dying husband, it is clear that the heart of human relationships and human love ultimately moves beyond anything that can be objectively described or measured. While the objective study of the cardiac effects of human interactions on coronary care patients is itself an extremely complex endeavor, understanding the heart of human relationships is not ultimately a process limited by complexity alone. There simply is a limit to science.

Nevertheless, from a scientific perspective, it was the complex nature of human interactions in coronary care units that first created serious problems for us. Before we initiated research in these hospital units, our investigations on the effects of human contact had usually been conducted within the quiet confines of research laboratories. Even when we ventured outside the laboratory, the environments in which our research was conducted were usually carefully controlled settings. The difference between these settings and work in a coronary care unit was difficult at first to reconcile. Just before beginning research in one of these units, we had been studying whether the cardiac system of horses responds to human contact. It had been a particularly beautiful spring morning, and few places could be further removed from the peaceful atmosphere of the countryside than a coronary care unit. The contrast was startling, and my initial reaction upon first entering an intensive-care environment was not unlike that reported by many patients who suddenly find themselves in similar hospital units. It was an overwhelming experience. At first I found it difficult even to glance at the patients lying quietly in their beds. Naïve though it seems in retrospect, I still remember being shocked by the realization that people really were struggling to survive even on a beautiful spring day.

For days that stretched into weeks and then into months, I watched rows of heartbeats move rhythmically across the central monitoring television screens, while the patients whose hearts were on display rested in beds 8 to 20 feet away. The patients' heartbeats usually moved across the screens in steady, trancelike rhythms, reminiscent of the monotonous clicks that measure a train's passage over a smooth but endless track. Occasionally the monotonous rhythm would suddenly change, and strange-looking beats would appear on the screen, causing a red light to flash.

Unlike a carefully controlled laboratory, this coronary care unit was a very complicated world. The patients included old and occasionally young, male and female, black and white, rich and poor, some had no formal education, while others were lawyers, physicians, or college deans. A variety of diagnostic labels such as atherosclerosis, pulmonary edema, congestive heart failure, myocardial infarction, ventricular tachycardia, and atrial fibrillation were attached to various patients' names. A barrage of different medications that had labels such as atropine, propranolol, quinidine, Valium, digoxin, Lanoxin, Coumadin, nitroglycerin, and Xylocaine were given to different patients. All of the factors which customarily appear in mortality statistics were no longer abstract numbers to me. They were, instead, individual patients struggling for their lives. The married, the single, the widowed, the divorced, the lonely, those who had been only children, those who had many siblings, those who had been orphaned or abandoned many years earlier by their parents, and those who seemed to have lives that were filled with love—over the period of the next few years, every type of patient seemed to appear in the unit.

Not only did the patients vary considerably during this period, but the atmosphere of the coronary care unit itself could change dramatically from one moment to the next. One moment the place could be very quiet and peaceful, and the next it could be filled with medical "alert teams" frantically trying to revive a patient whose heart had suddenly stopped beating. The types of human contact that could occur seemed almost limitless. Patients came in "contact" with each other by simply looking at the next bed; in a sense they were looking into a mirror, for there lay another human being also threatened with death. But one had to wonder whether the patients saw or came into "contact" with what we saw, or whether they viewed this world differently. Doctors visited patients; nurses came to and left each patient's bedside; anxious wives visited their husbands; men and women visited their critically ill parents; sometimes parents visited their stricken sons or daughters; priests, ministers, and rabbis visited their parishioners; cleaning ladies mopped beside patients' beds; prison guards occasionally sat quietly near the bed of a critically ill "patient-criminal"; dietitians discussed luncheon menus; young medical residents daily went on their ward rounds. And yet, for long periods during the day, the rhythmical flash of each patient's heartbeat was the only stimulus occurring in an otherwise tranquil environment. For some patients this constant rhythmical flash of their own heartbeats must have had the same impact that the rhythmical beat of the metronome had for the beleaguered citizens of Leningrad; it assured them that they were still alive and that they were not alone.

It was easy to see that human contact was very important to these patients. Many of them developed understandably strong attachments to the doctors and nurses in this unit, a staff that was, in many cases, the only barrier between them and death. But while the general impact of human contact was easy enough to observe, assessing its specific medical effects, especially on the heart, was a different matter.

Paradoxically, many of the coronary care medical personnel *already seemed to know the answer to our questions.* "Of course human contact affects the human cardiovascular system," a nurse commented after asking what we were trying to study. "Everyone knows that you have to measure a patient's blood pressure several times in order to get an accurate reading." "Everyone realizes that sometimes patients are frightened and anxious when a doctor first examines them," commented a medical resident, "that's why bedside manner is so important!" The answers to the questions we were asking seemed, at first glance, to be so obviously just "common sense" that a rather bewildering state of affairs only gradually became apparent. Everyone was so certain that human interactions, such as pulse taking, could affect patients' hearts that no one in this unit, or indeed in any coronary care unit, had ever systematically analyzed it. There were no scientific data about a phenomenon first recognized by Celsus 2,000 years ago and which everyone had subsequently assumed was "common sense." Nor did it take us very long to realize why there had been no systematic investigations in this area. For the search for scientific answers to this commonsense question had to be conducted in the most uncommon fashion.

A paramount consideration in studying human contact in coronary care units was the fact that the patients being observed were very sick human beings. Given this reality, it was clearly impossible to do anything to these patients that was not part of their routine clinical care. The experimental observations, therefore, had to be made in a social environment in which nothing was scientifically controlled. This was a dimension of human contact that scientists usually avoid—human contact that was chaotic and unpredictable, a large number of events occurring in a world where each patient could choose to attend to all or none of the social stimuli occurring around his or her bedside.

On the other hand, the heartbeat of each patient could be observed from a distance, without the patient's awareness. Physicians and nurses could also be observed interacting with patients, and usually neither the patients nor the medical personnel were consciously aware of the fact that they were being watched. Thus, at least theoretically, it was possible to determine whether these interactions affected the hearts of patients.

Several previous studies had suggested that human relationships are indeed an important part of coronary care. Dr. Klein and his colleagues at the Duke University Medical Center studied 14 patients who were transferred from their coronary care unit to an ordinary medical ward where their heart activity was no longer continuously monitored.[4] The first seven patients were moved abruptly, without advance notice and without having the coronary care nurse or personal coronary care physician visit them after their transfer. Of these seven patients, five had serious recurrent cardiovascular complications while still in the hospital. They complained of being lonely and depressed, and felt they had been abandoned by the coronary care team which had previously cared for them.[5] The next seven coronary care patients to be transferred out of this same unit were each prepared in advance for the transfer, and one of the coronary care nurses and the same physician followed them through the remainder of their stay in the hospital. While these seven patients also experienced some emotional reactions, none had any recurrent cardiovascular complications. When the relationship with the familiar medical team was not abruptly terminated, these patients experienced no cardiac difficulties upon transfer out of the unit.

In another type of intensive care unit, a metabolic ward, Dr. William Schottstaedt and his colleagues at the Oklahoma Medical School Hospital observed that various ward stresses could significantly alter certain vitally important hormones—and consequently alter the outcome of treatment. Interestingly, these investigators observed that "interpersonal difficulties were the most common source of stress to be associated with metabolic deviations. These accounted for twenty-eight of the forty-six stressful situations associated with such deviations. In general, they seemed to center on the most significant relationships. Interpersonal stresses arising between individuals without strong ties were less often associated with significant repercussions in the metabolic data."[6]

Drs. Stewart Wolf, Schottstaedt, and others then used this metabolic ward to study whether human interactions might alter levels of serum cholesterol in patients suffering from heart disease in an environment where diet and exercise could be rigidly controlled.[7] Their findings indicated that reassuring and supportive types of relationships could significantly lower the levels of serum cholesterol of patients in an intensive-care environment, while stressful human interactions could significantly elevate cholesterol levels. Within the hospital setting, the patients' serum cholesterol levels changed according to the nature of the human interactions they experienced. Perhaps one case they relate will help describe their general findings. The patient was a 49-year-old man who had had several previous heart attacks and a history of disrupted human relationships. During hospitalization, they reported,

> the patient seemed happy and reasonably relaxed, although very eager to please during the first few days of the study while receiving daily visits from his new woman friend. When she left town for a few days without telling him, however, he became anxious. Serum cholesterol concentration rose somewhat until she returned, revisited, and reassured him. During this visit, however, she had met another man whom she preferred. Her daily visits to the patient fell off and on November 13, 1957, she told him that she had abandoned the plan to marry him and would not see him again. He became intensely depressed. Again the serum cholesterol rose and the following day he had a recurrent myocardial infarction. Four days later he died (p. 384).

Observations such as these made it all the more imperative that the immediate effects of human contact on the coronary care patients' hearts be carefully examined. Yet it was difficult, from a scientific viewpoint, to know precisely where to begin or even precisely what to look for. Our first study began, therefore, by our simply plugging a recorder into the heart monitor of one of the patients, picked randomly from all the patients who happened to be in the unit that day, and recording that patient's heart rate all day long on a polygraph. Eventually the heart rates of 20 additional patients were recorded in this fashion. These patients had all been admitted to the coronary care unit at least 24 hours prior to our observations, in order to allow them to adjust to the unit and to recover somewhat from the initial shock of major cardiovascular difficulties. Each patient's heart rate was continuously recorded for an eight-hour period, and only one patient was monitored at a time. All events that occurred in the unit (e.g., any alarms, noises, crises, deaths, etc.) were marked on the polygraph immediately as they happened. In addition, all personal contacts with the patient, including physician's visits, nursing interactions, and family visits, were immediately marked and coded on the patient's heart rate record. The nature of these interactions was described in a log book by nurses who had been assigned the exclusive task of observing the patients. Since nurses were routinely assigned observational functions in the coronary care unit, it was easy to mesh this type of activity into the usual unit routine without arousing the attention of the unit's patients.

The observational techniques could not have been simpler, yet our attempts to analyze patients' heart reactions to various types of human contact quickly made it apparent why cardiologists had generally avoided this type of research. In order to detect any change in the patient's beat-to-beat heart rate, we usually had to run the recording paper 25 millimeters per second. Running recording paper at that speed for eight hours produced a paper record for one patient's heart rate that stretched for about .50 mile. Then to detect subtle changes in the heart rhythm of that patient, the distance between each and every heartbeat had to be visually examined. After we measured 20 patients for eight hours each, the records of the patients' heart rates stretched for almost 10 miles![8] Each patient's heart record and his or her reactions to human contact in the coronary care unit quickly became a meticulously detailed cardiac biography coded in mile upon mile of paper records. Were it not for the fact that patients' heart reactions to such routine events as pulse taking seemed at times to be so striking, these difficulties would have led us to abandon the study.

Since our chief concern was to study the heart reactions of patients in the typical coronary care setting without either the patient or the medical staff being aware of it, no attempt was made to control any of the interactions experienced by the patients. Since many of the interactions were quite complex—a nurse coming to the patient's bedside while a physician was examining a patient—attention was focused on interactions that were less complex, such as pulse taking, measurement of blood pressure, visits of relatives, and so on. When changes in heart rhythm were observed during such interactions, the entire context of these interactions had to be examined. (Part of the criteria for what was considered a less complex interaction included the stipulation that the patient rest quietly alone for a minimum of three minutes before and after any interaction, and that the environment be quiet during this period; this criterion was necessary in order to allow us to assess reactions to events such as pulse taking within the larger context of the patient's usual ongoing heart rate and rhythm.) Were abnormal beats occurring before the nurse came to the patient's bedside, or was the frequency of occurrence of such abnormal beats changed by the nurse's approach to the bedside? Were such cardiac changes limited to clinical interactions such as pulse taking, or were they a more general phenomenon of human contact with coronary care patients? Were such reactions regularly elicited from certain patients, or did they only occur infrequently? Were such reactions limited to coronary care patients with certain types of heart pathology, or did they occur in patients with different types of cardiovascular disorders?

These questions are especially important in view of the clinical situation faced almost daily by physicians. Cardiologists frequently observe abnormal heartbeats when they look at a patient's heart monitor or listen to the patient's heart with a stethoscope. The question at such times is whether these abnormal beats were occurring before the physician looked or listened—or are they the result of his very attempt to look at, or listen to, the patient's heart. Most clinicians have witnessed cases where significant heart reactions occurred when they or other people came to a patient's bedside. Most of these observations do not appear in textbooks but arise at social gatherings when one talks to physicians about bedside manner. Many physicians tend to shrug these observations off, because they cannot ever be certain that such heart changes would not have occurred by chance anyhow. Our studies began to indicate that there was a connection.

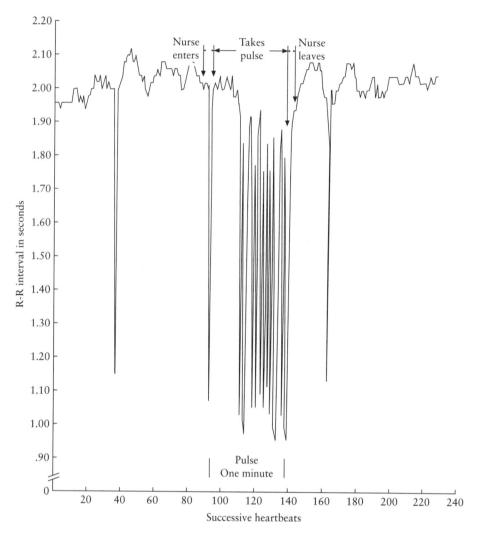

Figure 6.1   Effect of pulse taking on heart rate of patient with 2:1 block

Beat-to-beat heart rate of patient before, during, and after pulse taking by a nurse. Heart rate data are plotted such that 2.00 equals a heart (ventricular) rate of 30, while 1.00 equals a heart (ventricular) rate of 60, and so forth. R-R intervals refer to one aspect of the heartbeat.

A CASE STUDY

One of the very first patients monitored was a 72-year-old women who was in the coronary care unit because she had what is known as 2:1 heart block (Figure 6.1); that is, the upper portion of her heart (called the atrium) would begin the beat, but only every other beat would cause the remainder of her heart (the ventricles) to beat.

The very first human interactions monitored by us in this unit are shown in the following graphs. The first event was a routine pulse taking by a nurse, before and after which the patient rested quietly in bed for three minutes. During the pulse taking, the patient's heart rate began to vary from its pattern of 2:1 block, changing back and forth from 2° to 1° block. In essence, her heart began to change from 30 up to 60 beats per minute.

During two other episodes of pulse taking and one episode of blood pressure measurement, very similar cardiac reactions occurred. While this patient was still in heart block, however, there was one other episode of pulse taking during which there were no heart rate or heart rhythm changes. For three minutes prior to a sequence in which a nurse came to this patient's bedside simply to give her a pill, the patient's heart rate had been a regular 2:1 heart block with a rate of 35 beats per minute. But during the entire one minute the nurse was at her bedside, the patient's heart rate abruptly changed to a different mode of conduction and her heart rate was 70–75 beats per minute, only to change back abruptly to a rate of 35 beats per minute and 2:1 heart block for the three minutes after the nurse left the patient's bedside. A similar reaction occurred when the nurse brought this patient lunch.

Later that same day, the medicine (atropine) the cardiologist had prescribed took effect, and the patient was no longer in continuous 2:1 block. During this period we again monitored an episode of pulse taking. This time the beat-to-beat heart rate both before and after pulse taking was approximately 70–75 beats per minute, with only periodic episodes of heart block occurring. However, when the nurse took the patient's pulse, the heart rate was slightly elevated, the beat became quite rhythmic, and the periodic pattern of heart block was completely abolished.

Note that the episode of pulse taking shown in Figure 6.2 is an inverted mirror image of the cardiac reaction to pulse taking this same patient had shown earlier in the day. In light of the type of cardiac problems experienced by this patient and the medication she was given, it was not difficult for us to deduce the changes in the patient's nervous system that were producing these reactions. Understanding those physiological mechanisms, however, did not help us to understand why the nurse had had these effects on the patient's heart.[9]

We began to see heart rhythm changes in other patients, and occasional changes in the frequency of abnormal heartbeats when people were at a patient's bedside. Sometimes the frequency of these abnormal beats would increase, more often they would decrease, and sometimes there were no apparent changes, leading us to wonder whether these changes in arrhythmia were spontaneous fluctuations that would have occurred whether a person came to the bedside or not. The answer to this question soon became apparent.

For example, for one elderly woman, routine nursing interactions were the only human contact that occurred during the day. The patient had been in the coronary care unit for eight days, and therefore had become quite accustomed to the nursing staff and the unit routine. While her overall frequency of abnormal beats was low during the day of our observations, twice as many abnormal

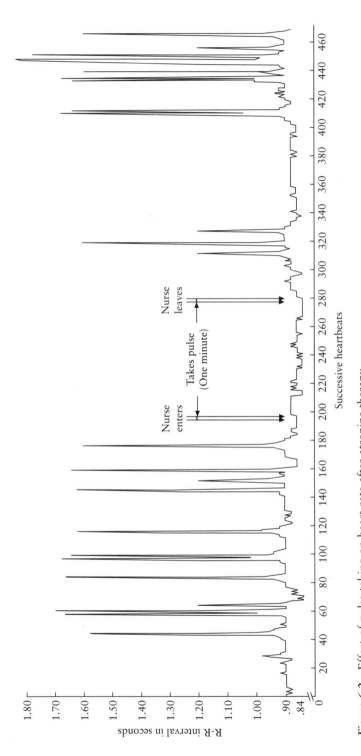

Figure 6.2 Effect of pulse taking on heart rate after atropine therapy

Beat-to-beat heart rate of patient before, during, and after pulse taking. Heart rate and rhythm were normal during pulse taking. Note the elimination of intermittent heart block during pulse taking.

heartbeats occurred when various nurses came to her bedside as when she was resting alone. To put it another way: there were twice as many abnormal beats during the 40 percent of the time that nurses were at her bedside.[10]

These observations of the effects of varying types of human contact on the frequency of cardiac arrhythmia only deepened the mystery. Why were these abnormal heartbeats occurring? Were these observations unusual? Were these patients unusual? Or were such heart reactions typical of coronary care patients?

The complex nature of these questions made it clear that to continue measuring every heartbeat in mile upon mile of records would be an overwhelming task. We were literally being buried in heart rate records and an ever-burgeoning catalogue of different types of human interactions. It also became increasingly apparent that many, many more patients would have to be monitored. Considering the numerous factors that might influence heart reactions, the many types of cardiac pathologies, the various patient personalities, and the variety of human interactions, we had no choice but to enlarge our sample of patients as quickly as possible. The only way to do that was to restrict the amount of time spent observing any one patient. What was needed was to concentrate on some type of human contact that was relatively simple yet experienced by all patients in the unit. Pulse palpation seemed to best fit this requirement. Every patient in the coronary care unit routinely had his or her pulse taken by a nurse every four hours, day or night, waking or sleeping. Furthermore, this was a human interaction which involved touch, was discrete, and of relatively short duration, required no conversation, and demanded no physical exertion on the part of the patient.

We thus began to examine the effects of pulse palpation on the heart rate and rhythm of over 300 coronary care patients, both during daylight hours and during the night when the patients were sleeping. Each pulse taking was examined only if the patient was resting alone for three minutes before and three minutes after this event. To summarize very briefly: after examining these patients it was clear that even the routine event of pulse palpation could alter the frequency of cardiac arrhythmia in coronary care patients. In some of the patients, indeed, pulse taking had the power to completely suppress arrhythmias that had been occurring.[11]

Most of the medical implications of these studies need not detain us here, except to point out that the simple act of touching can have important influences on patients' heart rate and rhythm. These observations did, however, raise many questions. Did pulse taking frighten the patients? After all, they were in coronary care units and were undoubtedly concerned with the status of their hearts. Or, conversely, did the pulse taking comfort them and reassure them that they were under continuous care? And what specifically led to the changes in the frequency of arrhythmia? Did the patients move physically in bed or change their manner of breathing in ways not noticed? Or was it an emotional response that influenced these heart rhythms? Any of these factors could have produced the heart reactions we were observing. An even larger question began to be of concern: was it only patients with cardiac pathology that reacted to human touch, or did patients without heart problems react similarly? These questions led us to shift our studies temporarily from coronary care units to one of the most acute clinical areas in any modern hospital, a shock-trauma unit.

HUMAN CONTACT IN A HOSPITAL SHOCK-TRAUMA UNIT

A few years ago the University of Maryland Hospital developed one of the first shock-trauma units in the United States. This unit, the Maryland Center for Emergency Services, became a prototype for similar units being developed through-out the country. The highly specialized Maryland Center was developed to cope with life-threatening medical emergencies, usually involving a patient who had suddenly experienced severe trauma and often had lapsed into a state of circu-latory shock and coma. About 60 percent of the 1,000 victims treated annually in this unit were flown in by a state-operated helicopter medical service. Typical patients included victims of serious automobile accidents, industrial accidents, or gunshot wounds. Most patients flown to this unit were in acute danger of death if multiple medical and surgical procedures were not immediately performed.

This shock-trauma unit itself was far more complex than a coronary care unit. The unit had 12 beds in an open rectangular area, in the center of which was a central monitoring station. Each bed unit was completely autonomous, with its own medical and patient care supplies: refrigerator, sink, running water, respirator, wall suction, wall air and oxygen, equipment for continuously monitoring the patient's electrocardiograms and blood pressure, and so forth. Each bed unit was equipped with all the facilities necessary to conduct almost every emergency medical procedure. At the central desk all patients' electrocardiograms, as well as a number of other bodily changes, were continuously monitored. A computer constantly scanned each bed, hourly printing out each patient's heart rate, blood pressure, temperature, respiration, and any other physiological data desired by the attending medical teams.

The possibility of monitoring the effects of human contact in the shock-trauma unit was of special interest because, unlike the patients in the coronary care unit, many of these patients were much younger, and most had no intrinsic heart pathology. Treatment for many of these patients involved the introduction of certain extreme medical procedures. One that was of special interest was the use of d-tubocurarine, a drug originally developed centuries ago by the Amazon Indians. The Indians placed the drug, curare, on the tips of arrowheads because it had the capacity to paralyze and kill wild animals immediately. In its modern medical use as d-tubocurarine, this drug temporarily paralyzes every muscle in the body, so that the patient cannot move, speak, open his eyes, or even breathe on his own without being artificially respirated. Yet curare still leaves a person perfectly aware of what is going on. If conscious, therefore, the patient can hear and feel what is going on in the world around him, but he cannot move any muscles. This drug was occasionally administered in the shock-trauma unit when patients had uncontrollable seizures, or when they were delirious or violently struggling against medical procedures being used to save their lives.

This clinical procedure allowed the exploration of certain questions raised by the coronary care observations. Would patients' hearts react to human contact when the patients themselves could no longer move or change their breathing pattern, or when the patients had no discernible cardiac disease? In extreme cases, would these patients react to human touch even if they were delirious or in deep comas?[12]

Two types of human interactions were studied. The first type consisted of relatively simple spontaneous clinical interactions, such as a doctor's visit, in which neither patient nor staff were aware they were being observed. The second type involved planned interactions in which nurses who were aware of the purpose of the study took the patient's pulse, held the patient's hand, or touched his arm and verbally comforted him with the following type of statement:

> (First name of patient), my name is (first name of nurse) and I am a nurse. I know you can't answer me when I talk to you even though you can hear me. That's because of your medication. You're receiving a drug called curare which has temporarily paralyzed you so that you are unable to respond in any way. The drug has also blocked your respiration, so there is a machine at your bedside breathing for you, which you may be able to hear. This medicine is an unpleasant but very necessary part of your therapy, so please try to relax and bear with it. As I said before, the effect will only be temporary, and once the drug is discontinued you will be able to move as before. We will try to anticipate your needs, since you are at present unable to communicate them to us. There is always a doctor or nurse at your bedside, so please try not to worry.

This statement was not memorized or delivered verbatim; rather, the nurse reacted to each patient in an individualized manner. Whenever possible, three-minute resting periods prior to and following both types of interactions were obtained.

Although a nurse holding a patient's hand and comforting him was among the simplest human interactions that we could analyze, even this most elementary human contact proved to be quite difficult to study within the context of the shock-trauma environment. Various clinical personnel were almost always at the patient's bedside, and it was not uncommon for as many as seven or eight physicians and four or five nurses to be around the patient. Then there were the telephones at the central station, which were constantly ringing. The intercom system frequently paged various physicians, and several patient monitoring devices also emitted noises. This complex array of stimuli frequently made it necessary to watch curarized patients for as long as four to five hours before a period would occur in which the patient was left alone for as long as seven minutes, the minimum time period necessary to evaluate patient reactions. Since patients were curarized for various periods of time, there was no precise way of determining whether the patient was conscious during the interactions. The research team relied on the attending physician's general assessment of mental status during periods when the curare effect was transiently reversed by a drug that counteracts its action. However, one of the patients was studied immediately after he was given d-tubocurarine. Since he was talking with the physician just

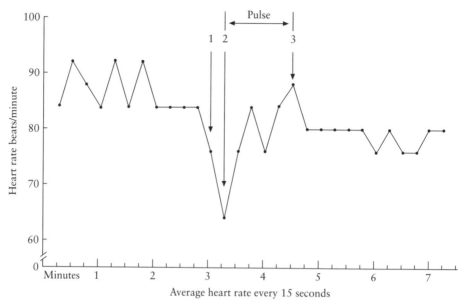

Figure 6.3 Effect of pulse taking on curarized woman

Patient's heart rate averaged every 15 seconds before, during, and after pulse taking by nurse. Note decrease in heart rate during pulse taking. Key: (1) nurse enters, (2) nurse takes pulse, and (3) nurse stops and leaves.

before he was given d-tubocurarine, it is reasonable to assume that he was conscious during these observations.[13]

In spite of the large number of environmental stimuli bombarding each patient, the common types of human contact seemed to produce dramatic changes in the patient's heart rate. For example, Figure 6.3 shows the heart rate of one 31-year-old woman critically injured in an automobile accident. Her heart rate slowed almost 20 beats per minute when a nurse quietly took her pulse. When the episode was recorded, this patient had been in a coma for two days. A similar change in heart rate was observed in a 30-year-old man who had suffered severe chest injuries in an accident. The nurse in this instance held his hand and quietly comforted him (Figure 6.4). The power of human contact on this patient's heart rate was again seen by us later in the day, quite by chance. As is shown in Figure 6.5, while we were monitoring this patient seven doctors came on medical rounds to his bedside to discuss his case.

After a few minutes they left, and several minutes later another physician came in to perform a tracheal suction on the patient. This uncomfortable procedure made it necessary for the physician to periodically turn off the patient's respirator during a one-minute period—at which point the patient could no longer breathe. It is difficult to imagine a more psychologically frightening or physically distressing sensation, and we may assume that the resulting heart rate increase was about as great as could be elicited under these extremely traumatic conditions.

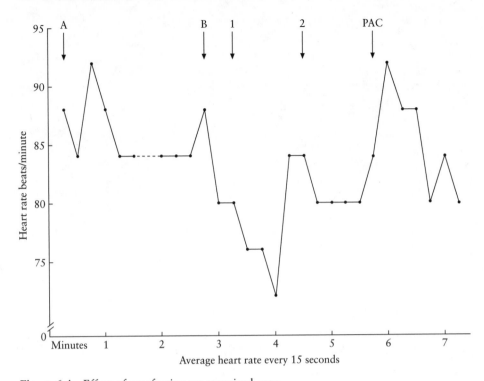

Figure 6.4   Effect of comforting on curarized man

Heart rate of patient before, during, and after comforting by nurse. Key: (A) nurse remaining quietly by bedside; and (B) nurse out; (1) nurse comforts patient; and (2) nurse leaves. PAC means premature atrial contraction, which was observed about one minute after second nurse comforted patient.

It is therefore of great interest to note that the heart rate increase was almost as great (although nowhere near as sustained) while the seven doctors chatted about this patient.

Finally, Figure 6.6 shows the heart rate change induced in an 11-year-old girl when a nurse quietly held her hand. This young girl had been struck by a car and had sustained a skull fracture and multiple fractures in her pelvis. She was in a coma when first brought to the shock-trauma unit and gradually recovered during the next eight days. Then she suddenly became restless, confused, and in great respiratory distress, and was curarized at this point. For the three minutes before the nurse approached her bedside, the girl's heart rate was cycling rather rhythmically from a maximum of 125 beats per minute to a low of 105 beats per minute. No unusual change in heart rate was observed during most of the period that the nurse quietly held her hand. However, just as the nurse let go of the girl's hand, her heart rate increased to a peak rate of 136 beats per minute and then fell to about 95 beats per minute before cycling back into the previous pattern. During the entire seven-minute period, the highest and lowest heart rates occurred within 30 seconds after the nurse let go of the patient's hand.

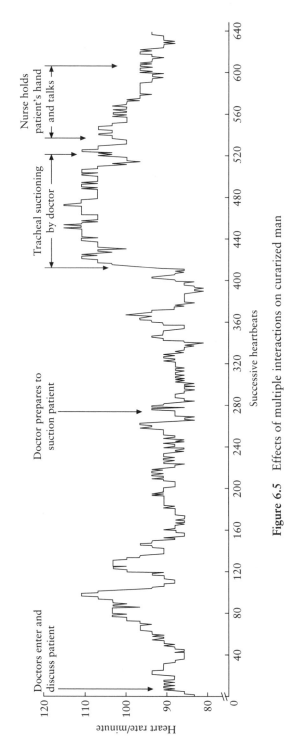

Figure 6.5 Effects of multiple interactions on curarized man

Beat-to-beat heart rate of patient during doctors' rounds, tracheal suctioning, and comforting by nurse.

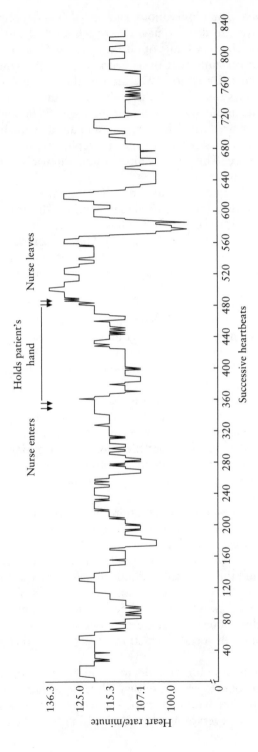

Figure 6.6 Effect of comforting on curarized girl

Beat-to-beat heart rate of patient before, during, and after nurse held patient's hand. Note increase and then abrupt decrease in heart rate at cessation of hand-holding.

It must be recognized that observations such as these—especially those of the two patients who were in deep comas, one of whom died shortly after our observations—take us to the very limits of our knowledge. It can never be established with 100 percent certainty that these heart rate changes would not have occurred by chance, and there is no way to repeat these observations to conclusively answer that question. All of these shock-trauma observations were unique and poignant human interactions, and from a scientific point of view this uniqueness must be recognized as both a strength and an unavoidable weakness. The events monitored in this study can never be replicated within the precise context of their occurrence. They were simply unique human interactions in a terribly traumatic environment.

The shock-trauma heart rate data did show that the cardiac changes seen in the coronary care unit were not unique to human beings with cardiac pathology. They also convinced us that the effects of holding a patient's hand could be seen even in the most intense of clinical environments. Human contact seemed to be all the more important to patients the more traumatic the environment became. If anything, the reaction of the heart rate to human contact seemed to increase in magnitude under these extreme conditions.

The magnitude of these reactions must also be viewed in the context of the acute clinical environment in which these measurements were taken. These patients, especially those in the shock-trauma unit, were literally bombarded by a wide array of changing environmental stimuli, any one of which could easily have had a greater impact on heart rate than the touch of one human hand. The "control periods" just before the human contact were by no means periods of quiet relaxation for the patients. It is also important to reemphasize that these patients varied from the very young to the very old and that they varied in terms of their cardiovascular pathology, physiological status, and the types of medicines they were being given. The fact that the effects of something as routine as human touch or quiet comforting could still be observed, despite all the factors that could potentially mask its influence, serves to underscore the vital importance it has for our hearts.

Like all scientific endeavors, these observations have posed far more questions than answers. Some conclusions do emerge, however. By no means should it be concluded that human contact is "dangerous" or "bad" for patients. Quite the opposite. Human contact seems to be desperately important to patients in these acute clinical settings, and the heart seems almost hyperreactive in these environments to even the most ordinary types of personal contact. It is our hope that by paying attention to the effects of various types of human contact and to the emotional context of these interactions, we may one day be able to isolate the types of patients and kinds of social interactions that produce therapeutic benefits for the heart.

From spending many hours observing doctors and nurses in these acute clinical areas, we have also come to recognize that while these individuals spend an extraordinary amount of time with their patients, very little of it is spent simply chatting with them. Almost everything physicians and nurses do is, of necessity, concerned with the patient's illness rather than with the patient himself. So even though a great deal of human contact takes place, some patients feel socially isolated and lonely. One can only speculate, but perhaps it is this peculiar aspect of social interactions in intensive-care units that makes the hearts of so many patients so sensitive to human contact. Dr. Gunnar Biörck, a Swedish cardiologist, recently reiterated Sir William Osler's advice on bedside manner when he wrote in the *American Heart Journal:*[14]

> Physicians should be careful of their own attitudes, from the time of the first contact with the patient, in taking the history and in making the physical and other examinations, because the first contact will, to a great extent, determine the future interrelationship between the patient and his physician. An optimistic attitude is essential. . . . In dealing with cardiac patients, much may be learned by listening to their heart with the stethoscope, but it may be even more important to listen to the patient himself without a stethoscope (p. 417).

Notes

1. Joel E. Dimsdale, "The Coping Behavior of Nazi Concentration Camp Survivors," *American Journal of Psychiatry* 131 (1974): 792–797.
2. James J. Lynch et al., "Psychological Aspects of Cardiac Arrhythmia," *American Heart Journal* (1977).
3. It is the occurrence of these abnormal beats which makes it imperative that a person be taken to a hospital as soon as possible after a heart attack. During this crucial period, even if a patient feels better, his life can be in mortal peril.
4. Robert F. Klein et al., "Transfer from a Coronary Care Unit: Some Adverse Responses," *Archives of Internal Medicine* 122 (1968): 104–108; see also W. Doyle Gentry, Gerard J. Musante, and Thomas Haney, "Anxiety and Urinary Sodium/Potassium as Stress Indicators on Admission to a Coronary Care Unit," *Heart and Lung* 2 (1973): 875–877.
5. Almost 20 years ago, Dr. Klaus Järvinen, a physician at a medical clinic of the University of Helsinki, raised the question of whether the medical rounds themselves could not be a danger to patients who had had a heart attack. He observed that 6 out of 39 patients stricken with an acute myocardial infarction who died after seven days of hospitalization did so during or shortly after ward rounds. Two of the cases involved a medical decision as to whether the patient should be discharged from the hospital upon the finish of the ward rounds. In another two cases, the ward rounds were made by the physician-in-chief, who only visited once or twice a week. (Klaus A. Järvinen, "Can Ward Rounds Be a Danger to Patients with Myocardial Infarction?" *British Medical Journal* 1 (1955): 318–320.)
6. William W. Schottstaedt et al., "Sociologic and Metabolic Observations on Patients in the Community of a Metabolic Ward," *American Journal of Medicine* 25 (1958): 248–257.
7. Stewart Wolf et al., "Changes in Serum Lipids in Relation to Emotional Stress during Rigid Control of Diet and Exercise," *Circulation* 26 (1962): 379–387.
8. These types of analysis can now be done by computers in a few minutes. Records that took weeks to analyze just a few years ago can now be evaluated in seconds.

9. James J. Lynch *et al.*, "The Effects of Human Contact on Cardiac Arrhythmia in Coronary Care Patients," *Journal of Nervous and Mental Disease* 158 (1974): 88–91.
10. Sue A. Thomas, James J. Lynch, and Mary E. Mills, "Psychosocial Influences on Heart Rhythm in the Coronary Care Unit," *Heart and Lung* 4, No. 5 (1975): 746–750.
11. James J. Lynch *et al.*, "Human Contact and Cardiac Arrhythmia in a Coronary Care Unit," *Psychosomatic Medicine* (1977); see also. M. E. Mills *et al.*, "The Effects of Pulse Palpation on Cardiac Arrhythmia in Coronary Care Patients," *Nursing Research* 25 (1976): 378–382.
12. James J. Lynch *et al.*, "Effects of Human Contact on the Heart Activity of Curarized Patients in a Shock-Trauma Unit," *American Heart Journal* 88 (1974): 160–169.
13. Our research team did not participate in any clinical decisions regarding these patients and had no prior knowledge as to when a patient might be curarized. We were able to monitor these patients only by remaining on 24-hour call.
14. Gunnar Biörck, "Social and Psychological Problems in Patients with Chronic Cardiac Illness," *American Heart Journal* 58 (1959): 414–417.

CHAPTER 7

Cancer and the Self: How Illness Constellates Meaning

Roger Levin

... all the diseases for which the issue of causation has been
settled ... have turned out to have a simple physical cause ...
and it is far from unlikely that something comparable will eventually be isolated for cancer ... It is diseases thought to be multi-
determined (that is, mysterious) that have the widest possibilities
as metaphors for what is felt to be socially or morally wrong.
                                                    (Sontag 1979)

... the cancer that had most likely lain dormant in his body
until then suddenly blossomed like a rose ... the hopelessness
pervading the entire country penetrated the soul to the body ...
                                                    (Kundera 1985)

... each civilization has its own kind of pestilence and can
control it only by reforming itself ...
                                                    (Dubos 1965)

Is cancer the pestilence of our time? Or is that kind of talk just ignorant superstition? Surely it seems we are in the midst of a cancer epidemic not solely attributable to the longevity of modern populations. With increasing frequency it strikes
not just the elderly but the young as well. We all feel at risk, as if it were literally
in the air. The probability of getting cancer, we often hear now, is about one-in-
four over the average lifetime. These are pretty terrifying odds.

Our collective terror of cancer is partly the result of still prevalent, if not quite
old-fashioned, beliefs about the inevitability of horrible, protracted suffering, bru-
tish therapies and eventual death following a cancer diagnosis. Of course cancer
is by no means always fatal, treatment is becoming little by little more humane,
and some people even survive terminal prognoses. But the fear still lingers in the
collective mind. I detect here evidence of a more shadowy foreboding, an inchoate sense of cancer's timeliness, its appropriateness to our social scene, as if an
obscure historical logic were somehow involved. This is what Foucault (1975)
has termed the historical individuality of pestilential disease in its time. Cancer

apparently shares that feature with all great epidemics of the past. And therein lies one of cancer's more troubling aspects: to hope to avoid or survive cancer is, with evident circularity, to find oneself out of pace, beyond one's historical time. This is perhaps the root of the stoicism once very commonly observed, though probably less so nowadays, in cancer patients. So the sense of inevitability for us attaches not only to the course of cancer illness, but as well and less visibly to the logic of its occurrence.

Is cancer then uniquely modern? Collectively we seem to feel so. Images of wild, uncontrolled cell growth imaginatively capture the worst of technological society, as if a pact with the demons of progress can set the natural order of things out of balance. We pay for our collective hubris. Here in our mythologies of cancer the personal and historical collide and interpenetrate. We think depression and unexpressed anger occasion the visitation of cancer. We think it shameful and contagious. True to our positivistic moral traditions, we value optimism and stoutness of heart in our citizens. Even our New Age ethos teaches that decisiveness and positive thought heal cancer. The ideal cancer patient now is a successful player. I get the sense of a civilization believing itself to be held hostage to its own driven will to power, a will thought capable in the absence of due diligence of turning in on itself—sour and malignant—in a crisis of faith.

Cancer patients stand accused primarily of a failure of will. Small wonder they have been shunned and shamed in our recent history, hidden like a consummate obscenity from public view. Defeatism is a moral outrage, a form of treason in a production driven economy. So the damage is to be limited and contained. We still wage war on cancer with knives and poisons and ray guns—no measure is thought too severe, too disfiguring in the effort to purge the body politic. In the New Age of consumption driven postmodern enlightenment we are more inclined to rehabilitate cancer patients than punish them, less inclined to isolate and destroy. So, today we cajole. We infuse cancer with the power of good thoughts, optimism, and above all will power! Good health has become a new ritual of patriotism, a market place for the public display of secular faith in the power of will. To lose faith in progress, the triumph of rationality over chaos (this is the subtext of cancer in our time, the mythic surround) is to bring down on oneself the demons of an essentially destructive natural order.

But what bearing has this metaphoric vernacular on the problem of physical illness? Readers familiar with Sontag's by now famous line of argument will agree, I think, that for her the metaphoric vernacular around cancer is thoroughly spurious. Of course, all vernacular discourse about illness, even the concept and definition of illness itself, is socially embedded and hence captive of dominant moral/political/economic agendas. The militarization of allopathic medical culture in cancer management is certainly a case in point. The blaming of cancer patients for their illness is another. Even holistic approaches, presumed to be revolutionary, are often subtly captive of dominant ideologies, as I shall detail further on. Illness metaphors reveal as much as they obscure of social processes. It is a matter of how we read them.

Sontag's reading of the idiom is reactionary in two ways. First, insofar as it seeks to limit the legitimate exploration of cancer issues to the search for simple physical causes, it reinstates the hegemony of the orthodox Cartesian paradigm of embodiment. Disease in the dualistic orthodoxy is presumed to inhabit a purely material machinelike body distinctly separate from the mind, the seat of consciousness (Leder 1984). Disease is knowable as the simply physical through reductive analyses unencumbered by the complexity of subjective meanings. Second, in its outright dismissal of the mysteriousness of cancer as merely superstition, her reading forbids the possibility, much less necessity, of critical self-reflection at either the personal or social level. In effect, there is then nothing to know about cancer beyond the simply material. This position is anachronistic even by the standards of allopathic medical science.

To the contrary, cancer poses a significant epistemic challenge to our culture since it is, in fact, still quite mysterious. Cancer is neither controllable nor for the most part well understood. Idiomatic metaphors about cancer engage that mystery and attempt to formulate a relevant discourse about what cancer means for us in terms of both the social/productive organization of modern culture and the texture of our personal lives situated in that concrete historical context. The capture of that idiom by the apparatus of social control must be deconstructed. The most thorough-going deconstruction of the captive imaginings about cancer will necessarily depend upon an understanding of how the embodied individual experiences illness meanings authentically. This is no less a project than the penetration of the opaque objectivity of the simply material body of disease, the overthrow of the positivistic paradigm of embodiment that forms the principal ideologic superstructure of technologic culture.

There is an open question about the socially critical status of authentic personal meanings, especially since personal self-actualization in our consumer culture has become one of the locations for the deployment of desire in the market by the structures of social control. This is one of the central issues in the current critical discussion of the contemporary culture of narcissism. A working assumption for me in these pages is that bodily felt experiencing is inherently resistant to social capture, but the demonstration of this assumption lies well beyond the scope of this essay. . . .

The task of this project is the deconstruction of cancer as a simply physical disease. I will develop instead the notion of cancer as an environment of bodily felt experiencing. Toward that end I will first look at the development of nineteenth-century medical discourse about disease as it enshrines and then transcends the notion of simple physical causes. I will suggest a way of understanding the interpenetration of material and nonmaterial features of illness environment. I will then assess the adequacy of postmodern twentieth century medical discourses to comprehend the place of meaning in illness. I will propose a view of embodiment that is adequate to the task. Finally, I will close with some observations about the current status of holistic thinking about cancer in light of the recent paradigmatic shift in medical thinking and the popularity of elements of ancient sacred healing traditions.

Cancer is a staggeringly complex phenomenon for which there are not, and likely will not be, simple understandings. Currently allopathic medical opinion tends to regard cancer as not one but many separate diseases. While I suspect this is partly an artifact of incomplete knowledge and an atomistic classificatory schema, it none-theless serves to underscore the extent of biologic variability encountered across the modern cancer phenomenon. Biologically suspect factors in the etiology of cancers are commonly thought to include: viral and fungal organisms, endogenous genetic/constitutional processes, exogenous environmental substances, and nutri-tion. Relatively little is still understood about how the interaction of these factors contributes to the appearance of symptomology. So the complexity is indeed great and cancer increasingly is viewed as multi-determined. In this atmosphere cancer research concentrates more and more on the regulatory environment of abnormal cell growth. Cancer medicine has moved steadily away from the lan-guage of first causes toward concepts of dynamically interactive fields. This brings medicine more in step with contemporary theoretical developments in physics, chemistry and biology which favor nonmechanically reductive models of reality (Capra 1983; Prigogine and Stengers 1984).

Paradoxically, the more adept modern hard-science technologies have become at penetrating deeper into the nexus of material reality the less convincing their mechanical/causal understanding. And this is certainly true of nineteenth-century bacteriologic science. Public health awareness prior to the development of the germ theory of pathogenic causes was dominated by attention to the cleanliness of the social environment (Starr 1982). Disease and moral condition were still conceptually interwoven. The origin of infectious disease was considered to re-side in the moral dimension of community history. The representation of disease as a moral configuration was characteristic of the premodern social perspective (Turner 1984). With the advent of the microscope and the identification of microbial pathogens, interest in the social/moral environment of disease waned. In effect the moral discourse about disease, the language of environments, was appropriated and subsumed by the medical domain.

And yet this reduction of the moral dimension of disease to simple material causes was also ultimately responsible for the transcendence of material reductive paradigms in the postmodern era. Toward the close of the last century the tech-nologically amplified vision of bacteriologic science revealed that the presence of pathogenic micro-organisms was a necessary but not sufficient cause of tuber-culosis. Roughly 10 percent of those who were demonstrably in contact with the tubercle bacillus became actively symptomatic. The concept of host resistance or susceptibility to pathogenic agents, the concept of an internal disease environment capable of mediating the effect of simple physical causes, arose as a direct result of the technologic capacity to extend the visible dimension of material reality.

The concept of host resistance, however, did not gain currency nor reveal its revolutionary impact upon the metaphysics of disease until the latter half of the present century. This was contingent upon changing epidemiological patterns, economic conditions and modes of knowledge in advancing industrial societies. The success of bacteriologic science in controlling acute infectious epidemics disclosed beneath the veil of contagion a new domain of chronic, debilitative noncontagious diseases that could not be attributed to pathogenic agency. And it was here that the conceptualization of the patient as a host environment was to become a central heurism in the construction of disease models along the leading edge of postmodern allopathy.

The patient-as-host is a decisioning matrix at the convergence of social/historical, psychological and biological lines of force. The locus of disease consequently shifts from external invasive agents to the internal invitational climate of a concretely situated host. No longer a passive receptacle, like a culture dish, for implanted pathogens, the host body becomes the dwelling place of a conscious social actor. Social context and motivated responding become legitimate arenas for medical discourse.

While the medical subsumption of community morality under the supervision of bacteriologic science constituted a concentration of medical focus, a contraction of social concerns to matters of physical substance, the concept of host resistance widened the field of view. It now legitimately included nonmaterial dimensions.

The technology that made possible the ascendency of a material-reductive discourse about disease ultimately rendered that perspective theoretically obsolete. Sentimental faith in the language of simple physical causes, the language of nineteenth-century naturalistic modernism, is now out of step with the paradigmatic shift implicit in postmodern medical science. The opening of the field of disease recognizes that bodily disease is an appropriate occasion for simultaneous, interpenetrating theoretic speculations—political, philosophic, historical, psychological as well as physiological (Turner 1984; Foucault 1975). We are no longer confined to the timeless physical body of disease. We are now permitted to ask the sentient, historically situated body about environments and meanings of environments.

Thus, critical inquiry into the relationship between cancer and the organization of industrial culture finds legitimate expression not only in the metaphoric vernacular around the popular perception of cancer but increasingly in the medical literature as well. Empirical support comes from a variety of comparative epidemiologic sources. Cancer incidence across divergent cultures, populations within cultures, and geographic regions is known to vary widely (Winter 1979). Urban populations, for instance, tend toward higher cancer fatality than rural. And a similar differential in incidence has been systemically reported for nonindustrial people, for example, Tibetans pre- and postexile (Choedrak 1983) and North American Indians pre- and postcontact with whites (Hoffman 1928). Socioeconomic status effects, occupational hazards, life-style strains, diet, and environmental pollutants either singly or in combination have all been implicated at one time or another in the etiologic picture of cancer as an industrial phenomenon. And yet, while epidemiologic speculation about cancer incidence remains largely tentative and controversial in regard to specific hypotheses, it is nonetheless on the whole highly suggestive of industrial culture effects in cancer (Wilkins 1974).

So the mysteriousness of cancer is not a matter of some as yet unknown simple physical cause. It seems likely that how we live, the environments we create, and the meanings of those environments are important factors. And this, of course, echoes the deep traditional wisdoms about the interdependence of the material and nonmaterial aspects of existence. The elder statesman of traditional Tibetan medicine, when asked if he could account for the phenomenon of cancer, attributed it to "industrial manufacture and restlessness of mind" (Choedrak 1983). Despite the theoretic shifts in contemporary disease models this is still a difficult notion for our medical culture to grasp, that the material and spiritual worlds are a unified whole.

DISEASE AND THE SACRED

The irrationality of the metaphoric vernacular around cancer is what disturbs critics like Sontag the most. I have suggested above that this irrationality is valuable in so far as it challenges our culture's critical self-knowledge. I want to look now a bit more closely at how that works.

Disease that is perceived as uncontrollable, beyond the technologic range of our culture's medicine, will likely become the subject of a significant discourse framed in nonrational terms. Cancer is an example. Tuberculosis was in its time. But with the discovery of the pathogenic bacillus, tuberculosis for the most part ceased to carry those metaphoric meanings. This should not be construed as evidence for the spuriousness of metaphoric talk, but rather for a certain cultural smugness as newly captive disease loses it critical cutting edge, its authority to ask questions about how we understand ourselves and the world we inhabit. The value-free stance of naturalistic medicine silences such talk. It presumes that rationality exhausts the knowable.

But the hierarchies of understandings that mediate social action in human ecosystems are not capable of being fully rationalized (Rappaport 1970). Even highly sophisticated analytic models of complex natural systems are in general not sufficiently exhaustive to allow precise prediction of outcomes of many sorts of social action. There are innumerable instances of uncontrolled results of exhaustively analyzed technical operations in our contemporary experience—for example, petro-chemical interventions in our food chain.

Natural ecosystems are teleologically more complex and less coherently coupled than even the most elegant laboratory analogues. Complex living systems, unlike machine systems, continuously create order in the matrix of relationships among their elements that is not given by the elements themselves. Such systems are modulated and ordered through the operation of relationships only some of which are likely to be amenable to deterministic analysis. Natural systems are not totally visible to technologic scrutiny.

Technologic operations tend to presume, contrary to fact, that any segment of a complex system which may be isolated for the purposes of analysis may be in practice isolated from the whole. This central tendency of atomistic approaches contributes significantly to an ecological hubris, a lack of basic respect for not completely understood endogenous regulatory processes. This translates into technologically amplified insensitivities to the maladaptive effects of social actions, principally the degradation of the biotic environment. Rappaport (1970) warned, therefore, that human activity must be informed by a large measure of respect for the living order which cannot be rendered causally transparent.

It is axiomatic that significant chunks of the collective belief systems of nontechnologic cultures can be naturalistically inaccurate without in any way impairing their adaptive capacity to regulate human activity in the natural world. People need not understand bacteriology, for example, to know that defecating in the public water supply is not a good idea. The religious fabric of cultural beliefs, for instance ritual relationships with the supernatural, will function in such cases to sustain an adaptive relationship with the environment. But it is not the dimension of material/causal facticity upon which religious beliefs rely for their adaptive value.

Rappaport rightly speculated that collective sacred understandings, grounded as they are in the commonality of nondiscursive personally felt experiences of organismic unity, provide a far better analogue of complex living ecosystems than analytic/technologic models. Thus, sacred discourse constellates the complex interrelatedness of living systems and empowers people to live adaptively in consonance with that wholeness. Sacred discourse is inherently mysterious as it leaps across the chasm of the inexplicable to the directly known.

My frank affection for disease metaphors, irrespective of their material facticity, has to do with an abiding sense that they are in our present positivistic climate one of the very last refuges of sacred discourse about illness. Disease, especially life-threatening disease, is the locus of collision for individual and collective, social and biological, material and nonmaterial, sacred and profane imperatives. Our metaphors struggle to comprehend the place of suffering and death, the possibilities for healing, in the complex scheme of things. Such matters are simply not subject to proof. And so our talk about them eschews the parsimonious logic of parts for the gestures that can embrace the whole.

In terms of the social/productive apparatus of technologic culture, the refusal to envision the wholeness of the living ecosystem in which we are inextricably embedded and to inform our actions with an appropriate respect for that intrinsically mysterious unity has encoded cancer directly into the organization of contemporary society. Carcinogenic potentials within the social body can be approached then as the cascades of ecologically maladaptive effects associated with the marginalization of sacred discourse in favor of atomistic, instrumental understandings of social process.

But the maladaptive effects of the marginalization of the sacred are not only a matter of external social/productive relations. My principal concern here is with our relation to ourselves and our capacity to constellate our own wholeness in a cultural context that utilizes the fragmentation of the individual self as an opportunistic strategy of the market economy. At the personal level cancer embodies this struggle of the self toward wholeness, the release of the self from the constraining identification with its objectified parts. Cancer is ultimately an invitation to journey to the interior of deeply, authentically personal meanings beyond the captive and conditioned partial self.

At this juncture I want to turn my attention to the two distinctive, though not wholly discontinuous, currents in twentieth-century allopathy that have inquired about disease as an environment of personal meanings. Both psychosomatic and behavioral medicine have contributed to the transition from the characteristically modern concern with specific causes to the postmodern conceptualization of a multidimensional interactive disease environment. Each, to the extent it has been captive of the reductionist ideologies of technological culture, has had to engage dialectically its own epistemological foundations in order to envision the new field of disease.

PSYCHOSOMATICS

Psychosomatic medicine at its prime during the third through fifth decades of this century set for itself the task of demonstrating psychological specificity in the siting and development of certain chronic degenerative diseases (Reiser 1975; Silverman 1968). The earliest systematic studies concentrated on detailed profiling of personalities in the chronically ill on a case by case basis (Dunbar 1935). While these first attempts were rich in clinical detail, they lacked theoretic coherence and ultimately contributed little to the understanding of specific disease etiologies. However, by the late 1930s psychosomatic medicine had acquired a determined theoretic perspective as the Chicago group around Franz Alexander pioneered the application of Freudian psychoanalytic concepts. Based on Freud's theory of neurosis, the essential pathogenic mechanism of degenerative illness was thought to be the innervation of organ systems associated with the damming of instinctual drive energies that a conflicted ego could not permit to be satisfied.

Since the formulation of neurotic innervation could not of itself account for specific symptomologies, a specificity hypothesis was added. The energy economies of psychosexual complexes were considered, then, to be symbolically encoded in target organ systems along a dimension of vegetative tonus (Alexander 1948). Thus, otherwise disparate illnesses, for example rheumatoid arthritis and hypertension, might be proximally classified. In this case, both conditions would exhibit the tonic quality of "constriction."

How drive energies got to be symbolically encoded at the level of the vegetative organs was the subject of unresolved debate throughout the history of psychosomatic medicine; it underscores the only marginal success research in the field had in coming to rest around the core project of mind-body unification.

The debate had its origins in Freud's early distinction between actual neurosis and psychoneurosis (Freud 1929). The former included a variety of seemingly simple physical symptoms like headache, muscular cramping, or organ irritability. An absence of meaning, or what Freud termed "signification in the mind" character- ized the actual neuroses. He considered them to be the result of unspecifiable metabolic toxins occasioned by sexual drive conflicts.

In contrast, the psychoneuroses were a class of symptomologies that arose as compensation or substitution around forbidden and repressed libidinal drives. Conversion, a subclass of psychoneurosis, involved the translation of such desires into a more or less transparent paralysis of the volitional body. Freud suggested in characteristically metaphoric style that the psychoneuroses formed around actual neuroses like an oyster pearl around a grain of sand. This implicit discontinuity between physical/metabolic mechanisms and epiphenomenal symbolic meanings was to haunt the steps of psychosomatic inquiry.

Franz Alexander, following Freud, defined a class of visceral neuroses that, un- like the compensatory meaning processes of conversion, functioned on the principle of direct metabolic innervation (Alexander 1939). The thrust of his argument was that while the volitional body seems capable of symbolization, the visceral body does not. This was at best a controversial view. Some researchers were more inclined toward the view that all psychosomatic illnesses, including those of the viscera, involved some kind of symbolic activity, if not strictly conversion.

In practice the whole field of psychosomatic medicine tended to frame the discussion of visceral disease against the backdrop of conversion. This in effect dichotomized the body of volition and the vegetative body, casting the latter as the true body, the dense body, the body alien to meaning. This was, of course, the traditional dualism of Cartesian orthodoxy somewhat in disguise.

With almost no exceptions analytic practitioners lent their attention to a relat- ively narrow range of diseases considered to be accessible to meaning. These came to be regarded as the psychosomatic diseases. Asthma, colitis, hypertension, migraine, rheumatoid arthritis, thyrotoxicosis, ulcers, and some skin conditions fell into this classification. These conditions presented themselves as concretely situated in their hosts' lives. While making the requisite theoretic genuflections to the notion that every disease is psychosomatic, the field nevertheless routinely defined itself as "bounded on one side by purely organic diseases and on the other by conversions" (Fenichel 1954, p. 307).

Conversion was uninteresting to psychosomatic medicine by virtue of the trans- parency of the volitional body. The bulk of diseases, however, were regarded as purely physical. They were unapproachable by virtue of their opacity, the density of the truly material body. Psychosomatic medicine bracketed beyond its field of view what it thought to be simply mind and simply body. What remained was neither transparent nor opaque but for the most part essentially murky in the no-man's-land between the dichotomized mind and body.

Psychosomatic medicine was a bit squeamish. It recoiled from the concrete body of disease, regarding it as base and dumb, without language. Psychosomatic discourse occurred at a certain remove from the newly visible body of disease

disclosed in the modern development of pathological anatomy and its technological amplifications as Foucault (1975) detailed it. Rather, it preferred to
converse in the abstract language of economies of desire and the structural
configurations of psychosexual energies. It was principally a language of formal
properties relevant to a very small range of primal mind-body interactions.

Thus, psychosomatic theory had little power to specify disease causes. Intra-
psychic drive conflicts produced multilayered, complex and highly idiosyncratic
interference patterns in the psychosexual personality that could be, in theory at
least, teleologically unraveled through analytic dialogue to the point of origina-
tion. But this was not a causal/predictive strategy and could not be extended to
populations. A persistent obstacle in this regard to the elaboration of predictive
models was the demonstrable ubiquity of the standard, presumably determinant,
conflictual drive elements even in healthy individuals lacking manifest organ
symptomologies. Alexander resorted to calling the evident yet thoroughly elusive
premorbid causative ingredients in individual disease incidence the "x-factor."
Psychosomatic medicine failed in its own terms to specify disease causes.

But psychosomatic medicine was not a language of experienced meanings
either. It valued that objective acumen of the analytic practitioner. As physical
medicine was ushered into the modern era by the anatomical dissection of corpses
the physician ceased to be a logician of correspondences and became the locus of
sensory observation (Foucault 1975). But to the extent that experience became
an essential ingredient of the medical encounter with disease, it was solely the
experience of the skilled clinician, as neutral observer, that was enshrined.
Psychosomatic medicine shared with physical medicine this naturalistic view of
the medical context.

As far as the psychosomatic patient was concerned, the symbolic epiphenomenal meanings of the primal body were not so much experienced by as attributed
to him or her. The objective of analytic dialogic disclosure was to bring the
patient into rational proximity with the intricately prefigured irrational relations
of desire. The patient as an experiencing self stood largely outside and subordinate to the formal properties of the system. The analytic diagnostician, rather than
performing an examination as an act of direct perception, deciphered the essential, logically prior, order of the psychosexual economy through the patient's
clues. The psychosomatic inquiry was basically a cryptographic project operated
upon the patient as a somewhat incidental object. In this respect, the analyst,
more logician of inferences than observer, was far closer to the premodern physician of classificatory medicine.

Characteristic of the premodern, preanatomical, medical perspective was the
independence of disease from the concrete body (Foucault 1975). Definition and
correspondences of formal elements had priority over the localization of disease
in tissues and organs. Disease inhabited a categorical space above the body. In
much the same way psychosomatic medicine remained aloof from both the body
of experienced meaning and the body of disease. It resembled more a rarified
nosology of primal desire than a deduction of specific psychological causes, despite its aspirations to predictive science.

And yet psychosomatic medicine was informed by a powerful mytho-poetic intuition of the resonance of mind and body. It had the courage to project the space of desire onto the visceral body at the occasion of disease. And so it installed in the public domain the legitimacy, once and for all, of inquiry into the personal meaning of illness. Behavioral medicine was eventually to take that inquiry far from the confines of psychosexual concepts and nosological predilections.

BEHAVIORAL MEDICINE

Behavioral medicine emerged as an identifiably distinct approach to the mind-body problem in disease around the mid 1970s (Gentry 1984). Although some psychodynamically oriented research has carried over, particularly visible in the attempts to identify personality traits contributory to chronic illness, the culture-wide climate of naturalistic positivism finds itself quite at home in behavioral attitudes toward illness. Perhaps the failure of psychodynamic approaches to delineate a coherent causal/predictive strategy has accelerated the turn toward frankly positivistic constructs about meanings. At any rate, the most significant aspect of the multidisciplinary approach of behavioral medicine has been the explosive technologic expansion of insight into biophysiological substrates of animal and human behavior. Current behavioral perspectives survey a very broad field of biological and psychosocial contributory factors in disease.

Early work on the physiological substrates of behavior concentrated on defensive organic responses to stressful stimuli. Selye's (1950) conceptualization of a general adaptive response envisioned a unitary, nonspecific response to all stressors. But this unifying heurism, while attractive, has generally come to be regarded since then as too parsimonious to account adequately for the observed intricacy of interactions involving central nervous system structures, neurohumoral pathways, and organ systems. Research advances in neuroanatomy, immunology, and endocrinology have both allowed for and required far greater specificity with regard to the biophysiologic substrates of emotional states and behavioral responses to stress (see for example Ader 1981).

Currently attention is focused on two neuroendocrine axes that function as the major chemical pathways of communication between the centers of the brain responsible for meaning processes and the rest of the body. Catecholamine pathways have been implicated in autonomic nervous system activation and thus in affective as well as visceral tonus. Corticosteroid pathways play a critical role in mediating immune responsiveness to disease processes.

While this new body of psycho/neuro/endocrinologic/immunologic literature is an impressive testimony to the intricacy of the relationships involved in disease mediation and the humbling incompleteness of knowledge about specific disease mechanisms, one conclusion is certainly in order. All physiologic systems, organ structures, and homeostatic processes in the human body, including perhaps most importantly immune functions traditionally thought to be autonomous, may be regarded as subject to the regulatory influence of central nervous system organizations of experienced meaning (Ader & Cohen 1984). The preponderance of scientific evidence—one source cites well over one thousand contributions to the literature in a recent six year period (Locke & Hornig-Rohan 1983)—now argues for a significant connection between mind and bodily disease.

Some researchers have begun to conceive of the neuroendocrine pathways as bi-directional vectors relating catecholamine activity to effort and relaxation and corticoid activity to depression and euphoria (Henry & Meehan 1981). In this way specific meaning states may be linked through neuroendocrine communication to specific disease susceptibility. Depression and suppression of immunocompetence is thought to be an exemplary case in point (Depue 1979).

But this is not only a powerful exposition of disease processes. Behavioral medicine has acquired almost unwittingly a heuristic tool for talking about wellness and extraordinary realities like yogic and shamanic ecstatic healing states.

While the expansion of scientific knowledge around molecular substrates of mind-body interaction has proceeded at break-neck pace, efforts to correlate psychosocial environment effects with disease onset have been generally disappointing. Animal experimentation throughout the 1970s consistently demonstrated a strong relationship between laboratory induced stress and lowered tumor resistance (see Riley 1975 for the classic study). This fueled interest in identifying epidemiologically premorbid human social stress factors, especially helplessness and depression. Results have been far from clear.

Studies of social support networks as factors in illness resistance have not achieved a strong consensus, though there is mild support for the hypothesis that social ties confer beneficial effects (Krantz & Glass 1984). The loss of a spouse is evidently a factor in increased cancer risk (Joseph & Syme 1982). But efforts to tally stressful life events in an arithmetic of illness susceptibility have proved confusing (Kasl 1983). Research into personality traits and coping styles as factors in disease incidence has produced divergent results (Lazarus 1982). The one notable exception in this last category is, of course, type "A" personality and coronary heart disease (Chesney & Rosenman 1983).

Dissatisfaction in the behavioral research community with many psychosocial studies has revolved around traditional methodological issues, especially retrospective design, which tends to confound cause and effect. But there are a few genuinely prospective studies that offer some corroborative evidence for the etiologic effect of psychosocial conditions (for example, Thomas *et al.* 1979).

While the methodological criticisms are to be taken seriously and there is much to be gained from carefully controlled doubly prospective longitudinal study of well populations, there is an over-arching problem that has gone largely unaddressed. The conceptual apparatus of behavioral research is still very poorly equipped to explore the dimension of experienced meanings. I think this may account for many divergencies (perhaps corroborations as well) in research results.

Constrained by the positivistic bias of behavioral precepts to study objectively construable things, the literature has armed itself with static constructs about experience. These constructs refer basically to four classes of observable behavioral indicators: states, traits, styles and events. The quantity of stressful life events or social ties will be measured. Evidence for specific attitudes, stressful emotions or coping styles will be tallied. But the subjective meaning of these indicators to the individuals in the studied populations will not be adequately investigated. So we don't really know what the presence or absence of behavioral indicators means about illness and actually experienced meanings.

This is evident in the frequently heated ecclesiastical discussions in the literature of the formal properties, durations, quality and intensity of stress, in which little attention is given to the subjectively experienced meaning of presumedly stressful conditions. As an aside, it is interesting to note that in engineering terms "stress" properly signifies the objectively measurable force applied externally to a mechanical system. "Strain" signifies the impact of stress force. So the language of stress is actually twice removed from the dimension of human experiencing. It is not at all clear what the volumes of literature on psychosocial "stress" tell us realistically about humans; this is evident in the widely divergent findings.

We need to know not merely that certain events occur, attitudes are espoused or behaviors are performed. We need to know what they indicate about felt meanings, especially if we are to apply study results to therapeutic contexts for prevention and/or healing.

This sort of confusion in the behavioral literature results from the use of constructs that deal with attributed experiences rather than with directly felt experiencing. More than twenty years ago Gendlin (1962) distinguished between the construct "experience," which consists of all possible conceptual contents whether or not they are actually present in awareness, and the referent "experiencing," which points only to immediately felt data. Though routinely confounded in the literature, experiences as conceptual contents and experiencing as felt presence are not equivalent. Certainly, as every therapist knows, explicit conceptualizations of experience may or may not accurately reflect what is actually going on in a deeply felt way.

As Schutz (1967, p. 216) warned, "It is methodologically inadmissible to interpret a given series of acts objectively . . . and then ascribe to them a subjective meaning." Yet this is what the behavioral literature does routinely out of a positivistic cynicism and insecurity about the reality or value of subjective experiencing.

In the wake of such methodological bias there have been frequent calls for the development of an interpretive science capable of researching subjective meaning processes from within but in a methodologically sound fashion. Gendlin (1962) observed, for instance, the relative ease with which direct reference to subjective experiencing may be integrated into positivistic research strategies both before and after operational steps without surrendering or altering such strategies. Thus, experiencing as such may even be quantified. More recently Rogers (1985) cited a number of well-developed heuristic, hermeneutic and phenomenological research approaches that all share a capacity for integrating nonreductionistic organization of experienced meanings into coherent investigative strategies. Nor has the recognition of the need for interpretive science been limited to humanistic social scientists. Thinkers on the leading edge of postmodern paradigmatic shifts in hard science frequently acknowledge the parallels between new acausal under-standings of elemental physical reality and interpretive approaches to meaning in psychology (Prigogine & Stengers 1984).

THE VISIBLE AND NOT SO VISIBLE

Psychosomatic medicine occupied a place analogous to pre-anatomical classi-ficatory physical medicine, which deciphered disease forms at considerable re-move from the density of the concrete material body. Psychosomatics actually defined the legitimate field of interest in terms of its relative opacity. Much as, according to Foucault (1975), the development of pathological anatomy rendered the impenetrable density of physical disease finally visible even in the enclosed tissues of the individual body, behavioral medicine effected an equally dramatic and revolutionary descent into the psychosomatic body of disease meanings.

This penetration of the not so visible occurred simultaneously but with un-equal clarity on two fronts: the technologic disclosure of molecular chemical substrates of behavior, the energic pathways linking the physiologic body with neurologic structures of meaning; and the broadening democratization of the field of meanings relevant to disease. The murky chasm between the mind and body of psychosomatic disease, conversed about in the hushed and rarified aristocratic formal language of desire, is revealed to be an energetic commerce of mind and body inputs languaged in an accessible vernacular of mechanical stresses.

On the face of it, the interactive mind-body field is now transparent not only to the scientific view but to the surveillance of the marketplace as well; witness the explosive expansion of the modern service sector devoted to the health of the "whole body". But this transparency may yet be deceiving. The descent of postquantum, postentropy elemental science into the subvisible interstices of the organization of matter deconstructed the traditional conceptual armamentarium of the knowledge of material reality. The organization of essential matter itself now resembles more the mysterious ineffability of mind than the solidity of machines (Prigogine & Stengers 1984). Bacteriologic science, I suggest, likewise installed and then ultimately overthrew the concept of simple physical causes in disease.

As the description of the material body of disease in naturalistic terms (now at the molecular and submolecular levels) seems to penetrate material density, the body as we know it becomes more elusive. The technologic instrumentation of neurobiology does not so much resolve the traditional discontinuity of the mind-body juncture into finer detail as radically dissolve it into the subtle energies of implicit, synchronic order, into pathways of communion.

At this new level of subtlety we lose not only the gross material body as we know it but the gross mind, the mind of mental and emotional contents. The projection of the structures of meaning onto the body of disease in behavioral medicine denies the dense body its absolute priority in disease, which had been a given of the naturalistic universe. Moreover, the neurohumoral gradient linking

the physical body and the body of meaning discloses a range of interactions beyond the boundaries of pathology. The far reaches of extraordinary realities and
capabilities fall within the disclosive range of a true biopsychology. This challenges
not only the physical but also the mental realities into which our world is con-
ventionally organized. Perhaps most significantly for behavioral research into the
environments of meaning around illness, the infinitely fine differentiations of
mind-body attunements implied by the neuroendocrine gradient far exceed the
resolving power of our most sophisticated psychological vocabularies.

The boundaries of our familiar emotional states—anger, sadness and so on—
begin to look crude and arbitrary. Emotional entities as such begin to lose their
objective solidity as well. The revolutionary significance of the postmodern discovery of the pathways of embodied meaning is the dissolution of both psychic
and physical entities as we customarily understand them into a fluid synchronic
process. Paradoxically, at this historic juncture behavioral medicine finds itself
conversing about human meanings in a curiously arcane and inadequate language of causal priorities among nonexistent entities quite as if the old verities
which it itself exploded still stood.

THE SUBTLE BODY OF MEANING

Now we need to say a bit more concretely what this embodiment of meaning
means in terms faithful to this new reality. Following Gendlin's (1962) philosophy of experiencing and the creation of meaning, we may distinguish abstract
conceptual "experiences" from presently felt "experiencing." This is, in fact, an
explication of the distinction between the psychic entities of the naturalistic metaphysics of psychology and the fluid process of embodiment implied by postmodern
psychoneuroendocrinology.

"Experiencing" is the presence in awareness of bodily felt preconceptual wholes,
implicit in which are an unlimited number of ways of symbolizing or making
explicit aspects of this whole presence. Experiencing is always larger, richer,
more complex than anything we can say about it, any way we at this particular
moment refer to it. But we can gain access to the implicit preconceptual whole
sense by letting the complexity emerge in explicit symbolizations that exactly fit
the whole experiencing. This exact fit between explicit symbolizations and the
flow of lived experiencing is the essence of the authentic self.

Since experiencing is implicit preconceptually, the fit of explicit symbolization
to it cannot be a relationship of logic. Yet as Gendlin discovered, it is hardly
random. To Gendlin, experiencing—unlike the Cartesian stance, which radically
separates the knower from the known—is an interactive unity in which the experiencing of meaning is never distinct from the situational context in which it
occurs. As Gendlin expressed it, "How one feels is not some after-event coming
on top of what happens, it is what happens" (Gendlin 1973, p. 324).

There is a purposive flow to experiencing, a temporal and valuative continuity
in the sense that experiencing always wants to be carried forward. Every moment

of experiencing implies still further specific situational relatedness, which will carry
the meaning of the situation on. We know this quite concretely for ourselves in
the way that, for example, with organismic imperatives only certain next steps
will seem right. When we are hungry, eating constellates as the next step and
then probably only certain foods will do at this moment, and so on. This is true
not merely for such basically simple situations but for all experiencing. The felt
continuity in experiencing, the rightness of fit of emergent symbolizations in the
explication of implicit experiencing, is the defining characteristic of experiential
process.

Experiencing is an organismic wholeness directly felt in the body. When experiencing proceeds in a way that is faithful to this organismic unity, a way Gendlin
(1981) calls focusing, explicit symbolizations are allowed to fit, as they emerge
step by step, the implicit whole felt sense rather than to be imposed upon it as a
limitation of our self-awareness; and the body consequently relaxes in distinctly
pleasurable releases of held tension. Conversely, experiencing that identifies the
self with objectified content conceptualizations and is thus stuck in symbolizations
that do not really fit, that have not organismically emerged from the implicit
whole felt sense, builds and holds tension in the body.

This latter condition, the various ways of not living in the embodied organismic
experiencing of felt wholeness, is the definition of pathology for Gendlin. Thus,
"the body forms any next behavior from all relevant aspects, but in troubles
there is no way to live all aspects further . . . there is no way to act or speak so
that all that is involved can be lived. Only on the plane of inward space and the
forming of a felt sense is there a way for the body to produce a next step that
takes everything relevant into account" (Gendlin 1974, p. 236).

In the absence of such felt whole sensing in the subtle energy body, we settle
for socially captive discursive relations with ourselves and the world. We have
ourselves as a collection of objectified entities: sensations, thoughts, feelings, concepts of self-reference that only inadequately carry the authentic whole meanings
implicit in our bodily lived inner subjective space. Routinely we reject, ignore,
tune out our ongoing experiencing that cannot readily be organized in the
customary, socially consensual, objectified ways of construing our inner reality.
Our rich sense of inherent connectedness, of our self with other, the world, the
cosmos, and of our self most profoundly within the wholeness of our own lives is
sacrificed to an atomized and thus diminished reality of thinly connected parts.
We cling tenaciously to this construction of an objective universe of clearly
bounded and separable entities.

This rather cynically mechanical view of reality conditions our relations to the
nonmaterial dimension of feeling and spirit. We deny what cannot be mechanically construed and verified by essentially deterministic proofs. Even our feeling
life is conducted this way as if it were a syllogistic exercise: this idea of me, and
then that one, therefore I should feel/be this way and no other. So we expend
enormous energy and effort constructing, defending and patching a reality of
acceptable self-reflexive forms that do not permit the fresh and spontaneous
creation of newly emergent modes of relatedness moment by moment in our

intrinsically open and unconditioned ground of experiencing. It is this limitation of our self-experiencing to objectified self-concepts that keep us painfully stuck in our troubles, isolated from the rich and genuine contact with ourself and others that we desire.

Relaxing into an openness toward the deep currents of felt experiencing, we descend from the material body of static, determinate entities (things, ideas, emotions) into the subtle body of resonant energies. This is the place where we feel shifts in the subtle tensions of the energy body as we penetrate the static density of our concepts about our feelings into the infinitely richer whole felt experiencing. The subtle body speaks to us of realities for which there can be no proof, for it dwells beyond the logic of our causal certainties in a field of infinitely subtle relatedness. It is here in the subtle body that dreaming unfolds beyond the constraints of linear time and material space. And it is in the subtle body that spirit reveals itself as the unbounded continuity of all existence. And most importantly for our discussion here, it is in the subtle body that disease constellates as inherently meaningful self-process and symptoms transform from defects in the mechanically construed body into explicit signs of the emergent implicit self.

The subtle body of felt meaning is the body of true interiority and uncondi-tioned subjectivity. While it is true that "bodies may be governed . . . embodiment is the phenomenological basis of individuality" (Turner 1984, p. 251).

DISEASE AND MEANING: THE CANCER CONNECTION

Psychoneuroendocrinological research strongly implicates depression and hope-lessness in the suppression of immunocompetence and hence in a decreased re-sistance to disease, in particular tumorogenicity. The mechanism principally indicated is increased corticosteroid activity, which when chronic tends to have deleterious effects on lymphatic tissues. While the state of current understand-ings still precludes any high degree of specificity with regard to depression and physiological correlates, a strong case has been made for depression as a final common pathway for a host of modern illnesses, cancer included (Depue 1979). Yet the epidemiological evidence for clinical depression as an etiological factor in particular cancers, while suggestive, is quite a bit less strong. It is hard to know what this means. It may signify that the artifactual parsimony of experimental conditions permits stronger findings than the "messy" conditions of real peoples' lives. This would argue in my view for the development of process-sensitive inter-pretive research methods rather than the static states/traits approach currently in vogue.

Further support for process-oriented research comes in the form of the major conundrum in the debate about the cancer-depression connection. It has to do with the issue of tumor latency. Conventional wisdom has it that tumors are commonly some thirty-to-forty years in the making. It is hard then to see how proximal life events, the loss of a spouse eighteen months prior to a cancer diagnosis, for example, might be causative. But the epidemiological literature, as I pointed out above, clearly points that way. It is commonly suggested in the literature that any observed depression in the vicinity of a cancer diagnosis may be an effect, not cause, of the cancer.

The puzzle intensifies when we consider the countless cases of cancer that commonly disregard prognostication of outcomes in both directions, for better or worse. William Boyd (1966), the eminent pathologist, was sufficiently moved by this phenomenon to collect clinical data on spontaneous, that is inexplicable, regressions in a variety of human cancers and to ruminate on the possible explanations. It seemed to him back then that far too little was known of the intricate cybernetics of cancer cell regulation to say anything conclusive about the temporal development of cancers. This is still largely the case today. But phenomenologically it seemed clear to Boyd that cancer growth was far more labile, both regressively and progressively, than it was customary to suppose.

This observation about clinically documented inexplicable regressions was buttressed by the high number (nearly 25 percent) of nonsymptomatic cancers unrelated to cause of death revealed in autopsy over the long course of Boyd's career. The presence of malignant tissue did not by itself seem to constitute disease, that is, illness in the sense one recognizes oneself to be sick.

Furthermore, Boyd was curious about the "phantom" ability of some cancers to disappear, sometimes quite rapidly, leaving paradoxical tissue evidence in support of their presumed existence. Boyd speculated that perhaps cancers can differentiate very quickly and become for all intents and purposes indistinguishable from normal surrounding tissue.

Overall, he was inclined toward the view that the phenomenology of cancer, if physicians did not arbitrarily exclude from their view these puzzling features for which there are not mechanical explanations, suggested it was not a "thing," an entity, but a process. The static histologic/morphologic snapshot used to diagnose and prognosticate could not, then, be expected to disclose the dimension of movement. In an analogous way, a high-speed snapshot of a ball thrown in the air would freeze the movement and then not reveal if the ball were on the way up or down.

Boyd did not hazard a guess about the relative weights of factors in the tumorogenic equation (genetics, toxins, psychic states, etc.). But there are some important speculations that may be drawn from his thinking. Cancer as a process-in-movement may not be reducible to cell morphologies, that is, momentary structural arrangements or contents. Cancer may be always present in the body as an interactive steady-state. This latter notion should not be confused with contemporary surveillance theory, which frames the discourse in terms of individual renegade cells. This steady-state may be highly labile and very sensitive to modulations of the whole body/mind system. In fact, the thresholds above which the process is perceived by the individual as disease symptomatic may vary as an aspect of the modulations.

Boyd did recommend as a result of his investigation into spontaneous remission that the medical community cease trying to kill cancer and instead concentrate on methods of inviting normal differentiation. Since in his view cancer was not an "it" there was nothing to kill but tissues that might be persuaded to different-iate normally. He suspected that the autopsy data argued for the possibility that a large number of people may live in balanced, non-ill relation to "cancer" for indefinite, perhaps extended, periods of time. One could wonder at this point whether the fine-comb approach in the technologic detection of cancers and the subsequent invasive treatment protocols does not in its own right account for a certain proportion of our high annual cancer fatality.

The ruminations above reinforce the central heurism of this paper: that cancer may best be thought of not as a disease entity but a relational process not separ-able from its subtle environmental context. In reducing cancer and life contexts to content entities and stripping them of their embedded contextual particularity, in assuming predictive lawfulness, the unfolding of individual process relationships as instances of unique and irreversible creativity is lost to our view. Contents are not, Gendlin (1974) reminded us, basic. They are created in the process of living, as aspects of that particular living. As a particular relational process moves forward through time, as it changes, so do the emergent contents. This particular movement is not repeatable. It can be grasped only as it unfolds its implicit order and only in ways that are respectful of the not fully knowable endogenous regulatory processes of the whole system. Cancer may be a good example of the kind of complex ecological process for which reductive discourse, the marginalization of the sacred respect for wholeness, is especially maladaptive at the individual level.

CASES

Let me cite a few representative cases from clinical practice to illustrate this point. These cases are not extraordinary; any clinician working with cancer patients in a way that respects and collaborates with embodied meaning process will have many similar stories to tell. But they are extraordinary because in some important respect each of them defies our customary understandings of how physical illness works. Those moments can only be comprehended as aspects of a contextual process in movement.

T. was a late-middle-aged luminary in the human potential movement. He had a passionately conflicted marriage with a woman who at the time I met him had just died of breast cancer. In the course of their often violent fighting, which lasted right up to her death, she had on a number of occasions accused him of giving her the cancer. In the limousine on the way home from the cemetary he suddenly recalled her accusation and felt in some unclear way he could not quite get a hold of that she had been right. He sank into remorse, feeling the weight of their emotional symbiosis, which even death could not lift. On the ride home he developed a mild cough, but it persisted for weeks. Not too long after he was admitted to hospital for tests and an inoperable lung cancer was diagnosed. He engaged me at that point to help him out. In very short order, for he was experienced and adept at self-processing, a sense began to form of his thwarted but passionate desire to create as an artist and to live his life as he never had at the service of that desire. He decided to refuse the treatment offered—he was considered terminal anyway—and to spend his last days on a remote beach somewhere breathing the life of an artist and writing the novel of his dreams. He went south. A couple of years later, his novel complete, he died up north of a heart attack. There was no trace of his cancer.

M. was a vibrant young mother who at the time I first saw her had just begun chemotherapy following a mastectomy. Her prognosis was regarded as quite good. This was reinforced by the energetic optimism and spiritual immersion that characterized her life. She was a real fighter and a gentle inspiration to everyone who met her, especially the members of her liberal protestant church, who genuinely revered her. As we worked together over the course of a year a different picture surfaced. She had been raised in a stridently puritanical religious setting and despite all her efforts felt unable to break out from underneath the oppression of her family values, which hung over her like a pall. Through focusing inwardly on her bodily felt sense of an inchoate freedom deep within her she was finally able to give birth to a kinesthetic symbolization of it, a kind of dream dance that perfectly constellated her emergent free self. Though she worked with this transformative symbol during our sessions she became disturbed that she was unable to give her life on the outside that vital quality. Working with her bodily felt sensing of this new whole context, transformed as it was by the dance of life but still not free, she was able to find what was in the way. The newly awakened but still implicit sexual energies that vivified her dream dance were totally unacceptable to her. She was still captive of her nuclear family. The very next session she reported a nagging pain in her lower back which she thought was a strain. I encouraged her to focus on it. She felt the cancer was there somehow and that it was now systemic. Diagnostic work-ups later in the week proved her right. She became steadily worse and died not too long after, still an inspiration to her shocked and unsuspecting friends.

B. is a tradesman, at retirement age when I met him a few years back. He had come from a strict and serious background, accustomed to independence, competence and undiminished energy. But there was a side to him that just wanted to grow and smell the flowers. So he was experiencing some difficulty integrating his new life circumstances. Following some health problems he was diagnosed leukemic at a major cancer center. He was given a poor prognosis, about eighteen months with treatment. He was advised to begin transfusion immediately, with chemotherapy to follow soon. But he felt that if he accepted transfusion it would be the beginning of the end, the sure road to death, and he was not ready to die. So he refused. Instead, he started to explore nutritional healing on his own. But he had trouble settling on any one plan of the many he tried. Each one somehow did not quite fit. So little by little he put together his own program guided mainly by what felt right for him. It featured vitamins, especially "C", which he took in megadoses. His history with psychological methods was similar. I never felt I succeeded in teaching him awareness work as I thought it should be done. But gradually I learned to trust his process, however it looked to me, and not interfere. His blood chemistry sometimes looks seriously leukemic, sometimes pretty healthy by normal standards. He always seems able to know implicitly when it is leukemic; it mirrors conflicts with his energies and expectations. The fluctuations continue. He is actively enjoying life several years now past the original terminal prognosis, without ever having any treatment.

N. was a bright and very caring middle-aged woman with grown children and a husband in the professions. Her marriage was unfulfilled. Her husband always seemed to her absorbed in his work and emotionally self-contained. Yet he leaned on her a lot. As a result her emotional needs went unmet. Their sexual life was by this time nonexistent. Her attempts at developing a career for herself once the kids were out of the house were verbally supported by her husband but, it seemed, shrewdly and passively undermined. Vacillating between staying in the marriage and leaving, she finally resolved to make a go of it. She determinedly planned activities the two of them could do together in the hopes of developing some emotional intimacy, but this strategy backfired. When they skied together he was competitive and much better at it; she usually felt worse after these events, alienated and resentful. One day on the slopes she fell, not badly, but it was a struggle to get up. Her husband, instead of being supportive, taunted and lectured about the proper way to fall and get up. She slumped back in the snow in a wave of despair and thought: I'll never do this again! Later that week a mild pain below her knee suggested to her that the fall had been perhaps worse than she thought. When it did not go away she saw a physician and a rare sarcoma was diagnosed. A very disabling surgery was performed, which saved her leg but left her lame. She completed a chemotherapy protocol and learned to walk on her leg despite the surgery. She was plucky and even taught herself how to use a brace to play tennis. At this time I began to work with her in group. She was generally reticent about her marital unhappiness and chose to concentrate on positive thinking. She seemed on the face of it to be doing well. But despite an optimistic prognosis, a couple of years after the initial diagnosis the cancer was found again around the knee and this time her leg was removed. Again, her recovery was nothing short of phenomenal. She attributed it to her indomitable spirit. But I felt her emotional life went largely unaddressed. She let fester a powerful romantic interest developed at the time of her first surgery without following it up. Her marriage continued to deteriorate beneath the surface. A few years elapsed during which she concentrated on learning to walk, keeping her spirits up and finding activities she could do. Her physicians finally informed her she was off the charts; she was cured. Within a year distant metastatic sites appeared. At this point her emotional life could no longer be contained. She made some efforts at trial separation, but they were half-hearted. As she grew weaker she fantasized leaving home and starting over, acknowledging to herself that in some way she had known all along that her unhappiness would probably kill her. She died a year and one-half or so after being declared officially cured.

These life stories are not principally stories of miraculous healing, though certainly such experiencing in the subtle body of meaning around cancers does genuinely, if rarely, occur. The range of meanings is as infinitely large and varied as the range of historic human possibilities itself. Thus, we do encounter in cancer patients not only simple modern naturalistic understandings of their disease process (the realization, for example, that the ionizing radiation of smoking has contributed to a lung cancer) but shamanic ones as well in which a frankly terminal cancer might present itself as a guided descent into esoteric knowledge through ritual dismemberment and miraculous rebirth. But a cautionary note is in order here, since our current cultural fascination with mystical healing can have a chilling and reifying effect upon the process of genuine self-knowledge around disease, as I shall elaborate further in a moment.

So here, in these cases, I have chosen to emphasize the more ordinary embeddedness of cancer in people's lives. While some cancer patients do present a classical picture of depression that seems on the face of it etiologic, it is also true that many do not. In fact, I am often struck by the seemingly robust psychological status of many patients I meet. From all indications N. fit what might be called the "fighter" profile so highly regarded these days. A spiritually engaged and upbeat woman with a healthy network of social support through her church, she tracked her cancer right off the charts. Her recovery from debilitating and demoralizing medical procedures was exemplary. And yet her life was stuck in a crucial respect and unfulfilled. The cancer spoke eloquently in her life of her courageous and extended struggle to understand her inner life and the tricky balance required to stand on her own in the context of relatedness to others.

For M., a similarly motivated fighter, her breast cancer constellated the difficulty she faced in accepting and living forward her deep sexual self. B.'s efforts to integrate his conflicted self-expectations with his available energies is mirrored in the fluid fluctuations of the leukemic process. The site of cancers speaks in this way directly to cancer patients about the critical arena in which the struggle for the wholeness of self is occurring.

Each of the above cases illustrates the remarkable synchronicity of the cancer process at the level of cells, organs and tissues with the felt meanings of the patients' lives. Often that synchronicity involves almost immediate shifts in the body of disease symptoms, sometimes apparently startling reversals in direction. M. was doing well when her inner work constellated her dream and its stuckness. The impasse was resolved in her death, which seemed more possible than carrying her sexual body forward.

For T., living out his heartfelt dream rid him of an incurable cancer. But he promptly died of heart failure. I am tempted to say his cancer was not a distinct illness but just one moment in his life-long struggle to find the heart for living. He succeeded and then stopped.

Death is an integral part of the process of living forward. Recently I saw an adolescent girl suffering with (not from) a horribly crippling and painful cancer. She continued to hold on despite all odds. Everyone around her marveled that she could live month after month in such a hopeless and weakened condition. Several hours after the birth of her sister's first child she died quietly. Not infrequently cancer patients predict with breathtakingly uncanny accuracy the moment of their deaths. Often the predictions seem to contradict the logic of their medical condition, but they are always meaningful in their lives.

Increasingly in clinical practice, if one keeps an open mind, the weight of such evidence argues that the symptoms of bodily disease and even death itself are not, as the mechanistic view would have it, discontinuities or dysfunctions. They are process continuities that arrive in a context of highly individual organismic meaningfulness. They are not extrinsic to life, things that happen to our patients. As with all contents of complex life processes, death is an intrinsic aspect of a particular living forward. Death, when it comes, is the meaningful next step in our patients' lives, no less authentic, no less right than a cure.

The scientific medical description of such intrinsic process continuities, despite the postmodern paradigmatic shift toward mind/body unity, is still inadequate to the task. Disease conditions that account for cancer onset and development are so complex as to elude deterministic specification. Minute variations along the biologic and psychologic dimensions will produce huge disease-outcome differences. In probabilistic terms we have no alternative but to describe such situations as essentially random. It is only just now that postmodern science is learning how to describe the irreversible, nonrandom emergence of order in such systems at the subvisible level of elemental matter. But we do know quite well how to describe disease-meaning systems in phenomenological terms respectful of the subtle synchronicity of the nondual bodymind.

CANCER IN THE NEW AGE

One passionate objection to this sort of thinking about cancer revolves around the fear that patients will be seduced into false hope for impossible cures and then blamed for their illness when the cure does not materialize. I have already argued that this concern may be rooted in sentimental attachment to naive naturalistic beliefs in the priority of the simply physical universe and that such beliefs are ideologically related to the moral agendas of the mechanisms of social control in our technological culture. But I do not wish to dismiss the matter out of hand. It is a more knotty issue than it might first appear.

Popular healing approaches rely for validation upon recent experimental evidence suggesting immune function may be subject to direct instruction by mental imaging (see, for example, Schneider et al. 1981). Study of cerebral laterality effects supports the view that activation of the right hemisphere through mental imaging may directly entrain neuroendocrine events that mediate depression and immunosuppression (Ley & Freeman 1984). And so it is then argued that imagery has the power to heal. In the New Age scripture this is the scientific basis of the efficacy of shamanic healing practices. This then sets up an all too facile equivalence basic to the subculture's view of itself between almost any contemporary imagery strategy and shamanism.

This way of thinking can be very problematic. Imaging instructions that produce desirable results in parsimonious experimental contexts are perhaps not so clearly efficacious when applied to illness situations in which both biologic and psychologic contexts are not nearly so simple. It is hard to be certain here, but my caution is based on the observation of many cancer patients for whom imaging instructions, even when performed correctly, seem not to do much. Cancer patients, after all, are immersed in dread of the disease and in a host of bad feelings, anxieties and physical sufferings from which imaging may momentarily distract them without touching anything deeply. Any potentially beneficial awareness practice may be used in that way to bypass rather than process and transform painful experience. So it is not enough just to give a set instruction. We have to know how it has concrete impact on experiential process in the particular individual.

The Cartesian bias of our technologic culture splits the body/mind into an intentional self-moving mind and a passive mechanical body. Both imaging instructors and cancer patients dwell at least to some extent within the constraints of this bias. As a result, imaging is often mutually construed as the application of positive/optimistic cognitive contents to a passive sick body. It is told to heal, or that it will. Of course, the body may fail at this extrinsic, content-specific task. This way of working may, indeed, set patients up for self blame.

I cannot emphasize too strongly that cancer therapists must respect and stay right with the emergent process of bodily felt meanings in individual patients in order to avoid further alienating them from a genuinely interior relation with themselves. In our thoroughly televised and media-captive culture we are all at sea in an ocean of disembodied images. I never assign cancer patients an imagery task to do with extrinsic imagery. I will work only with symbolizations, in whatever sensory modality, which have organismically emerged from the whole self. These symbolizations may then be elaborated or amplified in various exercises, but only these symbolizations shift the subtle body energies and thus have the power to transform. Since process-emergent symbolization is not given to, but comes from, the cancer patient, it does not oppress, it releases.

Generally speaking, shamanic (and some yogic) systems differentiate power from knowledge. Awareness practices working at different levels of the subtle body generate many nonordinary energy states that may from a certain point of view be regarded as powers. But the generation of these states may or may not be treated as an end in itself. At the highest levels esoteric subtle body disciplines are methods to develop contentless presence in the unlimited ground of awareness. Too tight fixation on specific powers of the subtle body as ends in themselves can arrest the development of open awareness. This is what distinguishes a sorcerer from a knowledge-holder. One knowledgeable observer has cautioned that people from technologic cultures tend erroneously to deify the shamanic vision contents when it is not the visions themselves but the shaman's ecstatic in-dwelling in the divinely infinite that is the real point (Wasson 1980).

Our New Age culture tends to flatten and trivialize shamanic process by reducing it to imagery contents and technologies as ends. While our emulation of mystical healing rites seems to promise a resacralization of medical discourse, a retrenchment of what Turner (1984) identified as the central historic tendency of the modern secular order toward redeployment of moral stewardship from religious to medical institutions, the situation is somewhat contradictory.

The development in the modern era of the germ theory of disease established the dominance of scientific medical naturalism, which extracted from the social/moral organization a presumed value-free medical perspective which constituted "a second-order moral framework . . . masked by the language of disease" (Turner 1984, p. 214). The principal conceptual apparatus of this scientific ascendency was the bifurcation of the spiritual and natural orders. The disclosure in the scientific discourse of postmodern behavioral medicine of the neurohumoral synchronicity of mind and body threatens, as I have suggested, to dissolve that dualism, Without a doubt, the disclosure of the unitary subtle body, heretofore confined to the domain of spiritual disciplines, represents a potential respiritualization of the social perception of health.

And yet to the extent that this contemporary "spiritual" talk about health remains captive to a reductionist social agenda, it constitutes a further, veiled and hence deeper, degradation of the sacred. Currently our medical morality projects health as a life style. This is not to be confused with the ideal of the productive citizen of the industrial era. It is preeminently a consumer morality. We prefer fit, sexually attractive, stress-free, fun-loving citizens, the "hard bodies" of up-scale consumers who drive the postmodern economy. The marketing of hard bodies in all manner of self-improvement has become itself an enormously invasive industry. With the expenditure of some few hundred dollars for a weekend workshop we are now even assured of becoming real shamans ourselves.

Our culture in this way sentimentalizes and simultaneously plunders ancient sacred traditions in the service of opportunistic economic imperatives. With the deployment of sex, health and wisdom as instruments of the consumer market we have more thoroughly objectified and commoditized body and spirit than at any previous time in human history. This systematic degradation of our phylogenetic wisdoms accumulated across the millennia of human history is a dangerously maladaptive trend. It threatens to lead us even further from the self-knowledge of organismic wholeness which is the sacred ground of all living systems.

Conclusion

Cancer may well be the pestilential challenge of our time that can awaken us to the need for critical self-reflection and reform. The atomized and specialized knowledges of our technological culture have imparted to us impressive powers to act upon the social and natural worlds. We have virtually banished infectious disease from the planet. And yet the reductionist focus of our specialized knowledges has left us powerless to comprehend the relationship of parts to the whole. This is reflected at every level of social organization. Our productive economy degrades the biotic environment at a scale the impact of which we can as yet barely comprehend. Our ascendant medical culture, just now beginning to imagine the synchronicity of the mind and body, still finds itself lacking the philosophic vision to conduct an exploration of disease as an aspect of meaningfully lived experience. The alternative medical discourse, while promising a respiritualization and revisioning of health, suffers itself the reductionist habit of confounding particular ideas and methods with the emergent process of the self. And cancer patients are themselves alienated from the wholeness of their physical/emotional lives, unable to carry essential aspects of their deep selves forward in meaningfully embodied ways.

Cancer constellates the basic human condition of relatedness. The physical devastation of cancer undermines the solid, immovable facticity of the discrete material body and our compelling notions of the bounded reality of things upon which we have come to rely. We penetrate the veil of objectivity that separates our self from others and parts of our own self from its intrinsic wholeness. We discover that the corporeal and spiritual, physical and emotional dimensions of existence are not separate but a single synchronous experiencing of the subtle embodied self, and that this inner felt synchronicity perfectly mirrors the vast interconnectedness of the living universe of which we are a part. Cancer is an invitation to heal—literally—to regain wholeness, an invitation extended to ourselves as emergent individuals and to our culture at large.

References

Ader, R. ed., *Psychoneuroimmunology*. New York: Academic Press, 1981.

Ader, R. & Cohen, N., "Behavior and the immune system," in Gentry, W. D., ed., *Handbook of Behavioral Medicine*. New York: Guilford Press, 1984.

Alexander, F., "Emotional factors in essential hypertension." *Psychosomatic Medicine*, vol. 1, 1939.

—— "Present trends and the future outlook," in Alexander, F. & French, T. M., eds., *Studies in Psychosomatic Medicine*. New York: Ronald Press, 1948.

Boyd, W., *The Spontaneous Regression of Cancer*. Springfield, Ill.: Charles C. Thomas, 1966.

Capra, F., *The Turning Point*. New York: Bantam, 1983.

Chesney, M. & Rosenman, R., "Specificity in stress models: examples drawn from type 'A' behavior," in Cooper, C. L., ed., *Stress Research: Issues for the Eighties*. New York: John Wiley, 1983.

Choedrak, T., First International Convention on Tibetan Medicine. Venice, Italy, April, 1983. Oral commentary.

Depue, R. A., ed., *The Psychobiology of the Depressive Disorders*, New York: Academic Press, 1979.

Dubos, R., *Man Adapting*. New Haven: Yale University, 1965.

Dunbar, F. H., *Emotions and Bodily Changes*. New York: Columbia University, 1935.

Fenichel, O., *The Collected Papers of Otto Fenichel*, second series. New York: W. W. Norton, 1954.

Foucault, M., *The Birth of the Clinic*. New York: Vintage Books, 1975.

Freud, S., "Ordinary neurosis," in *A General Introduction to Psychoanalysis*. New York: Simon & Schuster, 1929.

Gendlin, E. T., *Experiencing and the Creation of Meaning*. Glencoe, Ill.: Free Press, 1962.

—— "Experiential Psychotherapy," in Corsini, R., ed., *Current Psychotherapies*. Itasca, Ill.: Peacock, 1973.

—— "Client-centered and experiential psychotherapy," in Wexler, D. & Rice, L., eds., *Innovations in Client-centered Therapy*. New York: John Wiley, 1974.

—— *Focusing*. New York: Bantam, 1981.

Gentry, W. D., "Behavioral medicine: a new research paradigm," in Gentry, W. D., ed., *Handbook of Behavioral Medicine*. New York: Guilford Press, 1984.

Henry, J. P. & Meehan, J., "Psychosocial stimuli, physiological specificity and cardiovascular disease," in Weiner, H. M. *et al.*, eds., *Brain, Behavior and Bodily Disease*. New York: Raven Press, 1981.

Hoffman, F. L., *Cancer among North American Indians*. Prudential Press, 1928.

Joseph, J. G. & Syme, S. L., "Social connection and the etiology of cancer," in Cohen, J. *et al.*, eds., *Psychosocial Aspects of Cancer*. New York: Raven Press, 1982.

Kasl, S. V., "Pursuing the link between stressful life experiences and disease: a time for reappraisal," in Cooper, C. L., ed., *Stress Research: Issues for the Eighties*. New York: John Wiley, 1983.

Krantz, D. S. & Glass, D. C., "Personality, behavior patterns and physical illness: conceptual and methodological issues," in Gentry, W. D., ed., *Handbook of Behavioral Medicine*. New York: Guilford Press, 1984.

Kundera, M., *The Unbearable Lightness of Being*. New York: Harper & Row, 1985.

Lazarus, R. S., "Stress and coping as factors in health and illness," in Cohen, J. *et al.*, eds., *Psychosocial Aspects of Cancer*. New York: Raven Press, 1982.

Leder, D., "Medicine and paradigms of embodiment," *Journal of Medicine & Philosophy* (1984) 9: 29–43.

Ley, R. G. & Freeman, R. J., "Imagery, cerebral laterality and the healing process," in Sheikh, A., ed., *Imagination and Healing*. New York: Baywood Publishing, 1984.

Locke, S. & Hornig-Rohan, M., eds., *Mind and Immunity: Behavioral Immunology*. New York: Institute for the Advancement of Health, 1983.

Prigogine, I. & Stengers, I., *Order out of Chaos*. New York: Bantam, 1984.

Rappaport, R., "Sanctity and adaptation," *Io* (1970) 7: 46–71.

Reiser, M., ed., "Psychosomatic medicine," in *American Handbook of Psychiatry*, vol. 4. New York: Basic Books, 1975.

Riley, V., "Mouse mammary tumors: alteration of incidence as apparent function of stress," *Science* (1975) 189: 465–467.

Rogers, C., "Toward a more human science," *Journal of Humanistic Psychology* (1985) 25, 4: 7–24.

Schneider, J., *et al.*, *Imagery and Neutrophil Function: a Preliminary Report*. Michigan State University Department of Psychiatry, 1981.

Schutz, A., *The Phenomenology of the Social World*. Evanston, Ill.: Northwestern University, 1967.

Selye, H., "The physiology and pathology of exposure to stress: a treatise based on the concepts of the general adaptation syndrome and the diseases of adaptation," Montreal: Acta, 1950.

Silverman, S., *Psychological Aspects of Physical Symptoms*. New York: Appleton-Century-Crofts, 1968.

Sontag, S., *Illness as Metaphor*. New York: Vintage, 1979.

Starr, P., *The Social Transformation of American Medicine*. New York: Basic Books, 1982.

Thomas, C. B., *et al.*, "Family attitudes reported in youth as potential predictors of cancer," *Psychosomatic Medicine* (1979) 41: 287–302.

Turner, B. S., *The Body and Society*. New York: Basil Blackwell, 1984.

Wasson, R. G., *The Wondrous Mushroom: Mycolatry in Mesoamerica*. New York: McGraw-Hill, 1980.

Wilkins, W. L., "Social stress and illness in industrial society," in Gunderson, E. K. E. & Rahe, R. H., eds., *Life Stress and Illness*. Springfield, Ill.: Charles C. Thomas, 1974.

Winter, R., *Cancer-causing Agents*. New York: Crown, 1979.

CHAPTER 8

Illness as Metaphor and AIDS and Its Metaphors

Susan Sontag

ILLNESS AS METAPHOR, CHAPTER 7

Cancer is generally thought an inappropriate disease for a romantic character, in contrast to tuberculosis, perhaps because unromantic depression has supplanted the romantic notion of melancholy. "A fitful strain of melancholy," Poe wrote, "will ever be found inseparable from the perfection of the beautiful." Depression is melancholy minus its charms—the animation, the fits.

Supporting the theory about the emotional causes of cancer is a growing literature and body of research, and scarcely a week passes without a new article announcing to some general public or other the scientific link between cancer and painful feelings. Investigations are cited—most articles refer to the same ones—in which out of, say, several hundred cancer patients, two-thirds or three-fifths report being depressed or unsatisfied with their lives, and having suffered from the loss (through death or rejection or separation) of a parent, lover, spouse, or close friend. But it seems likely that of several hundred people who do *not* have cancer, most would also report depressing emotions and past traumas: this is called the human condition. And these case histories are recounted in a particularly forthcoming language of despair, of discontent about and obsessive preoccupation with the isolated self and its never altogether satisfactory "relationships," which bears the unmistakable stamp of our consumer culture. It is a language many Americans now use about themselves.[1]

Investigations carried out by a few doctors in the last century showed a high correlation between cancer and that era's complaints. In contrast to contemporary American cancer patients, who invariably report having feelings of isolation and loneliness since childhood, Victorian cancer patients described overcrowded lives, burdened with work and family obligations, and bereavements. These patients don't express discontent with their lives as such or speculate about the quality of its satisfactions and the possibility of a "meaningful relationship." Physicians found the causes or predisposing factors of their patients' cancers in grief, in worry (noted as most acute among businessmen and the mothers of large families), in straitened economic circumstances and sudden reversals of fortune, and in overwork—or, if the patients were successful writers or politicians, in grief, rage, intellectual overexertion, the anxiety that accompanies ambition, and the stress of public life.[2]

Nineteenth-century cancer patients were thought to get the disease as the result of hyperactivity and hyperintensity. They seemed to be full of emotions that had to be damped down. As a prophylaxis against cancer, one English doctor urged his patients "to avoid overtaxing their strength, and to bear the ills of life with equanimity; above all things, not to 'give way' to any grief." Such stoic counsels have now been replaced by prescriptions for self-expression, from talking it out to the primal scream. In 1885, a Boston doctor advised "those who have apparently benign tumors in the breast of the advantage of being cheerful." Today, this would be regarded as encouraging the sort of emotional dissociation now thought to predispose people to cancer.

Popular accounts of the psychological aspects of cancer often cite old authorities, starting with Galen, who observed that "melancholy women" are more likely to get breast cancer than "sanguine women." But the meanings have changed. Galen (second century A.D.) meant by melancholy a physiological condition with complex characterological symptoms; we mean a mere mood. "Grief and anxiety," said the English surgeon Sir Astley Cooper in 1845, are among "the most frequent causes" of breast cancer. But the nineteenth-century observations undermine rather than support late-twentieth-century notions—evoking a manic or manic-depressive character type almost the opposite of that forlorn, self-hating, emotionally inert creature, the contemporary cancer personality. As far as I know, no oncologist convinced of the efficacy of polychemotherapy and immunotherapy in treating patients had contributed to the fictions about a specific cancer personality. Needless to say, the hypothesis that distress can affect immunological responsiveness (and, in some circumstances, lower immunity to disease) is hardly the same as—or constitutes evidence for—the view that emotions cause diseases, much less for the belief that specific emotions can produce specific diseases.

Recent conjecture about the modern cancer character type finds its true antecedent and counterpart in the literature on TB, where the same theory, put in similar terms, had long been in circulation. In his *Morbidus Anglicus* (1672), Gideon Harvey declared "melancholy" and "choler" to be "the sole cause" of TB (for which he used the metaphoric term "corrosion"). In 1881, a year before Robert Koch published his paper announcing the discovery of the tubercle bacillus and demonstrating that it was the primary cause of the disease, a standard medical textbook gave as the causes of tuberculosis: hereditary disposition, unfavorable climate, sedentary indoor life, defective ventilation, deficiency of light, and "depressing emotions."[3] Though the entry had to be changed for the next edition, it took a long time for these notions to lose credibility. "I'm mentally ill, the disease of the lungs is nothing but an overflowing of my mental disease," Kafka wrote to Milena in 1920. Applied to TB, the theory that emotions cause diseases survived well into this century—until, finally, it was discovered how to cure the disease. The theory's fashionable current application—which relates cancer to emotional withdrawal and lack of self-confidence and confidence in the future—is likely to prove no more tenable than its application to tuberculosis.

In the plague-ridden England of the late sixteenth and seventeenth centuries, according to the historian Keith Thomas, it was widely believed that "the happy man would not get plague." The fantasy that a happy state of mind would fend off disease probably flourished for all infectious diseases, before the nature of infection was understood. Theories that diseases are caused by mental states and can be cured by will power are always an index of how much is not understood about the physical terrain of a disease.

Moreover, there is a peculiarly modern predilection for psychological explanations of disease, as of everything else. Psychologizing seems to provide control over the experiences and events (like grave illnesses) over which people have in fact little or no control. Psychological understanding undermines the "reality" of a disease. That reality has to be explained. (It really means; or is a symbol of; or must be interpreted so.) For those who live neither with religious consolations about death nor with a sense of death (or of anything else) as natural, death is the obscene mystery, the ultimate affront, the thing that cannot be controlled. It can only be denied. A large part of the popularity and persuasiveness of psychology comes from its being a sublimated spiritualism: a secular, ostensibly scientific way of affirming the primacy of "spirit" over matter. That ineluctably material reality, disease, can be given a psychological explanation. Death itself can be considered, ultimately, a psychological phenomenon. Groddeck declared in *The Book of the It* (he was speaking of TB): "He alone will die who wishes to die, to whom life is intolerable." The promise of a temporary triumph over death is implicit in much of the psychological thinking that starts from Freud and Jung.

At the least, there is the promise of a triumph over illness. A "physical" illness becomes in a way less real—but, in compensation, more interesting—so far as it can be considered a "mental" one. Speculation throughout the modern period has tended steadily to enlarge the category of mental illness. Indeed, part of the denial of death in this culture is a vast expansion of the category of illness as such.

Illness expands by means of two hypotheses. The first is that every form of social deviation can be considered an illness. Thus, if criminal behavior can be considered an illness, then criminals are not to be condemned or punished but to be understood (as a doctor understands), treated, cured.[4] The second is that every illness can be considered psychologically. Illness is interpreted as, basically, a psychological event, and people are encouraged to believe that they get sick because they (unconsciously) want to, and that they can cure themselves by the mobilization of will; that they can choose not to die of the disease. These two hypotheses are complementary. As the first seems to relieve guilt, the second reinstates it. Psychological theories of illness are a powerful means of placing the blame on the ill. Patients who are instructed that they have, unwittingly, caused their disease are also being made to feel that they have deserved it.

ILLNESS AS METAPHOR, CHAPTER 8

Punitive notions of disease have a long history, and such notions are particularly active with cancer. There is the "fight" or "crusade" against cancer; cancer is the "killer" disease; people who have cancer are "cancer victims." Ostensibly, the illness is the culprit. But it is also the cancer patient who is made culpable. Widely believed psychological theories of disease assign to the luckless ill the ultimate responsibility both for falling ill and for getting well. And conventions of treating cancer as no mere disease but a demonic enemy make cancer not just a lethal disease but a shameful one.

Leprosy in its heyday aroused a similarly disproportionate sense of horror. In the Middle Ages, the leper was a social text in which corruption was made visible; an exemplum, an emblem of decay. Nothing is more punitive than to give a disease a meaning—that meaning being invariably a moralistic one. Any important disease whose causality is murky, and for which treatment is ineffectual, tends to be awash in significance. First, the subjects of deepest dread (corruption, decay, pollution, anomie, weakness) are identified with the disease. The disease itself becomes a metaphor. Then, in the name of the disease (that is, using it as a metaphor), that horror is imposed on other things. The disease becomes adjectival. Something is said to be disease-like, meaning that it is disgusting or ugly. In French, a moldering stone façade is still *lépreuse*.

Epidemic diseases were a common figure for social disorder. From pestilence (bubonic plague) came "pestilent," whose figurative meaning, according to the *Oxford English Dictionary*, is "injurious to religion, morals, or public peace—1513"; and "pestilential," meaning "morally baneful or pernicious—1531." Feelings about evil are projected onto a disease. And the disease (so enriched with meanings) is projected onto the world.

In the past, such grandiloquent fantasies were regularly attached to the epidemic diseases, diseases that were a collective calamity. In the last two centuries, the diseases most often used as metaphors for evil were syphilis, tuberculosis, and cancer—all diseases imagined to be, preeminently, the diseases of individuals.

Syphilis was thought to be not only a horrible disease but a demeaning, vulgar one. Anti-democrats used it to evoke the desecrations of an egalitarian age. Baudelaire, in a note for his never completed book on Belgium, wrote:

> We all have the republican spirit in our veins, like syphilis in our bones—we are democratized and venerealized.

In the sense of an infection that corrupts morally and debilitates physically, syphilis was to become a standard trope in late-nineteenth- and early-twentieth-century anti-Semitic polemics. In 1933 Wilhelm Reich argued that "the irrational fear of syphilis was one of the major sources of National socialism's political views and its anti-Semitism." But although he perceived sexual and political phobias being projected onto a disease in the grisly harping on syphilis in *Mein*

Kampf, it never occurred to Reich how much was being projected in his own persistent use of cancer as a metaphor for the ills of the modern era. Indeed, cancer can be stretched much further than syphilis can as a metaphor.

Syphilis was limited as a metaphor because the disease itself was not regarded as mysterious; only awful. A tainted heredity (Ibsen's *Ghosts*), the perils of sex (Charles-Louis Philippe's *Bubu de Montparnasse,* Mann's *Doctor Faustus*)—there was horror aplenty in syphilis. But no mystery. Its causality was clear, and understood to be singular. Syphilis was the grimmest of gifts, "transmitted" or "carried" by a sometimes ignorant sender to the unsuspecting receiver. In contrast, TB was regarded as a mysterious affliction, and a disease with myriad causes—just as today, while everyone acknowledges cancer to be an unsolved riddle, it is also generally agreed that cancer is multi-determined. A variety of factors—such as cancer-causing substances ("carcinogens") in the environment, genetic makeup, lowering of immuno-defenses (by previous illness or emotional trauma), characterological predisposition—are held responsible for the disease. And many researchers assert that cancer is not one but more than a hundred clinically distinct diseases, that each cancer has to be studied separately, and that what will eventually be developed is an array of cures, one for each of the different cancers.

The resemblance of current ideas about cancer's myriad causes to long-held but now discredited views about TB suggests the possibility that cancer may be one disease after all and that it may turn out, as TB did, to have a principal causal agent and be controllable by one program of treatment. Indeed, as Lewis Thomas has observed, all the diseases for which the issue of causation has been settled, and which can be prevented and cured, have turned out to have a simple physical cause—like the pneumococcus for pneumonia, the tubercle bacillus for tuberculosis, a single vitamin deficiency for pellagra—and it is far from unlikely that something comparable will eventually be isolated for cancer. The notion that a disease can be explained only by a variety of causes is precisely characteristic of thinking about diseases whose causation is *not* understood. And it is diseases thought to be multi-determined (that is, mysterious) that have the widest possibilities as metaphors for what is felt to be socially or morally wrong.

TB and cancer have been used to express not only (like syphilis) crude fantasies about contamination but also fairly complex feelings about strength and weakness, and about energy. For more than a century and a half, tuberculosis provided a metaphoric equivalent for delicacy, sensitivity, sadness, powerlessness; while whatever seemed ruthless, implacable, predatory, could be analogized to cancer. (Thus, Baudelaire in 1852, in his essay *"L'Ecole païenne,"* observed: "A frenzied passion for art is a canker that devours the rest. . . .") TB was an ambivalent metaphor, both a scourge and an emblem of refinement. Cancer was never viewed other than as a scourge; it was, metaphorically, the barbarian within.

While syphilis was thought to be passively incurred, an entirely involuntary disaster, TB was once, and cancer is now, thought to be a pathology of energy, a disease of the will. Concern about energy and feeling, fears about the havoc they wreak, have been attached to both diseases. Getting TB was thought to signify a defective vitality, or vitality misspent. "There was a great want of vital power . . . and great constitutional weakness"—so Dickens described little Paul in *Dombey and Son*. The Victorian idea of TB as a disease of low energy (and heightened sensitivity) has its exact complement in the Reichian idea of cancer as a disease of unexpressed energy (and anesthetized feelings). In an era in which there seemed to be no inhibitions on being productive, people were anxious about not having enough energy. In our own era of destructive overproduction by the economy and of increasing bureaucratic restraints on the individual, there is both a fear of having too much energy and an anxiety about energy not being allowed to be expressed.

Like Freud's scarcity-economics theory of "instincts," the fantasies about TB which arose in the last century (and lasted well into ours) echo the attitudes of early capitalist accumulation. One has a limited amount of energy, which must be properly spent. (Having an orgasm, in nineteenth-century English slang, was not "coming" but "spending.") Energy, like savings, can be depleted, can run out or be used up, through reckless expenditure. The body will start "consuming" itself, the patient will "waste away."

The language used to describe cancer evokes a different economic catastrophe: that of unregulated, abnormal, incoherent growth. The tumor has energy, not the patient; "it" is out of control. Cancer cells, according to the textbook account, are cells that have shed the mechanism which "restrains" growth. (The growth of normal cells is "self-limiting," due to a mechanism called "contact inhibition.") Cells without inhibitions, cancer cells will continue to grow and extrude in a "chaotic" fashion, destroying the body's normal cells, architecture, and functions.

Early capitalism assumes the necessity of regulated spending, saving, accounting, discipline—an economy that depends on the rational limitation of desire. TB is described in images that sum up the negative behavior of nineteenth-century *homo economicus*: consumption; wasting; squandering of vitality. Advanced capitalism requires expansion, speculation, the creation of new needs (the problem of satisfaction and dissatisfaction); buying on credit; mobility—an economy that depends on the irrational indulgence of desire. Cancer is described in images that sum up the negative behavior of twentieth-century *homo economicus*: abnormal growth; repression of energy, that is, refusal to consume or spend.

TB was understood, like insanity, to be a kind of one-sidedness: a failure of will or an overintensity. However much the disease was dreaded, TB always had pathos. Like the mental patient today, the tubercular was considered to be someone quintessentially vulnerable, and full of self-destructive whims. Nineteenth- and early-twentieth-century physicians addressed themselves to coaxing their tubercular patients back to health. Their prescription was the same as the enlightened one for mental patients today: cheerful surroundings, isolation from stress and family, healthy diet, exercise, rest.

The understanding of cancer supports quite different, avowedly brutal notions of treatment. (A common cancer hospital witticism, heard as often from doctors as from patients: "The treatment is worse than the disease.") There can be no question of pampering the patient. With the patient's body considered to be under attack ("invasion"), the only treatment is counterattack.

The controlling metaphors in descriptions of cancer are, in fact, drawn not from economics but from the language of warfare: every physician and every attentive patient is familiar with, if perhaps inured to, this military terminology. Thus, cancer cells do not simply multiply; they are "invasive." ("Malignant tumors invade even when they grow very slowly," as one textbook puts it.) Cancer cells "colonize" from the original tumor to far sites in the body, first setting up tiny outposts ("micrometastases") whose presence is assumed, though they cannot be detected. Rarely are the body's "defenses" vigorous enough to obliterate a tumor that has established its own blood supply and consists of billions of destructive cells. However "radical" the surgical intervention, however many "scans" are taken of the body landscape, most remissions are temporary; the prospects are that "tumor invasion" will continue, or that rogue cells will eventually regroup and mount a new assault on the organism.

Treatment also has a military flavor. Radiotherapy uses the metaphors of aerial warfare; patients are "bombarded" with toxic rays. And chemotherapy is chemical warfare, using poisons.[5] Treatment aims to "kill" cancer cells (without, it is hoped, killing the patient). Unpleasant side effects of treatment are advertised, indeed overadvertised. ("The agony of chemotherapy" is a standard phrase.) It is impossible to avoid damaging or destroying healthy cells (indeed, some methods used to treat cancer can cause cancer), but it is thought that nearly any damage to the body is justified if it saves the patient's life. Often, of course, it doesn't work. (As in: "We had to destroy Ben Suc in order to save it.") There is everything but the body count.

The military metaphor in medicine first came into wide use in the 1880s, with the identification of bacteria as agents of disease. Bacteria were said to "invade" or "infiltrate." But talk of siege and war to describe disease now has, with cancer, a striking literalness and authority. Not only is the clinical course of the disease and its medical treatment thus described, but the disease itself is conceived as the enemy on which society wages war. More recently, the fight against cancer has sounded like a colonial war—with similarly vast appropriations of government money—and in a decade when colonial wars haven't gone too well, this militarized rhetoric seems to be backfiring. Pessimism among doctors about the efficacy of treatment is growing, in spite of the strong advances in chemotherapy and immunotherapy made since 1970. Reporters covering "the war on cancer" frequently caution the public to distinguish between official fictions and harsh facts; a few years ago, one science writer found American Cancer Society proclamations that cancer is curable and progress has been made "reminiscent of Vietnam optimism prior to the deluge." Still, it is one thing to be skeptical about the rhetoric that surrounds cancer, another to give support to many uninformed doctors who insist that no significant progress in treatment has been made, and that cancer is not really curable. The bromides of the American cancer establishment, tirelessly hailing the imminent victory over cancer; the professional pessimism of a large number of cancer specialists, talking like battle-weary

officers mired down in an interminable colonial war—these are twin distortions
in this military rhetoric about cancer.

Other distortions follow with the extension of cancer images in more grandiose
schemes of warfare. As TB was represented as the spiritualizing of consciousness,
cancer is understood as the overwhelming or obliterating of consciousness (by
a mindless It). In TB, you are eating yourself up, being refined, getting down
to the core, the real you. In cancer, non-intelligent ("primitive," "embryonic,"
"atavistic") cells are multiplying, and you are being replaced by the non-you.
Immunologists class the body's cancer cells as "nonself."
    It is worth noting that Reich, who did more than anyone else to disseminate
the psychological theory of cancer, also found something equivalent to cancer in
the biosphere.

> There is a deadly orgone energy. It is in the atmosphere. You can demonstrate it
> on devices such as the Geiger counter. It's a swampy quality. . . . Stagnant, deadly
> water which doesn't flow, doesn't metabolize. Cancer, too, is due to the stagnation
> of the flow of the life energy of the organism.

Reich's language has its own inimitable coherence. And more and more—as its
metaphoric uses gain in credibility—cancer is felt to be what he thought it was,
a cosmic disease, the emblem of all the destructive, alien powers to which the
organism is host.
    As TB was the disease of the sick self, cancer is the disease of the Other.
Cancer proceeds by a science-fiction scenario: an invasion of "alien" or "mutant"
cells, stronger than normal cells (*Invasion of the Body Snatchers, The Incredible
Shrinking Man, The Blob, The Thing*). One standard science-fiction plot is mutation, either mutants arriving from outer space or accidental mutations among
humans. Cancer could be described as a triumphant mutation, and mutation is
now mainly an image for cancer. As a theory of the psychological genesis of
cancer, the Reichian imagery of energy checked, not allowed to move outward,
then turned back on itself, driving cells berserk, is already the stuff of science
fiction. And Reich's image of death in the air—of deadly energy that registers
on a Geiger counter—suggests how much the science-fiction images about cancer
(a disease that comes from deadly rays, and is treated by deadly rays) echo the
collective nightmare. The original fear about exposure to atomic radiation was
of genetic deformities in the next generation; that was replaced by another fear,
as statistics started to show much higher cancer rates among Hiroshima and
Nagasaki survivors and their descendants.
    Cancer is a metaphor for what is most ferociously energetic; and these energies
constitute the ultimate insult to natural order. In a science-fiction tale by Tommaso
Landolfi, the spaceship is called "Cancerqueen." (It is hardly within the range of
the tuberculosis metaphor that a writer could have imagined an intrepid vessel
named "Consumptionqueen.") When not being explained away as something
psychological, buried in the recesses of the self, cancer is being magnified and

projected into a metaphor for the biggest enemy, the furthest goal. Thus, Nixon's bid to match Kennedy's promise to put Americans on the moon was, appropriately enough, the promise to "conquer" cancer. Both were science-fiction ventures. The equivalent of the legislation establishing the space program was the National Cancer Act of 1971, which did not envisage the near-to-hand decisions that could bring under control the industrial economy that pollutes—only the great destination: the cure.

TB was a disease in the service of a romantic view of the world. Cancer is now in the service of a simplistic view of the world that can turn paranoid. The disease is often experienced as a form of demonic possession—tumors are "malignant" or "benign," like forces—and many terrified cancer patients are disposed to seek out faith healers, to be exorcised. The main organized support for dangerous nostrums like Laetrile comes from far-right groups to whose politics of paranoia the fantasy of a miracle cure for cancer makes a serviceable addition, along with a belief in UFOs. (The John Birch Society distributes a forty-five-minute film called *World Without Cancer.*) For the more sophisticated, cancer signifies the rebellion of the injured ecosphere: Nature taking revenge on a wicked technocratic world. False hopes and simplified terrors are raised by crude statistics brandished for the general public, such as that 90 percent of all cancers are "environmentally caused," or that imprudent diet and tobacco smoking alone account for 75 percent of all cancer deaths. To the accompaniment of this numbers game (it is difficult to see how any statistics about "all cancers" or "all cancer deaths" could be defended), cigarettes, hair dyes, bacon, saccharine, hormone-fed poultry, pesticides, low-sulphur coal—a lengthening roll call of products we take for granted have been found to cause cancer. X-rays give cancer (the treatment meant to cure kills); so do emanations from the television set and the microwave oven and the fluorescent clock face. As with syphilis, an innocent or trivial act—or exposure—in the present can have dire consequences far in the future. It is also known that cancer rates are high for workers in a large number of industrial occupations. Though the exact processes of causation lying behind the statistics remain unknown, it seems clear that many cancers are preventable. But cancer is not just a disease ushered in by the Industrial Revolution (there was cancer in Arcadia) and certainly more than the sin of capitalism (within their more limited industrial capacities, the Russians pollute worse than we do). The widespread current view of cancer as a disease of industrial civilization is as unsound scientifically as the right-wing fantasy of a "world without cancer" (like a world without subversives). Both rest on the mistaken feeling that cancer is a distinctively "modern" disease.

The medieval experience of the plague was firmly tied to notions of moral pollution, and people invariably looked for a scapegoat external to the stricken community. (Massacres of Jews in unprecedented numbers took place throughout Europe in 1347 and 1348, then stopped as soon as the plague receded.) With the modern diseases, the scapegoat is not so easily separated from the patient. But much as these diseases individualize, they also pick up some of the metaphors of epidemic diseases. (Diseases understood to be simply epidemic have become less useful as metaphors, as evidenced by the near-total historical amnesia about the influenza pandemic of 1918–19, in which more people died than in the four years of World War I.) Presently, it is as much a cliché to say that cancer is "environmentally" caused as it was—and still is—to say that it is caused by mismanaged emotions. TB was associated with pollution (Florence Nightingale thought it was "induced by the foul air of houses"), and now cancer is thought of as a disease of the contamination of the whole world. TB was "the white plague." With awareness of environmental pollution, people have started saying that there is an "epidemic" or "plague" of cancer.

AIDS and Its Metaphors, Chapter 3

Because of countless metaphoric flourishes that have made cancer synonymous with evil, having cancer has been experienced by many as shameful, therefore something to conceal, and also unjust, a betrayal by one's body. Why me? the cancer patient exclaims bitterly. With AIDS, the shame is linked to an imputation of guilt; and the scandal is not at all obscure. Few wonder, Why me? Most people outside of sub-Saharan Africa who have AIDS know (or think they know) how they got it. It is not a mysterious affliction that seems to strike at random. Indeed, to get AIDS is precisely to be revealed, in the majority of cases so far, as a member of a certain "risk group," a community of pariahs. The illness flushes out an identity that might have remained hidden from neighbors, jobmates, family, friends. It also confirms an identity and, among the risk group in the United States most severely affected in the beginning, homosexual men, has been a creator of community as well as an experience that isolates the ill and exposes them to harassment and persecution.

Getting cancer, too, is sometimes understood as the fault of someone who has indulged in "unsafe" behavior—the alcoholic with cancer of the esophagus, the smoker with lung cancer: punishment for living unhealthy lives. (In contrast to those obliged to perform unsafe occupations, like the worker in a petrochemical factory who gets bladder cancer.) More and more linkages are sought between primary organs or systems and specific practices that people are invited to repudiate, as in recent speculation associating colon cancer and breast cancer with diets rich in animal fats. But the unsafe habits associated with cancer, among other illnesses—even heart disease, hitherto little culpabilized, is now largely viewed as the price one pays for excesses of diet and "life-style"—are the result of a weakness of the will or a lack of prudence, or of addiction to legal (albeit very dangerous) chemicals. The unsafe behavior that produces AIDS is judged to be more than just weakness. It is indulgence, delinquency—addictions to chemicals that are illegal and to sex regarded as deviant.

The sexual transmission of this illness, considered by most people as a calamity one brings on oneself, is judged more harshly than other means—especially since AIDS is understood as a disease not only of sexual excess but of perversity. (I am thinking, of course, of the United States, where people are currently being told that heterosexual transmission is extremely rare, and unlikely—as if Africa did not exist.) An infectious disease whose principal means of transmission is sexual necessarily puts at greater risk those who are sexually more active—and is easy to view as a punishment for that activity. True of syphilis, this is even truer of AIDS, since not just promiscuity but a specific sexual "practice" regarded as unnatural is named as more endangering. Getting the disease through a sexual practice is thought to be more willful, therefore deserves more blame. Addicts who get the illness by sharing contaminated needles are seen as committing (or completing) a kind of inadvertent suicide. Promiscuous homosexual men practicing their vehement sexual customs under the illusory conviction, fostered by medical ideology with its cure-all antibiotics, of the relative innocuousness of all sexually transmitted diseases, could be viewed as dedicated hedonists—though it's now clear that their behavior was no less suicidal. Those like hemophiliacs and blood-transfusion recipients, who cannot by any stretch of the blaming faculty be considered responsible for their illness, may be as ruthlessly ostracized by frightened people, and potentially represent a greater threat because, unlike the already stigmatized, they are not as easy to identify.

Infectious diseases to which sexual fault is attached always inspire fears of easy contagion and bizarre fantasies of transmission by nonvenereal means in public places. The removal of doorknobs and the installation of swinging doors on U.S. Navy ships and the disappearance of the metal drinking cups affixed to public water fountains in the United States in the first decades of the century were early consequences of the "discovery" of syphilis's "innocently transmitted infection"; and the warning to generations of middle-class children always to interpose paper between bare bottom and the public toilet seat is another trace of the horror stories about the germs of syphilis being passed to the innocent by the dirty that were rife once and are still widely believed. Every feared epidemic disease, but especially those associated with sexual license, generates a preoccupying distinction between the disease's putative carriers (which usually means just the poor and, in this part of the world, people with darker skins) and those defined—health professionals and other bureaucrats do the defining—as "the general population." AIDS has revived similar phobias and fears of contamination among *this* disease's version of "the general population": white heterosexuals who do not inject themselves with drugs or have sexual relations with those who do. Like syphilis a disease of, or contracted from, dangerous others, AIDS is perceived as afflicting, in greater proportions than syphilis ever did, the already stigmatized. But syphilis was not identified with certain death, death that follows a protracted agony, as cancer was once imagined and AIDS is now held to be.

That AIDS is not a single illness but a syndrome, consisting of a seemingly open-ended list of contributing or "presenting" illnesses which constitute (that is, qualify the patient as having) the disease, makes it more a product of definition or construction than even a very complex, multiform illness like cancer. Indeed, the contention that AIDS is invariably fatal depends partly on what doctors decided to define as AIDS—and keep in reserve as distinct earlier stages of the disease. And this decision rests on a notion no less primitively metaphorical than that of a "full-blown" (or "full-fledged") disease.[6] "Full-blown" is the form in which the disease is inevitably fatal. As what is immature is destined to become mature, what buds to become full-blown (fledglings to become full-fledged)—the doctors' botanical or zoological metaphor makes development or evolution into AIDS the norm, the rule. I am not saying that the metaphor creates the clinical conception, but I am arguing that it does much more than just ratify it. It lends support to an interpretation of the clinical evidence which is far from proved or, yet, provable. It is simply too early to conclude, of a disease identified only seven years ago, that infection will always produce something to die from, or even that everybody who has what is defined as AIDS will die of it. (As some medical writers have speculated, the appalling mortality rates could be registering the early, mostly rapid deaths of those most vulnerable to the virus—because of diminished immune competence, because of genetic predisposition, among other possible co-factors—not the ravages of a uniformly fatal infection.) Construing the disease as divided into distinct stages was the necessary way of implementing the metaphor of "full-blown disease." But it also slightly weakened the notion of inevitability suggested by the metaphor. Those sensibly interested in hedging their bets about how uniformly lethal infection would prove could use the standard three-tier classification—HIV infection, AIDS-related complex (ARC), and AIDS— to entertain either of two possibilities or both: the less catastrophic one, that *not* everybody infected would "advance" or "graduate" from HIV infection, and the more catastrophic one, that everybody would.

It is the more catastrophic reading of the evidence that for some time has dominated debate about the disease, which means that a change in nomenclature is under way. Influential administrators of the way the disease is understood have decided that there should be no more of the false reassurance that might be had from the use of different acronyms for different stages of the disease. (It could never have been more than minimally reassuring.) Recent proposals for redoing terminology—for instance, to phase out the category of ARC—do not challenge the construction of the disease in stages, but do place additional stress on the *continuity* of the disease process. "Full-blown disease" is viewed as more inevitable now, and that strengthens the fatalism already in place.[7]

From the beginning the construction of the illness had depended on notions that separated one group of people from another—the sick from the well, people with ARC from people with AIDS, them and us—while implying the imminent dissolution of these distinctions. However hedged, the predictions always sounded fatalistic. Thus, the frequent pronouncements by AIDS specialists and public health officials on the chances of those infected with the virus coming down with "full-blown" disease have seemed mostly an exercise in the management of public opinion, dosing out the harrowing news in several steps. Estimates of the percentage expected to show symptoms classifying them as having AIDS within five years, which may be too low—at the time of this writing, the figure is 30 to 35 percent—are invariably followed by the assertion that "most," after which comes "probably all," those infected will eventually become ill. The critical number, then, is not the percentage of people likely to develop AIDS within a relatively short time but the *maximum* interval that could elapse between infection with HIV (described as lifelong and irreversible) and appearance of the first symptoms. As the years add up in which the illness has been tracked, so does the possible number of years between infection and becoming ill, now estimated, seven years into the epidemic, at between ten and fifteen years. This figure, which will presumably continue to be revised upward, does much to maintain the definition of AIDS as an inexorable, invariably fatal disease.

The obvious consequence of believing that all those who "harbor" the virus will eventually come down with the illness is that those who test positive for it are regarded as people-with-AIDS, who just don't have it . . . yet. It is only a matter of time, like any death sentence. Less obviously, such people are often regarded as if they *do* have it. Testing positive for HIV (which usually means having been tested for the presence not of the virus but of antibodies to the virus) is increasingly equated with being ill. Infected *means* ill, from that point forward. "Infected but not ill," that invaluable notion of clinical medicine (the body) "harbors" many infections), is being superseded by biomedical concepts which, whatever their scientific justification, amount to reviving the antiscientific logic of defilement, and make infected-but-healthy a contradiction in terms. Being ill in this new sense can have many practical consequences. People are losing their jobs when it is learned that they are HIV-positive (though it is not legal in the United States to fire someone for that reason) and the temptation to conceal a positive finding must be immense. The consequences of testing HIV-positive are even more punitive for those selected populations—there will be more—upon which the government has already made testing mandatory. The U.S. Department of Defense has announced that military personnel discovered to be HIV-positive are being removed "from sensitive, stressful jobs," because of evidence indicating that mere infection with the virus, in the absence of any other symptoms, produces subtle changes in mental abilities in a significant minority of virus carriers. (The evidence cited: lower scores on certain neurological tests given to some who had tested positive, which could reflect mental impairment caused by exposure to the virus, though most doctors think this extremely improbable, or could be caused—as officially acknowledged under questioning—by "the anger, depression, fear, and panic" of people who have just learned that they are HIV-positive.) And, of course, testing positive now makes one ineligible to immigrate everywhere.

In every previous epidemic of an infectious nature, the epidemic is equivalent to the number of tabulated cases. This epidemic is regarded as consisting *now* of that figure plus a calculation about a much larger number of people apparently in good health (seemingly healthy, but doomed) who are infected. The calculations are being made and remade all the time, and pressure is building to identify these people, and to tag them. With the most up-to-date biomedical testing, it is possible to create a new class of lifetime pariahs, the future ill. But the result of this radical expansion of the notion of illness created by the triumph of modern medical scrutiny also seems a throwback to the past, before the era of medical triumphalism, when illnesses were innumerable, mysterious, and the progression from being seriously ill to dying was something normal (not, as now, medicine's lapse or failure, destined to be corrected). AIDS, in which people are understood as ill before they are ill; which produces a seemingly innumerable array of symptom-illnesses; for which there are only palliatives; and which brings to many a social death that precedes the physical one—AIDS reinstates something like a premodern experience of illness, as described in Donne's *Devotions*, in which "every thing that disorders a faculty and the function of that is a sicknesse," which starts when we

> are preafflicted, super-afflicted with these jelousies and suspitions, and apprehensions of Sicknes, before we can cal it a sicknes; we are not sure we are ill; one hand askes the other by the pulse, and our eye asks our own urine, how we do. . . . we are tormented with sicknes, and cannot stay till the torment come. . . .

whose agonizing outreach to every part of the body makes a real cure chimerical, since what "is but an accident, but a symptom of the main disease, is so violent, that the Phisician must attend the cure of that" rather than "the cure of the disease it self," and whose consequence is abandonment:

> As Sicknesse is the greatest misery, so the greatest misery of sicknes is solitude; when the infectiousnes of the disease deterrs them who should assist, from comming; even the Phisician dares scarse come. . . . it is an Outlawry, an Excommunication upon the patient. . . .

In premodern medicine, illness is described as it is experienced intuitively, as a relation of outside and inside: an interior sensation or something to be discerned on the body's surface, by sight (or just below, by listening, palpating), which is confirmed when the interior is opened to viewing (in surgery, in autopsy). Modern—that is, effective—medicine is characterized by far more complex notions of what is to be observed inside the body: not just the disease's results (damaged organs) but its cause (microorganisms), and by a far more intricate typology of illness.

In the older era of artisanal diagnoses, being examined produced an immediate verdict, immediate as the physician's willingness to speak. Now an examination means tests. And being tested introduces a time lapse that, given the unavoidably industrial character of competent medical testing, can stretch out for weeks: an agonizing delay for those who think they are awaiting a death sentence or an acquittal. Many are reluctant to be tested out of dread of the verdict, out of fear of being put on a list that could bring future discrimination or worse, and out of fatalism (what good would it do?). The usefulness of self-examination for the early detection of certain common cancers, much less likely to be fatal if treated before they are very advanced, is now widely understood. Early detection of an illness thought to be inexorable and incurable cannot seem to bring any advantage.

Like other diseases that arouse feelings of shame, AIDS is often a secret, but not from the patient. A cancer diagnosis was frequently concealed from patients by their families; an AIDS diagnosis is at least as often concealed from their families by patients. And as with other grave illnesses regarded as more than just illnesses, many people with AIDS are drawn to whole-body rather than illness-specific treatments, which are thought to be either ineffectual or too dangerous. (The disparagement of effective, scientific medicine for offering treatments that are *merely* illness-specific, and likely to be toxic, is a recurrent misconjecture of opinion that regards itself as enlightened.) This disastrous choice is still being made by some people with cancer, an illness that surgery and drugs can often cure. And a predictable mix of superstition and resignation is leading some people with AIDS to refuse antiviral chemotherapy, which, even in the absence of a cure, has proved of some effectiveness (in slowing down the syndrome's progress and in staving off some common presenting illnesses), and instead to seek to heal themselves, often under the auspices of some "alternative medicine" guru. But subjecting an emaciated body to the purification of a macrobiotic diet is about as helpful in treating AIDS as having oneself bled, the "holistic" medical treament of choice in the era of Donne.

NOTES

1. A study by Dr. Caroline Bedell Thomas of the Johns Hopkins University School of Medicine was thus summarized in one recent newspaper article ("Can Your Personality Kill You?"): "In brief, cancer victims are low-gear persons, seldom prey to outbursts of emotion. They have feelings of isolation from their parents dating back to childhood." Drs. Claus and Marjorie Bahnson at the Eastern Pennsylvania Psychiatric Institute have "charted a personality pattern of denial of hostility, depression and of memory of emotional deprivation in childhood" and "difficulty in maintaining close relationships." Dr. O. Carl Simonton, a radiologist in Fort Worth, Texas, who gives patients both radiation and psychotherapy, describes the cancer personality as someone with "a great tendency for self-pity and a markedly impaired ability to make and maintain meaning-ful relationships." Lawrence LeShan, a New York psychologist and psychotherapist (*You Can Fight for Your Life: Emotional Factors in the Causation of Cancer* [1977]), claims that "there is a general type of personality configuration among the majority of cancer patients" and a world-view that cancer patients share and "which pre-dates the development of cancer." He divides "the basic emotional pattern of the cancer patient" into three parts: "a childhood or adolescence marked by feelings of isolation," the loss of the "meaningful relationship" found in adulthood, and a subsequent "conviction that life holds no more hope." "The cancer patient," LeShan writes, "almost invariably is contemptuous of himself, and of his abilities and possibilities." Cancer patients are "empty of feeling and devoid of self."
2. "Always much trouble and hard work" is a notation that occurs in many of the brief case histories in Herbert Snow's *Clinical Notes on Cancer* (1883). Snow was a surgeon in the Cancer Hospital in London, and most of the patients he saw were poor. A typical observation: "Of 140 cases of breast-cancer, 103 gave an account of previous mental trouble, hard work, or other debilitating agency. Of 187 uterine ditto, 91 showed a similar history." Doctors who saw patients who led more comfortable lives made other observations. The physician who treated Alexandre Dumas for cancer, G. von

Schmitt, published a book on cancer in 1871 in which he listed "deep and sedentary study and pursuits, the feverish and anxious agitation of public life, the cares of ambition, frequent paroxysms of rage, violent grief" as "the principal causes" of the disease. Quoted in Samuel J. Kowal, M.D., "Emotions as a Cause of Cancer: 18th and 19th Century Contributions," *Review of Psychoanalysis*, 42, 3 (July 1955).

3. August Flint and William H. Welch, *The Principles and Practice of Medicine* (fifth edition, 1881), cited in René and Jean Dubos, *The White Plague* (1952).

4. An early statement of this view, now so much on the defensive, is in Samuel Butler's *Erewhon* (1872). Butler's way of suggesting that criminality was a disease, like TB, that was either hereditary or the result of an unwholesome environment was to point out the absurdity of condemning the sick. In Erewhon, those who murdered or stole are sympathetically treated as ill persons, while tuberculosis is punished as a crime.

5. Drugs of the nitrogen mustard type (so-called alkylating agents)—like cyclophosphamide (Cytoxan)—were the first generation of cancer drugs. Their use—with leukemia (which is characterized by an excessive production of immature white cells), then with other forms of cancer—was suggested by an inadvertent experiment with chemical warfare toward the end of World War II, when an American ship, loaded with nitrogen mustard gas, was blown up in the Naples harbor, and many of the sailors died of their lethally low white-cell and platelet counts (that is, of bone-marrow poisoning) rather than of burns or sea-water inhalation.

Chemotherapy and weaponry seem to go together, if only as a fancy. The first modern chemotherapy success was with syphilis: in 1910, Paul Ehrlich introduced an arsenic derivative, arsphenamine (Salvarsan), which was called "the magic bullet."

6. The standard definition distinguishes people with the disease or syndrome "fulfilling the criteria for the surveillance definition of AIDS" from a larger number infected with HIV and symptomatic "who do not fulfill the empiric criteria for the full-blown disease. This constellation of signs and symptoms in the context of HIV infection has been termed the AIDS-related complex (ARC)." Then follows the obligatory percentage. "It is estimated that approximately 25 percent of patients with ARC will develop full-blown disease within 3 years." Harrison's *Principles of Internal Medicine*, 11th edition (1987), p. 1394.

The first major illness known by an acronym, the condition called AIDS does not have, as it were, natural borders. It is an illness whose identity is designed for purposes of investigation and with tabulation and surveillance by medical and other bureaucracies in view. Hence, the unselfconscious equating in the medical textbook of what is empirical with what pertains to surveillance, two notions deriving from quite different models of understanding. (AIDS is what fulfills that which is referred to as either the "criteria for the surveillance definition" or the "empiric criteria": HIV infection plus the presence of one or more diseases included on the roster drawn up by the disease's principal administrator of definition in the United States, the federal Centers for Disease Control in Atlanta.) This completely stipulative definition with its metaphor of maturing disease decisively influences how the illness is understood.

7. The 1988 Presidential Commission on the epidemic recommended "de-emphasizing" the use of the term ARC because it "tends to obscure the life-threatening aspects of this stage of illness." There is some pressure to drop the term AIDS, too. The report by the Presidential Commission pointedly used the acronym HIV for the epidemic itself, as part of a recommended shift from "monitoring disease" to "monitoring infection." Again, one of the reasons given is that the present terminology masks the true gravity of the menace. ("This longstanding concentration on the clinical manifestations of

AIDS rather than on all stages of HIV infection [i.e., from initial infection to seroconversion, to an antibody-positive asymptomatic stage, to full-blown AIDS] has had the unintended effect of misleading the public as to the extent of infection in the population. . . .") It does seem likely that the disease will, eventually, be renamed. *This* change in nomenclature would justify officially the policy of including the infected but asymptomatic among the ill.)

CHAPTER 9

Holistic Medicine

Fred Frohock

ALTERNATIVE THERAPIES

All healing therapies begin with the assumption that the individual to be treated is ill or damaged in some way. The healer's task is to find and realize the method or condition that will make the patient better. Any effective therapy requires a response from the patient. Individuals who do not respond to therapy at either conscious or unconscious levels cannot be helped. The body is an obvious target of treatment in modern medicine. But sometimes the beliefs of the patient are more decisive than physiological responses, and on occasion can even control the body's powers of rejuvenation.

These rudimentary observations are as true of the most technological, allopathic medicine as they are of spiritual healing. All therapy helps the person to heal herself, though sometimes medical intervention can be crucial in restoring health and avoiding death. But the methods and conditions of effective therapy differ widely even when these truisms are accepted. Western medicine today relies on a mechanistic view of the body that inclines physicians to regard illness as a malady caused by bacteria, viruses, or organic damage (for example, genetic flaws). The goal of therapy is a restoration of that equilibrium defining the healthy organism. Today this restoration is usually accomplished with modern medicine and/or surgical techniques.

The healing therapies that are regarded as nonstandard or unconventional from allopathic perspectives generally have a different view of the individual, of health and illness, and the range of methods and conditions that can successfully heal. Nonstandard therapies tend to regard individuals in holistic terms. Individuals are seen as singular wholes and as constituent parts of some larger reality. The problem is that an abundance of evidence and argument suggests that individuals are more complex and fragmented than commonly thought. Rival social and intellectual contexts can provide competing definitions of the individual, so that societies often present different selves with no changes in psychic references.

Also, the brain seems to be a heterogeneous arrangement that can contain multiple selves within a single physical endowment.

Nonstandard therapy uses a wide and interesting range of justifications to prove that the whole individual is better than the fragmented self, for example that the individual as an integrated whole can respond more effectively to treatment and is closer to a more complete equilibrium extending to both body and mind. Even the duality of body-mind is rejected in most holistic medicine. In its place is a unity of mental and physical domains. The healthy individual is one who is in a state of harmony achieved by subordinating the self to a larger purpose. This purpose meets the enduring interests of the individual. Health, and the therapy that secures health, is as much a matter of attitude as physical condition.

It is the effort to connect the integrated self with reality, however, that most sharply distinguishes nonstandard from more conventional therapy. Traditional faith healing claims interventionist powers for a reality outside sensory experiences. Health is achieved by a healer who acts as an instrument for these powers, primarily by the laying on of hands or invocation of special healing forces by words and thought. Another form of faith healing attempts to realign individuals with reality, a kind of restoration of a cosmic balance between the individual and the universe. Christian Science aims at such a harmony, and a number of recent therapies use various meditative techniques to achieve this comprehensive equilibrium. The result of such an equilibrium is said to be the amelioration of certain pathological states, and on occasion the eradication of illness in its entirety. This latter type of meditative healing joins paranormal experiences with therapy.

THERAPEUTIC TOUCH

The spiritual efforts found in the Pentecostal and charismatic traditions stress the interventionist type of healing. Practitioners in these traditions heal by touch and prayer. One recent variation on such healing that bridges some of the differences with meditative types of healing is "therapeutic touch." This form of healing is conducted by a healer who attempts to diagnose and cure a variety of ailments by a noninvasive sweeping of the body with her hands. The method is squarely in the tradition of spiritual healings that stress the laying on of hands. The assumptions informing therapeutic touch, however, are similar to those found in meditative healing, especially the belief that the sick individual must be brought back into a natural balance with nature.

Therapeutic touch is based on the belief that a universal life-energy field flows through all living organisms. This energy field flows freely and naturally through all healthy organisms, nourishing all parts of body and mind. Illness is an obstruction or disorder of this energy field within individuals. The causes of such disruption are many, including emotional distress and disease agents (bacteria, viruses). The aim of the therapy is to remove the energy obstructions and restore harmony within the individual and between the individual and the environment.

A typical exercise of therapeutic touch begins with the healer engaged in a private effort to relax and bring her mental powers into focus. When centered —her body and mind at rest—the therapist then assesses the condition of the petitioner. The assessment is conducted by sweeping the subject's energy field, moving the hands over the subject's body at a distance of three to five inches from the surface of the skin. The assessment is done quickly, usually lasting no more than fifteen to twenty seconds. Therapists report that a healthy energy field feels unbroken, exudes a continuous sensation of gentle warmth or vibration, and is accessible to the therapist. The assumption is that a healthy person is engaged in continuous and beneficial energy transfers with others and with the environment, and this vibrant exchange can be sensed quickly and accurately in therapeutic touch.

Illness sends different signals. If the subject is sick, the sweep of his or her body will reveal areas of congestion, deficit, or imbalance in the energy field. Therapists report feelings of heaviness or pressure, sometimes diffuse and sometimes concentrated around an area of the body, when illness is present. A blocked area is described as cold, sometimes empty of energy. The therapist who senses such emptiness will report the area as the site of an illness, for example ulcers in the lower abdominal areas or pneumonia in the lower areas of the chest. Therapists claim to be able to feel an energy depletion in all illnesses. The sensations here are those of drawing or pulling, "as though a stream of very fine water bubbles were being pulled through one's hands." Energy deficits are said to be located under congested areas of the energy field. A sensation of discomfort in the hands, a prickly feeling, or a feeling of disruption or thickness can indicate an imbalance in the energy field. Therapists believe that these sensations suggest that an organ of the body is malfunctioning.

The techniques for sensing illness can be taught through meditation exercises and practice sessions. But some practitioners seem to have more talents than others in these exercises. The workshops in which these skills are taught always include practice seminars in which a subject suffering from some undisclosed illness is assessed by each member of the workshop. Then the assessments are evaluated, using the physical condition of the subject as a baseline. Though sensing illness may be a latent ability we all have to some degree, some members of each workshop will typically surpass the others and some will have only marginal abilities to sense illness. Since the subject's illness may not correspond to his or her own feelings or symptoms, even the gifted individual practicing therapeutic touch is instructed to seek validation of impressions with another practitioner if possible.

The therapy following the assessment is remarkably uniform. Practitioners of therapeutic touch try to clear energy congestion by sweeping it downward (said to be its natural direction of travel) towards the legs and out through the feet. Beginning at the head of the subject and moving down to the feet, the practitioner uses downward sweeping motions of the hands, as if urging smoke or water to move. Sometimes the feet must be "opened" by exerting gentle pressure under the arches, or by massage, to facilitate the flow of energy. The release of congestion is designed to alleviate illnesses (like migraines, colds, etc.) and help rebalance the subject's energy field.

One of the more dramatic techniques in therapeutic touch is the therapist's attempt to transfer energy directly to a subject. In these efforts the therapist consciously tries to be the instrument or conduit to allow universal energy forces to enter her body and go into the subject's body. This method is used if the therapist senses a depletion in the subject's energy field. These deficits are sometimes felt around wounds or injuries, though even local deficits indicate that the whole energy field is depleted. In an energy transfer the therapist leaves her hands near the subject, at the site of the local deficit if one is sensed, and allows energy to flow into the subject's field. Therapists often report a sensation of pulling, of energy flowing through the hands until the subject's energy levels feel whole again and the flow stops on its own or at the subject's suggestion. It is possible, according to therapists, to force too much energy into a subject's field. The overburdened recipient will then feel restless, impatient, or dizzy.

The aim of therapeutic touch is to restore the subject's energy field by rebalancing it, removing congestion, repairing breaks and rough edges by smoothing out the troubled areas, replenishing energy levels, and in general stroking and tuning the field until it is in a healthy integrated state, flowing easily and continuously. The illness is said to be helped, and sometimes overcome entirely, by bringing the individual to a holistic state of equilibrium.

Patients say that they can feel the effects of therapeutic touch. The first response almost always is one of relaxation, often indicated by words like "I feel so relaxed right now." Respiration and heartbeat often slow down, sometimes immediately at the very beginning of therapy. Subjects also feel warmth when the therapist's hands hover over an area of the body. Sometimes a tingling sensation occurs, and sometimes the subject claims that he can feel the congestion of energy being moved down to the area of the feet and out of the body. Sometimes the subject feels nothing during a session and still feels good at the completion of the therapy. Most subjects report that they feel better after the therapy.

Are there physiological effects that correspond to these subjective reports? Evidence indicates that there are. Psychogenic diseases respond to therapeutic touch. Some types of headaches, asthma, and gastrointestinal disturbances (including colic and constipation) are especially responsive. In fact, many patients with stress-related illnesses seem to improve with therapeutic touch. These effects are not surprising, for the strong psychological connections that often arise between therapist and patient would almost surely produce psychophysiological benefits. It is surprising, however, that these benefits seem to follow even when the subject is skeptical of the therapy. The only attitudinal impediments to a successful outcome seem to be denial of illness and a hostility toward the therapist.

There also is evidence that therapeutic touch accelerates healing of somatic illnesses. Pain is alleviated and sometimes eliminated by the therapy. Wounds can heal more rapidly. One frequently cited study introduces evidence that the wounds of mice who had received a kind of laying-on-of-hands treatment (similar to therapeutic touch) healed more quickly than those of a control group of mice who did not receive the treatment. A more recent experiment monitored the healing process of two sets of identical-sized, surgically administered dermal wounds, one subject to therapeutic touch and the other not. The therapist in this experiment was isolated from the subjects and treated only the wound on the subject's arm, which was extended through a hole in a wall to the control room. Subjects were told that their wounds were simply being monitored by instruments in the control room. The wounds treated by the therapeutic touch practitioner improved more rapidly than the untreated wounds.

In both experiments, the placebo effect was nullified, in the first case by the obvious fact that the subjects were mice and in the second case by the use of double blinds (isolation of the practitioner and the subjects' ignorance that therapeutic touch was being employed). The beneficial effects of the therapy seemed to be independent of the subjects' attitudes. Other experiments have provided evidence that the hemoglobin level of subjects in therapeutic touch can be increased. In these and similar efforts, a physiological change seems to be brought about by the techniques of therapeutic touch in and of themselves.

THEORY AND PRACTICE

The temptation is strong to divide therapeutic touch into two domains, one containing its metaphysical assumptions and the other laying out its practical effects. Something seems to be going on in the therapy that cannot be adequately explained with material assumptions. Thousands of health professionals have attended therapeutic touch workshops and presumably have learned a method of healing that is a clear alternative to conventional medical practice. The outcomes of the therapy do benefit patients, and sometimes the effects are transforming. This practical side of therapeutic touch is widely acknowledged, although it is still disputed within mainstream medicine. It is also important to note that the modern techniques of therapeutic touch originated in practice, apart from theory of any sort.

The genesis story of therapeutic touch is repeated by almost all practitioners trying to explain the therapy. Oskar Estabany, a former colonel in the Hungarian cavalry, was confronted one evening with a problem. He loved animals, horses in particular, and his horse had become ill and did not seem likely to survive. He spent the night with the horse, contriving a cure from his instincts and religious impulses. His efforts included massages and caresses, prayers and exhortations. In the morning, to his astonishment, the horse was well. He used these pragmatic techniques on other ill horses with remarkable success, then slowly and reluctantly expanded them to include humans. When he retired, he immigrated to Canada and joined a research group studying healing. He had no theory to explain what he did. He regarded his ability to heal as a special gift, often referring to himself (in the manner of faith healers past and present) as an instrument or channel for the healing powers of God (in this case, Jesus Christ).

The research group Estabany had joined evolved the theory of healing that later provided the explanation for therapeutic touch. The evolution illustrates a standard pattern of concept formation. The members of the group were studying the practice of healing. The early efforts were inductive. They included observing and cataloging acts of healing, generalizing the observed techniques, and trying to duplicate what they were observing. More than collating the facts was required to explain the practice, however. A theory or philosophy was needed. The key participants in the group drew this theory from a variety of sources but stressed Eastern literatures. Sanskrit, for example, provides the word *prana*, which is a kind of energy roughly translated as vitality and conceptually linked to regeneration. The group members began to accept the Eastern doctrine that *prana* is the organizing energy of life itself and that health is an excess of this energy. They also accepted the notion of a transfer of energy. The healer was viewed as someone with an abundance of *prana* and the power to channel this energy to ill persons.

The vocabulary of this Eastern approach to healing was adopted and expanded to the current view of energy fields in therapeutic touch. The *chakra* (or "wheel") is postulated as the mechanism that modulates and distributes *prana*. Living persons are seen as enclosed in an etheric field extending one to six inches from the body. The idea of an equilibrium explains the simultaneous stability and interactive motion of this energy field. In this philosophical perspective, humans are no longer defined as solid entities. They are regarded as forms of energy in a symbiotic relationship with their environments. It is then but a short step to extend the theory to the healing act, now seen as a successful restoration of a damaged energy field.

There is nothing unusual or perverse in this pattern of concepts. They fit the known facts, and in standard fashion begin to define the facts by influencing observations. But the temptation to divide therapeutic touch into theory and practice is strong precisely because of its pragmatic origins. If it works, it works without introducing the elaborate ontologies that currently offer explanations for the practice. Healing occurred before a theory was attached to the practice and occurs today among subjects who know little, if anything, about energy fields. Further, and this is the case with all explanatory theories, alternative theories and rival philosophies may be equally effective in explaining the causal chains of healing in therapeutic touch.

The one thing we do know is that therapeutic touch can improve the conditions of ill or damaged life forms in ways not explained adequately by conventional medicine. How and why the improvement occurs is open to discussion.

SULZMAN

William Sulzman became interested in religious movements and metaphysical problems in high school. In his senior year, he wrote a brief essay on comparative religion. His theme was that there is one God who speaks through many different religions. He was a practicing Protestant at the time but open to the appeals of competing religions. Years later, when he came to New York City after college to study Spanish at the Latin American Institute, he reconstructed these ideas for a conversation exam near the end of his first term. The instructor in the course was a member of the Theosophy Society. She identified the ideas as congenial with theosophy and gave Sulzman pamphlets about the movement.

Sulzman scanned the history of theosophy quickly and easily. The society was founded in New York City in 1875 by Madame Blavatsky, a seer who had traveled extensively in the East (especially in India). Blavatsky, like many Westerners, had become intrigued with the philosophical ideas of the East, in large part because they seemed to combine rather than separate religion and science. They also contained vast stretches of mystical thinking and experiences. Blavatsky appropriated a variety of doctrines and fused them into a complicated system of thought that addressed all of reality. The Theosophy Society was formed to disseminate these ideas to others.

Sulzman began studying the philosophy elaborated by Blavatsky, sometimes spending more time on these works than on his Spanish. In fact, he switched from Spanish to English philosophy publications to make sure he was absorbing the right ideas. His instructor continued to assist him, making sure that he got the more sensible interpretations of theosophy rather than the bizarre offshoots of the movement. He continued studying theosophy throughout his two year stint in the Army. When he returned to New York, he realized that he had accepted the basic ideas, so he joined the Society.

Even a rough sketch of theosophy can suggest how complex the system of thought is. Basically, and without the elaborations found in the major works of the movement, theosophy recognizes a seven-dimensional reality with corresponding individual forms in each dimension. The lowest dimension is the physical, that reality encountered and constructed in sensory experience. The physical body is the individual form located in this dimension, along with an etheric double. The etheric body is the instrument connecting the body to higher planes of reality. It both permeates the physical body and surrounds it as an energy field. It exists in the etheric dimension of reality (consisting of undetected electromagnetic areas).

A second dimension of reality houses the astral body. It is this body that is said to travel in out-of-body experiences. When at rest in the physical body, it can be seen (by those with the requisite abilities) as an aura, a spectrum of many colors that represent virtues and vices. In theosophy, the astral body is the locus of consciousness and the processor of data sensed by the physical body. Higher dimensions of reality are progressively more abstract and distant from the sensory world. The individual's task is to progress to higher states in successive incarnations.

Sulzman believes the most vital parts of theosophy are its unifying powers. It provides him with a view of the personality as a changing unity—feeling, acting, sensing, moving—against a more comprehensive background that fixes meaning on these changes. This larger context allows him to see events from a long-range perspective, not in any way diminishing their importance but calming and reassuring him when bad things happen. His creative energies increase dramatically when he realizes that there is more to existence than this life here and now. He is able to see himself and others within a transcendent reality that guides his efforts to achieve higher states of consciousness.

Sulzman believes that everything is part of a cosmic whole. For him, the highest state of consciousness and the lowest, inert rock are different aspects of one unchangeable reality. Like the violent emergence of empirical reality from a primordial big bang, all of reality for Sulzman derives from some common origin. He points out that water, steam, and ice look radically different from one another but are each manifestations of H_2O. In similar fashion, a human being may appear to be different from an insect, but the two forms of life are expressions of the same reality.

Meditation is crucial for Sulzman in gaining access to the foundations of reality. He has sensed in meditation the truth that all individual humans are processes or waves in a kind of cosmic sea, having existence from one perspective but only parts of a larger whole when viewed correctly. Sulzman does not denigrate human consciousness. Like classical theorists, he regards the individual mind as a transforming feature of the universe. In the absence of thinking and reflection as it occurs through the instrumentation of the cerebral cortex, the universe might be nothing, or perhaps just a passive state with none of the intelligible properties that consciousness recognizes. Sulzman believes that individual consciousness is a remarkable product that focuses reality in unique ways. His point is simply that the goal of human life is to move beyond this state by realizing the transcendent unity of reality within the self.

The fundamental law of the universe in theosophy is karma. This law states that an individual is the result of all of the acts in one's previous lives. One consequence of this understanding is that human action must be seen as an incremental effort set against the inertia of all earlier incarnations. Most people find this thought both encouraging and daunting. Actions must be judged from a time perspective considerably longer than the measure of any one person's life, and the chances of reaching an enlightened state must be measured against the additive consequences of a long history of past lives. *Destiny* is a good interpretation of karma, meaning that life is determined by forces beyond individual control. Yet followers of theosophy, like William Sulzman, believe that the effort must be made to attain this enlightened state, for the whole point of human life is to transcend it by moving to a higher dimension of reality.

Sulzman uses the idea of a connected yet layered reality to explain healing. He practices therapeutic touch. He admits that he does not fully understand how the therapy works. He does know that successful therapy requires that the healer be properly centered. For him this means that the center of one's being is stilled, the emotion and the intellect quieted, a harmony and connection to a universal order carefully set in a place at a conscious level. Then compassion must occur, a feeling for the person to be healed that is not exactly love or sympathy but a reflective concern for the other. Sulzman believes that in this mental state energy can be sent out to another person that will help the healing process.

Sulzman learned therapeutic touch from the originators. He took the early experimental classes organized by Dora Kunz in New York City. Kunz would bring a patient into the group of fifteen or twenty students and ask each student in the class to diagnose the patient's illness. The students would go over in pairs and sweep the patient's body with their hands. Then Kunz would move around the room and ask each student, "What did you feel?"

Sulzman remembers one woman Kunz brought in who looked perfectly normal in every respect. When it was his turn, he placed his hands over the woman's body while she sat quietly in a chair. Something felt different to Sulzman around the woman's eyes. Yet she was not wearing glasses, and she obviously was having no trouble seeing. Kunz went around the room asking for diagnoses, and Sulzman reported, "Well, I felt something around the eyes." Kunz nodded and went on to the next person until each student had offered an opinion on the woman's condition. Most centered the diagnoses on the woman's torso—the liver, the heart, the lungs, and so on. After everyone had spoken, Kunz announced that the woman had glaucoma. Sulzman was the only member of the class who had sensed a problem in the woman's eyes.

Sulzman was able to demonstrate this diagnostic talent in a number of subsequent classes. He found that it was better for him to work in back of the patient. He believes this was because he then avoided eye contact and a lapse into sentimentality. Time after time he and the other students would work on patients under Kunz's direction. Kunz would ask both the patient and the students what they felt during the sessions. Sulzman would get to a certain point on the patient's back and feel this tremendous heat pouring through his hands, often so much heat that later (when he conducted his own healing sessions) he would sometimes touch the back of his hand to the patient's skin to see if the heat came from that direction. It never did. The heat he felt was in his own hands as he diagnosed disease and then, later, began healing. Often in Kunz's classes another similarly gifted student would also feel heat around the same particular site on a patient's body and corroborate the diagnosis Sulzman offered.

The healing sessions Sulzman later conducted on his own were gratifying to him and to his patients. He kept everything simple and never considered himself a professional healer. He administers therapeutic touch mainly to friends and family on a need basis. He enjoys most those sessions with individuals who are skeptical (since he admits that believers could be imagining the cures). On one evening he and his wife were at the One World Festival (they do Scottish dancing) and one of the dancers came in for the performance looking awful. She showed every sign of coming down with the flu and felt as bad as she looked. The only reason she had even appeared was for the sake of the dance team Sulzman and his wife had organized for the festival.

Sulzman went over to her and asked her to sit quietly for a moment. "Why," she asked, "what are you going to do?" He passed his hands above the surface of her body and she immediately started feeling a heat go through her. Sulzman remembers her saying, "My God, this is amazing, what are you doing?" He said, "Does it bother you?" She said no. He asked her to keep quiet and talk about it later. The result was a dramatic improvement in her condition. No cure, no complete healing of the flu. But her energy level went up and she was able to dance without discomfort.

Sulzman sees the main effects of therapeutic touch in exactly this kind of rapid increase of energy levels. He believes that all therapy, conventional and unconventional, helps the body heal itself. He is convinced that therapeutic touch infuses energy into individuals from a higher level, and from this level into the whole person straight down through to the physical body. For this reason, he does not believe that healing works if the healer stays at the surface level of purely personal contact. It is not the charisma of the healer that is decisive, Sulzman believes, but the ability of the healer to address the whole person and release that deeper, more powerful energy that can radiate through the patient's entire being. Sulzman gives special attention to local sites of illness on the patient's body, but he aims his efforts at the whole energy field.

Not everyone accepts unconventional healing. Sulzman knows this. Once he was standing next to one of the male dancers in his troupe when the man complained of back pain. Sulzman spontaneously ran his hand down the dancer's back without touching him and felt a withdrawal of heat at a certain location. He touched the dancer's back at that spot and said, "It's there, isn't it?" The dancer looked at him and said, "You're weird."

But what Sulzman thinks is weird is that the scientific community has been so reluctant to examine therapeutic touch with an open mind. In his ideal world, both the healer and the patient would be scrutinized carefully according to the canons of the best empirical inquiry. Much healing fraud and many gullible patients would be dismissed in such an inquiry. But he believes a strong and broad residue would remain. Somewhere between utter skepticism and complete gullibility Sulzman sees that rock-hard universal reality which is accessible to the human intellect and the source for genuine healing.

MEDITATIVE HEALING

The goal of meditative healing is an abandonment of the discrete self and a fusion of healer and patient for a brief time during the healing session. No direct healing occurs. Healing is the consequence of the momentary transformation in both individuals. An altered state of consciousness is said to produce therapeutic benefits because both individuals enter a different reality. The healer attempts to bring to the one seeking therapy the healing forces of the larger natural world.

An individual viewing meditative healing from the outside may see nothing extraordinary even when the session is successful in reaching a different state of reality. In a two-person healing session, the therapist and patient typically sit across from one another in comfortable positions, perhaps even reclining in lounge chairs or on a sofa. Both individuals fall silent at the onset of the session and each begins meditating. The goal is to sense and merge with the other in the different reality sought through meditation. Nothing may appear to be happening because the two participants are engaged in mental efforts. The fusion, if it occurs, is psychic, not physical, and may involve no discernible movement at all. At the end of a brief period of time, say ten to fifteen minutes, the session ends and each individual usually relates the experience to the other.

In one session a man and a woman (who is the therapist) sit in her New York City apartment late in the afternoon meditating together in a healing session. The man's thoughts rocket in several directions as he tries to control his psychic energies and escape his physical fatigue. He is extremely relaxed, with good feelings seeming to radiate throughout his body. He thinks at first of becoming one with the objects in the room and tries to enter the inert state of being that is represented by the ashtray in front of him, the large painting of a woman in a leotard, two glass art objects of uncertain lineage, the coffee table. Then his thoughts suddenly jump to Key West, Florida, where he grew up, and then he is in St. Mary Star of the Sea Catholic Church where he served as an altar boy in his early youth. He can feel the Sunday morning heat and movement in the church while mass is being performed. At the corner of his right field of vision he can see the therapist. She raises her arms in a kind of supplication. The man's vision becomes more concrete as he allows the apartment setting to dominate again his meditation. After a few more moments pass the therapist sighs and says, "All right, tell me what you felt." He describes his experience and asks her to relate her own. She tells him that she felt his presence very strongly, though with enough space within it for the freedom of others, and that the two of them did become one during the session. The man is pleased that the session was successful and the two part amicably, almost fondly.

The meditation occurred on a Friday afternoon. That weekend the man had vivid dreams on successive nights. The first provided him with what he is convinced are fresh and important insights into his marriage. The second night he dreamed that he had a near-death experience, one so detailed that in the dream he reached out to crush some dry leaves in one of his hands to test tactile sensation. The sensations were so impressive that he concluded in the dream that he was not dreaming, that the experience was real. Skeptics among his friends offered an empirical interpretation of the dreams. When they heard that he had been suffering from a mild viral infection during the interviews, they explained the vivid dreams as neural activity stimulated by the effects of an active virus. Friends knowledgeable about psychic matters offered a different interpretation. They accepted his report as routine and told him that the meditation freed some blockages in his psyche. The vivid dreams were simply the natural result of his union with the therapist in an altered reality. Again, two incompatible but plausible (in context) explanations comfortably accord with the experiences.

What is the union of individuals that some claim occurs in psychic experiences? What does it mean to say that two individuals are one? Setting aside colloquial uses of language (as in mythical and unrealistic accounts of marriage), the merger of individual identities can mean several things. Arguably, the most common meaning is a transfer of one individual identity to the circumstances of another individual. When we wonder what it is to be another, we usually mean to ask what it would be like to have that person's profession, income, house, perhaps spouse and children. The commonplace attempts of academics and others (including political leaders) to enter the life world of certain classes of individuals fall under this category. The professional, for example, who lives on the street for a period of time to see what it is like to be homeless, or stays in prison to get a sense of incarceration, or tries to live at an income below the poverty line to see what it is like to be poor, or cohorts with rich people to see what being rich is like—any ethnographic or participant-observation experience is an effort to see the world from the circumstances of the other. The merger is largely (perhaps entirely) at the contextual level.

The limitations of such efforts are well known and even standard by now. In addition to the obvious drawback that such experiences are usually voyeuristic, the fantasies of a dilettante, it is easy to point out that even serious excursions into ways of life inevitably miss that which is most distinctive about the experience being investigated—its permanence. Trial marriages, prison visits, and temporary poverty do not duplicate the essential features of these experiences, for by definition they avoid the contextual traps that hold the occupants in their social conditions. Also, the visitor in other people's lives does not tap into the effects the conditions have on the perceptions of others. Try to imagine, as the reader of this book, what your perception would be like if the circumstances of life had denied you the possibility of reading a single book before this one in your entire life. What would you be like?

The main point, however, is that circumstantial identification is not identification with the self. More ambitious efforts are required to be the other. The nearest point away from the self as a discrete identity is the economic exercise of "extended sympathy." Here the individual tries to see the world from the perspective (and the circumstances) of the other. A variety of devices are used in this exercise. Imaginative renditions, as in fiction, are crucial. One individual reconstructs the views of another and tries to transport himself inside the other's perspective. The identity of the transported individual is not abandoned. The exercise asks this question, what is it like for me to be you while I retain some sense of myself?

The difficulty with this interpretation of extended sympathy is finding a balance between the two identities. The task is more or less demanding on different features of the self and the other. One can more easily imagine entering the emotive consciousness of a different other, becoming chronically angry or sentimental, and so on, than taking on the intellectual apparatus of another who is mentally distant. What would it be like to see the world through Einstein's eyes, or from the view of someone who is afflicted with Down's syndrome? It is not easy to see how one's own identity can be maintained while assuming the perspective of another who has the mental endowment to structure reality in radically different ways.

A more radical interpretation of extended sympathy beckons. One might try to become the other without maintaining self-identity in the exercise. Here the same problem of extending self to other occurs. But the effort can be imagined with others who are less like the self, the genius even, or the mentally retarded, so long as the original self can be abandoned completely and the other's mental resources are reasonable continuations of the self (not, say, a species distant from the human, like a hawk or spider). But finding the vocabulary to render the other's mental perspective intelligible is another matter. It may be impossible to translate such experiences back to one's own reality.

Meditative healing identifies this different reality as the site for fusion between healer and patient. The problems of identity that occur in sensory reality are unimposing in a dimension of experience that has already denied the separation of individuals as distinct egos. The key to success, then, becomes whether one can enter this other reality even if translation is impossible.

EDWARDS

Philip Edwards is a microbiologist with long-standing interests in the paranormal and psychic healing. A few years ago he signed up for a course on meditation given at a local college. One book on the reading list was Lawrence LeShan's *The Medium, the Mystic, and the Physicist*. Edwards read the book and immediately knew that he had to find out more about psychic healing. The instructor in the course turned out to be a close friend of LeShan and was able to steer Edwards into one of the training seminars LeShan had organized to disseminate the healing techniques he had developed. The workshop Edwards joined was taught by Joyce Goodrich, an instructor LeShan had trained himself.

The training sessions were held in an old house in Connecticut that had once been a Catholic monastery. The group of twelve students included a wide assortment of what Edwards considered ordinary people: a couple of therapists, a former priest, nurses, psychologists. They began with simple breathing exercises, attempts at visualization (imagining positive connections between the self and the world), some brief meditations, all interspersed with Goodrich's instruction on changing realities to make healing possible. On the fourth day, the group began deeper meditations, designed in particular to open the heart and generate compassion.

It was at that point that Edwards discovered emotions he had never encountered before. He simply opened up, his feelings flowing out in tears that seemed never to stop. He and the person next to him in the meditations began keeping a roll of toilet paper between them, sharing the tissues in wiping away their tears. By the time the group entered the stage of healing meditations, Edwards felt he was completely receptive to new realities. The instructor stressed that no healing as such was to be attempted; rather, the individuals were to try to move into a different level of consciousness with the other person in mind and then merge with that person in the altered state of mind.

The exercises involved one person in the group acting as patient, a kind of practice subject who would lie down in the middle of the group while the others would try to move into the altered state of consciousness along with the acting patient. The group was instructed to use visualization. One suggestion was to visualize one's self and the other person as being two trees, and then visualize the root systems under the ground intertwining. Another suggestion was visualizing two streams entering the ocean and becoming one. Those with religious backgrounds were urged to use religious imagery. Edwards had no religious background at all. He used natural visualization, utilizing his early training in physics to imagine persons as constituted by space and atoms and having the possibility of synthesizing with one another.

Edwards reports merging with the others on two occasions in the five-day session. It was, in his words, "a weird experience." He remembers the visualizations as seeming to take on a life of their own, controlling his thoughts and perceptions. He cannot find words to describe the experience, except that he tends to see them as field-effect phenomena where the individual enters a reality that is continuous in all respects. He believes that language breaks up experience into separate items and so is inadequate as an instrument to explain the merger experiences he had.

Edwards also refuses to use his training in scientific methodology to explain the experiences. As a physical scientist, he is used to isolating phenomena and performing experiments on them. But he sees the experiences in the healing workshop as relationships, and he believes that reducing any relationship to an isolated datum would be to deny its essentially connective nature. He also believes that experiences are inadequately depicted in the limited concepts of classical physics.

Edwards does not claim to have lost his identity, even momentarily, in the experience. He says that in two healing meditations he became one with the other person with some sense that he was still himself. He did not feel any contradiction in the experience. There was always a duality of self and other, but he was able somehow "to see how things are from the inside of somebody else." He sensed his subconscious taking over in a group that became like a close family. In his words: "One thing that I did was visualize myself with a person who was the healer. And then, with my eyes closed, at one point we just kind of teamed together and became one entity. That was not something I was trying to do. It just happened. It was a spontaneous merging in the visualization."

It is in this state of individual fusion that Edwards believes psychic healing occurs. One person does not consciously, intentionally, do something to another. It is the connecting in itself, he thinks, that produces the therapeutic benefits.

There was one apparent instance of a dramatic healing in the workshop. It turned out that a woman in the group had been diagnosed earlier as suffering from Lou Gehrig's disease. Both the Hershey Medical Center and Johns Hopkins had confirmed the presence of the disease. On the last day of the workshop, Goodrich told the group what the woman's problem was and asked for a real rather than a simulated healing session. The group went through the healing routine with the woman. Edwards remembers that the session was very emotional, the energy level in the room so high that it was almost palpable. After the workshop ended, the woman went back to both the Hershey Center and Hopkins. Edwards says no trace of the disease could be found. The physicians at both centers concluded that they had misdiagnosed the illness. Edwards stayed in contact with the woman for two or three years after that traumatic session. She is still well and healthy as far as he knows.

Edwards does not practice psychic healing regularly, though he continues the meditation exercises. He did go back for a second workshop, but has not really kept up with the training or literature. The experience did convince him that everything is more connected than he had ever realized, and so consciousness in one part of the system is going to affect other parts. He is also convinced that the healing power of the body can be augmented with meditation. These connections for him are as natural as anything he studies in the physical sciences.

KASTER

Gloria Kaster is a psychotherapist. In the 1960s she was one of many therapists trying to break from conventional methods of treatment. She was intrigued by what she now regards as putative distinctions between mind and body, in particular by the ways in which the states of the body affect the mind (rather than the reverse). Her work explored body awareness, or how individuals can have a type of physical knowledge without being conscious of it. In her therapy sessions, some strange things occurred when she introduced techniques to make individuals more aware of their bodily responses to the environment. In one sequence of awareness sessions, she noticed that the members of the therapy group were picking up on each other's habits. Unconscious mimicry occurred. Some individuals began responding to the mental images of others. One person would be having trouble with another person in the group and say she imagined a horrible person, a witch, for example. The person so transmogrified in the other's thoughts would begin feeling bad, even without knowing that she was the target of these negative feelings. Kaster knew that these transferences should not be happening according to every scientific principle she had ever learned. But they *were* happening. So she began trying out a different, more controversial way of conceptualizing what she was observing. She began thinking that energy from one body could go into another.

Love relationships seemed especially appropriate for this concept of energy transference. A typical situation would be what the romantic calls love at first sight. People would be drawn to one another in almost magnetic fashion, often against all reasonable understandings of self-interest. After awhile the relationship would sour and the couple could not understand why. If the contact was prolonged, the individuals could end up hating one another. Kaster would have couples in therapy who would literally become ill in each other's presence and wanted nothing more than to escape the relationship and perhaps even destroy the other. This came from people who a short time before were completely, absolutely in love with each other.

Kaster began using an energy-transfer metaphor in trying to understand this pattern of behavior. She speculated that in the early stages of a relationship (the love part), each individual was giving energy to the other, which was absorbed successfully. Then, as the energy transfer continued, the givers would feel drained. They were made sick by the depletion of some kind of psychic energy, something lost in the intense love relationship. Kaster recognized that this metaphor sounds like the wildest kind of superstition if introduced as an explanation for any type of human behavior. But then the standard psychological categories could not explain the emotive pattern of attraction and revulsion either. All Kaster knew at this stage in her therapy work was that some kind of tacit response was occurring that the participants could not grasp or even control at the conscious level of the self, no matter how successful their therapy might be in recovering forgotten and repressed experiences.

At about this time, Kaster began exploring the literature in parapsychology to see if any helpful insights or theories could be found there. Nothing seemed relevant in this work. But she did come across an advertisement for a seminar on psychic healing conducted by Lawrence LeShan. She called LeShan and asked him whether the seminar was to be about psychic healing, or was he going to do psychic healing. LeShan answered, "We are going to do psychic healing." Kaster said, "Sign me up."

It was at this seminar that Kaster saw a more refined way to state her intuitions about energy transfer. LeShan described his thesis on Type I and II healings. In Type I healing, individuals meditate and enter that different reality that encourages the body (or mind) to heal itself. The wisdom of the universe and the organism will bring about the proper therapy. All the therapist does in the meditative session is seek a harmony between the larger natural world and the patient. Type II healing is closer to magic. The therapist finds and uses powers that can heal or harm depending on their use. Kaster remembers LeShan warning the group about the danger of Type II healing, even in its more benign forms as the "laying on of hands" of faith healing traditions. It is too narrow a focus for healing, she remembers LeShan telling the class, and can lead to a blowup in other bodily illnesses even when curing the immediate problem. LeShan used her metaphor of energy transfer to explain the danger in Type II healing. Putting energy into one part of the body can cause other vectors and domains of the energy field to go out of balance. At last Kaster had a theoretical reference for her intuitions.

In the weeks and months following her first seminar in psychic healing, Kaster studied everything she could find on the subject. Events in her life convinced her of the truth of these claims for healing powers and meditations. Once she was a member of a leaderless therapy group of therapy group leaders (a kind of therapist-heal-yourself session without anyone to direct it). The group was meeting on the terrace of a sixteenth-floor apartment in New York City overlooking Central Park West. She remembers the setting as beautiful. But the man sitting next to her was feeling very depressed and was more than willing to share his depression with others. It turned out that his wife was very sick with renal failure and he had to get a dialysis machine into their home to treat her. It was a genuinely sad story, and as the man told it he became more and more depressed.

Kaster was distressed over the man's situation and thought he needed to be picked up a bit emotionally. So she began transferring energy to him in the way she had learned in Type II healing. The man kept talking with no awareness of what Kaster was doing, but his demeanor became more cheerful, a note of optimism began appearing in the accounts he was providing of his life. Then he got up from the sofa and went over to stand by the railing overlooking Central Park. By this time he was telling the group how great he felt, so good in fact that he thought he could actually spread his wings and fly across the park. Kaster started pulling back the energy so fast that she felt like she was running across a psychic landscape. The man came down from his emotional high and returned to the sofa with more moderate perspectives on his life and powers. Kaster came away from the session with a renewed appreciation of the dangers in Type II healing.

On another occasion she was in the audience during a performance by one of the Living Theatre ensembles. At the end of the play, the actors gathered on stage and, in a gesture common in the 1960s, invited the audience to join hands with them. Kaster was at the theater that evening with a black judge in the city's judicial system. The man, according to Kaster, was very uptight and wanted nothing to do with tribal superstitions and the like. Nevertheless, he joined hands with her and the others. Kaster knew what was coming. She could feel the energy move from her hands through his body. The judge said (in atypical language for him), "Wow, I can feel it, it's going through me." It was indeed, according to Kaster. Only she was "turned off" by the display of public energy transfer on that evening because she regarded it as exploitive. Real, but also very show biz in that setting.

Kaster believes that there is something in the universe that we do not understand and cannot name. This something, which she calls theos (Greek for god), is for Kaster the energy that heals. In meditation a reality can be reached where theos suffuses everything. In this sense, Kaster believes pantheism is true of the reality known during the altered state of consciousness. God is in us and in everything in that world sought and found through meditation. In ordinary reality polytheism reigns. Theos is distributed as diverse pockets of energy. It can be found in a mountain, in a tree, in a spring, in the stones of the Wailing Wall in Jerusalem, in cathedrals, at Lourdes. Kaster believes that this energy can be owned, packaged, bought and sold, exchanged for other bunches of energy. It is a commodity no stranger to her than nuclear energy, electricity, or gravity. She believes that theos can be used for good or bad purposes (white or black magic) and is the stuff that is stored by shamans and sorcerers to practice their magic. Type II healing depends on pockets of theos used in the therapy sessions. She can feel this energy as a psychic current whenever she touches some source where it has accumulated.

The healing Kaster practices in her therapy sessions is meditative. Her patients do not completely abandon their identities in meditation, though she confesses to a chronic puzzlement over exactly who or what we are in ordinary reality.

She points out that individuals sit in chairs that are mostly empty space, congeries of particles joined by forces that are not really understood. Persons are also compositions of space and particles. She sees no insurmountable problem in merging these different compositions with each other, one person with another and persons with their surrounding reality. She sees no individual identity that will resist fusion with a reality that is, after all, continuous with persons. Separateness, she feels, is an illusion.

All matter, both living and inert, is part of the natural world and has equal status in Kaster's ontology. This view leads to well-known perplexities. It implies that the HIV virus and the human body have equal standing in nature. How, then, can therapy designed to eradicate the virus from its human host be justified? Kaster, like many healers, sees the human person as an organism with the power to reach an optimal state of equilibrium. This balance may be expressed as an internal and external harmony (or balance within the self, and between the self and nature). A human being in a state of harmony will have an immune system that can defend the body against the HIV virus. The ideal state for humans is one free of illness, and it is this state that can be achieved through successful meditation. (Presumably the HIV virus does not meditate and so is at a comparative disadvantage.) Kaster does not avoid modern medicine, however. If she is coming down with pneumonia, she goes for an antibiotic without a second thought. But meditation is the more basic approach for her. It does not address disease. It is a method for healing the whole person.

There is also no doubt in Kaster's mind that a few individuals have special healing abilities. Some can easily bring others to the proper meditative levels and release the energies needed to heal the person. Others can appropriate and direct bundles of healing energies at appropriate illnesses and to sites on the body. She reports that when she is the recipient of a powerful healing she finds that her lips will curl up automatically in a little smile. The first time it happened she thought, "like the Mona Lisa," which she reminds us is a painting of a model who was being lavished with all the immediate attention of one of the geniuses of the era. That smile—the feeling of well-being—represents for Kaster the glow of a deliberate type of meditative healing.

The thoughtful reader will also recall the languid smile of the model in Goya's *Naked Maja*. Or the compassion and grief of the Virgin Mary in Michelangelo's *Pietà*. Or, at a more melancholy level, the sad smile of Thomas Canterbury's mother as she died with the comfort of a beneficent and swift passage from life.

LeShan

Lawrence LeShan entered the field of the paranormal because, at one point in his life, he was "very, very tired." He has a doctorate in psychology. His graduate training included the usual empirical methods required of all psychology students, including statistics and research designs. To this day he can run a rat through a maze, though he no longer remembers why anyone bothered to run rats through mazes. He even claims to have invented the ideal maze back in the early 1940s, twenty years too late for most research agendas.

The United States Army summoned LeShan for a tour of duty during World War II. There he received what he still considers superb training in clinical psychology, a field he maintains the Army invented to meet its own medical needs. He spent three years in a psychiatric hospital, working, learning, trying not to do any harm to the patients while attempting to master the main approaches in psychotherapy of the time. He still regarded himself as an experimental psychologist, however, and to this day defines his work in research terms. Put simply, LeShan sees a problem he wants to solve, finds someone (a foundation, a business, an individual) to pay for the research, and does the work.

After leaving the Army, LeShan began working exclusively with dying people, primarily terminally ill cancer patients. His research project was aimed at developing different and more effective psychotherapy for the medically hopeless. The work was exceptionally demanding and conducted with little knowledge of what might work. LeShan did forge a number of effective techniques and supporting theories in the fifteen years he devoted to this effort. But in the end he burned out, even before the phrase was invented. He had always believed that objectivity in psychotherapy is absurd and best deciphered as the therapist's ability to support the mental growth of the patient. This commitment to the patient turned out to be both affirmation and destruction. His patients responded well until they died. LeShan ended up exhausted. He walked away and began looking for something else.

The field of parapsychology intrigued him for perverse reasons. He had always regarded claims for psychical experiences with the usual skepticism of those in conventional forms of psychology. But he was also intrigued by the number of outstanding intellects who took parapsychology seriously. Some of the leading thinkers of the past and current century have accepted the paranormal— individuals like William James, Gardner Murphy—and LeShan wanted to know why. He even whimsically considered discovering and naming the disease afflicting all these famous people, perhaps calling it the LeShan syndrome. It would describe a complicated intellectual failing that at once led scholars into a pseudoacademic discipline while allowing them to do very good work in their own fields.

So LeShan began his studies. In solid Aristotelian fashion he reviewed the literature, sure that he would be able to discover the academically fatal attraction and dismantle it. But many of the research designs, statistics, and data he encountered were impressively tight. He could not find the flaws he had been sure were there. He read further. It began to seem to him that parapsychology was legitimately describing a different way for humans to relate to one another, to communicate and be with one another, and that this set of relations might be the most important task that he could possibly be involved with at this time in his life and in human history. He decided to enlist.

LeShan's first working assignment was with Eileen Garrett, a psychic with a wide reputation for unusual powers. Garrett had invited him to monitor the experiments that psychic investigators conducted with her. LeShan's job was to ensure that the research was methodologically sound. He did this for five years. He came away from this working relationship with two conclusions. One was that Garrett was an ethical and highly principled woman. The other was that she had extraordinary gifts that suggested the validity of paranormal experiences.

LeShan observed Garrett doing things that could not be explained with the standard scientific frameworks he had absorbed for his research in psychology. Very often these feats would be accomplished under LeShan's own experimental conditions. Some of the more impressive exercises were carried out in assisting the police. LeShan says that a man would be on the national missing persons list, someone Garrett had never met and knew nothing about. LeShan would bring her a piece of the shirt the man wore the day before. She would then, according to LeShan, make very specific statements about where the man was or what he was doing: that he was going to Mexico on a bus, or sitting on a porch with some people dressed in outlandish clothes, or that he had lost all the hair on his body. That kind of statement would emerge and turn out to be very accurate. LeShan came to believe that sometimes people had information they couldn't possibly have had, very specific information, and the only way to explain this phenomenon was with psychic frameworks.

Once, in the late 1960s, LeShan was conducting an experiment with Garrett in veridical dreaming. Each morning at 2:00 A.M. a man in Brooklyn would pick out a picture using a random number selector and look at it, concentrating as hard as he could. Then he would call Garrett, waking her up, and ask her to recall her dreams. He would write down the description she provided. Sometimes Garrett would write the report. Then, later, experimenters would try to identify common features of the picture and written report. It is a widely used experiment, and variations on it seem endless.

One morning Garrett came into LeShan's office and related a strange dream. She said that Whately Carington, a well-known psychic researcher who worked with her in the 1920s , had come into her room during the night. This nocturnal presence was especially odd since Carington had died in 1947. Carington told her that she had to do two things for him. One, Garrett was to take care of his wife "because she needs you very badly at this moment." Second, Carington complained that all his papers were being ruined because they were under a bed and a wallaby was sleeping on them. LeShan remembers that he and Garrett giggled a bit, and then the researcher came in and reported an absolute bust for the morning's correlation. The dream had nothing to do with the picture.

The next day Garrett reported having a variation on the same dream. This time Carington had come into her room in an angry state. He said to her that he had asked her to do something for his wife and she had done nothing. He told her it was a very serious situation. He was so mad, Garrett reported, that he had thrown her out of bed. She had awakened on the floor.

Garrett was troubled. "I know myself," she told LeShan. She felt that they should do something about the situation. A group effort began to locate Carington's wife. Someone called Garrett's secretary and instructed her to join the search efforts. Someone else called the Society for Psychic Research in London. No one knew where Mrs. Carington was. Finally Garrett called someone very high in Internal Revenue, someone she both knew and had something on. He reluctantly agreed to assist in the efforts. An hour later he called back and said that Carington's wife lived in a cottage out on the moors in Devon. Garrett made one more demand. "Call the Devon tax office and on any excuse send one of their people out there." The man agreed to make the request.

Six hours later the phone rang. Yes, Mrs. Carington is fine, the Devon tax office reported. She is in the hospital. The tax assessor had gone out to her cottage and found her. She was lying on the floor with a broken hip. She had been in that position for two days, eaten one apple, soiled herself, no one expected for two more days. She would almost certainly have died had not the tax assessor appeared.

Later Garrett arranged a search for the despoiled papers. They were found also, under the designated person's bed, but they were absolute useless nonsense—a collection of tax bills, laundry lists, things that should have been thrown out years ago. The second part of the spiritual request did not match the profundity of the first part. But LeShan had witnessed the report of the dream, taken part in the effort to locate Mrs. Carington, was present in the office when the phone call came through reporting the rescue. He cannot stretch empirical frames of explanation to fit such situations without giving up his sanity.

Still, even after his five years with Garrett, LeShan remained puzzled and uncertain about the paranormal. One problem that persistently bothered him was the theory-deprived state of paranormal inquiry. The study of the paranormal had started as a set of theories in search of data. The acceptance of spiritual causes and mystical explanations, after all, can be traced to the origins of human history. But then the various mechanistic and general empirical approaches to experience celebrated in modern science displaced spiritual theories of being. The anomaly, on LeShan's understanding, was that the data on paranormal events began accumulating more rapidly under scientific controls. The result was a mass of data looking for a theory. LeShan resolved to provide such theory and the techniques for teaching psychic skills, or find a method to explain away what he was observing.

But why turn to psychic healing? LeShan has a pragmatic approach to theory. He insists on subjecting theories to tests of usefulness when deciding on his research priorities. The paranormal is important to him because it demonstrates that people are related to one another in some way beyond the senses, and this knowledge is important in a secular age of isolated individualism. But LeShan also requires that theory be expressed in language that fits reality and that it be made into a practical tool. Which part of the paranormal can be a useful tool? Telepathy? No, electronic communication will always be better. Clairvoyance? No, because if you want to find out what is in a sealed envelope, get a letter opener. But psychic healing might be useful, for the restoration of health can always be improved, even given the advances in conventional medicine. So LeShan moved into psychic healing.

The first question he raised in his early inquiries is basic enough. Is there a phenomenon? He reviewed the data and concluded that even in the best cases 90 percent of the claims had to be thrown out. The patient forgot to mention that he had received a penicillin injection that morning, or the placebo effect could explain the improvement—that sort of disqualifying consideration discredited most of the best psychic healings. Also, spontaneous remissions fall within medical expectations, and many healings could be explained that way. But he found some cases, maybe 10 percent of the very best, that he couldn't throw out easily. To do so would be to stretch coincidence or spontaneous remissions too far. LeShan looked at these cases with one controlling question: How does psychic healing work when it succeeds?

LeShan pressed this question on healers from the ancient Greeks to the present, scanning written explanations and interviewing serious healers when possible. He catalogued four types of accounts. One, God healed. Two, spirits did it. Three, energy brought healing. Or, four, it was mysterious, inexplicable. None of these met LeShan's intellectual needs. God requires human hands to work, he believes, and so the first explanation devolves to human levels, which leaves the causal powers still unexplained. He refused to do research on spirits, since they seem to appear and disappear at will, leaving the filed healing effect too glibly explained as "the spirits are not here." He viewed energy as a hopeless variable. Healers "didn't know anything more about energy than a cat knows about Christmas." They mixed it literally and metaphorically, sometimes referring to the energy in a Picasso painting, the energy in a group discussion, the energy in an electric light bulb. It made no sense to LeShan.

But he did isolate two categories that appealed to his sense of intellectual economy and decorum. One category was heterogeneous and could be set aside. It consisted of the full range of idiosyncratic things that healers did. They would line up facing in some geographical direction, or they would chant, sing hymns, pray, or they would wash themselves, whatever—all of the different groups of healers would have specific rituals that often distinguished them from each other. But they all did one single thing, a move that was generalizable to all of the healers he studied. It constituted LeShan's second category. At some point in their procedures, all of the healers changed their consciousness. They claimed to have shifted away from the conventional or commonsense reality where the world is a uniform whole. Most of the healers he scrutinized did not regard this shift as important, but to LeShan it looked like the critical variable. And it was a variable he could isolate and study empirically.

LeShan began trying to change his own consciousness. Meditation seemed to be the key. He studied and used every meditative technique he could find. Ever the pragmatist, LeShan saw meditation as an instrument to alter the state of one's mind, much like Nautilus machines are tools to change one's body. He followed a strict regimen, meditated six to eight hours a day, five days a week, for about a year and a half, surpassing some of the most assiduous body builders in dedication to craft. He would try each of the various meditative techniques for about six weeks, carefully evaluating the method for its effectiveness. Then he would retain the methods that worked, discard those that failed. He also paid careful attention to the explanations offered for the steps purporting to lead from ordinary consciousness to the "world of one" consciousness. At the end of his studies and efforts, he felt he had identified and mastered (at a reasonable level) a set of procedures that could take him to the altered state of consciousness found in psychic healings.

At this point he was still skeptical. It was when he started getting results as a healer that "scared the living hell out of me" that he became a believer. His first case was pure drama. A woman came to him with severe arthritis in her hands. She had not been able to close her fingers into a first for over a year. There was a heavy calcium overlay on the joints. LeShan recalls that at that point in his work he had to have absolute silence to ensure the level of concentration needed to enter the different state of consciousness. (Later he learned how to do it even while at Times Square.) The woman's family tip-toed into the next room, and he was left with a "patient" who asked him, "What do I do?" LeShan had no idea. He asked her what she wanted to do. She said that there was an article in the *New York Times* that she had been trying to read. LeShan said, "Fine. Read it." Then, while the woman read the *Times*, LeShan shifted his consciousness several times, clearly holding the altered state for maybe two or three seconds (as much as he can achieve even now, he humbly reports). In this state he and the other person in the focus of his consciousness are one, and he claims to enter a universe of inexorable logic where all things flow into each other. Separateness is revealed as an illusion.

At the end of the meditation, LeShan turned to the woman and asked, "What did you feel?"

She answered, "Nothing."

LeShan persisted. "What happened?"

"Nothing," she replied. Her family came into the room and asked her what had happened.

"Nothing," she said, "except that in Washington, D.C., the politicians are doing . . . ," going on to relate the contents of the article she had read.

"How are your hands?" they asked.

"Just the same," she said, and at that point she raised them up to demonstrate and flapped them back and forth. Somehow complete mobility had been restored. Both LeShan and the woman's family virtually went into shock. The woman did also when she realized what had happened. X rays taken thirty-six hours later revealed a 50 percent reduction in the calcium overlay. LeShan had no idea where that calcium had gone. He did know that if that level of calcium were injected suddenly into the lymphatic system the patient would be lucky to survive. He didn't, and doesn't, know what happened. But that is the kind of result he says he started to get through psychic healing.

LeShan admits that a good healer who is honest will admit to maybe a 20 percent success rate, one in five cases that are genuine cures, *on a good day*. He considers himself a moderately competent healer, a good hack. The theories he studied suggest that healers must be in a state of grace, or possessed of a personality quirk, to work their craft successfully. He has never noticed either of these two features in his own set of characteristics. Nor has he ever had a paranormal experience. He has simply observed them in others. Yet meditative healing worked when he tried it. So he regarded it not as an arcane talent, but as a set of acquirable skills. He resolved to teach these skills to others.

The training sessions he developed with Joyce Goodrich were the result of this resolution. When he first put them together in California, he developed the reputation of conducting the only residential seminars where everybody slept in their own beds. This was not because of LeShan's moral concerns, but because the participants were so exhausted at the end of the day that they looked forward only to sleep. He works novitiates hard. He uses techniques that urge meditation of body, emotions, and mind (or intellect). LeShan believes that the fastest progress is made by jolting individuals back and forth between these three types of meditations, the day consisting of a constant shifting from one to the other. Everyone is also placed in the role of both healer and subject. The sessions are intense. LeShan claims that 80–90 percent of the participants get it at the end of a five- to six-day seminar. Some are more successful than others. But in his experience, success is correlated with practice, not some innate talent (whatever that means). Meditation for LeShan is a very tough discipline, and he is all business in teaching and using it.

The screening methods used in the seminars do not seem very rigorous from an outsider's point of view. Using interviews, the seminar conveners screen out those people on power trips. They also make every candidate promise that they will never (a) take money or gifts for their healing efforts, or (b) treat anyone who is not under a doctor's care. Also, they try to deny admission to those who have rigid personalities. Otherwise, a wide variety of individuals seek and gain admission.

One mark of a developed science is that the researchers know why things do *not* work as well as why they do. LeShan, though, has no idea why healing fails. He claims that we have working knowledge of only one of the three variables that seem to operate in psychic healing. One is what the healer should do. This is where LeShan claims knowledge. A second is what the patient should do. Here LeShan admits to ignorance. The third variable comprises a set of factors that he argues cannot even be identified, much less used as explanatory devices. Here LeShan classifies all of the considerations in mystic philosophies from the beginning of history: Homer's gods, spirits of all types, God in every religion, karma—the concepts, in short, that explain what leads to success or failure in some grand sense beyond the immediate pragmatics of the experience.

LeShan's approach to this third set of factors is at once tentative and ambitious. He reads the esoteric schools (those who advance philosophical or theological explanations for psychic healing) as agreeing on two ways of being in the universe, the way of the one and the way of the many. We are half divine, half empirical self, part mind and part body. All of the philosophies of psychic healing agree that full humanness requires both of these dimensions of reality. LeShan believes (with many others) that we are highly practiced experts in the way of the many, able to negotiate our journey through a sensory reality that we often take as the only level of being. But he maintains that denying the way of the one is to distort existence. It is to cut ourselves off from that spiritual nourishment that provides the needed balance away from the way of the many. For LeShan, the effective healer invites the person into the way of the one for a moment, allowing the person to realize a human potential that is beyond that fixed by the sensory world. In this sense, LeShan asserts, there is technically no psychic healing as such. There is self-healing, made possible by entrance into a different and vital level of being.

LeShan professes ignorance about the extent of such healing possibilities. He claims success in speeding the mending of fractured bones and wounds, alleviating arthritis and bursitis, migraines, and so forth. But he regards psychic healing as an undeveloped field, with knowledge gaps so great that no limits can be set on what might be possible. He concedes that there are probably only six or seven experiments in the paranormal field that really stand up before any bar of science. They are tight and convincing but limited in number and scope. In LeShan's view, paranormal studies have not advanced since the year 1800. He says this cannot be said of any other field, including medicine, dentistry, painting, sculpture, and architecture, though he might be persuaded to concede philosophy as a regressive case.

The puzzle for LeShan is not the status of neurology. He admits that we know what is going on in only a few small areas of the brain. But the deeper conundrum as he sees it is in the connections between the functions of the brain and consciousness, the bridges between the electrochemical changes in the physical brain and the complex functions of the conscious self. He still regards Descartes as having made the first heroic effort to connect body and mind, but with little success. LeShan quotes Arthur Eddington's famous observation approvingly: "The brain function resembles consciousness as a telephone number resembles the subscriber."

In the early 1940s, LeShan was working his way toward a master's degree and was teaching a speech class that addressed the problem of stuttering. Children would come in convinced that they were beginning to stutter because, like the centipede that couldn't walk when asked how he did it, others had pointed out a small speech impediment and had made them self-conscious. They wanted to learn how to take conscious control of their speaking abilities. LeShan's technique was to convince them to lose control and forget their "problems." One day he gave the students an unusual assignment. They were to listen to Lowell Thomas, the master radio commentator at the time, and count the flubs he made. The students said Thomas never made a mistake. LeShan said, "Count them tonight." They concentrated. Lowell Thomas made twelve errors. The students were elated. The point was made that everyone committed errors. But then LeShan was inspired to go further. He asked the class to relate the news Thomas had delivered. They had no idea. They hadn't been listening. They had given up the symphony for the notes.

LeShan uses this story to illustrate levels of reality. One can construe reality as a seamless garment, fixed at a holistic level, or one can see it as a place where discrete items define experience. Either way is valid in LeShan's approach. But psychic healing requires that the individual shift consciousness, move from the notes to the music, and know in the shift that the universe is constructed as a uniform whole where one's own consciousness fuses with the other's consciousness. LeShan believes that this shift can be achieved through a teachable method of meditation, sometimes by the numbers and sometimes tailored for the particular person, but in either case leading to remarkable and only partially explained healings of both body and mind.

LeShan greatly admires Gertrude Schmeidler and loves her metaphor for the paranormal. Imagine being in a forest where we keep hearing the noises of a large animal thrashing about. We see branches waving and broken off, large footprints, bark sheared off trees, stool droppings. We smell the animal. We sense its presence. We know there is something huge in this forest, even though we have not seen it. LeShan believes that we occasionally even have a photograph of it. This usually terrifies people into a kind of irrational denial, because to accept the photograph, to see the animal, to believe in the paranormal, would require abandoning conventional understandings of reality. LeShan is convinced that this is impossible for most people, and so he sees the paranormal chronically being denied, even though its presence is everywhere around us.

PART III

The Physician and the Patient

CHAPTER 10

The Physician and the Patient

From this hospital bed
I can hear an engine
breathing – somewhere
in the night:

– Soft coal, soft coal,
soft coal!

And I know it is men
breathing
shoveling, resting –
William Carlos Williams, excerpt from *The Injury*

SCIENTIFIC MEDICINE AND THE PHYSICIAN

The doctor–poet William Carlos Williams writes of the uneasy bedside meeting of the person and the machine, the patient transposed as a machine. Contemporary physicians, patients and health care systems in most parts of the world reflect this uneasiness. The body, which still is a person, is also acting like a machine. The realization that bodies are also people complicates the task of medicine, for people have emotions, character and unpredictability. This chapter surveys the nervous attempts to mesh human and machine in the encounters between physicians and patients.

Medical interventions are often predicated on more than an analogy of a machine – the body is not just *like* a machine, but *is*, in important respects, a machine. The increasingly common high-technology medical procedures such as scans, computer imaging, organ transplants, radiotherapy and chemotherapy for long-term conditions such as cancer, heart disease and AIDS are predicated quite explicitly on the idea of the body as a machine. The philosophy that justifies such procedures is in most contemporary biomedicine unabashedly materialist. That is, it assumes that life can be described in terms of *material* (rather than spiritual or intangible) forces which can be observed with the eye or perceived directly and unproblematically with the senses. From repeated observations and experiments in clinical and laboratory settings, laws of cause and effect can be formulated in precise, perhaps even mathematical terms. In medical genetics, for example, DNA is described in the language of geometry – the famous 'double helix'. Bodily functions and body parts are described in ever smaller – hence 'reduced' – units. DNA is a reduction of the genes; genes are a reduction of complex physical (and increasingly, mental and behavioural) traits; these traits are themselves a reduction of complex phenomena relating to the person that the doctor or clinician has observed and has further 'reduced' from the wider psychological, social and historical context.

This materialism in medicine is a form of reductionism, in that it attempts to describe observed or reported bodily processes, diseases or states at some more abstract level. The task of the physician imbued with this philosophy is to transform the rich complexity of what is observed and the multifaceted talk, conduct or story of the patient into something that is meaningful in diagnostic terms. As Waitzkin (1983: ch. 6; 1991) has demonstrated in his research analysing the micropolitics of doctor–patient interactions, it is important to strip away the social and emotional contexts of patients' presentations, in order to arrive at the physical problem and the corresponding medical intervention. Once such a reduction has been accomplished, the path is open to diagnosis and treatment. Although the social context of a patient's presentation is not ignored, Waitzkin's research (1991: 259) suggests that it is marginalized and not considered intrinsic to solving the health problem at hand. Others have argued that this marginalization actually damages health. Thus, Finkler (1991: 126) contends that, '[b]y not incorporating information about the family and life world in which the patient is embedded, the medical consultation aggravates rather than allays the crisis for the patient and accentuates the drama'.

Contemporary medicine considers itself a scientific activity and appeals to the social institutions and imagery of 'science' as a source of legitimacy, probity and integrity. Science, in turn, concerns itself with 'systematic' explanations of phenomena in terms of cause and effect. Using experimental research methods, it arrives at explanations through the isolation of an object of study (the body, organs, behaviour etc.) and the specification of conditions and applications for which causality holds. For example, microbes might be established as the cause of disease through some named channel of infection of the body. Through such procedures, medicine as a branch of science aims to identify facts and formulate general laws. In medicine, laws appear in the correspondence between diagnostic taxonomies – names for ailments – and illness states which are elaborated as to their onset, course, duration and outcome. Over time, through laboratory and clinical experience, facts accumulate, and on this basis symptoms of disease, disease states and remedies can be named and entered into the knowledge base. The aim of these endeavours is to formulate predictive forms of knowledge so that facts about the body in general and individual clinical histories in particular can be deployed to predict the trajectories that illness will take.

Through recording actual clinical consultations, or the 'medical encounter', sociologists and anthropologists have illustrated many of these aspects of contemporary biomedicine. The consultation is the forum in which biomedical theory and scientific assumptions meet lay expressions of the experience of illness. In the encounter, the personal, social and psychological contexts of sickness that are brought by the patient are translated by the physician into terms that are intelligible in biomedicine. This does not mean that physicians are rude or inconsiderate, only that an important part of their job is translation. In her study of physicians in Mexico, Finkler (1991) draws attention to the orchestrating of patients' presentations into a medical script. In keeping with the Western individualistic idea of a continuous narrative self, the contextual information regarding social roles, work, marriage and sex, for example, is rendered into what may be clinically significant to the physical body. The work of the physician is pressed into persuading patients to see their bodies and illnesses in biomedical terms. Thus, the belief in the heritability of illness is encouraged by frequent questioning about patients' parents' ailments, as this segment from one of Finkler's (1991: 130) transcripts shows:

DOCTOR: From May 1986 till the present you had an alteration in arterial pressure. It goes up and it goes down. It relaxes. Do you sweat?
PATIENT: It goes up and down in the morning, when it is very high and very low.
D: And how did you get it?
P: Well . . .
D: Do you study? Work? Or what do you do?
P: I work and I study.
D: What kind of work do you do and what are you studying?
P: I work in an auditor's office.
D: Auditor.
P: And I am studying public accountancy.
D: Are there people in your family – father, mother, grandfather – that have high blood pressure?
P: I don't know.
D: Your mother, what did she die of?
P: Heart.
D: What heart problem did she have?
P: I don't know. I was one and a half years old.
D: Did anyone have angina pectoris, heart arrest, or, what was the problem? You should ask your father what she had.
P: I think she had a heart operation.
D: She had a heart operation. Probably she had a traumatic problem, maybe the valvular, due to rheumatism, rheumatic cardiopathy. You were two and a half?
P: A year and a half.
D: A year and a half, correct. And your father is alive? What health problems does he have?

Science views itself as an 'advanced' system of thought and practice because it is predicated on reason and what it presents as 'objective' methods of apprehending the physical world. As such it has become a cosmology, a totalizing and definitive view of the universe and what is universal. It sees itself, as philosopher of science Thomas Kuhn (1962) famously pointed out in *The Structure of Scientific Revolutions*, as progressing in a linear manner. Each new generation of scientists considers itself to be building upon the foundations inherited from the previous generation. Most scientists believe that science is a superior system for generating understanding and knowledge, and, following the popular evolutionary metaphor, scientists represent science as chronologically subsequent to other ways of understanding the world. Science is built up incrementally through continuous augmentations of knowledge, which are made possible by 'discoveries', 'break-throughs' and research employing methods of investigation which are accepted as objective by the community of scientists. Non-Western and previous systems of explanation are held by many contemporary scientists to be poor relations, infused with the biases of religion and superstition. In fact, some prominent medical historians discount much of Western medical history prior to the twentieth century (see Thomas, 1983). As Lester King (1982: 6) remarks of his own medical training in the 1930s, 'the great rush of progress produced the viewpoint that modern medicine differed markedly from that of the past, and that only now, in what we call the electronic age, was medicine at *last* truly scientific.' Concomi-tantly, it has also been assumed that, with time, other forms of medical therapy – folk healing, alternative therapies and the like – would disappear as medical science made ever more progress in conquering disease. The sheer superiority of the methods, technology and efficacy of biomedicine would expose such alterna-tives as increasingly marginal to the modern world (O'Connor, 1994: 17).

Important to the legitimation of science is the assumption that, in contrast to religious and other systems of knowledge, its procedures are objective and value free. The construct of objectivity, as sociologist Will Wright (1992: 23) has explained, gives science a 'desperate privilege', so that in Western societies, knowledge is virtually equated with the achievements of science. In relation to medicine, the doctor, as a 'professional', stands outside both personal and social prejudices. The patient is perceived purely in terms of the illness or disorder in question. In this way, objectivity is thought to be achieved, so that whatever is discovered about disease will be all the more valid. This is in marked opposition to other forms of knowledge and other healing systems, which are often con-ceived by medical scientists to be simply incorrect and at variance with what is known about the workings of the human body and disease. In his illuminating discussion of clinical medicine in connection with anthropology, Good (1994: 8) makes this point well:

> Medical knowledge . . . is constituted through its depiction of empirical biological reality. Disease entities are resident in the physical body; whether grossly apparent, as the wildly reproducing cells of a cancer, or subtly evident through their effects, as in the disordered thoughts and feelings of schizophrenia or major depression, dis-eases are biological, universal, and ultimately transcend social and cultural context. Their distribution varies by social and ecological context, all medical scientists agree, but *medical knowledge does not*. [Emphasis added]

The laws of Western medical science are conceived of as universal laws of health. From the vantage point of biomedicine, other forms of knowledge can be both misleading to the patient and dangerous. In order to arrest and cure many medical conditions, quick professional identification of the ailment is deemed necessary. Other approaches to healing, it is argued, may extend the progress of the disease, exacerbate impairments, weaken the patient and make healing more difficult. Thus, in Mexico, for example, physicians complain that patients go to folk practitioners as a first resort, and this means that medical disorders are often too far advanced to cure by the time patients arrive at their medical clinics (Finkler, 1985: 58). Partly for these reasons, but quite transparently for professional self-interest as well, the medical profession has consistently opposed or dislodged both alternative medical practices such as homœopathy and chiropractic (see Nicholls, 1988; Wardwell, 1992) and indigenous systems of healing. As Arnold (1988: 18) has pointed out in relation to medicine in European colonies, 'seeing itself as rational, scientific and universalistic, western medicine defined itself in opposition to the presumed irrationality and superstition of indigenous medicine. The customs and beliefs of the people were treated as obstacles to overcome, obscurantism to be brushed aside by the new scientific age.'

This is not to say that other Western sciences, including the social sciences, do not share this ethnocentrism and condescension towards non-Western and non-materialist ideas about illness and healing procedures. Much of the literature in the sociology of illness behaviour, health psychology and even medical anthropology shares with biomedicine an empiricist and materialist understanding of illness and holds, at least implicitly, pejorative views of non-biomedical and non-Western approaches (see Good, 1994: 37–47).

Summarizing, Berliner (1984: 30) has characterized contemporary scientific medicine as having three major philosophical components: (1) the assumption that all disease is *materially* generated by specific aetiological agents such as bacteria, parasites, physiological and genetic malformations and internal chemical imbalances; (2) a passive patient role; and (3) the use of invasive manipulation to restore or maintain the human organism at a statistically derived equilibrium. In relation to the assumption of material causality, the germ theory of illness has provided a standard by which concrete cause-and-effect linkages can be made. With the discovery of microbes through the lens of the microscope by Louis Pasteur in 1859 and Robert Koch's finding of the tubercle and diphtheria bacilli in 1882, diseases were perceived as the products of hitherto unseen microorganisms inhabiting, or 'invading' as later medical rhetoric would have it, the body.[1] The invention of the microscope made possible the germ theory of illness, as gradually specific microbes were found to be involved in infectious diseases such as cholera, typhoid and tuberculosis that claimed high rates of mortality in the nineteenth century. These microbes, for medical scientists, were proof of specific material aetiology.

Germ theory assumes a specific biological cause of bodily malfunctioning and posits a radical distinction between sickness and health. At a practical level, this has major implications for the role both of the physician and of treatment. Because germ theory is predicated upon the technology of the microscope, it encourages physical separations between doctor and patient and between patients and their bodies or body parts (Reiser, 1978: 90). With the proliferation of machine technologies, the doctor immerses him or herself less in the patient's overall situation and more in the machinery used to render symptoms intelligible.

In terms of treatment, the germ theory of illness implies that medical work ought to concentrate on eliminating or neutralizing the microbe rather than limiting environmental exposure to it. Within this framing of disease the objectives of medical research narrow to the solving of biological puzzles. The emphasis is on the disease process once it has occurred, rather than on other social, psychological or environmental possibilities. The germ theory assumes the pathogen is external, biological in nature and hence politically and socially neutral.

The germ theory signals a general process – the trend towards the specification of ever smaller units of pathology and, hence, causality. Whereas the Hippocratic, pre-Cartesian view of sickness may have been open not only to what today we refer to as 'environmental' factors, but also to cosmic factors, as causes of illness, the view that emerged after the Enlightenment and took shape in the doctrine of specific aetiology is one in which ever larger units of causality (the cosmos, the environment and the person) are 'reduced' to ever smaller agents (the cell, the microbe, the molecule, genes and DNA). As we saw in part II, this does not mean that non-material factors are necessarily not considered, but that when they are considered they are explained in terms of a concrete material process within the corpus of medical science.

The major implication for doctor–patient relations of the appeal to science as a means of apprehending disease is that the two parties are removed from each other. As medical technology alienates the doctor from the patient and the patient from his or her body, 'science' likewise distances the two parties from each other, especially as living, feeling human beings. Although more immediate personal interaction takes place in clinical settings, the knowledge that flows from this is subordinate to that which is obtained from medical instruments. This was one of the major findings of Renee Anspach's (1993) ethnographic study of a neonatal intensive care unit in the United States. Anspach (1993: 81–2) shows that the knowledge nurses contribute to the assessment of very ill infants and their parents – at once intimate and personal – is 'devalued data'.

By emphasizing laboratory training in the natural sciences, medical education encourages an 'objective', technological and clinical outlook on the healing process, and, perhaps in order to harden the emotions of students, one of the first exercises in medical school is the dissection of a cadaver. In the first part of this book, Foucault described this sensibility:

> In the rational space of disease, doctors and patients do not occupy a place as of right; they are tolerated as disturbances that can hardly be avoided: the paradoxical role of medicine consists, above all, in neutralizing them, in maintaining the maximum difference between them, so that, in the void that appears between them, the ideal configuration of the disease becomes a concrete, free form . . .

In North America, the influential Flexner Report in 1910 established laboratory methods and detached objectivity as the standards to be upheld in medical education. Concentrating on the requisites of effective scientific training in the workings of the body, Flexner said little about the doctor–patient relationship.

However, the pronouncements that he did make on the subject depict the patient, like the microscope, as a source of data: 'The student is to collect and evaluate facts. The facts are locked up in the patient. To the patient he must therefore go. Waiving the personal factor, always important, that method of clinical teaching will be excellent which brings the student into close and active relation with the patient . . .' (Flexner, 1960: 92–3) Ever the scientist, Flexner disdained that which was not based on established methods of data collection. Thus, '[g]ratuitous speculation is at every stage foreign to the scientific attitude of mind' (Flexner, 1960: 53).

Recently, however, medicine has succumbed to creative impulses which have moved many of its practitioners to speculate on the specifically human dimensions of their work, moving away from the coldly detached model of the physician collecting facts at the bedside. This is especially apparent in the writings of numerous physicians, especially in the United States, who have reflected on the intricate details of their work and relations with patients. These reflections expose many of the difficulties in the neutralization of the doctor and patient that Foucault suggests is paradigmatic. Although one obviously cannot pronounce on all of the published writings of physicians, it is safe to argue that many in this genre, even those who are self-consciously humanistic, reproduce the fundamental scientific assumptions of biomedicine. We will take one physician–writer as an example – **Oliver Sacks**.

In works such as *Awakenings* (1973), *A Leg to Stand on* (1984) and *The Man Who Mistook His Wife for a Hat* (1985), the neurologist Oliver Sacks has become renowned for his descriptive and metaphorical renderings of the experiences of his neurological patients. In our first reading in this section, 'The Last Hippie', Sacks's approach to the predicament of his patient, Greg F., is almost anthropological. That is, it is not prosaic and clinical, but ethnographic in the manner of anthropologists seeking to engage in the life-worlds of their 'natives'.[2] While Sacks is empathic towards his patient, his own grounding in biomedical doctrines is evident from the start. Greg's involvement with the Krishna Consciousness movement – which expounds a distinctly non-materialist view of the world – is portrayed as youthful exuberance and folly. The spiritual interpretation of Greg's condition which Sacks tells us the movement proffered, that he was an 'illuminate', is dismissed and becomes the contrast upon which a materialist account of illness is constructed. The phenomenology of Greg's condition – his amnesia, his blindness, the nuances of his relationships with others and the discovery of the restorative power of music – is presented in rich detail by Sacks. All, however, is a product of a basic underlying substrate of 'memory mechanisms' and neurological functions, which in Greg's case have been damaged by a tumour. Observations of Greg are peppered with analogies to other patients who have definitive neurological conditions. We have in Sacks's evocative story a picture of Greg's social and emotional (although at some points Sacks doubts whether Greg has any emotions) world, but it is one that almost always rests on the authority of scientific medicine and relates back to or is explained by neurophysiology.[3]

THE ROLE OF THE PATIENT

We may legitimately enquire as to what role the patient plays in scientific medicine. Where is the patient as a subject and the world that he or she inhabits? The American sociologist Talcott Parsons (1951: 439–47), in his famous discussion of the role of medicine in the 'social system', defined various roles and responsibilities of the patient and coined the term 'sick role' to characterize the social situation of the patient. Fundamentally, the patient is someone who has asked for help in areas in which he or she does not possess expert knowledge. It is socially recognized that individuals when they are sick are not competent to help themselves. They are expected to do all they can to improve their health, but in doing so must yield to the advice and ministrations of the expert physician. This deference is necessary in order that the sickness be socially legitimated and the sick person relieved of his or her ordinary responsibilities and obligations. In many ways the key to the sick role lies in the legitimation of the sickness of the patient by the doctor. In this process, the patient has no choice but actively to seek to be well and to do so through compliance with the physician's prescriptions. According to Parsons, the stability of society hinges to some degree on this legitimation process.

A more recent analysis of the role of the patient is provided by Bologh (1981), who depicts scientific medicine as involving the alienation of the physical self from the social (we could also add psychological) self of the patient. For Bologh, scientific medicine is not centrally concerned with social aspects of illness such as differences in mortality and morbidity based on social criteria such as poverty, occupation and environmental factors. The role of expert is adopted by the physician and one of vulnerability by the patient. The expert role further conveys a monopolization of legitimate and pertinent knowledge – it is for the patient only to 'report' to the physician; physicians do not communicate to patients as human beings, but as bodies in the abstract, analogous to the communication between a garage mechanic and the owner of a car. Patients are made to feel that for the most part their health and recovery are beyond their own immediate control. Their illnesses are often invisible – biological, chemical, physiological, genetic – requiring expert intervention into realms which are, for most patients, esoteric.

As a passive object, the patient is open to exploitation through 'trial-and-error' methods, through exploratory surgery or as an 'interesting case' in the service of the advancement of medical science. Patients' bodies are literally the raw material upon which medical pedagogy takes place. This is especially the case in teaching hospitals, where the restoration of the health of the patient is not the only agenda. Young medical students must learn their trade upon patients' bodies. Hospitals are the setting for continuous clinical experiments, research projects and trials of numerous technologies and pharmacological agents. Although patients must provide 'informed consent', it is doubtful how meaningful this term is when patients may be in pain, under medication and in a strange environment. In his ethnographic study of hospital nurses, Chambliss (1996: 130–1) notes several examples of painful procedures carried out on patients for the benefit of medical pedagogy, including some experimentation on dying patients.

It is this sense of personal alienation that one derives from reading our second selection in this section. In **Arthur Frank's** account of his period of hospitalization, ' "I" seemed to exist beyond the horizon of their interest.' Rather like Foucault's comment that the patient is an 'external fact' to the disease, for Frank as a patient you become 'a spectator to your own drama'. Frank is acutely aware both of the fact that he has been made into a depersonalized object at the hands of his physicians and that his own body and his sense of it have been taken over by the physicians. He chooses the metaphor of colonization to describe what has become of his body and even personhood. Like the domination exerted by colonial powers, '[t]he hospital had created its own version of my identity.' In this connection, it might be instructive to compare Frank's perspective with that of Sacks, who is on the other side of the medical encounter. Is Greg F. a colonized person? Surely we cannot know, because Greg 'speaks' only through Sacks's narration. Greg's personality – his quirkiness, his spirituality and his attachment to music – are filtered through Sacks's clinical encounters and explained in terms of medical pathology.

While the neurological patients in Oliver Sacks's vignettes are seldom able to speak about their condition, patients generally have become more informed not only about biomedicine but about the different paradigms and ways of knowing about health. This has become especially apparent now that ailments with no definitive biomedical diagnosis or treatment have appeared. These include conditions such as Myalgic Encephalomyelitis (ME), Chronic Fatigue Syndrome (CFS) and Gulf War Syndrome. As sociologist **Lesley Cooper** argues in the third reading in this section, the reluctance of doctors to legitimate the experiences of sufferers from these conditions with a definitive diagnostic label has led to acute doctor–patient conflict. ME represents a fundamental disagreement between doctors and patients as to what constitutes illness and, in the Parsonian sense, disrupts entry into the sick role. Thus, 'what were to the sufferers severe symptoms of pain, depression and fatigue were trivialised by doctors, who saw them as common experiences not worthy of being brought to a doctor's attention'. In the context of this conflict, sufferers have taken it upon themselves to learn as much as possible about their ailment, and, in the face of physician resistance to considering their pain seriously, they have explored many different healing sources. The ME sufferers studied by Cooper do not conform to the characteristics of the biomedical patient that many sociologists have described. Likewise, their sufferings do not fit the existing models of illness, which legitimate only observable physical signs and symptoms and material origins. For Parsons (1951: 442–3), the emotional drama for patients and those close to them was a byproduct of sickness. It made it difficult for patients to have an 'objective' understanding of their conditions and all the more necessary for physicians to be diplomatic.

With time, the requirement for deference from patients, implied in Parsons's analysis, seems to be eroding. For ME sufferers and perhaps others with 'well-defined' conditions, the emotions produced by illness have been directed towards confronting physicians and seeking alternatives. Over the last few decades, concerns over the sexist treatment of women patients have led to the formation of all-female Well Women clinics. British feminists have contended that physicians base diagnoses on essentialist stereotypes and reinforce traditional female subservience and a conservative view of women in society (see Foster, 1989). A fairly consistent finding in surveys is a high level of patient dissatisfaction with medical dominance as it is manifested in gynaecological and obstetric consultations. One recent study in Trinidad and Tobago found 'an apparent insensitivity to the patient's condition, evasion of direct questions, deliberate use of medical jargon and expressed unwillingness to give information' as well as 'some evidence of negligence, incompetence, malpractice and evasive practices in addition to the pervasive presence of poor communication' (Phillips, 1996: 1,424–5).

The depersonalization of the patient along with the limited success of biomedicine in healing chronic diseases and publicity regarding the damaging effects of many of its techniques and procedures have precipitated moves on the part of patients to explore alternative or complementary medicine. Surveys in Britain have demonstrated the growing attraction of alternative medical therapies such as chiropractic, homeopathy, reflexology and acupuncture (see Sharma, 1992). A significant number of physicians in Britain have even trained themselves in techniques such as homeopathy which rely on completely contrary assumptions to biomedicine (Nicholls, 1988: 4). One of the most important factors in this drift to alternative medicine, at least in Britain and the United States, is the quality of the medical encounter (see Taylor, 1984). In particular, consultations with British general practitioners in the NHS are perceived by large segments of the population to be brusque, authoritarian, detached and infused with the attitudes and sensibilities of a rigid social class system. Alternative medical practitioners, on the other hand, spend vastly more time with their patients and are generally more attentive to patients' emotional and social situations

The popularity of alternative medicine illustrates a further shift away from patient passivity and deference. In a survey of lay people in medical consultations in Australia, Lupton (1997) notes both 'consumerist' and 'passive' stances among patients, depending on context. Although it cannot be considered in any detail here, a more consumerist approach to health on the part of patients has been fostered by the increasing commercialization of medicine. As the more intimate exchanges of the fee-for-service general practitioner model of care have gradually given way to 'managed' health care in corporate Health Maintenance Organizations (HMOs) in the United States (see Starr, 1982), patients have been encouraged to treat their health as they would any other marketed commodity. Doctors, likewise, are governed by the regulations and payment parameters of the corporation that employs them. Because they are paid on a per case basis, they have every incentive to make the consultation as brief and to the point as possible. The combination of detached clinical attitudes, inculcated in medical schools, with corporate control of health care facilities and services encourages the development of mechanical doctor–patient relationships. These trends establish the context for the widely reported deterioration in doctor–patient relations in the United States (see DeVita, 1995).

'Market-oriented' health systems have profound implications for the doctor–patient relationship. Instead of basing a commitment to a physician on trust, patients need to be able to compare the costs and benefits of health services on a number of different dimensions. The situation is not appreciably different in countries with well-developed public health care systems. Within state-run health services, patients are increasingly required to know the intricacies of bureaucratic doctrines and procedures regarding their 'rights'. In Britain, for example, the recent health care reforms restructured the relationships between units of health care such as hospitals, clinics and community services and Health Authorities. The once unitary system was fragmented to separate 'purchasers' from 'providers' and to enable contracts between them to determine which 'packages of care' would be made available to 'consumers'. While many people in Britain still seek health care as they did before the reforms, the procedures have become more complicated, and the character of the care a patient receives may depend on how well he or she is able to recognize the advantages and disadvantages of different routes through the system – or outside the system, as many more Britons are now subscribers to private health care plans (see Klein, 1995).

The main difference between seeing a physician and buying a commodity, however, is that health decision-making may be a life-and-death issue. The heightened risk in making decisions about how sickness will be treated – or not, as the case may be – underscores the increased inequality between buyer and seller in this realm. Although consumers have become more knowledgeable about their health, the esoteric biomedical knowledge possessed by physicians puts the patient at a distinct disadvantage, and this is exacerbated by state legitimation of biomedicine over other medical approaches. Thus, if patients opt out of biomedical treatment, they are often regarded as contributing to their own illness, especially if their condition worsens.

PROFESSIONALISM AND RATIONAL MEDICINE

The fact that doctors are socially designated as professionals is a vital consideration in regard to their roles and relationship with patients. Professions developed out of medieval guilds, which were informal organizations of artisans and craftsmen that specified particular criteria for admission such as skill, apprenticeship and patronage to others in the guild. Admission to the guild and subsequent regulations of conduct were strictly delineated by the governing bodies of guilds. Max Weber, perhaps the first sociologist to theorize the importance of professionalism, was to term this power 'social closure', meaning that guilds, and later 'professions', could determine their own membership through the enumeration of specific entry criteria. For Weber, professionalism was a part of the general development of processes of rationality in the West, processes which coincide

with the imposition of the world-view of the European Enlightenment and which
were linked to ever more 'rational' and hence tightly controlling forms of social
domination.[4] The professional was in Weber's analysis an expert bureaucrat,
trained in a particular field to dispense knowledge dispassionately within the
larger framework of rules and regulations devised by the organization of which
the professional was a part. The professional as a bureaucrat exerted power and
control through monopolizing legitimate knowledge – and hence being able to
name what counts as truth.

Some critics have argued that, because of the narrow focus on specialist
domains, professionals produce nothing but reductionistic knowledge. In the
philosopher Alfred North Whitehead's (1975: 233) view, professionals have
a single knowledge base and 'professionalized knowledge is supported by a
restricted acquaintance with useful subjects subservient to it'. That is, in contrast
to the educated classes of the past, professionals have little general knowledge
and no substantial knowledge of the larger realms of human inquiry that may
form the context for their own specialism. What results from professionalism is,
again in Whitehead's words, 'minds in a groove' which contemplate only a limited
set of abstractions extracted from a larger unit of analysis, which is then discarded. Professionalism represents a shift away from the more open, ecumenical
and less compartmentalized knowledge said to characterize earlier periods in
European history and non-Western cultures today. Contemporary observations
about 'dumbing down' and the 'closing of the American mind' (Bloom, 1987)
could easily apply to the sensibilities and outlooks of professionals in medicine,
science and social science in their quests for ever more refined and specialized
knowledge.

Parsons (1951: 435), while recognizing the physician as a specialist 'whose
superiority to his fellows is confined to the specific sphere of his technical training and expertise', took a benevolent view of the profession as a vocation based
on the ideals of service to the community, the pursuit of higher knowledge for its
own sake, disinterested devotion to tasks and 'affective neutrality'. As such,
professionals were constrained by a set of norms of conduct and practice which
precluded them from taking financial advantage of particular situations. A set of
internal regulations for dealing with issues that were ethical in nature was contained within the professional organization. Friedson (1970) extended Parsons's
ideas by stating that the distinguishing mark of a profession was organized and
legitimate autonomy. In addition to the power of social closure, the profession
has the right to control its own work and determine how the work is to be done
with minimal interference.

The professional autonomy manifested in medicine was termed 'medical dominance' by Friedson, who argued that the privileges of physicians relied on the
patronage of the state. That is, the state endorsed the medical self-perception to
be service- and community-oriented and consequently conferred upon medics
autonomy denied to other public and private bureaucrats. As a consequence of
medical dominance, doctors are free to determine the time, character, setting and
even the emotional tone of their consultations with patients. These features of

the doctor–patient relationship have been illustrated in a number of ethnographic studies. In *The Ceremonial Order of the Clinic*, Phil Strong (1979) observed that doctors even had the power to control the emotional response of mothers to the news of their children's illnesses. In a survey of medical encounters, Baker et al. (1997) found that 'negative emotions' are generated by the need of physicians to ask questions of a moral nature. An ethnographic study of medical interviews between doctors and female patients undergoing sensitive procedures such as PAP smears and breast examinations found that doctors dominated every aspect of the interaction and controlled the decision-making processes (Fisher, 1986). That doctors are able to organize, supervise and regulate other groups within the medical division of labour further validates the concept of medical dominance. Doctors could control workers as diverse as medical record librarians, medical technicians, occupational therapists, psychologists, social workers, secretaries and, of course, nurses.

However, the move towards more purely 'market-oriented' structures of health care has meant that doctors have become less autonomous and less empowered to control vast swathes of the medical workforce. The commercialization of health care that has come into operation around the world has meant that 'medical dominance' has increasingly been made subservient to managerial and economic interests. Consequently, medical judgements regarding the appropriate treatment for patients and the ethic of patient care are highly influenced by the needs of health care organizations and funders to make profits and limit costs. Physicians are increasingly accountable not to their patients or to professional codes of ethics, but to vast economic conglomerates. However, as Gray (1991: 203) has argued, the conflict between the professional fiduciary ethic to patients and the business ethic is a consequence not simply of the rise in for-profit health care providers, but of the increasing entrepreneurial activities of physicians themselves. Physicians in the United States are among the ranks of investors in diagnostic technologies, prescription drugs and medical products and equipment. These investments further compromise medical judgements and sway decision-making in the direction of products and services in which physicians may have financial stakes.

Medical dominance in Britain has also been curtailed. Under the Conservative government health reforms of the 1980s and 1990s, doctors who could formerly determine the character of patient consultations and their own working hours and conditions have found themselves accountable to armies of managers overseeing, costing and controlling much of their work. Physicians' accountability is increasingly to meeting 'targets' set by public social policies. Likewise in Canada, the Federal government has recently attempted to 'rationalize' health care through control over insurance parameters. This has curbed the power of medicine and increased the autonomy of para-professionals (see Coburn, 1993).

In contemporary health care systems, a vast number of economic and other values, including those of the increasingly well-informed patient, need to enter into the decision-making process. The plethora of considerations impinging on clinical consultations renders the detached, professional Hippocratic model of the physician increasingly archaic. The new, 'postmodern' medicine does not operate according to any fixed, immutable principles or ethical codes, but through a certain anarchistic plurality. In characterizing the new medicine, Veatch (1991: 264) describes the changes as follows:

> The most basic concepts are no longer meaningful. The most basic practices no longer make sense. The notions of 'clinical judgement', of treatments being 'medically indicated' or 'treatments of choice', of the 'medically correct thing to do', of 'medically safe and effective', the practice of writing prescriptions and of ordering treatments – they all collapse in a conceptual muddle.

Related to these trends towards the commercialization of medicine, the loosening of the endorsement of biomedicine by the state and public cynicism as to the quality of the medical consultation has been a movement towards recognition of alternative or complementary medicine by the medical establishment. In 1993 both the British Medical Association (BMA) and the National Institutes of Health (NIH) in the United States softened their attitudes to alternative medicine. The NIH advocated the allocation of more research funds to these systems of healing, and the BMA also recommended more research and encouraged GP referrals to alternative practitioners (see Angier, 1993; British Medical Association, 1993).

SHAMANISM, HEALING AND THE ENGLISH

Although this may at first glance seem contrary to all that has been said regarding the physician as bureaucrat and as professional, there is a sense in which we could look at the doctor in Western culture as similar to the shaman in other cultures. The shaman acts as a channel or medium for the spirits which govern the lives of members of many societies. Similarly, the physician is a representative of science. Both spiritual worlds and scientific worlds rely on faith in particular premises for their social legitimation. Although science attempts to bypass this by appealing to 'objectivity', such a construct is itself a human one, relying on shared assumptions within the scientific community as to how 'reality' and 'truth' are to be ascertained and which techniques of observation count as valid. Scientific procedures, methods and assumptions are 'objective' only insofar as they are invested with such qualities by people. Objectivity is itself a subjective concept. Therefore, both Western medicine and shamanism rely on faith for their legitimacy (see Rogers, 1982: 167), and it is the faith of patients in the curative powers of any healing system that ultimately sustains it.

As has been observed, the placebo influences scientific medicine a great deal across Western cultures (Payer, 1988: 27), and much healing relies upon both a personal relationship between healer and sufferer and the ability to mobilize healing powers in the sufferer by psychological means (see Frank, 1963). Even a sober academic such as Parsons (1951: 445) admits that 'even if he [the physician] is not in general tending in our society to take the place formerly occupied by the clergy . . . he at least has very important associations with the realm of the sacred'. A spiritual or non-materialist element, as we saw in part II, is vital to healing. Thus, it is ironic, as the philosopher Jacob Needleman (1985: 10) has pointed out, because of the influence of the metaphysical Pythagoras upon Hippocrates, that scientific medicine 'springs from the greatest mystical teachings'.

The language of magic infuses medical and scientific writing, especially in discussions of great discoveries, landmarks in medical history and new technologies. Thus, Mark Graubard's introduction to a 1960s edition of William Harvey's *On the Motion of the Heart and Blood in Animals* (1962: 1), for example, states that the book 'is universally regarded as a classic because it constitutes, metaphorically speaking, a magic window through which the inquirer into the nature of science can discern its most hidden meanings and mode of advancement'. The writer here saves himself from a lapse into metaphysics with the assurance that the 'magic window' is only metaphorical.

In many respects the detached objectivity and rationalism with which the doctor is invested is itself mystical. The building of rational order out of human and natural chaos, which is the project of post-Enlightenment science, as the physician and anthropologist Michael Taussig (1987: 37) has argued, is an 'objectivist fiction'. The power of the doctor, like the power of the shamans in the Putumayo whom Taussig wrote about, owes itself to the magic with which it has been invested by patients. 'Yet everyone accorded the doctors great respect, and the faith, which was a magical faith, in the medical wonders of modern science,' Taussig (1987: 276) remarks of the people in Puerto Tejado, Colombia with whom he lived, 'was restrained only by the fact that few could afford it . . .'.

Most patients do not know the scientific explanations for their ailments. They are not generally aware of the complex webs of causality in the same way as a physician. Similarly, the shaman's patient would not usually be conscious of the exact alignment of spiritual powers that the shaman invokes in order to cure them. In fact, in England the lack of knowledge and hence the resort to spiritual belief in the power of the doctor may be greater than in other cultures. Payer's (1988) comparative research suggests that the English tend to know little about their bodies. One study in 1970 showed that only 42 per cent of a sample of English patients could give the right location of their heart and only 20 per cent the location of their stomach (Payer, 1988: 112). According to Payer, English patients are more stoical than others. Their social codes emphasize self-control, rather than exploration of symptoms.

For the English ex-patriot **John Berger**, in our final reading in this section, the English are particularly culturally deprived. They have far fewer ways of recognizing themselves than people in other societies. A great deal of their experience, especially emotional, goes unnamed. Like Cooper's ME sufferers naming is the key to healing for Berger; it gives the patient's complaint a legitimacy and helps neutralize cultural deprivation. 'It' has an independent existence, signifying that the patient is not malingering. If healing is to proceed, though, it can only be based on an intense personal involvement of the physician with the patient – one that is quite subtle in the case of Berger's Dr Sassall, but which is professional and self-consciously scientific in the stance of Oliver Sacks towards Greg F. This involves a *recognition* which can form the basis for healing. Lack of recognition, failure to recognize oneself in the outside world, is, Berger urges, the major cause of unhappiness. Hence, the doctor performs a service merely by naming and hence 'validating' the patient. To do this, the doctor must be recognizable by the patient – as a comparable person, as a member, albeit higher-status, of the locality.

The model of the doctor presented in the reading relates to the 1960s, an era when medical authority in Britain was less hemmed in by state and economic forces. In many ways – and this is somewhat paradoxical given many of the features of medical dominance already discussed – it is the relative freedom from institutional and bureaucratic strictures that promotes public faith and trust in the curative power of the doctor. The kinds of involvement, going far beyond the purely mechanical, that Sassall maintained with his patients in the Forest of Dean would now largely be impossible in most Western health systems. As medicine succumbs to commercial and bureaucratic control, it enters the realm of the mundane, everyday capitalist world and sheds whatever links it had with the sacred. In doing so, perhaps it also loses an important part of its powers of healing.

Notes

1. It should not be assumed that medical 'discoveries' suddenly flower into practical applications. They are the products of the social conventions of medical scientists themselves (see Kuhn, 1962). As Parsons (1951: 433) points out, Pasteur's work was for a long time opposed by the French Academy of Medicine, and the importance of his discoveries was not recognized until several years later.
2. In fact, Sacks describes his approach as 'anthropological' and 'naturalistic'. See Brawarsky (1997: 1,092).
3. For critical commentaries on the writings of Sacks see Rose (1988) and Hunter (1995).
4. This is articulated in Weber's concept of legitimation in 'Politics as a Vocation' (see Gerth and Mills, 1946: 77–128), in his discussion of bureaucracy in 'Bureaucracy' (Gerth and Mills, 1946: 196–244) and in the reference to the 'iron cage' of modern society at the end of *The Protestant Ethic and the Spirit of Capitalism*.

References

Angier, Natalie (1993), 'US Opens the Door Just a Crack to Alternative Forms of Medicine', *New York Times*, 10 January, 1, 13.

Anspach, Renee (1993), *Deciding Who Lives: Fateful Choices in the Intensive Care Nursery*, Berkeley, CA: University of California Press.

Arnold, David (1988), 'Introduction: Disease, Medicine and Empire', in David Arnold (ed.), *Imperial Medicine and Indigenous Societies*, Manchester: Manchester University Press, 1–26.

Baker, Patricia, William Yoels and Jeffrey Clair (1997), 'Emotional Expression during Medical Encounters: Social Dis-ease and the Medical Gaze', in Veronica James and Jonathan Gabe (eds), *Health and the Sociology of Emotions*, Oxford: Blackwell, 173–200.

Berliner, Howard (1984), 'Scientific Medicine since Flexner', in J. Warren Salmon (ed.), *Alternative Medicine*, London: Tavistock, 30–56.

Bloom, Allan (1987), *The Closing of the American Mind*, London: Penguin.

Bologh, Roslyn Wallach (1981), 'Grounding the Alienation of Self and Body', *Sociology of Health and Illness*, 3(2): 188–206.

Brawarsky, Sandee (1997), 'Street Neurologist with a Sense of Wonder', *The Lancet*, 350 (October 11): 1,092–3.

British Medical Association (1993), *Complementary Medicine: New Approaches to Good Medical Practice*. Oxford: Oxford University Press.

Chambliss, Daniel (1996), *Beyond Caring: Hospitals, Nurses and the Social Organization of Ethics*, Chicago, IL: University of Chicago Press.

Coburn, David (1993), 'State Authority, Medical Dominance and Trends in the Regulation of the Health Professions: The Ontario Case', *Social Science and Medicine*, 37(2): 129–38.

Department of Health (1991), *Women Doctors and Their Careers: Report of the Joint Working Party*, London: HMSO.

DeVita, Elizabeth (1995), 'The Decline of the Doctor–Patient Relationship', *American Health*, June: 63–7.

Finkler, Kaja (1985), *Spiritualist Healers in Mexico: Successes and Failures of Alternative Therapeutics*, South Hadley, MA: Bergin and Garvey.

—— (1991), *Physicians at Work, Patients in Pain: Biomedical Practice and Patient Response in Mexico*, Boulder, CO: Westview Press.

Fisher, Sue (1986), *In the Patient's Best Interests: Women and the Politics of Medical Decisions*, New Brunswick, NJ: Rutgers University Press.

Flexner, Abraham (1960) [1910], *Medical Education in the United States and Canada: A Report to the Carnegie Foundation for the Advancement of Teaching*, New York: Arno Press and *The New York Times*.

Foster, Peggy (1989), 'Improving the Doctor/Patient Relationship', *Journal of Social Policy*, 18(3): 337–61.

Frank, Jerome (1963), *Persuasion and Healing: A Comparative Study of Psychotherapy*, New York: Schocken.

Friedson, Eliot (1970), *Profession of Medicine*, New York: Dodd, Mead.

Gerth, Hans, and C. Wright Mills (1946) (eds), *From Max Weber: Essays in Sociology*, New York: Oxford University Press.

Good, Byron (1994), *Medicine, Rationality and Experience: An Anthropological Perspective*, Cambridge: Cambridge University Press.

Gray, Bradford (1991), *The Profit Motive and Patient Care: The Changing Accountability of Doctors and Hospitals*, Cambridge, MA: Harvard University Press.

Harvey, William (1962) [1628], *On the Motion of the Heart and Blood in Animals*, Chicago, IL: Gateway Editions.

Hunter, William (1995), 'Your Friendly Neighborhood Neurologist: Dr. Oliver Sacks and the Cultured View of Physicians', *Journal of Popular Culture*, 28(4): 93–102.

King, Lester (1982), *Medical Thinking: A Historical Preface*, Princeton, NJ: Princeton University Press.

Klein, Rudolf (1995), 'Big Bang Health Care Reform – Does It Work? The Case of Britain's 1991 National Health Service Reforms', *Milbank Quarterly*, 73(3): 299–337.

Kuhn, Thomas (1962), *The Structure of Scientific Revolutions*, Chicago, IL: University of Chicago Press.

Lupton, Deborah (1997), 'Consumerism, Reflexivity and the Medical Encounter', *Social Science and Medicine*, 45(3): 373–81.

Needleman, Jacob (1985), *The Way of the Physician*, London: Arkana.

Nicholls, Phillip (1988), *Homoeopathy and the Medical Profession*, London: Croom Helm.

O'Connor, Bonnie Blair (1994), *Healing Traditions: Alternative Medicine and the Health Professions*, Philadelphia, PA: University of Pennsylvania Press.

Parsons, Talcott (1951), *The Social System*, New York: Free Press.

Payer, Lynn (1988), *Medicine and Culture*, London: Gollancz.

Phillips, Daphne (1996), 'Medical Professional Dominance and Client Dissatisfaction: A Study of Doctor–Patient Interaction and Reported Dissatisfaction with Medical Care among Female Patients at Four Hospitals in Trinidad and Tobago', *Social Science and Medicine*, 42(10): 1,419–25.

Reiser, Stanley Joel (1978), *Medicine and the Reign of Technology*, Cambridge: Cambridge University Press.

Rogers, Spencer (1982), *The Shaman: His Symbols and His Healing Power*, Springfield, IL: Charles Thomas.

Rose, Jacqueline (1988), '"The Man Who Mistook His Wife for a Hat" or "A Wife is Like an Umbrella" – Fantasies of the Modern and Postmodern', in Andrew Ross (ed.), *Universal Abandon*, Minneapolis, MN: University of Minnesota Press, 237–50.

Sacks, Oliver (1973), *Awakenings*, New York: E. P. Dutton

—— (1984), *A Leg to Stand on*, New York: Harper and Row

—— (1985), *The Man Who Mistook His Wife for a Hat*, London: Picador.

Sharma, Ursula (1992), *Complementary Medicine Today*, London: Routledge.

Starr, Paul (1982), *The Social Transformation of American Medicine*, New York: Basic.

Strong, P. M. (1979), *The Ceremonial Order of the Clinic: Parents, Doctors and Medical Bureaucracies*, London: Routledge.

Taussig, Michael (1987), *Shamanism, Colonialism and the Wild Man: A Study in Terror and Healing*, Chicago, IL: University of Chicago Press.

Taylor, Rosemary (1984), 'Alternative Medicine and the Medical Encounter in Britain and the United States', in J. Warren Salmon (ed.) *Alternative Medicine*, London: Tavistock, 191–227.

Thomas, Lewis (1983), *The Youngest Science: Notes of a Medicine Watcher*, New York: Viking Penguin.

Veatch, Robert (1991), *The Patient–Physician Relation: The Patient as Partner, Part 2*, Bloomington and Indianapolis, IN: Indiana University Press.

Waitzkin, Howard (1983), *The Second Sickness: Contradictions of Capitalist Health Care*, New York: Free Press.

—— (1991), *The Politics of Medical Encounters: How Patients and Doctors Deal with Social Problems*, New Haven, CT: Yale University Press.

Wardwell, Walter (1992), *Chiropractic History and the Evolution of a New Profession*, St Louis, MO: Mosby.

Weber, Max (1958), *The Protestant Ethic and the Spirit of Capitalism*, New York: Scribner's.

Whitehead, Alfred North (1975) [1925], *Science and the Modern World: Lowell Lectures 1925*, London: Fontana.

Witz, Ann (1992), *Professions and Patriarchy*, London: Routledge.

Williams, William Carlos (1969), *Selected Poems*, New York: New Directions.

Wright, Will (1992), *Wild Knowledge: Science, Language, and Social Life in a Fragile Environment*, Minneapolis, MN: University of Minnesota Press.

CHAPTER 11

The Last Hippie

Oliver Sacks

1.

Greg F. grew up in the 1950s in a comfortable Queens household, an attractive and rather gifted boy who seemed destined, like his father, for a professional career—perhaps a career in songwriting, for which he showed a precocious talent. But he grew restive, started questioning things, when he was fifteen; started to hate the conventional life of his parents and neighbors, and the cynical, bellicose administration of the country. His need to rebel, but equally to find an ideal and a guide, to find a leader, crystallized in the "Summer of Love," in 1967. He would go to the Village, and listen to Allen Ginsberg declaiming all night; he loved rock music, especially acid rock, and, above all, the Grateful Dead.

Increasingly he fell out with his parents and teachers—was truculent with the one, secretive with the other. In 1968, a time when Timothy Leary was urging American youth to "tune in, turn on, and drop out," Greg grew his hair long and dropped out of school, where he had been a good student; he left home and went to live in the Village, where he dropped acid, and joined the East Village drug culture—searching, like others of his generation, for utopia, for inner freedom, and for "higher consciousness."

But "turning on" did not satisfy Greg, who stood in need of a more codified philosophy, doctrine, and way of life. In 1969 he gravitated, as so many young acid heads did, to the Swami Bhaktivedanta, and his society for Krishna Consciousness, on Second Avenue. And under his influence, Greg, like so many others, stopped taking acid, finding his religious exaltation a replacement for his acid highs. "The only radical remedy for dipsomania," as William James wrote, "is religiomania." The philosophy, the fellowship, the chanting, the rituals, the austere and charismatic figure of the swami himself came like a revelation to Greg, and he became, almost immediately, a passionate devotee and convert.[1] Now there was a center, a focus, to his life. In those first, exalted weeks of his conversion, he wandered around the East Village, dressed in saffron robes, chanting the

Hare Krishna mantras; and early in 1970, he took up residence in the main temple in Brooklyn. His parents objected at first, then went along with this. "Perhaps it will help him," his father said, philosophically. "Perhaps—who knows?—this is the path he needs to follow."

Greg's first year at the temple went well, he was obedient, ingenuous, devoted, and pious. He is a Holy One, said the swami, one of us. Early in 1971, now deeply committed, Greg was sent to the temple in New Orleans. His parents had seen him occasionally when he was in the Brooklyn temple, but now all communication from him virtually ceased.

One problem arose in Greg's second year with the Krishnas—he complained that his vision was growing dim, but this was interpreted, by his swami and others, in a spiritual way: he was "an illuminate," they told him; it was the "inner light" growing. Greg had worried at first about his eyesight, but was reassured by the swami's spiritual explanation. His sight grew still dimmer, but he offered no further complaints. And indeed, he seemed to be becoming more spiritual by the day—an amazing new serenity had taken hold of him. He no longer showed his previous impatience or appetites, and he was sometimes found in a sort of daze, with a strange (many said "transcendental") smile on his face. It is beatitude, said his swami: he is becoming a saint. The temple felt he needed to be protected at this stage—he no longer went out or did anything unaccompanied—and contact with the outside world was strongly discouraged.

Although Greg's parents did not have any direct communication from him, they did get occasional reports from the temple—reports filled, increasingly, with accounts of his "spiritual progress," his "enlightenment," accounts at once so vague and so out of character with the Greg they knew that, by degrees, they became alarmed. Once they wrote directly to the swami, and received a soothing, reassuring reply.

Three more years passed before Greg's parents finally decided they had to see for themselves. His father, a man of nearly fifty when Greg was born, was now elderly and in poor health, and feared that if he waited longer he might never see his "lost" son again. On hearing this, the temple finally permitted a visit from Greg's parents. In 1975, then, not having seen him for four years, they visited their son in the temple in New Orleans.

When they did so, they were filled with horror: their lean, hairy son had become fat and hairless; he wore a continual "stupid" smile on his face (this at least was his father's word for it); he kept bursting into bits of song and verse, and making "idiotic" comments, while showing little deep emotion of any kind ("like he was scooped out, hollow inside," his father said); he had lost interest in everything "current"; he was disoriented—and he was totally blind. The temple, surprisingly, acceded to his leaving—perhaps even they felt now that his ascension had gone too far, and had started to feel some disquiet about his state.

Greg was admitted to the hospital, examined, and transferred to neurosurgery. Brain imaging had shown an enormous tumor of the pituitary gland, destroying the adjacent optic chiasm and tracts, and extending on both sides into the frontal lobes. It also reached backward to the temporal lobes, and downward to the forebrain, or diencephalon. At surgery, the tumor was found to be benign, but it had swollen to the size of a small grapefruit or orange, and though the surgeons were able to remove it entirely, they could not undo the damage it had already done.

Greg was now not only blind, but gravely disabled neurologically and mentally —a disaster which could have been prevented entirely had his first complaints of dimming vision been heeded, and had medical sense, and even common sense, been allowed to judge his state. Since, tragically, no recovery could be expected, or very little, Greg was admitted to Williamsbridge, a hospital for the chronically sick, a twenty-five-year-old boy for whom active life had come to an end, and for whom the prognosis was "hopeless."

2.

I first met Greg in April 1977, when he arrived at Williamsbridge Hospital. Lacking facial hair, and childlike in manner, he seemed younger than his twenty-five years. He was fat, Buddha-like, with a vacant, bland face, his blind eyes roving at random in their orbits, while he sat motionless in his wheelchair. If he lacked spontaneity, and initiated no exchanges, he responded promptly and appropriately, and with wit, when I spoke to him. But his answers were short, never expanded the question, never gave rise to associations or reflection. Between questions, if the time was not filled, there tended to be a deepening silence; and if this lasted for more than a minute, he would fall into Hare Krishna chants, or to a soft muttering of mantras. He was still, he said, "a total believer," devoted to the group's doctrines and aims.

I could not get any consecutive history from him—he was not sure, for a start, why he was in the hospital, and gave different reasons when I asked him about this; first he said, "Because I'm not intelligent," later, "Because I took drugs in the past." He knew he had been at the main Hare Krishna temple ("a big red house, 439 Henry Street, in Brooklyn"), but not that he had subsequently been at their temple in New Orleans. Nor did he remember that he started to have symptoms there—first and foremost a progressive loss of vision. Indeed he seemed unaware that he had *any* problems: that he was blind, that he was unable to walk steadily, that he was in any way ill.

Unaware—and indifferent. Ill, blind, incorrigibly disabled, he had been dumped in a hospital for the chronically sick with no prospect of ever getting out or recovering; but nothing of this seemed real to him at all. He seemed bland, placid, emptied of all feeling—it was this unnatural serenity which his Krishna brethren had perceived, apparently, as "bliss," and indeed, at one point, Greg used the term himself. "How do you *feel*?" I returned to this again and again. "I feel blissful," he replied at one point. "I am afraid of falling back into the material world." At this point, when he was first in the hospital, many of his

Hare Krishna friends would come to visit him; I often saw their saffron robes in the corridors. They would come to visit poor, blind, blank Greg, and flock around him; they saw him as having achieved "detachment," as an enlightened one.

Questioning him about current events and people, I found the depths of his disorientation and confusion. When I asked him who was the president, he said "Lyndon," then, "the one who got shot." I prompted, "Jimmy . . ." and he said, "Jimi Hendrix," and when I roared with laughter, he said maybe a musical White House would be a good idea. A few more questions convinced me that Greg had virtually no memory of events much past 1970, certainly no coherent, chronological memory of them. He seemed to have been left, marooned, in the Sixties—his memory, his development, his inner life since then had come to a stop.

His tumor, a slow-growing one, was huge when it was finally removed in 1976; but only in the later stages of its growth, as it destroyed the memory system in the temporal lobe, would it actually have prevented the brain from registering new events. But Greg had difficulties—not absolute, but partial—even in remembering events from the late Sixties, events which he must have registered perfectly at the time. So, beyond the inability to register new experiences, there had been an erosion of existing memories (a retrograde amnesia) going back several years before his tumor had developed. There was not an absolutely sharp cut-off here, but rather a temporal gradient, so that figures and events from 1966 and 1967 were fully remembered, events from 1968 or 1969 partially or occasionally remembered, and events after 1970 almost never remembered.

It was easy to demonstrate the severity of his immediate amnesia. If I gave him lists of words, he was unable to recall any of them after a minute. When I told him a story and asked him to repeat it, he did so in a more and more confused way, with more and more "contaminations" and misassociations—some droll, some extremely bizarre—until within five minutes his story bore no resemblance to the one I had told him. Thus when I told him a tale about a lion and a mouse, he soon departed from the original story and had the mouse threatening to eat the lion—it had become a giant mouse and a mini-lion. Both were mutants, Greg explained when I quizzed him on his departures. Or possibly, he said, they were creatures from a dream, or "an alternative history" in which mice were indeed the lords of the jungle. Five minutes later, he had no memory of the story whatever.

I had heard, from the hospital social worker, that he had a passion of music, especially for rock-and-roll bands of the Sixties; I saw piles of records as soon as I entered his room, and a guitar lying against his bed. So now I asked him about this, and with this there came a complete transformation—he lost his disconnectedness, his indifference, and spoke with great animation about his favorite rock bands and pieces—above all, of the Grateful Dead, "I went to see them at the Fillmore East, and in Central Park," he said. He remembered the entire program in detail, but "my favorite," he added, "is 'Tobacco Road.'" The title evoked the tune, and Greg sang the whole song with great feeling and conviction—a depth of feeling of which, hitherto, he had not shown the least sign. He seemed transformed, a different person, a whole person, as he sang. "When did you hear them in Central Park?" I asked.

"It's been a while, over a year maybe," he answered—but in fact they had last played there eight years earlier, in 1969. And the Fillmore East, the famous rock-and-roll theater where Greg had also seen the group, did not survive the early 1970s. He went on to tell me he once heard Jimi Hendrix at Hunter College, and Cream, with Jack Bruce playing bass guitar, Eric Clapton, lead guitar, and Ginger Baker, a "fantastic drummer." "Jimi Hendrix," he added reflectively, "What's he doing? I don't hear much about him nowadays." We spoke of the Rolling Stones and the Beatles—"Great groups," Greg commented, "but they don't have the soul, they don't space me out, the way the Dead do. What a group," he continued, "there's no one like them. Jerry Garcia—he's a saint, he's a guru, he's a genius. Mickey Hart, Bill Kreutzmann, the drummers are great. There's Bob Weir, there's Phil Lesh; but Pigpen—I love him."

This narrows down the extent of his amnesia. He remembers songs vividly from 1964 to 1968. He remembers all the founding members of the Grateful Dead, from 1967. But he is unaware that Pigpen, Jimi Hendrix, and Janis Joplin are all dead. His memory cuts off by 1970, or before. He is caught in the Sixties, unable to move on. He is a fossil, the last hippie.

At first I did not want to confront Greg with the enormity of his time loss, his amnesia, or even to let involuntary hints through (which he would certainly pick up, for he was very sensitive to anomaly and tone)—so I changed the subject, and said, "Let me examine you."

He was, I noted, somewhat weak and spastic in all his limbs, more on the left, and more in the legs. He could not stand alone. His eyes showed complete optic atrophy—it was impossible for him to see anything. But strangely, he did not seem to be aware of being blind, and would *guess* that I was showing him a blue ball, a red pen (when in fact it was a green comb and a fob watch that I showed him). Nor indeed did he seem to "look"; he made no special effort to turn in my direction, and when we were speaking, he had often failed to "face" me, to "look" at me. When I asked him about seeing, he acknowledged that his eyes weren't "all that good," but added that he enjoyed "watching" the TV. "Watching" TV for him, I observed later, consisted of following with attention the soundtrack of a movie or show, and inventing visual scenes to go with it (even though he might not even be looking toward the TV). He seemed to think, indeed, that this was what "seeing" meant, that this was what was meant by "watching TV," and that this is what all of us did. Thus he had apparently lost the very idea of seeing.

I found this aspect of Greg's blindness, his singular blindness to his blindness, his no longer knowing what "seeing" or "looking" meant, deeply perplexing. It seemed to point to something stranger, and more complex, than a mere "deficit," to point, rather, to some radical alteration within him in the very structure of knowledge, in consciousness, in identity itself.[2]

I had already had some sense of this when testing his memory, finding his confinement, in effect, to a single moment—"the present"—uninformed by any sense of a past (or a future). Given this radical lack of connection and continuity in his inner life, I got the feeling, indeed, that he might not have "an inner life" to speak of, that he lacked the constant dialogue of past and present, of experience and meaning, which constitutes consciousness and inner life for the rest of us. He seemed to have no sense of "next," and to lack that eager and anxious tension of anticipation, of intention, that drives us through life.

Some sense of ongoing, of "next," is always with us. But this sense of movement, of happening, Greg lacked; he seemed immured, without knowing it, in a motionless, timeless, moment. And whereas for the rest of us, the present is given its meaning and depth by the past (hence it becomes "the remembered present," in Gerald Edelman's term), as well as being given potential and tension by the future, for Greg it was flat and (in its meager way) complete. This living-in-the-moment, which was so manifestly pathological, had been perceived in the temple as an achievement of "higher consciousness."

3.

Greg seemed to adjust to Williamsbridge with remarkable ease, considering he was a young man being placed, probably forever, in a hospital for the chronically ill. There was no furious defiance, no railing at fate, no sense, apparently, of indignity or despair. Compliantly, indifferently, Greg let himself be put away in the protective environment, the backwater of Williamsbridge. When I asked him about this, he said, "I have no choice." And this, as he said it, seemed wise and true. Indeed, he seemed eminently philosophical about it. But it was a philosophicalness made possible by his indifference, his brain damage.

His parents, so estranged from him when he was rebellious and well, came daily, doted on him, now that he was helpless and ill; and they, for their part, could be sure, at any time, that he would be at the hospital, smiling and grateful for their visit. If he was not "waiting" for them, so much the better—they could miss a day, or a few days, if they were away; he would not notice, but would be cordial as ever the next time they came.

Greg soon settled in, then, with his rock records and his guitar, his Hare Krishna beads, his Talking Books, and a schedule of programs—physiotherapy, occupational therapy, music groups, drama. Soon after admission he was moved to a ward with younger patients, where with his open and sunny personality he became popular. He did not actually know any of the other patients or the staff, at least for several months, but was invariably (if indiscriminately) pleasant to them all. And there were at least two special friendships, not intense, but with a sort of complete acceptance and stability. His mother remembers "Eddie, who had MS . . . they both loved music, they had adjacent rooms, they used to sit together, . . . and Judy, she had CP, she would sit for hours with him too." Eddie died, and Judy went to a hospital in Brooklyn; there has been no one so close for many years. Mrs. F. remembers them, but Greg does not, never asked for them, or about them, after they had gone—though perhaps, his mother thought, he was sadder, at least less lively, after they had gone, for they stimulated him, got him talking and listening to records and inventing limericks, joking and singing; they pulled him out of "that dead state" he would otherwise fall into.

A hospital for the chronically ill, where patients and staff live together for years, is a little like a village or a small town: everybody gets to meet, to know, everybody else. I often saw Greg in the corridors, being wheeled to different programs, or out to the patio, in his wheelchair, with the same odd, blind, yet searching look on his face. And he gradually got to know me, at least sufficiently to know my name, to ask, each time we met, "How're you doing, Dr. Sacks? When's the next book coming out?" (a question which rather distressed me in the seemingly endless interim between the publication of *Awakenings* and *A Leg to Stand On*, an eleven-year period in which I thought I would never write again).

Names, then, he might learn, with frequent contact; and in relation to them he would recollect a few details about each new person. Thus he came to know Connie Tomaino, the music therapist—he would recognize her voice, her foot-falls, immediately—but he could never remember where or how he had met her. One day Greg began talking about "another Connie," a girl called Connie whom he'd known at high school. This other Connie, he told us, was also, remarkably, very musical—"How come all you Connies are so musical?" he teased. The other Connie would conduct music groups, he said, would give out song sheets, play the piano-accordion at sing songs at school. At this point, it started to dawn on us that this "other" Connie was in fact Connie herself, and this was clinched when he added, "You know, she played the trumpet." (Connie Tomaino is a professional trumpet player.) This sort of thing often happened with Greg, when he put things into the wrong context, or failed to connect them with the present; it was particularly startling to hear him talk to Connie about "another" Connie.

His sense of there being two Connies, his segmenting Connie into two, was characteristic of the bewilderments he sometimes found himself in, his need to hypothesize additional figures because he could not retain or conceive of an identity in time. With consistent repetition Greg might learn a few facts, and these would be retained. But the facts were isolated, denuded of context. A person, a voice, a place would slowly become "familiar," but he remained unable to remember where he had met the person, heard the voice, seen the place. Specifically, it was context-bound (or "episodic") memory which was so grossly disturbed in Greg—as is the case with most amnesiacs.

Other sorts of memory were intact; thus Greg had no difficulty remembering or applying geometrical truths which he had learned in school. He saw instantly, for example, that the hypotenuse of a triangle was shorter than the sum of the two sides—thus his semantic memory, so-called, was fairly intact. Again, he not only retained his power to play the guitar, but actually learned to type while at Williamsbridge—so his procedural memory was also unimpaired.

Finally, there seemed to be some sort of slow habituation or familiarization—so that he became able, within three months, to find his way about the hospital, to go to the coffee shop, the cinema, the auditorium, the patio, his favorite places. This sort of learning was exceedingly slow, but once it had been achieved, it was tenaciously retained.

4.

It was clear that Greg's tumor had caused damage that was complex and curious. First, it had compressed or destroyed structures of the inner, or medial, side of both the temporal lobes—in particular, the hippocampus and its adjacent cortex, areas crucial for the capacity to acquire new memories. Episodic amnesia such as Greg's follows destruction of these regions, not only in human beings, but in some experimental animals as well. With such an amnesia, the ability to acquire information about new facts and events is devastated—there ceases to be any explicit or conscious remembrance of these. But while Greg is so often unable to recall events or encounters or facts to consciousness, he might nonetheless have an unconscious or implicit memory of them, a memory expressed in performance or behavior. Such implicit ability to remember allowed him to become slowly familiar with the physical layout and routines of the hospital and with some of the staff, and to make judgments on whether certain persons (or situations) were pleasant or unpleasant.[3]

While explicit learning requires the integrity of the medial temporal lobe systems, implicit learning may employ more primitive and diffuse paths, as do the simple processes of conditioning and habituation. Explicit learning, however, involves the construction of complex percepts—syntheses of representations from every part of the cerebral cortex—brought together into a contextual unity, or "scene." Such syntheses can be held in mind for only a minute or two—the limit of so-called "immediate" memory—and after this will be lost unless they can be shunted into permanent memory. Thus higher-order memorization is a multistage process, involving the transfer of perceptions, or perceptual syntheses, from immediate to permanent memory.[4] It is just such a transfer which fails to occur in people with temporal lobe damage. Thus amnesiacs may have perfect, intact "immediate" memories, but lack the ability to transfer them into permanent memory. Greg can repeat a complicated sentence with complete accuracy and understanding the moment he hears it, but within three minutes, or sooner if he is distracted for an instant, he will retain not a trace of it, or any idea of its sense, or any memory that it ever existed.

Larry Squire, a neuropsychologist at the University of California, San Diego, who has been a central figure in elucidating this shunting function of the temporal lobe memory system, speaks of the brevity, the precariousness, of immediate memory in us all; all of us, on occasion, suddenly lose a perception or an image or a thought we had vividly in mind ("Damn it," we may say, "I've forgotten what I wanted to say!"), but only in amnesiacs is this precariousness realized to the full.

Yet while Greg, no longer capable of transforming his perceptions or immediate memories into permanent ones, remains stuck in the Sixties, when his ability to learn new information broke down, he has nevertheless adapted somehow and absorbed some of his surroundings, albeit very slowly and incompletely.[5]

Some amnesiacs, like Jimmie (the Korsakov's patient whom I described in "The Lost Mariner"[6]) have brain damage largely confined to the memory systems of the diencephalon and medial temporal lobe; others, like Mr. Thompson (described in "A Matter of Identity"[7]) are not only amnesiac, but have frontal lobe syndromes as well; yet others—like Greg, with immense tumors—tend to have a third area of damage as well, deep below the cerebral cortex, in the forebrain, or diencephalon. In Greg, this widespread damage has created a very complicated clinical picture, with sometimes overlapping or even contradictory symptoms and syndromes. Thus though his amnesia is chiefly caused by damage to the temporal lobe systems, damage to the diencephalon and frontal lobes also has a part. Similarly there are multiple origins for his blandness and indifference, for which damage to the frontal lobes, diencephalon, and pituitary gland is in varying degrees responsible. In fact, Greg's tumor first caused damage to his pituitary gland; this was responsible not only for his gain in weight and loss of body hair but also for undermining his hormonally driven aggressiveness and assertiveness, and hence for his abnormal submissiveness and placidity.

The diencephalon is especially a regulator of basic functions—of sleep, of appetite, of libido, etc. And all of these were at a low ebb with Greg—he had (or expressed) no sexual interest; he did not think of eating, or express a desire to eat, unless food was brought to him; and, if he was not stimulated, he fell not into sleep, but into a sort of daze—though he could be "awakened" from this as long as a stimulus was present.

Thus, left alone, Greg would spend hours in the ward without spontaneous activity. This inert state was at first described by the nurses as "brooding"; it had been seen in the temple as "meditating"; my own feeling was that it was a profoundly pathological mental "idling," almost devoid of content, of affect, of attention, and even of arousal. It was difficult to give a name to this state, so different from alert, attentive wakefulness, but also, clearly, quite different from sleep—it had a blankness resembling no normal state. It reminded me somewhat of the vacant states I had seen with some of my post-encephalitic patients, and, as with them, went with profound damage to the diencephalon. But as soon as I talked to him, or if he was stimulated by sounds (especially music) near him—and with his blindness he now showed a heightened sensitivity to these, an almost exclusively auditory orientation—he "came to," "awakened," in an astonishing way.

Once Greg is "awakened," once his cortex comes to life, one sees that this animation itself has a strange quality—an uninhibited and quirky quality of the sort one tends to see when the orbital portions of the frontal lobes (i.e., the portions adjacent to the eyes) are damaged, a so-called orbito-frontal syndrome.[8] The frontal lobes are the most complex part of the brain, concerned not with the "lower" functions of movement and sensation, but the highest ones of integrating all judgment and behavior, all imagination and emotion, into that unique identity which we like to speak of as "personality" or "self." Damage to other parts of the brain may produce specific disturbances of sensation or movement, of language or of specific perceptual, cognitive, or memory functions. Damage to the frontal lobes, in contrast, does not affect these, but produces a subtler and profounder disturbance of "identity."

And it was this—rather than his blindness, or his weakness, or his disorientation, or his amnesia—which so horrified his parents when they finally saw Greg in 1975. It was not just that he was damaged, but that he was changed beyond recognition, had been "dispossessed," in his father's words, by a sort of simulacrum, or changeling, which had Greg's voice and manner and humor and intelligence but not his "spirit" or "realness" or "depth"—a changeling whose wisecracking and levity formed a shocking counterpoint to the fearful gravity of what had happened.

This sort of wisecracking, indeed, is quite characteristic of such orbito-frontal syndromes—and is so striking that it has been given a name to itself: *Witzelsucht*, or "joking disease." Some restraint, some caution, some inhibition, is destroyed, and patients with such syndromes tend to react, immediately and incontinently, to everything around them, and everything within them—to virtually every object, every person, every sensation, every word, every thought, every emotion, every nuance and tone.

There is an overwhelming tendency to wordplay and puns. Once when I was in Greg's room another patient walked past. "That's Bernie," I said. "Bernie the Hernie," quipped Greg. Another day, when I visited him he was in the dining room, awaiting lunch. When a nurse announced, "Lunch is here," he immediately responded, "It's time for cheer"; when she said, "Shall I take the skin off your chicken?" he instantly responded, "Yeah, why don't you slip me some skin." "Oh, you want the skin?" she asked, puzzled. "Nah," he replied, "it's just a saying."

He is, in a sense, preternaturally sensitive—but it is a sensitivity that is passive, without selectivity or focus. There is no differentiation in such a sensitivity— the grand, the trivial, the sublime, the ridiculous, are all mixed up and treated as equal.[9] There may be a childlike spontaneity and transparency about such patients, in their immediate and unpremeditated (and often playful) reactions. And yet there is something ultimately disquieting, and bizarre, because the reacting mind (which may still be highly intelligent and inventive) loses its coherence, its inwardness, its autonomy, its "self," and becomes the slave of every passing sensation. There is now, it seems, no boundary, no "psychological distance" (as Lhermitte would say), between Greg and his environment—he seizes it, he is seized by it, he cannot distinguish himself from it.

Though, as a neurologist, I had to speak of his "syndrome," his "deficits," I did not feel this was adequate to describe Greg. I felt, one felt, he had become another "kind" of person; that though his frontal lobe damage had taken away his identity in a way, yet it had also given him a sort of identity or personality, albeit of an odd and perhaps primitive sort.

Dreaming and waking, for us, are usually distinct—dreaming is enclosed in sleep, but enjoys a special license, because it is cut off from external perception and action; while waking perception is constrained by reality.[10] But in Greg the boundary between waking and sleep seems to break down, and what emerges is a sort of waking or public dream, in which dreamlike fancies and associations and symbols proliferate, and weave themselves into the waking perceptions of the mind. These associations are often startling and sometimes surrealistic in quality. They show the power of fancy at play, and, specifically, the mechanisms— displacement, condensation, "over-determination," etc.—which Freud has shown to be characteristic of dreams.

One felt all this very strongly with Greg; that he was often in some intermediate, half-dreamlike state,[11] in which, if the normal control and selectivity of thinking was lost, there was a half-freedom, half-compulsion of fantasy and wit. To see this as pathological was necessary, but insufficient: it had elements of the primitive, the childlike, the playful. Greg's absurdist, often gnomic utterances, combined with his seeming serenity (actually blandness), gave him an appearance of innocence and wisdom combined, gave him a special status on the ward, ambiguous but respected, a Holy Fool.

If Greg was alone, in a corridor, he seemed scarcely alive; but as soon as he was in company, he was a different person altogether. He would "come to," he would be funny, charming, ingenuous, sociable. Everyone liked him; he would respond to anyone at once, with a lightness and a humor and an absence of guile or hesitation; and if there was something too light or flippant or indiscriminate in his interactions and reactions, and if, moreover, he lost all memory of them in a minute, well, this was one of the results of his disease. Thus one was very aware, in a hospital for chronic patients like ours, a hospital where feelings of melancholy, of rage, and of hopelessness simmer and preside, of the virtue of a patient such as Greg—who never appeared to have bad moods, who, when activated by others, was invariably cheerful, euphoric.

He seemed, in an odd way, and in consequence of his sickness, to have a sort of vitality, or health—a cheeriness, an inventiveness, a directness, an exuberance, which other patients, and indeed the rest of us, in small doses, found delightful. And where he had been so "difficult," so tormented, so rebellious, in his pre-Krishna days, all this anger and torment and angst now seemed to have vanished; he seemed to be at peace. His father, who had had a terrible time in Greg's stormy days, before he got "tamed" by drugs, by religion, by tumor, said to me in an unbuttoned moment, "It's like he had a lobotomy," and then, with great irony, "Frontal lobes—who needs 'em?"[12]

5.

In a note about Greg of March 1979, I reported that "games, songs, verses, converse, etc. hold him together completely . . . because they have an organic rhythm and stream, a flowing of being, which carries and holds him." I was strongly reminded here of what I had seen with my amnesiac patient Jimmie, how he seemed held together when he attended Mass, by his relationship to and participation in an act of meaning, an organic unity, which overrode or bypassed the disconnections of his amnesia.[13] And what I had observed with a patient in England, a musician with profound amnesia from a temporal lobe encephalitis, unable to remember events or facts for more than a few seconds, but able to remember, and indeed to learn, elaborate musical pieces, to conduct them, to perform them, and even to improvise at the organ.[14] In Greg's case, of course, there was not just an amnesia, but a severe frontal-lobe syndrome as well, tending to "shallow" him, to remove genuine feeling and meaning, to replace these with a sort of indifference or frivolity.

Music, songs, seemed to bring Greg what, apparently, he lacked, to evoke in him a depth to which he otherwise had no access. Music was a door to a world of feeling, of meaning, a world in which Greg could, if only for a while, recover himself. Music drew back the constraints of the disease, aroused him from his blandness, released him from his levity. One felt Greg was "a different person" at such times—this was a phrase everyone used. He no longer seemed to have a frontal lobe syndrome at such times, but was (so to speak) temporarily "cured" by the music. Even his EEG, so slow and incoherent most of the time, became calm and rhythmical with music.

I observed, in this same note, that he not only had an excellent musical memory for songs of the Sixties, but was also able to learn new songs—even though, apparently, he could not absorb new "facts"; it was apparent that quite different memory mechanisms were involved.

He also possessed the ability to learn verses and limericks (these too have a rhythm and impetus of their own, very different from mere "facts"). Soon after his admission, I tested him with the following limerick:

> Hush-a-bye baby
> Hush quite a lot
> Bad babies get rabies
> And have to be shot

Greg immediately repeated this, without error, laughed at it, asked if I'd made it up, and compared it to "something gruesome, like Edgar Allan Poe." But two minutes later he could not recall it. When I repeated it each time I met him for a month, he did learn it, and thereafter recited it whenever he met me. What, I wondered, if one gave him political or satirical limericks, limericks not about babies and rabies, but about the current national or world situation? Would these, indeed, enable him to grasp some meaning?

It seemed natural, at this time, given Greg's blindness, and the revelation of his potentials for learning, that he should be given an opportunity to learn Braille. Arrangements were made with the Jewish Institute for the Blind for him to enter intensive training, four times a week. It should not have been a disappointment, nor indeed a surprise, that Greg was unwilling to learn any Braille—that he was startled and bewildered at finding this imposed on him, and cried out, "What's going on? Do you think I'm blind? Why am I here, with blind people all around me?" Attempts were made to explain things to him, and he responded, with impeccable logic, "If I were blind, I would be the first person to know it." The institute said they had never had such a difficult patient, and the project was quietly allowed to drop. And indeed, with the failure of the Braille program, a sort of hopelessness gripped us, and perhaps Greg too. We could do nothing, we felt; he had no potential for change.

Greg by this time had had several psychological and neuropsychological evaluations, and these, besides commenting on his memory and attentional problems, had all spoken of him as being "shallow," "infantile," "insightless," "euphoric." It was easy to see why they had thought this; Greg was like this for much of the time. But was there a deeper Greg beneath his illness, beneath the shallowing effect of his frontal lobe loss and amnesia? Early in 1979, when I questioned him, he said he was "miserable . . . at least in the corporeal part," and added, "It's not much of a life." At such times, it was clear that he was not just frivolous and euphoric, but capable of deep, and indeed melancholic, reactions to his plight. The comatose Karen Ann Quinlan was then very much in the news, and each time her name and fate were mentioned, Greg became distressed and silent. He could never tell me, explicitly, why this so interested him—but it had to be, I felt, because of some sort of identification of her tragedy with his own. Or was this just his incontinent sympathy, his falling at once into the mood of any stimulus or news, falling almost helplessly, mimetically, into its mood?

This was not a question I could decide at first, and perhaps too I was prejudiced against finding any depths in Greg, because the neuropsychological studies I knew of seemed to disallow this possibility. But these studies were based on brief evaluations, not on long-continued observation and relationship of a sort which is, perhaps, only possible in a hospital for chronic patients, or in situations where a whole world, a whole life, is shared with the patient.[15]

Greg's "frontal lobe" characteristics—his lightness, his quick-fire associations, were fun; but beyond this there shone through a basic decency and sensitivity and kindness. One felt that Greg, though damaged, still had a personality, an identity, a soul.[16]

When he came to Williamsbridge we all responded to his intelligence, his high spirits, his wit. All sorts of therapeutic programs and enterprises were started at this time, but all of them—not just the learning of Braille—ended in failure. The sense of Greg's incorrigibility gradually grew on us, and with this we started to do less, to hope less. Increasingly, he was left to his own devices. He slowly ceased to be a center of attention, the focus of eager therapeutic activities—more and more he was left to himself, left out of programs, not taken anywhere, quietly ignored.

And it is easy, even if one is not an amnesiac, to lose touch with current reality in the back wards of hospitals for the chronically ill. There is a simple round which has not changed in twenty, or fifty, years. One is awakened, fed, taken to the toilet, and left to sit in a hallway; one has lunch, is taken to bingo, has dinner, and goes to bed. The television may indeed be left on, blaring, in the television room—but most patients pay no attention to it. Greg, it is true, enjoyed his favorite soap operas and westerns, and learned an enormous number of advertising jingles by heart. But the "news," for the most part, he found boring and, increasingly, unintelligible. Years can pass, in a sort of timeless limbo, with few, and certainly no memorable, "markers" of the passage of time.

As ten years or so passed, Greg showed a complete absence of development, his talk seemed increasingly dated and repertorial, for nothing new was being added to it, or him. The tragedy of his amnesia seemed to become greater with the years, although his amnesia itself, his neurological syndrome, remained much the same.

6.

In 1988 Greg had a seizure—he had never had one before (although he had been on anticonvulsants, as a precaution, since the time of his surgery)—and in the seizure broke a leg. He did not complain of this, he did not even mention it; it was only discovered when he tried to stand up the following day. He had, apparently, forgotten it as soon as the pain eased, and as soon as he had found a comfortable position. His not knowing that he had broken a leg seemed to me to have similarities to his not knowing he was blind, his inability, with his amnesia, to hold in mind an *absence*. When the leg caused pain, briefly, he knew something had happened, he knew it was there; as soon as the pain ceased, it went from his mind. Had he had visual hallucinations or phantoms (as the blind sometimes do, at least in the first months and years after losing their sight), he could have spoken of them, said, "Look!" or "Wow!" But in the absence of actual visual input, he could hold nothing in mind about seeing, or not-seeing, or the loss of a visual world. In his person, and in his world, now, Greg knew only presence, now absence. He seemed incapable of registering any loss—loss of function in himself, or of an object, or a person.

In the summer of 1990, Greg's father, who had come every morning before work to see Greg, and would joke and chat with him for an hour, suddenly died. I myself was away at the time for several weeks, and hearing the news on my return, I hastened to Greg, who had been given the news, of course, when it happened. And yet I was not quite sure what to say—had he been able to absorb this new fact? "I guess you must be missing your father," I ventured.

"What do you mean?" Greg answered. "He comes every day. I see him every day."

"No," I said, "he's no longer coming . . . He has not come for some time. He died last month."

Greg flinched, turned ashen, became silent. I had the impression he was shocked, doubly shocked, at the sudden, appalling news of his father's death, and at the fact that he himself did not know, had not registered, did not remember. In this instant, then, he was doubly devastated—not only by the death of his father, but by the sudden revelation of his own amnesia. "I guess he must have been around fifty," he said.

"No, Greg," I answered, "he was well up in his seventies."

Greg grew pale again as I said this. I left the room briefly; I felt he needed to be alone with all this. But when I returned, a few minutes later, Greg had no memory of the conversation we had had, of the news I had given him, no idea that his father had died.

Very clearly, at least, Greg showed a capacity for love and grief. If I had ever doubted Greg's capacity for deeper feeling, I no longer doubted it now. He was clearly devastated by his father's death—he showed nothing "flip," no levity, at this time.[17] But would he have the ability to mourn? Mourning requires that one hold the sense of loss in one's mind, and it was far from clear to me that Greg could do this. One might indeed tell him that his father had died, again and again. And every time it would come as something shocking and new, and cause immeasurable distress. But then, in a few minutes, he would forget, and be cheerful again; and was so prevented from going through the work of grief, the mourning.[18]

I made a point of seeing Greg frequently in the following months, but I did not again bring up the subject of his father's death. It was not up to me, I thought, to confront him with this—indeed it would be pointless and cruel to do so; life itself, surely, would do so, for Greg would discover his father's absence.

I made the following note on November 26, 1990: "Greg shows no conscious knowing that his father has died—when asked where his father is, he may say, 'Oh, he went down to the patio,' or 'He couldn't make it today,' or something else plausible. But he no longer wants to go home, on weekends, on Thanksgiving, as he so loved to—he must find something sad or repugnant in the fatherless house now, even though he cannot (consciously) remember or articulate this. Clearly he has established an *association* of sadness."

Toward the end of the year Greg, normally a sound sleeper, started to sleep poorly, to get up in the middle of the night, and wander gropingly for hours around his room. "I've lost something, I'm looking for something," he would say when asked—but what he had lost, what he was looking for, he could never explain. One could not avoid the feeling that Greg was looking for his father, even though he could give no account of what he was doing, and had no explicit knowledge of what he had lost. But, it seemed to me, there was perhaps now an implicit knowledge, and perhaps too a symbolic (though not a conceptual) knowing.

7.

Greg had seemed so sad, since his father's death, that I felt he deserved a special celebration—and when I heard, in August of 1991, that his beloved group, the

Grateful Dead, would be playing at Madison Square Garden in a few weeks, this seemed just the thing. Indeed, I had met one of the drummers in the band, Mickey Hart, earlier in the summer, when we had both testified before the Senate about the therapeutic powers of music, so arrangements were made for Greg to come to one of the concerts.[19]

We received tickets for the concert at the last minute, and I had given Greg no warning, not wanting to disappoint him if we failed to get seats. But when I picked him up at the hospital and told him where we were going, he showed great excitement. We got him dressed swiftly, and bundled him into the car. As we got into midtown, I opened the car windows, and the sounds and smells of New York came in. As we cruised down 33rd Street, the smell of hot pretzels suddenly struck him; he inhaled deeply, and laughed, "That's the most New York smell in the world."

There was an enormous crowd converging on Madison Square Garden, almost all in tie-dyed T-shirts—I had hardly seen a tie-dyed T-shirt in twenty years, and I myself began to think we were back in the Sixties, or perhaps that we had never left them. I was sorry that Greg could not have seen this crowd; he would have felt himself one of them, at home. Stimulated by the atmosphere, Greg started to talk spontaneously—very unusual for him—and to reminisce about the Sixties:

> Yeah, there were the be-ins in Central Park. They haven't had one for a long time —over a year, maybe, can't remember exactly.... Concerts, music, acid, grass, everything.... First time I was there was Flower-Power Day....
>
> Good times ... lots of things started in the Sixties—acid rock, the be-ins, the love-ins, smoking.... Don't see it much these days.... Allen Ginsberg—he's down in the Village a lot, or in Central Park. I haven't seen him for a long time. It's over a year since I last saw him....

Greg's use of the present tense, or the near-present tense; his sense of all these events, not as far distant, much less as terminated, but as having taken place "a year ago, maybe" (and, by implication, likely to take place again, at any time); all this, which seemed so pathological, so anachronistic in clinical testing, seemed almost normal, natural, now that we were part of this Sixties crowd sweeping toward the Garden.

Inside the Garden we found the special place reserved for Greg's wheelchair near the soundboard. And now Greg was growing more excited by the minute; the roar of the crowd excited him—"It's like a giant animal," he said—and the sweet, hash-laden air—"What a great smell," he said, inhaling deeply. "It's the least stupid smell in the world."[20]

As the band came onstage, and the noise of the crowd grew greater, Greg was transported by the excitement, and started clapping loudly, and shouting in an enormous voice, "Bravo! Bravo!" then, "Let's go!" followed by "Let's go, Hypo," followed, homophonously, by "Ro, Ro, Ro, Harry-Bo." Pausing a moment, Greg said to me, "See the tombstone behind the drums? See Jerry Garcia's Afro?" with such conviction that I was momentarily taken in, and looked (in vain) for a tomb-stone behind the drums—before realizing it was one of Greg's confabulations—and at the now-gray hair of Jerry Garcia, which fell in a straight, unhindered descent to his shoulders.

And then, "Pigpen!" Greg exclaimed, "You see Pigpen there?"

"No," I replied, hesitantly, not knowing how to reply. "He's not there. . . . You see, he's not with the Dead anymore."

"Not with them?" said Greg, in astonishment. "What happened—he got busted or something?"

"No, Greg, not busted. He died."

"That's awful," Greg answered, shaking his head, shocked. And then a minute later, he nudged me again. "Pigpen! You see Pigpen there?" And, word for word, the whole conversation repeated itself.

But then the thumping, pounding excitement of the crowd got him—the rhyth-mic clapping and stamping and chanting possessed him—and he started to chant, "The Dead! The Dead!," then with a shift of rhythm, and a slow emphasis on each word, "We want the Dead!" And then, "Tobacco Road, Tobacco Road," the name of one of his favorite songs, until the music began.

The band began with an old song, "Iko, Iko," and Greg joined in with gusto, with abandon, clearly knowing all the words, and especially luxuriating in the African-sounding chorus. The whole vast Garden now was in motion with the music, eighteen thousand people responding together, everyone transported, every nervous system synchronized, in unison.

The first half of the concert had many earlier pieces, songs from the Sixties, and Greg knew them, loved them, joined in. His energy and joy were amazing to see; he clapped and sang nonstop, with none of the weakness and fatigue he generally showed. He showed a rare and wonderful continuity of attention, every-thing orienting him, holding him together. Looking at Greg transformed in this way, I could see no trace of his amnesia, his frontal lobe syndrome—he seemed at this moment completely normal, as if the music was infusing him with its own strength, its coherence, its spirit.

I had wondered whether we should leave at the break midway through the concert—he was, after all, a disabled, wheelchair-bound patient, who had not really been "out" on the town, at a rock concert, for more than twenty years. But he said, "No, I want to stay, I want it all"—an assertion, an autonomy, I rejoiced to see, and had hardly ever seen in his compliant life at the hospital. So we stayed, and in the interval went backstage, where Greg had a large hot pretzel, and then met Mickey Hart and exchanged a few words with him. He had looked a little tired and pale before, but now he was flushed, excited by the encounter, charged and eager to be back for more music.

But the second half of the concert was somewhat strange for Greg: more of the songs dated from the mid- or late Seventies, and had lyrics which were unknown to him, though they were familiar in style. He enjoyed these, clapping and singing along wordlessly, or making up words as he went. But then there were newer songs, radically different, like "Picasso Moon," with dark and deep harmonies, and an electronic instrumentation such as would have been impossible, unimaginable, in the 1960s. Greg was intrigued, but deeply puzzled. "It's weird stuff," he said, "I never heard anything like it before." He listened intently, all his musical senses stirred, but with a slightly scared and bewildered look, as if seeing a new animal, a new plant, a new world, for the first time. "I guess it's some new, experimental stuff," he said, "something they never played before. Sounds futuristic . . . maybe it's the music of the future." The newer songs he heard went far beyond any development that he could have imagined, were so beyond (and in some ways so unlike) what he associated with the Dead, that it "blew his mind." It was, he could not doubt, "their" music he was hearing, but it gave him an almost unbearable sense of hearing the future—as late Beethoven would have struck a devotee if it had been played at a concert in 1800.

"That was fantastic," he said, as we filed out of the Garden, "I will always remember it. I had the time of my life." I played CDs of the Grateful Dead in the car on the way home, to hold as long as possible the mood and memory of the concert. I feared that if I stopped playing the Dead, or talking about them, for a single moment, all memory of the concert would go from his mind. Greg sang along enthusiastically all the way back, and when we parted at the hospital, he was still in an exuberant concert mood.

But the next morning when I came to the hospital early, I found Greg in the dining room, alone, facing the wall. I asked him about the Grateful Dead—what did he think of them? "Great group," he said, "I love them. I heard them in Central Park and at the Fillmore East."

"Yes," I said, "you told me. But have you seen them since? Didn't you just hear them at Madison Square Garden?"

"No," he said, "I've never been to the Garden."

EPILOGUE

Greg has no recollection of the concert, seemingly—but when I was sent a tape of it, he immediately recognized some of the "new" pieces, found them familiar, was able to sing them. "Where did you hear that?" I asked as we listened to "Picasso Moon."

"I can't remember," he said, "didn't hear it, anything like it, at the Central Park concert."

I had wondered whether hearing the songs, and especially hearing a tape of the concert itself, with all the sounds of coughing, clapping, singing, and background noise, would bring back the memory of Madison Square Garden. "It was a big concert," I said. "You went there a few nights ago."

"I don't remember it," he said, "but that's a real big noise—huge. The place must be as big as a stadium." But he could not be more specific. Then he became puzzled: "Were you there with me?"

Thus Greg remembers the music—and something about it evokes my presence too—but he cannot say when or where he heard it, he cannot give a frame or context to his learning.

Smells are sometimes even more evocative than music; and the percepts of smells, generated in a very primitive part of the brain—the "smell brain," or rhinencephalon—may not go through the complex, multistage memory systems of the medial temporal lobe. Olfactory memories, neurally, are almost indelible; thus they may be remembered despite an amnesia. It would be fascinating to bring Greg hot pretzels, or hash, to see whether their smells could evoke memories of the concert. He himself, the day after the concert, spontaneously mentioned the "great" smell of pretzels—it was very vivid for him—and yet he could not locate the smell in place or time. I have visited him, played him tapes, several times, and now, when I arrive, and he hears my voice, he lights up, and greets me as a fellow Deadhead. Thus he has not only acquired new knowledge, he has acquired a new relation to me; he sees me (so to speak) in a new light.

A recently published paper from Endel Tulving and his colleagues at the University of Toronto suggests that factual learning may indeed be possible, and put to use, even in patients with the densest amnesia. Thus they note that "amnesiacs can learn new factual information, despite [their] inability to recollect the learning episodes," and that though such learning may be slow and laborious, its long-term retention, once learned, is entirely normal. They add, with regard to their own patient, K. C., that

> his newly-acquired knowledge represented [for him] ordinary facts of the world . . .
> he thought other people would know "rays softened asphalt" [one of his learned
> sentences] as well as they would know that "dogs chase cats."

They conclude that their patient "could generalize from his new knowledge, and did not see it, or treat it, as an isolated, 'free' fragment."

Although Tulving and his colleagues were specifically concerned with their subjects' ability to learn some hundreds of short sentences, they allude to other sorts of learning amnesiacs have been found capable of—learning statements of facts about people, places, and things; learning new computer-related vocabulary or simple computer commands. Such learning, they stress, is invariably slow and inefficient, but it does occur.

With music, for whatever reasons—whether because of his musical giftedness, or the fact that musical memory may use different memory paths—learning for Greg is neither slow nor inefficient, but swift, automatic, and enjoyable. Moreover, music does not consist of sparse propositions (like "rays softened asphalt"), but is rich with emotion, association, and meaning. Songs, quicker than anything, can evoke a character, an epoch, a world—what Thomas Mann, in *The Magic Mountain*, calls "the world behind the music."

It is easy to show that simple information can be embedded in songs; thus we can give Greg the date every day, in the form of a jingle, and he can readily isolate this, and say it when asked—give it, that is, without the jingle. But what does it mean to say, "This is December the 19th, 1991," when one is sunk in the profoundest amnesia, when one has lost one's sense of time and history, when one is existing from moment to moment in a sequenceless limbo? "Knowing the date" means nothing in these circumstances. Could one, however, through the evocativeness and power of music, perhaps using songs with specially written lyrics—songs which relate something valuable about himself or the current world —accomplish something more lasting, deeper? Give Greg not only "facts," but a sense of time and history, of the relatedness (and not merely the existence) of events, an entire (if synthetic) framework for thinking? This is something which Connie Tomaino and I are trying to do now. We hope to have an answer in a year.

Notes

I am grateful to Elkhonon Goldberg, who has performed neuropsychological evaluations on Greg F., and has provided, in his articles and personal contact, invaluable insights about frontal lobe function; to Concetta Tomaino, the music therapist at "Williamsbridge," who has worked closely with Greg for years; to Larry Squire, who has been helpful in discussing mechanisms of memory and problems of amnesiacs; to Mickey Hart, who showed a compassionate interest in Greg and made it possible for us to see the Grateful Dead in concert; to Greg's parents; and above all, to Greg himself.

1. The swami's unusual views are presented, in summary form, in *Easy Journey to Other Planets* by Tridandi Goswami A. C. Bhaktivedanta Swami, published by the League of Devotees, Vrindaban (no date, one rupee). This slim manual, in its green paper cover, was handed out in vast quantities by the swami's saffron-robed followers, and it became Greg's Bible at this stage.
2. Another patient, Ruby G., was in some ways similar to Greg. She too had a huge frontal tumor, which, though it was removed in 1973, left her with amnesia, a frontal lobe syndrome, and blindness. She too did not know that she was blind, and when I held up my hand before her and asked, "How many fingers?" would answer, "A hand has five fingers, of course."

   A more localized unawareness of blindness may arise if there is destruction of the visual cortex. Such patients may not know that they are blind; they have lost the very idea of "seeing" and "light," but are otherwise intact. But frontal-lobe unawarenesses are far more global in nature—thus Greg and Ruby were not only unaware of being blind, but unaware (for the most part) of being ill, of having devastating neurological and cognitive deficits, and of their tragic, diminished position in life.

   Goldberg and Barr have recently speculated on the mechanisms that underlie these different forms of unawareness. See Elkhonon Goldberg and William B. Barr, "Three possible mechanisms of unawareness of deficit," in *Awareness of Deficit After Brain Injury: Clinical and Theoretical Issues*, edited by George P. Prigatano and Daniel L. Schachter (1991). An amnesia such as Greg's, indeed, is a profound alteration in the entire structure of consciousness, knowledge, and identity—this is strongly brought out by Israel Rosenfield in a forthcoming book, *The Strange, Familiar and Forgotten: An Anatomy of Consciousness* (1992).

3. That implicit memory (especially if emotionally charged) may exist in amnesiacs was shown, somewhat cruelly, in 1911, by Edouard Claparède, who when shaking hands with such a patient whom he was presenting to his students, stuck a pin in his hand. Although the patient had no explicit memory of this, he refused, thereafter, to shake hands with him.

4. The development of a special high-speed, multistage transfer system for explicit memory seems to be a recent development in evolution, one which perhaps parallels the development of consciousness itself (see Gerald Edelman, *The Remembered Present*, 1990). It is present in higher mammals, but absent in lower animals, as is consciousness itself. Thus although a rat or monkey could have amnesia, it seems doubtful whether a slug or frog could.

5. Luria too remarks on this, in *The Neuropsychology of Memory* (1976), and speaks of all his amnesiac patients, if hospitalized for any length of time, as acquiring "a sense of familiarity" with their surroundings.

6. *The New York Review*, February 16, 1984. Reprinted in *The Man Who Mistook His Wife for a Hat* (Harper and Row, 1987).

7. *Granta*, No. 16 (Summer, 1985), reprinted in *The Man Who Mistook His Wife for a Hat*.

8. One may see two quite different, indeed opposite, sorts of frontal lobe syndromes. Damage to the outer, or lateral, portions of the frontal lobes tends to cause profound apathy and immobility, while damage to the inner or medial portions causes the opposite, a state of wisecracking and excitement. Although Greg has damage to both, it is especially the medial portions of his frontal lobes which have been compressed by the tumor, hence he shows, predominantly, an excitatory syndrome.

9. Luria has provided immensely detailed, at times almost novelistic, descriptions of frontal-lobe syndromes—Luria, *Human Brain and Psychological Processes* (1966)—and sees this "equalization" as the heart of such syndromes.

10. Rodolfo Llinás, of New York University, comparing the electrophysiological properties of the brain in waking and dreaming, postulates a single fundamental mechanism for both—a ceaseless "inner talking" between cerebral cortex and thalamus, a ceaseless interplay of image and feeling, irrespective of whether there is sensory input or not. When there is sensory input, this interplay integrates it to generate "waking consciousness," but in the absence of sensory input it continues to generate brain states, those brain states we call fantasy, hallucination, or dreaming. Thus waking consciousness is dreaming—but dreaming constrained by external reality. R. R. Llinás and D. Paré, "On Dreaming and Wakefulness," *Neuroscience*, Vol. 44, No. 3 (1991), pp. 521–535.

11. In 1963, when I first smoked some marijuana, I found it had a singular effect, releasing strings of word rhymes and homonyms which rushed, involuntarily, with great speed through my mind. This immediately made me think of the mechanism of jokes and dreams, and of the forced wordplay in frontal lobe syndromes and schizophrenia. This is "Undermind," I said to myself—and was intrigued to have, through a reversible intoxication, a brief experience of what, in patients, is usually permanent.

12. A fascinating account of such a natural "lobotomy" is related by Lytton Strachey concerning Dr. North, a master of Trinity College, Cambridge, in the seventeenth century. Dr. North, it is evident, was a man with severe anxieties, and tormenting obsessional traits, who was hated and dreaded by the fellows of the college for his punctiliousness, his moralizing, and his merciless severity. Until one day, in college, he suffered a stroke.

> His recovery was not complete [Strachey tells us]; his body was paralyzed on the left side; but it was in his mind that the most remarkable change occurred. His fears had left him. His scrupulosity, his diffidence, his seriousness, even his morality—all had vanished. He lay on his bed, in reckless levity, pouring forth a stream of flippant observations, and naughty stories, and improper jokes. While his friends hardly knew which way to look, he laughed consumedly, his paralyzed features drawn up in a curiously distorted grin. . . . Attacked by epileptic seizures, he declared that the only mitigation of his sufferings lay in the continued consumption of wine. He, who had been so noted for his austerity, now tossed off, with wild exhilaration, glass after glass of the strongest sherry.

Strachey gives us here a precise and beautifully described picture of a frontal lobe stroke altering the personality in a major and, so to speak, "therapeutic" way.

13. The nature of the "organic unity," at once dynamic and semantic, which is central to music, incantation, recitation, and all metrical structures, has been most profoundly analyzed by Victor Zuckerkandl, in his remarkable book *Sound and Symbol* (two volumes, Princeton University Press, 1973). It is typical of such flowing dynamic-semantic structures that each part leads on to the next, that every part has reference to the rest. Such structures cannot be perceived, or remembered, in part—they are perceived and remembered, if at all, as wholes.

14. This patient is the subject of a remarkable BBC film made by Jonathan Miller, *Prisoner of Consciousness* (November 1988).

15. The great French neurologist F. Lhermitte is especially sensitive to this, and instead of just observing his patients in the clinic, he makes a point of visiting them at home, taking them to restaurants or theaters, or for rides in his car, sharing their lives as much as possible. It is impossible to fully understand frontal lobe syndromes in the impoverished and constraining atmosphere of the clinic, and such a "naturalistic" or "ecological" approach is essential.

16. Mr. Thompson, who also had both amnesia and a frontal lobe syndrome, by contrast often seemed "desouled." In him the wisecracking was manic, ferocious, frenetic, and relentless; it rushed on like a torrent, oblivious to tact, to decency, to propriety, to everything, including the feelings of everyone around him. Whether Greg's (at least partial) preservation of ego and identity is due to the lesser severity of his syndrome, or to underlying personality differences, is not wholly clear. Mr. Thompson's premorbid personality was that of a New York cabbie, and in some sense his frontal lobe syndrome merely intensified this. Greg's personality was less aggressive, more childlike, more passive from the start—and this, it seemed to me, even colored his frontal lobe syndrome.

17. This is in distinction to Mr. Thompson, who with his more severe frontal lobe syndrome had been reduced to a sort of nonstop, wisecracking, talking machine, and when told of his brother's death quipped, "He's always the joker!" and rushed on to other, irrelevant things.

18. The amnesiac musicologist in the BBC film *Prisoner of Consciousness* shows something both similar and different. Every time his wife goes out of the room, he has a sense of calamitous, permanent loss. When she comes back, five minutes later, he sobs with relief, saying, "I thought you were dead."

19. Mickey Hart himself has written fascinatingly about the mind-altering, body-altering powers of rhythm, *Drumming at the Edge of Magic: A Journey into the Spirit of Percussion* (1990).

20. Jean Cocteau, in fact, said this of opium. Whether Greg was quoting this, consciously or unconsciously, I do not know.

References

Edelman, Gerald M. *The Remembered Present: A Biological Theory of Consciousness.* Basic Books (1989).
Goldberg, Elkhonon, and William B. Barr. "Three Possible Mechanisms of Unawareness of Deficit." In George P. Prigatano and Daniel L. Schachter (Eds.). *Awareness of Deficit after Brain Injury: Clinical and Theoretical Issues.* Oxford University Press (1991).
Hart, Mickey. *Drumming at the Edge of Magic: A Journey into the Spirit of Percussion.* HarperSanFrancisco (1990).
Lhermitte, F., B. Pillon, and M. Serdaru. "Human Autonomy and the Frontal Lobes." *Annals of Neurology*, 19(4) (1986): 326–43.
Llinás, R. R., and D. Paré. "On Dreaming and Wakefulness." *Neuroscience*, 44(3) (1991): 521–35.
Luria, A. R. *Human Brain and Psychological Processes.* Harper and Row (1966).
—— *The Neuropsychology of Memory.* Halsted Press (1976).
Rosenfield, Israel. *The Strange, Familiar, and Forgotten: An Anatomy of Consciousness.* Knopf (1992).
Squire, Larry, and Stuart Zola-Morgan. "The Medial Temporal Lobe Memory System." *Science*, 253 (September 20, 1991): 1,380–6.
Tulving, Endel, C. A. Gordon Hayman, and Carol A. Macdonald. "Long-Lasting Perceptual Priming and Semantic Learning in Amnesia: A Case Experiment." *Journal of Experimental Psychology*, 17(4) (July 1991): 595–617.
Zuckerkandl, Victor. *Sound and Symbol*, vol. 1: *Music and the External World*; vol. 2: *The Musician.* Princeton University Press (1973).

CHAPTER 12

The Body as Territory and as Wonder

Arthur W. Frank

I have put my body in the hands of physicians off and on since the day I was born. But until I was critically ill I never felt I was putting my life in their hands. Life-threatening illness gave doctors a new dimension of importance for me. I had never expected so much from them or been so sensitive to their shortcomings. How medicine treats the body is an essential part of the story of illness, but it is never more than half of the story. The other half is the body itself. Life-threatening illness also gave my body a new dimension of importance. I had never been so sensitive to its shortcomings, nor had I realized how much I could expect of it. These two stories, the story of medicine taking the body as its territory and the story of learning to wonder at the body itself, can only be told together, because illness is both stories at once.

After the ultrasound a physician said, "This will have to be investigated." Hearing this phrase, I was both relieved and offended. The relief was that someone was assuming part of the burden of worrying about what was happening to me. But I was also offended by his language, which made my body into medicine's field of investigation. "I" had become medicine's "this". The physician did not even say, "We'll have to find out what's wrong with you," which would have been a team of real people ("we") speaking to another person ("you"). "This will have to be investigated" was not addressed to me at all. The physician was speaking as if to himself, allowing me, the patient, to overhear.

"This will have to be investigated" assumes that physicians will do the investigation, but they too are left out of the phrase, anonymous. "Will have to be" suggests the investigation happens of its own necessity. Why should a physician speak this way? Because if in the course of this investigation mistakes are made (as the physician who spoke had already mistaken my diagnosis), no individual physician is responsible. The mistakes are just part of a process; they too "have to be." I imagine he spoke out of fear as well as uncertainty. He responded by making himself and other physicians anonymous. And I had to be made equally anonymous.

I, my body, became the passive object of this necessity, the investigation. I could imagine how native people felt when European explorers arrived on their shores, planted a flag, and claimed their land on behalf of a foreign monarch who would bring cirvilization to the savages. To get medicine's help, I had to cede the territory of my body to the investigation of doctors who were as yet anonymous. I had to be colonized.

The investigation required me to enter the hospital. Fluids were extracted, specialists' opinions accumulated, machines produced images of the insides of my body, but the diagnosis remained uncertain. One day I returned to my room and found a new sign below my name on the door. It said "Lymphoma," a form of cancer I was suspected of having. No one had told me that this diagnosis, which later proved to be wrong, had been confirmed. Finding it written there was like the joke about the guy who learns he has been fired when he finds someone else's name on his office door. In this case my name had not been changed, it had been defined. "Lymphoma" was a medical flag, planted as a claim on the territory of my body.

This colonization only became worse. During chemotherapy a nurse, speaking to Cathie, referred to me as "the seminoma in 53" (my room number). By then the diagnosis was correct, but it had crowded out my name entirely. The hospital had created its own version of my identity. I became the disease, the passive object of investigation and later of treatment. Nameless, how could I be a person who experiences?

The ill person actively tries to make sense of what is happening in her body. She tries to maintain a relationship between what is happening to her body and what is going on in the rest of her life. When a person becomes a patient, physicians take over her body, and their understanding of the body separates it from the rest of her life. Medicine's understanding of pain, for instance, has little to do with the ill person's experience. For the person, pain is about incoherence and the disruption of relations with other people and things; it is about losing one sense of place and finding another. Medicine has no interest in what pain means in a life; it can see pain only as a symptom of a possible disease. Medicine cannot enter into the experience; it seeks only cure or management. It does offer relief to a body that is suffering, but in doing so it colonizes the body. This is the trade-off we make in seeking medical help.

If the treatment works, the passivity is worth it. When I am ill, I want to become a patient. It is dangerous to avoid doctors, but it is equally dangerous to allow them to hog center stage in the drama of illness. The danger of avoiding doctors is immediate and physical, but if we allow them to dominate the drama, they will script it to include only disease. By saying "This will have to be investigated," my physician claimed center stage and scripted the drama to follow; the person within my body was sent out into the audience to watch passively.

What did I, as patient, want from physicians and the medical staff? I did not expect to become friends with them. In the hospital I had such fleeting contact with so many specialists, and nurses appeared to rotate through shifts so rapidly, that exchanging anything more than conventional pleasantries would have been artificial. The relationship of patient to staff is peculiar, unlike any other. We discussed intimate matters, but this talk did not make us close. As treatment providers, they saw my intimate concerns in the context of their general categories of disease and the progress of treatment.

Relationships between patients and medical staff, whether physicians or nurses, involve people who are intimate with each other but rarely become intimates of each other. For a truly intimate relationship people need a sharing of time and personal history and a recognition of each other's differences. Medical intimacy categorizes rather than recognizes, and it is one-sided. The patient's life and body are an open book, or chart, to the medical staff. The staff sometimes share their experiences with patients, but in my memory these moments are the exceptions. More important, physicians and nurses can choose what they will tell a patient about themselves, and whether they will say anything at all. There is the real asymmetry, which becomes more complicated during moments that are critical in the patient's life but represent just another day's work for the staff. The staff cannot match the patient's emotional intensity on such occasions, but they should not expect the patient to mimic their professional calm.

I may not expect emotion or intimacy from physicians and nurses, but I do expect recognition. Another person, whose experience I want to honor, said it is no small thing to have cancer—to realize you are becoming ill, to suffer that illness and risk death, to be dying or to have returned to the living and be starting life over again with the knowledge of your own mortality. It is no small thing to have your body rearranged, first by disease and then by surgical and chemical interventions intended to cure that disease. Critical illness takes its travelers to the margins of human experience. One step further and someone so ill would not return. I want that journey to be recognized.

I always assumed that if I became seriously ill, physicians, no matter how overworked, would somehow recognize what I was living through. I did not know what form this recognition would take, but I assumed it would happen. What I experienced was the opposite. The more critical my diagnosis became, the more reluctant physicians were to talk to me. I had trouble getting them to make eye contact; most came only to see my disease. This "it" within the body was their field of investigation; "I" seemed to exist beyond the horizon of their interest.

Medical staff often believe they are involved in the patient's personal life. When I was admitted to the hospital, the resident doing my intake physical made a point of saying he was now getting to the "social history." Cathie and I were curious to know what the hospital considered important as social history. The resident then asked what my job was. I answered and waited for the next question; he closed the chart. That was it, nothing more. What bothered us was the illusion that he had found out something. The resident took his inquiry into my social history seriously and seemed to have no sense of how little he learned. The irony of there being only one question completely escaped him. He was filling in a category, employment, to give himself an illusion of having recognized me as a "social" being.

The night before I had surgery, I was visited by an anesthesiologist who represented the culmination of my annoyance with this nonrecognition. He refused to look at me, and he even had the facts of the planned operation wrong. When he was leaving I did the worst thing to him I could think of: I made him shake hands. A hand held out to be shaken cannot be refused without direct insult, but to shake a hand is to acknowledge the other as an equal. The anesthesiologist trembled visibly as he brushed his hand over mine, and I allowed myself to enjoy his discomfort. But that was only a token of what I really wanted. I wanted him to recognize that the operation I was having and the disease it was part of were no small thing.

The kind of recognition I wanted changed over the course of my illness. While seeking diagnosis I felt that I was in a struggle just to get physicians to recognize the disease; once I got them onto the stage of my illness, the problem was to keep it my drama, not theirs. The active roles in the drama of illness all go to physicians. Being a patient means, quite literally, being patient. Daily life in the hospital is spent waiting for physicians. Hospitals are organized so that physicians can see a maximum number of patients, which means patients spend maximum time waiting. You have to be patient. Maybe the doctor will come this morning; if not, maybe this afternoon. Decisions about treatment are stalled until the doctor's arrival; nurses and residents don't know what's happening. Hopes, fears, and uncertainty mount.

When the physician does arrive, he commands center stage. I write "he" because this performance is so stereotypically masculine, although women physicians learn to play it well enough. The patient hangs on what brief words are said, what parts of the body are examined or left unattended. When the physician has gone, the patient recounts to visitors everything he did and said, and together they repeatedly consider and interpret his visit. The patient wonders what the physician meant by this joke or that frown. In hospitals, where the patient is constantly reminded of how little he knows, the physician is assumed not only to know all but to know more than he says.

In becoming a patient—being colonized as medical territory and becoming a spectator to your own drama—you lose yourself. First you may find that the lab results rather than your body's responses are determining how you feel. Then, in the rush to treatment, you may lose your capacity to make choices, to decide how you want your body to be used. Finally, in the blandness of the medical setting, in its routines and their discipline, you may forget your tastes and preferences. Life turns to beige. It is difficult to accept the realities of what physicians can do for you without subordinating yourself to their power. The power is real, but it need not be total. You can find places for yourself in the cracks.

I want to affirm the importance, both for yourself and for those around you, of holding onto the person you still are, even as medicine tries to colonize your body. Disease cannot be separated from other parts of a person's identity and life. Disease changed my life as husband, father, professor, and everything else. I had to learn to be dependent. I was unreliable in practical matters and often in emotional ones as well, and incapable of doing tasks that I had considered normal. It was no small thing to rediscover myself as I changed.

I have learned that the changes that begin during illness do not end when treatment stops. Life after critical illness does not go back to where it was before. A danger of allowing physicians to dominate the drama of illness is that they leave as soon as the disease is resolved to their satisfaction or when they have done all they can. Then the ill person and those around him are left to deal with the consequences of what has not been recognized. If the ill person dies, those who survive must deal with all that was not said, the unfinished business of a life closed out in a setting where dying is a problem of management, not a continuity of experience. And those ill persons who recover must recover not only from the disease but from being a patient. This recovery will proceed far more smoothly if the person within the patient has been recognized throughout the period of illness and recovery.

Continuing to recognize myself as the person undergoing the illness, reclaiming my body as my territory while I was in settings dominated by what was relevant to medicine alone, was no easy business.

What authorizes medicine to claim the body as its territory? Every day society sends us messages that the body can and ought to be controlled. Advertisements for prescription and nonprescription drugs, grooming and beauty advice, diet books, and fitness promotion literature all presuppose an ideal of control of the body. Control is good manners as well as a moral duty; to lose control is to fail socially and morally. But then along comes illness, and the body goes out of control.

In society's view of disease, when the body goes out of control, the patient is treated as if he has lost control. Being sick thus carries more than a hint of moral failure; I felt that in being ill I was being vaguely irresponsible. Of course, the problem is not that I or any other ill person has "lost" control; the problem is that society's ideal of controlling the body is wrong in the first place. But rather than give up this ideal, society sends in physicians to prove that bodies can be controlled. Physicians justifiably think it is their duty to restore, in the name of society, the control that the sick are believed to have lost. Control, or at least management, becomes a medical ideal.

A cousin who had cancer wrote to me about a meeting she had with her doctor in which she asked more questions than he apparently thought appropriate. He accused her of "trying to control" her treatment, and asserted that he was "in control." This story is not uncommon, though it seems to happen more often to women patients than to men. The real question is not who is in control, but whether anyone is. One lesson I have learned from illness is that giving up the idea of control, by either myself or my doctors, made me more content. What I recommend, to both medical staff and ill persons, is to recognize the wonder of the body rather than try to control it.

Wondering at the body means trusting it and acknowledging its control. I do not mean that we should stop trying to change the direction the body is taking.

I certainly did all I could, and I value all that my physicians did, to use treatment to change the direction my body was taking. Wonder and treatment can be complementary; wonder is an attitude in which treatment can best proceed. To think that any of us was controlling the body through treatment is another illusion. That my body responded to medical interventions did not mean it was being "successfully" controlled. Rather we should wonder at what "it" did. I use the word "it" here because the body worth wondering at is not the creature of my conscious mind. It is not an extension of "I." Instead, my mind is an extension of my body. I claim little credit for the wonder of my body.

Wonder is almost always possible; control may not be. If the ill person can focus on an ideal of wonder in place of control, then living in a diseased body can recover some of its joy. I did not think this up; I learned it from my body one morning in the rain.

While my investigation was still in the outpatient stage, I used to walk to the hospital for diagnostic tests. One morning I was scheduled to have a pyelogram, a kind of X-ray to test kidney functioning. Cathie was teaching and needed the car. It was pouring rain, coming down in buckets. Any sane person would have called a taxi, but I had cancer and no aspirations to sanity. I wanted to walk. Preparation for the pyelogram required taking massive laxatives to empty the intestine, so in addition to my sleeping problems, I had spent the night in the bathroom.

But as wrecked as I was, when I started walking I began to feel better. I was outside and moving and really very happy. First my feet began to get wet, then my pants, and soon the water was dripping inside my jacket, but that didn't matter. Here was the world of people going to work, of puddles and grass and leaves, and I was able to be part of it. Getting wet was the least of my problems. My problem was going into the hospital, or, more specifically, not coming out again. I feared that the pyelogram's results would mean I couldn't leave the hospital; soon the world I was walking through would be closed off to me. Not today probably; I half realized that before any results were available and medical judgment took over, I would have escaped. But I did not know how many more walks I might have. So I did not lapse into thinking about what I was going to do once I got where I was going; that day I experienced the trip. And I realized that I owed it to illness to be able to see that green September day so very clearly.

I did not want to arrive at the hospital, yet I knew I couldn't slosh around outside much longer. For the first time since the ultrasound several days before, I felt pleasantly relaxed about whatever was to happen. Going inside out of the rain, I wondered at what the body could still do for me, as diseased as I knew it must be. That day I stopped resenting "it" for the pain I had felt and began to appreciate my body, in some ways for the first time in my life. I stopped evaluating my body and began to draw strength from it. And I recognized that this body was me.

Later, when I was admitted to the hospital, the strange progress of my disease had relieved most of the pain, and I started exercising again. Exercising in a hospital is not easy. In Canadian hospitals one gets a private room only by the luck of the moment of arrival or by having some very infectious disease. I was lucky in my timing. I took advantage of my privacy to lift weights Cathie brought for me. Nurses would come in to record my vital signs and find I was out running up and down stairs. Their tolerance was more remarkable than my eccentricity.

Running on the stairs, experiencing the strength I still had, gave me a feeling that my body was doing what it wanted. Through exercise I began to discover what I wanted. Exercise was a way of keeping myself at center stage of my illness. When I had surgery, these activities had to end, but they got me through the period of finding "Lymphoma" written under my name. The hospital had its labels for me, but I could hold onto my identity, which was still rooted in my body, tumorous or not.

Exercising was also a way of telling myself that I would come back from cancer, that my body was still worth taking care of. This affirmation was not, however, a deal. I did not think exercise was part of any cure. It was the way I wanted to live out my life with illness, a way to keep living the life I had, regardless of the progress of disease. Exercise was my expression of wonder at the body.

The arts of being ill and of practicing medicine should converge in mutual wonder at the body. A physician who does not have this sense of wonder seeks only to cure diseases. Sometimes he succeeds, but if cure is the only objective, not achieving it means he has failed. For the artful physician, wonder precludes failure. The physician and the ill person enter into a relationship of joint wonder at the body, in which failure is as irrelevant as control. The ill person who finds a physician to join in this wonder is fortunate. The body is not a territory to be controlled by either the physician's treatment or the patient's will. Those patients whose physicians remain rooted in disease and cure have to accept medical treatment for what it is, and learn to wonder alone or with other care-givers.

I hope that what I call wonder at the body will not be confused with the particular ways I used my body. It happened that I learned about my body by walking to the hospital and by exercising while I was a patient there, but these activities were not essential to continuing the process of wonder. After surgery I did not have many choices for using my body, and chemotherapy gave me even fewer, since by then I could not read. But I found other sources of coherence, particularly in music. At night when I put my head into a Walkman and listened to Bach, I could forget the implications of being in a hospital. Orchestral music was too busy when heard through my cheap headphones, but Glenn Gould playing the Goldberg Variations brought me a peace and identity my environment could not provide. Only later did I learn that Bach wrote the variations for an insomniac prince.

Listening to that music became an activity for my body. I love running most when moving is pervaded by a sense of rhythm, and listening to Bach's music gave me a sensation of movement. The origins of music are inseparable from dance, and dance is one of the great metaphors of life itself. Until I was ill I had never heard so clearly the dance in the music, and life in the dance. Illness taught me that beyond anything I can do, the body simply is. In the wisdom of my body's being I find myself, over and over again.

CHAPTER 13

Myalgic Encephalomyelitis and the Medical Encounter

Lesley Cooper

INTRODUCTION

In the history of twentieth century western medicine several 'syndromes' have been denied the legitimate status of 'organic disease'. I shall entitle these syndromes 'non-diseases' or 'illegitimate illnesses', because they neither fit the category of organic disease, nor do they have the status of legitimate illnesses. Hypoglycaemia (Singer *et al*. 1984), repetitive strain injury (RSI) (Arksey 1994), candidiasis, multiple chemical sensitivity, myalgic encephalomyelitis (ME) and chronic fatigue syndrome (CFS) are all examples of such non-diseases, being generally defined in terms of symptoms, with uncertain aetiology and pathogenesis. Sufferers often look perfectly well, and standard medical tests fail to find any clearly demarcated abnormalities. For instance, at present there is no accepted definitive test for ME, even though a number of studies have shown that the condition can be diagnosed on the basis of specific highly complex pathologies using extremely sophisticated technologies (see below). Given the context of scientific uncertainty, different specialties of medicine, both from within and outside of scientific medicine, construct opposing theories on aetiology which are usually centred on the question of whether the syndrome is primarily psychological or physical.

ME, or CFS as it is otherwise labelled, is perhaps unique amongst these syndromes in that estimates of prevalence have been much higher than estimates of other diseases – most literature quotes an estimate of 150,000 sufferers in Britain, and it has perhaps been the most vociferously contested of all such 'non-diseases'. In the last twenty years, the disease status of ME has been passionately debated in the scientific and medical community, whilst the controversy has had extensive coverage in the lay and medical press. Those committed to the validation of ME/CFS succeeded in getting the illness recognised by Parliament in 1987 (Private member's bill, Jack Ashley), and in initiating a Task Force, a body set up in conjunction with the government and the ME charity *Westcare*. The Task

Force Report, published in 1994, validated the condition, whilst the government response to this report in the form of the Royal Colleges' *Report on Chronic Fatigue Syndrome*, published on 2 October [1997], also recognised that the condition existed as a valid illness. However, the latter report decreed that the term ME or Myalgic Encephalomyelitis should no longer be used, and still spoke of the condition as 'existing in the grey area between mind and body' with no single aetiology, and with an emphasis on psychological causes and management. As the editor of the *Lancet* stated, 'Psychiatry has won the day for now' (Lancet 1996). Meanwhile, a number of physicians still doubt the existence of ME as a legitimate disease process. The Task Force Report itself states: 'We should start by recognising that we have to deal with a condition which some believe does not exist as a true disease and which certainly grades into a number of other conditions' (1994: 78).

The assumption in this paper is that both disease and illness are theoretical and culturally bound constructs representing a particular abstraction of the empirical world (Rosenberg 1992). This view is contrary to the traditional conception of disease and illness which, whilst arguing for the cultural construction of illness, regards disease as an objective fact. Unlike Kleinman (1980: 78) and others, who argue that illness is the behavioural and societal response to the disease, where disease is in their terms ontologically prioritised over the illness, I would argue that illness can be framed as sufferers' social and cultural response to symptoms. *Disease* can then be viewed as the doctor's subjective, culturally bound assessment of the 'reality' of their patient's *illness*, based on a mixture of empirical observations, and theoretical, intersubjective, negotiated and ideological knowledge (Young 1981: 380).

Whereas this is the case for all disease nomenclature, this understanding is particularly apposite for the terms used to name the symptoms of ME, as they are vigorously contested both within the medical community and by patient groups. The latter prefer the term ME, as opposed to psychiatrists and some medical researchers who use the term CFS or Chronic Fatigue Syndrome. In the history of ME, definitions, nomenclature and classifications have varied from country to country, and also amongst groups of researchers. Terms have been based on place (such as 'Akureyri Disease' after an epidemic in a town in Iceland), on symptoms, and on hypothesised aetiologies, often reflecting different ideologies and interests of the groups involved. As the Government-funded Task Force reports, the issue of nomenclature is not just a semantic problem: 'It encompasses serious disagreements', which have 'sadly led to ill will and abusive remarks, on such questions as whether the syndrome or some form of it exists, whether it is "real" or "organic" or "merely" psychological' (1994: iii). Those who wish to 'psychologise' the condition have been accused of constructing the term Chronic Fatigue Syndrome in order to sustain this belief, whilst those who wish to construct ME as a physical disease insist on calling it 'Myalgic Encephalomyelitis' (the term translates into inflammation of the brain). Where generally a biomedical disease name represents the symbolic legitimation of the ideology of expertise (Habermas 1970: 81), I would argue that in this particular arena, the label

ME has come to serve as a symbol for the usurpation of power from doctors by patients.

With this in mind, I wish to bracket the label ME in that it is a problematic construct and does not necessarily bear any clearly defined relation to bodily experiences of pain and fatigue. The implication of this for this paper is that when I speak of 'sufferers' I do not mean sufferers of *ME*, but sufferers of such bodily experiences of pain and incapacity, which have been presently *labelled* as ME; I make this distinction so as not to be accused of 'ontological gerrymandering'.[1] Given this bracketing of the label, it has to be accepted that the symptoms described by the term are often severe and chronically disabling. Exhaustion, severe muscle fatigue and pain have been the most widely reported symptoms, whilst sufferers have also complained of depression, severe headaches, weakness, dizziness, concentration difficulties and memory loss, all of which show great variability in terms of remissions and relapses (Hyde 1992).

Amongst advocates of the organicity of the condition are individual sufferers, sufferers' organisations, medical research scientists, and individual doctors. They base their arguments on laboratory-based evidence of persistent or reactivated viral infection (Archard *et al.* 1988, Archard 1992), disturbances in immune function, structural and functional abnormalities in the central nervous system, hypothalamic and neuro-transmitter abnormalities (Dinan 1995, Demitrack *et al.* 1991), and abnormalities in the blood flow to the brain (Costa *et al.* 1992). Confusion and credibility are further confounded by the fact that there are several differing theories of aetiology within the 'believers' camp. The dominant theory is that the illness is caused by a persisting virus, and the contending theory is that it is caused by the persistence of immunity damage due to a virus or other stressors such as environmental toxins (Hilgers and Frank 1994). 'Believers' argue that any depression that patients suffer is either caused by the pathological abnormalities of the disease, or the psychological, emotional and social consequences of having such a severe chronic illness (Ray 1992: 101).

Proponents of the psychological paradigm have questioned the somatic basis of ME advocating a psychosomatic or depressive hypothesis (Wessely 1990, 1994). According to this paradigm the condition is attributed to one or all of the following factors: immune suppression caused by depression, a constitutional neural weakness of which prior major depressive disorder is an indicator, and a tendency for the patient to somatise depression through physical symptoms. Those who hold this view argue that such diagnoses as ME are 'fashionable' labels, self diagnosed by individuals who wish their emotional and psychological distress to be legitimised as an organic illness. The evidence cited for this are studies done by psychiatrists of a high incidence of psychiatric disturbance among those who claim to have the illness or who fulfil the criteria for CFS (Taerk 1987, Wessely and Powell 1989, Katon and Walker 1993). Psychiatrists argue that attributing an aetiological role to psycho-social factors does not deny legitimate access to the sick role, whilst sufferers argue vehemently in the self help journals and in the press against being labelled as mentally ill, even if that does mean that they are given an entry point into the sick role.

Sufferers of ME are more likely to diagnose their condition than their doctors, and often come to the consultation armed with considerable knowledge. This state of affairs results in doctors' concern that diagnosis is controlled more by the patient than the doctor (Scott et al. 1995), the underlying inference being that these patients may not warrant legitimate access to the sick role; that they may be malingering. These kinds of behaviours are seen to cause difficult doctor–patient relationships by both patients (Interaction 1993) and doctors (Scott et al. 1995). Sufferers who are faced with disbelief and dismissal by doctors and other medical professionals feel angry and let down by the welfare system and the medical community. Stories of patients suffering at the hands of social workers, psychiatrists and GPs abound in the popular press and in the journals of the sufferers' groups. The Report of the Royal Colleges declares that the constructive therapeutic alliance between doctor and patient and the administration of a biopsychosical approach is the key to recovery for ME sufferers. In the light of the following analysis this declaration may be a little Utopian.

Given the background context of political and medical controversy, and the uncertainty of the label, I would argue that sufferers' own understandings and experiences are essential to an analysis of the political and social framework of ME. This paper is an attempt at an uncovering of these experiences. The respondents in the study reported here perceived major problems in their inter-actions with the medical profession. Their attempts at obtaining a diagnosis were constantly rejected, their symptoms were dismissed and disbelieved, and they were often labelled as bored housewives or depressed adolescents. Consequently, acting no longer as passive agents when their needs were not met, respondents actively pursued their own paths to knowledge and challenged the authority and status of their GPs and consultants. The supposition I wanted to investigate in this paper is that, if patients cannot find in the doctor someone who will diagnose, name, and accept their illness, they are more likely to challenge their doctors, and perhaps the legitimacy of medicine itself than patients with more easily diagnosed 'legitimate' illnesses.

The literature on the issue of patient satisfaction with, and legitimation of, mainstream medicine is confusing and contradictory. Willis (1994: 64) argues that, with the growth and success or alternative medicine, clinical rather than scientific legitimacy has become increasingly important. Calnan (1988) contends that although consumer studies of patient satisfaction with medical care have tended to show, with some exceptions, that patients are rarely critical of medical practice, the general public is ambivalent as a whole about modern medicine. In his study of the lay evaluation of medical practice he suggests some scepticism amongst patients about the value of biomedicine but faith in individual doctors. This is shown in their ranking of doctors' personal and relational practices above their perceived clinical scientific competence. This finding is borne out by MacCormack (1981), who uses a Weberian model of legitimacy to place medical power in the healers themselves – that is in health care; authority is vested in particular (bodies) individuals and their practices, recognised in the community as healers. Their authority is independent of the knowledge base of their particular practice, but invested in loyalty to (the body of) healers themselves. According to the more recent study done by Williams and Calnan (1996) men and women were ambivalent about the value of modern medicine and had a varying amount of faith in their family doctors according to the quality of the relationship they had with them.

The concept of legitimacy derives from Max Weber (1968) and has more recently been developed by Habermas (1975) and Beetham (1991). Legitimacy has been defined as a 'politico-legal process whereby a set of practices is accepted as authoritative and becomes dominant through the political process of justification' (Willis 1994: 55). Doctors' politico-legal legitimacy rests upon the basis of both scientific and clinical legitimacy (Willis 1994: 65). In the first case doctors are privy to the special knowledge of scientific medicine. They normally have control over both the production and reproduction of this knowledge, their institutionalised authority being based on it. However, whilst on a macro level, their institutionalised knowledge/power and authority are granted by the state, on a micro level, the legitimacy of their individual authority, their clinical legitimacy, is constituted by those in a subordinate position to them. Patients, being those who are in a position of subordinate power, have to continue to legitimate doctors' authority and power, in order for the power dyad of doctor–patient to work. In this study patients report that they have challenged their doctors' authority, and it is on the basis of this finding that I will discuss the question of the de-legitimisation of the medical profession as a whole.

METHODOLOGY

The analysis in this paper is based on the collection of data over a two-year period. This material was obtained through a postal survey of doctors' attitudes to ME, interviews with doctors, researchers and psychiatrists, attendance at international conferences and a review of papers in medical journals. More specifically, for the purposes of this paper, ten life history interviews were undertaken with sufferers of ME. Contacts were made through the local organiser of the self-help group, Irene, with whom a relationship had developed over time.[2] Irene is a fifty-five-year-old, single woman who has been chronically ill since 1971. She was severely ill and bedridden at the time of initial contact, living on a diet of potatoes and bottled water as she had experienced severe adverse reactions to all foods. Despite this, she was extremely active in running the local group providing advice and information, and organising occasional talks by experts.

Respondents were chosen from a list of names of sufferers who had contacted her for help or information on the illness in the last five years, on the basis of advice as to whether possible respondents would be co-operative or not. Many sufferers are not in contact with either local or national self-help groups, possibly because they do not need any extra advice or support as they are already obtaining this from their local GP. As ME gains credibility as a disease, and as more and more information about its nature is disseminated, GPs are more likely to give advice and support to patients who have this illness. Other sources I have investigated show that a growing proportion of GPs now accept these conditions.[3] Those sufferers who go to self-help groups may do so because they have not received satisfactory advice and help from elsewhere. On the basis of this assumption, no generalisation can be made about the concerns of all sufferers of ME; conclusions based on the following accounts can only be made with the understanding that only those who have been in touch with self-help groups have had these experiences and these kinds of feelings.

Most contacts were made by telephone, and seven individuals agreed to be interviewed. The other three interviewees were obtained by contacting another local self-help group organiser, who placed an advertisement for me in the local newsletter. Out of ten respondents, three had been involved in disseminating and researching information on ME, all as non-professionals. The ratio of men to women reflected the overall ratio for the condition (which has been estimated at something like 70 per cent women to 30 per cent men[4]), in that there were seven women and three men. There was a varying degree of disability, from those who were bedridden to the majority who could manage day-to-day tasks but had not entirely recovered. All respondents were interviewed in their own homes, as some found it difficult to travel. In one case I interviewed the mother rather than the daughter, as the daughter was too ill to speak for any length of time.

The methodology used in the collection and analysis of the following material is based on the concepts of 'narrative' or 'story'. Telling stories is arguably one of the significant and natural ways that individuals construct and express meaning. There has been considerable disagreement about different definitions of the term 'narrative', but usually narratives have been defined as stories about past events, as discrete unities with a beginning and an end. Chanfrault-Duchet defines a 'real' narrative as one that 'reveals the existence of a form that can be identified through specific features and that corresponds to a particular discursive and literary genre: the life story' (1991: 79). Following Plummer (1995) and Mishler (1986), in interviewing respondents I wished to participate in the construction of their responses as stories, stories which hopefully would have a general coherence, a beginning, a middle and an end, in which both the structure and the content implied certain concerns and frames. With this in mind, my intention was to impose as little framework on respondents' narratives as possible, and within a loose interview schedule they were encouraged to tell their own 'story' of their illness, including what had been happening in their lives before the illness onset, the events leading up to their illness and their illness experiences. Despite this encouragement, two kinds of interview evolved: those where respondents told stories and those where questions were answered. Those respondents who were concerned to tell stories took control of the direction of the interview, focusing on some central concerns and framing their narratives in a particular fashion. In the case of the latter these stories centred on the illness 'career' of the respondent and their interactions with members of the medical profession. It is on these accounts, which constituted about two-thirds of my sample, that I will focus.

When it came to analysing the data obtained, I found myself confronted by a tension that has probably confronted most other researchers who use oral history techniques or open-ended interviews. Was I to approach my material as data that were giving access to the facts about my chosen area? Were my respondents accurately reconstructing what happened to them since they became ill? The information elicited form these interviews is obviously one-sided. When patients speak of their experiences with doctors, no attempt can be made, given the limitations of this paper, to give a voice to the professionals who play such a large part in their narratives. However, there is much more to these narratives than an objective account of reality. The techniques and style of oral history do not exclude a relationship with the real world, but even if it is recognised that stories are socially and culturally framed; this does not mean that they are fabrications: they bear a relationship to real, lived life. The question to be asked is what kind of relationship? People have to be seen as speaking their own truths of their experiences as they see them. Ambiguity of meaning and alternative readings of the same material are permitted with this kind of perspective. These stories, I hope, can become not merely 'data' from which certain analytical and theoretical understandings can be drawn: more than this, the accounts can be perceived as attempts at making sense of problematic experiences, as empowering and healing experiences in their own right, and as political narratives.

Several writers have argued that the narratives we tell are often involved in a critical relationship of self with the societal status quo (Plummer 1995), and that by focusing on the relationship between narrative structures and socio-symbolic contents the researcher can explore the relationship between the self and society (Chanfrault-Duchet 1991). The following narratives, being based on 'experiential knowledge', can be seen as an 'epistemological challenge' (Kelleher 1994: 116, Williams and Popay 1994: 123). When sufferers experience symptoms which doctors refuse to recognise because they cannot be fitted into any known legitimate disease entity, then it is likely that the intensity of this challenge will increase.

THE NARRATIVES

In the following discussion of my respondents' narratives it has to be noted that the three male patients had not shared many of the women patients' experiences. Two of the men had found that their GPs accepted their condition without really questioning it, even though they may have preferred not to have it labelled as ME, and one had the good fortune to find the only pro-active GP in the area very early on in his illness career. The numbers of respondents are so few in this study that it would be foolish to generalise on the implications of this observed gender difference.

Most, but not all, respondents related their stories within the broad framework of an 'illness career', and this framework provided a coherence and structure for their stories. An illness career can be defined as a progression of an individual through a series of positions in an institution or a social system, each having implications for the social status of the person concerned. Some respondents introduced other themes into their narratives; one woman, for instance, was concerned with her family's attitudes and reactions to her illness. Nonetheless, a major part of all the respondents' narratives was focused on framing an unknown set of physical and mental symptoms as a problem that could be defined, made meaningful and possibly solved by the institution of medicine, rather than by other means. The typical illness career began with sufferers starting to experience various inexplicable symptoms, severe enough to warrant giving up work or school. Often, because the symptoms were so mysterious, they were ignored or not 'given in to':

> Like most people I refused to give in at first I didn't realise there was anything wrong. It was May the first symptoms started arriving . . . I had an ear infection, a terrible ear infection, I was in a lot of pain and I didn't stop working, I carried on . . . I was in dreadful pain and I think, gradually when you look back you can see all the things falling into place, I started to say things back to front, couldn't count with money, I was getting very tired when I woke up in the morning, it was as if I hadn't been to sleep, all those sorts of things – and it got to Christmas and I collapsed (GB, 55-year-old, female, been ill 8 years, much better at time of interview).

Respondents often attempted to place their illnesses and its onset within the circumstances and emotions of their personal lives, so that causes of their illness were attributed to personal stress and traumatic events. One woman, who had a Down's syndrome child at the age of 25, associated her illness throughout the whole of the interview with the stress caused by looking after her daughter. Within the first few minutes of commencing her narrative, she had connected the stress of the birth of her daughter to contracting viral meningitis which developed into what was later diagnosed as ME, even though the latter event was many years after the first:

> She had always been poorly. She wasn't expected to live. I nursed her through so much which obviously really exhausted me. Yes I think it was the fact that I was stressed out and rundown when I got this virus, . . . But there again I don't think I'd have had ME if I hadn't had Rachel (AB, female, 52 years old, been ill 12 years, mobile but did not go very far outside own home).

One woman's story revolved around her dismissal from her job as a teacher which she believed was grossly unfair:

> I had stress at work which resulted in me being suspended and losing my job and the whole thing just became bigger. It was noticeable, and the day I went for my appeal against dismissal, the day after that I physically collapsed. The doctor had to come out. I hadn't been as bad as that before. I think it was the stress that triggered it (HP female, 45 years old, been ill 8 years, mobile but only able to do part-time work).

These attempts to make sense of illness in terms of biographical events are not specific to sufferers of 'illegitimate' illnesses (Williams and Popay 1994: 123), but in the face of uncertainty as to the scientific medical causes of their condition, and what was seen as a lack of understanding on behalf of their GPs, they were relied upon to give meaning and structure to an otherwise chaotic world.

DIAGNOSIS

Diagnosis of an illness has been seen to be vital to the psychological and emotional well being of the patient by both medical historians (Rosenberg 1992) and medical sociologists. A recent study by Woodward (1995) based on interviews with fifty people diagnosed with ME/CFS found that patients were much happier after a diagnosis of ME/CFS – despite the ambiguity and stigma of this label – as the diagnosis provided a rational and a structured meaning system for their experiences of disability and illness.

Sufferers in this study found themselves seeing a number of doctors and consultants in an effort to find a diagnosis. The act of diagnosis was seen as a key even in the illness career, and a major part of the narratives was concerned with the difficulties in obtaining an acceptable diagnosis. Tests invariably gave negative results, visits to the psychiatrist proved unrewarding, as did visits to various consultants. Respondents often did not obtain a diagnosis for several years. Irene, the local contact, had become ill in 1971 and was not diagnosed with ME until 1987. A typical comment was:

> It was three years before we knew it was ME. At first we clutched onto everything that might be a diagnosis and no doctor could tell us what was wrong. . . . (EB, 19 years old, female, been ill 6 years, mobile but unable to work or study).

This lack of a credible diagnosis led to problems with employers and family. By not being allowed full and decisive entry into the sick role, sufferers found that their social position was eroded, their social identity devalued and stigmatised, whilst they found it difficult to obtain legitimate absence from work or disability benefit. Interactions with doctors were thereafter conflictual and emotional. Respondents at this point perceived themselves as being at 'rock bottom', where the outlook was bleak and where positive support from physicians was nil. The turning point came when respondents discovered ME, often from newspaper or magazine articles, and diagnosed themselves, or were diagnosed by a 'pro-ME' professional who accepted the condition and recommended management and possible treatment routes. A teenager who had spent years trying to obtain a diagnosis finally read about it in a teenage magazine:

> We read this article in *Just 17* Magazine about a young girl who was ill at home and had got ME . . . As I read this article I thought this is what I've got and my friends started ringing me up to say it (EB).

This diagnosis, especially when it was a self diagnosis, marked as it usually was by conflict and denial on the part of their own GP, could be seen as a symbolic turning point in respondents' change in attitudes towards their doctors. From then on, many of those I talked to expressed the belief that they had improved psycho-socially, if not physically, as the illness was given a label and the patient had finally found some respite from the chaos and anarchy of their illness. This appears to be the case despite the uncertainty and stigma surrounding the label ME.

At this point in the illness career, the label ME became both a symbol of the sufferer's own newly acquired empowerment, and of the threat to the doctor's position of authority. An ex-school teacher, whose wife also came down with the illness, commented:

> Well my doctor was calling it Post Viral Syndrome . . . I joined the ME Association because it was in the news with Clare Francis in 1988. We sort of guessed what it was but at no point did we get diagnosed with the magic words ME. We were certainly not diagnosed by the doctor. . . . He was very cagey about calling it ME . . . (TT, male, 47 years old, been ill for 8 years).

When symptoms are eventually labelled as Myalgic Encephalomyelitis or Chronic Fatigue Syndrome this is often done in a manner that nonetheless denies the validity of the label. One woman whose daughter was ill recounted that the paediatrician off-handedly mumbled a diagnosis of ME or glandular fever but said that he did not believe in it, and advised the mother not to get in touch with the ME Society. When another woman tentatively suggested their own diagnosis of ME, she was told: 'ME does not exist . . . it's all in your head!'

Even when a diagnosis is made, the stigma of the label of ME sometimes results in embarrassment and stress. Irene, who had other, more respectable, diagnosed conditions stated:

> I know what I'm doing but I'm treated as if I don't, as if I'm in the wrong, and that's another aspect, yeah another reason why I keep the ME down the bottom of the list. . . . I was just left with a feeling 'Oh Irene's made a fuss again' . . . that's the sort of attitude they have towards ME people you see, and that's why I do push the ME out the way, why I don't use it as a diagnosis (Irene W, female, been ill for 20 years, bedridden).

MISUNDERSTANDING AND DISBELIEF

Respondents, with only the rare exception, reported that many people, and particularly doctors, misunderstood the nature of their illness. They complained to their doctors of multiple, vague symptoms, often with little physical sign of an organic disease. Various tests prove negative, and, according to both sufferers and doctors, they did not *always* look terribly ill.[5] These individuals expressed the belief that they experientially 'knew' that something was wrong, and expected their doctors to take this knowledge and transfer it into their own understanding. However doctors and patients did not share the same understanding of simple descriptive terms. When patients talked of 'fatigue', they explained afterwards that they meant something different from what was commonly understood by the term. To sufferers, fatigue means being so tired they cannot brush their hair or even sit up in bed. To doctors 'fatigue' may simply mean a term to describe a common occurrence in the general population as a result of modern-day stress. Thus, what were to the sufferers severe symptoms of pain, depression and fatigue were trivialised by doctors, who saw them as common experiences not worthy of being brought to a doctor's attention. This breakdown of a shared meaning system, where the same term signifies different experiences, led to confusion and uncertainty. The common gap between medical and lay approaches in which neither party can find a common language was widened with respect to ME, where patients' experiences and doctors' understandings appeared to be so markedly incommensurate.

Female respondents gave accounts of invariably being dismissed and disbelieved by their doctors, despite in many cases experiencing quite severe symptoms. They recounted stories of doctors who labelled them as 'malingerers', 'school phobics', or 'bored housewives'. One informant who had worked as a health visitor for most of her life had this to say:

> I had an hour with this chap and he just insulted me all the time . . . He was a consultant physician . . . it was obvious from the onset that he was trying to either break me down or I don't know what he was trying to do . . . or make me come to my senses or something. But it was a bullying tirade . . . that's all I can tell you. It started off with him bumping the table saying 'all right cards on the table now what's wrong with you? Something wrong with your marriage?' (HM, female, age 60 years, health visitor, ill 19 years, functioning and mobile but coughed constantly and still quite unwell)

Often, it was recounted that standard tests done did not reveal any abnormal pathology. Much of the misunderstanding, as far as the patients were concerned, stemmed from doctors' misunderstanding their symptoms as mere depression rather than as a severe physical illness in which depression played just one part. A female sufferer described the attitude of one particular doctor to both herself and her friend:

> I had got a list of symptoms – . . . one written down was mild depression. Having to give up work and be ill at the same time was bound to cause a slight depression – I mean I wasn't gaga or on antidepressants or anything but I was fed up having to be at home and not feeling well. Of course having the depression written down on a piece of paper he said 'Oh you women, that's all you ever say . . . you're depressed.' 'Bored Housewife Syndrome' that's what he called it. He told my friend she'd got too many children – she'd got four children. He said she got four children . . . he told her 'Oh you housewives you've got too many children' (GB).

Often treatments such as antibiotics and antidepressives given to patients did not work, and in fact made symptoms worse. This exacerbated the conflictual relationship:

> *After the Septrin?* It worsened and that was the point. When I went back to the doctor he was confidently expecting me to be better and I said I don't understand this, I think I feel worse. And of course I don't think he believed me either because he'd, I suppose he'd made a judgement and he'd given me the antibiotics and I, and it was my fault I wasn't responding and it was sort of that sort of attitude – yeah you're not co-operating with us very well (HMc).

Even though relationships with their doctors deteriorated, patients kept on insisting they were ill, as sick role legitimacy and diagnostic certainty were still goals to be achieved and patients had to stay within the state medical system to achieve them. Attempts to attain legitimacy took on a moral face as patients took pains to show that they were really ill and 'good' or 'normal' patients: that they themselves were not deviant although they might have a 'deviant' illness, and that they were trying as best they could to get better:

> One thing also I've learnt is psychiatrists and doctors don't like you in a wheelchair. So my immediate thing I said to him was 'Do you mind if I sit in an ordinary chair?' and he looked at me and said 'Why?' I said 'I feel more normal there'. I didn't tell him, you know, something I had learnt, you know, what I say to them (Irene W).

Part of playing the game of the good patient was to try and not incite the doctor by 'provoking' him with knowledge procured from other sources, particularly the self-help groups:

> When I last saw him I gave him some literature from ME and he got a bit up-tight. That was the only time I provoked him that far (TT).

PUBLIC MYTH–PRIVATE BELIEF: THE SOCIAL STOCK OF KNOWLEDGE

Sufferers in this study came to their doctor with several expectations and needs. They needed to obtain relief of their symptoms, to have their pain and suffering named; in order to create some meaning out of a confusing plethora of symptoms, and to obtain validation of their illness to achieve entry into the sick role. As part of the social stock of knowledge (Berger and Luckman 1967), sufferers assume that the doctor *should* be able to help.

> I went back to the doctor and she said she couldn't help. I asked 'where do I go from here?' and she just shrugged her shoulders and said there was nothing she could do really (EB).

Another way of viewing this social stock of knowledge is as myth. Thompson writes about the power of myth as a force that shapes and frames narratives in oral history, arguing for the universality of myth as a constituent of human experience. These interviews can be seen as both expressing and confronting an underlying myth, that of the doctor as a figure of both symbolic authority within society and as symbolic healer within our deeper consciousness. The implicit assumption that the doctor has the authority and knowledge to diagnose is challenged by these respondents in the stories of encounters with doctors as they fall foul of their assigned role. Some told of a specific turning point in their perception of doctors, and of a moment of defiance. Those rare doctors who did not challenge this myth were treated with the utmost esteem and deference. The ways that these doctors were treated in the narrative, those who gave support and the 'right' diagnosis, and those who denied the illness, exemplify the myths of 'idealisation' and 'demonisation' (Thompson 1990: 15). Respondents had experienced such frustration in their attempts to satisfy their internalised expectation of the doctor's power to heal, to name and legitimate their 'disease', that they held those doctors that fell short of their expectations in great contempt, 'demonising' them. Evidence for this demonisation can be found throughout the accounts, not so much in the actual statements but in the underlying message, and in the tone of voice of respondents when they spoke of their encounters with doctors. Evidence for the alternative capacity to idealise doctors is borne out by the response of those respondents who had met a particular doctor who took their suffering seriously, and entered into a warmer, more personal and emotional relationship with them:

> He is a wonderful doctor, a lovely, lovely man and without him I don't think I would have been able to have taken it, I really don't. He really has gone into it in great depth. . . . But on the very first day I saw him I said 'Do you think I am ill?' And he said 'yes', and I tapped my head and said 'Do you think it is all in here?' And he said 'No – I can see you are ill!' And, of course, then he knew that I was ill and he went out of his way to see how he could treat me. I mean, he sat in this house on many occasions crying with me because I was so upset at the time and he was so upset that he couldn't actually help (KC, male, ex-mayor, ill 12 years, mobile but unable to work).

This particular doctor represented this patient's only hope, without him, he said, he couldn't have carried on. This doctor was spoken of so highly by various respondents, not because he carried the hope for a quick fix or a cure but simply because he accepted his patients as fellow human beings, whose suffering needed to be understood and accepted.

FIGHTING BACK

When doctors fell foul of their assigned role, contradicting the 'stock knowledge' of their patients, sufferers told of a specific turning point in their perception, of a moment of defiance when they challenged not only a particular individual, but their own internalised myth of the 'doctor'. The mother of a young girl who was seriously ill to the point where she could not eat recounted:

> ... that would be the eruption of the volcano if you like cos Dr X the paediatrician in C came to see her the next morning (our GP thought she needed a brain scan), and he came up to Kate and patted her on the head, she hated to be touched, and he patted her on the head and said 'Don't worry Kate we know where your brain is don't we', and walked off. And I was *so angry* I thought I don't care if the whole hospital hears me and I'm not one to given to shouting and hollering, but I'd had enough, and he walked off ... (AC, mother of KC, 14 years old, ill for two years, bedridden).

A young girl who had been sent to a psychiatric hospital had this to say:

> Yeah, I don't trust them at all, I don't trust doctors, because I knew I was ill and they were saying I weren't and I knew they were wrong ... I'm not frightened anymore I used to be but I'm not frightened, I will say what I think, you know ... I think actually after the day hospital, I couldn't put up with it anymore I spent at that point two and half years being pushed around by this specialist and that specialist, being pushed around from pillar to post, and I just said 'No More' and that was the turning point ... (EB).

Some of my informants had collected their own information. For instance, the health visitor had undertaken her own research using facilities available to her because of her contact with medical institutions. She believed she had more medical knowledge of her condition than her own GP. When sufferers started to take a more active role in the diagnostic process, sometimes diagnosing themselves, and pushing for other consultants or doctors who could give a more definitive diagnosis, they recounted that doctors could not accept this threat to their professional knowledge and power, and attempted to retain control not only over the patient but also over their claim to knowledge, often becoming angry and abusive. One young respondent, EB, who had discovered through avenues other than the NHS that she had severe sensitivities to food and to various pharmaceuticals, including anti-depressants and pain killers, recounted how various doctors had denied her own right as a patient to obtain and act upon her own knowledge of her illness, and her own body:

> Dr Y said, I know too much, he said he likes his patients to go in without any knowledge of what's wrong with them 'cos he, 'cos I'm liable to say I'm not taking that 'cos I know that makes me ill, whereas someone who doesn't have that knowledge will take it you see, he doesn't like that, he wants ... also his approach is, I should be taken away from the family and he basically told my parents I've got to be handed over to him, he's got to have complete control over my life basically. I said to him 'I've got to accept this illness and I won't get better'. He said 'You don't have to accept that, I can cure you, I will cure you!' (EB).

When the mother of a young patient asked for a second opinion, from some-one who was known to be 'pro-ME', she experienced this kind of response:

> He went absolutely scarlet, he went red in his face, we stood in the corridor of the ward, I mean I felt very vulnerable because my daughter was fading away in front of me, nobody could tell me what was wrong with her, and I felt as though I was asking for something I shouldn't be asking for, and it was as though I was sort of undermining his judgement, but I didn't think he had a judgement, I didn't think he'd said anything really, and I said 'Could I have this Dr Z?' and he went red in the face, I'll never forget, he was lost for words he didn't know what to say, and in the end I forget what he called him but it wasn't very complimentary – silly old crank or that old buffoon, or words to that effect . . . and he said 'Oh if you want to see him take her to see him a day out will do her good!' I stood there absolutely speechless, I felt awful, I said to him 'Can't he come and see her here?' 'Not in my hospital!' he said and walked off. He was absolutely furious and he realised that I must have gone behind his back if you like and gone to the ME society even though he'd asked me not to (AC).

CONCLUSION

The research reported here highlights the dilemmas that the issue of diagnostic uncertainty and disease legitimacy delivers to both doctors and patients. The respondents in the study experienced serious difficulties in their interactions with doctors. As has been found elsewhere (Ware 1992), they found themselves misunderstood and disbelieved. This kind of response has been labelled as 'psychogenic dismissal' whereby dismissed patients suffer iatrogenic psychological injury when their symptoms are dismissed as being all in the mind.[6] The taken-for-granted, every-day reality of an individual becomes disrupted by serious unknown illness, and as Taussig points out, 'This gives the doctor a powerful point of entry into the patient's psyche, and almost amounts to a destructuration of the patient's conventional understandings and social personality' (1980: 4). When the patient experiences psychogenic dismissal, they can be said to be experiencing double disruption of this taken-for-granted reality.

Respondents found it difficult to obtain a satisfactory diagnosis, and because of a lack of diagnosis, they could not get easy entry into the sick role (Parsons 1951). Acceptance into the sick role legitimates an illness. It can also be seen as the ritual exculpation and legitimation of the patient (Young 1976). Naming an illness with an authenticated biomedical disease label is the ticket for entry into the sick role. Thus the *name* becomes the symbol for this legitimation and exculpation. Respondents failed to receive a bona-fide disease label, and thus a full passage into the sick role. Consequently the majority were not allowed passage into a state of legitimate patienthood free from responsibility and blame for their illness state. Also more concretely, their social position was to some extent eroded, their social identity devalued and stigmatised, and they found it difficult to obtain legitimate absence from work or disability benefit.

Furthermore, when confronted by patients who had obtained a diagnosis of ME from elsewhere, or gone to the self-help groups for advice, doctors sometimes became angry and abusive. This finding duplicates that of another study (Scott *et al.* 1995).

As a result of these serious assaults on patients' beliefs and expectations, respondents often began to challenge their individual doctors and to some extent experienced a demystification of doctors' 'Aesculapian authority'.[7] However, although respondents often expressed the feeling that they no longer trusted doctors, their most common action was either to challenge their existing GP or to change doctors, until they found a GP or consultant in whom they could invest their loyalty. Patients appeared to be just as willing to idealise as to demonise their doctors. Thus, although the symbolic authority of the doctor had taken some battering, and doctors were no longer on the pedestal on which they had previously been placed, respondents appeared content either to challenge or to accept the authority of individual doctors, rather than to challenge the medical profession or medicine as a whole.

It is a major step to move from challenging individual doctors to an actual rejection of the institution of medicine. The existence of the ME self-help groups and the institution of alternative medicine do challenge modern medicine by privileging lay experience and knowledge, thus providing an opportunity to resist the domination of the life world by the expert system of medicine (Kelleher 1994: 104–117). The hostility shown towards the ME self-help groups by some doctors and psychiatrists leads one to surmise that these groups do represent a perceived threat, but only a small percentage of those who suffer from ME belong to them and the two main groups, the *ME Association* and *Action for ME*, still rely upon the discourses of scientific medicine to legitimate the 'organicity' of the disease.[8]

Outside the self-help groups, alternative medicine, and particularly clinical ecology, has actually begun to provide an alternative paradigm. A survey conducted in the US suggested that 40 per cent of CFS patients eventually dropped out of mainstream medicine (Johnson 1996: 584). Sufferers who go to clinical ecology practitioners, for instance, find that their illness is totally legitimated, whilst responsibility for their illness is placed outside themselves and laid at the feet of environmental pollutants. Three respondents in this study, all of whom had developed some degree of food and chemical sensitivity, had used the facilities of alternative medicine. Nonetheless, these three were otherwise very much concerned to stay within the NHS domain.

Aronowitz (1992) points out that radical epistemological critiques of bio-medical models of disease have been rare, and the case of ME is no exception. Whilst sufferers may wish their understanding of their own symptoms and bodily experiences, their *illness*, to be prioritised over existing medical knowledge, they still argue for the acceptance of ME as an organic 'disease'. The legitimacy of doctors as holders of authoritative knowledge may be questioned in individual cases. Nonetheless, as a profession which holds the rights to possession of scientific medical knowledge, and as gatekeepers to social and community support, they are not seriously challenged.

Notes

1. Ontological gerrymandering is the term used by Woolgar and Pawluch (1985: 218) in order to argue their case that in the area of the analysis of the construction of social problems, 'one category of claims is laid open to ontological uncertainty and then made the target for explanation in terms of the social circumstances which generated them; at the same time the reader is asked to accept another category of claims on faith'.
2. Irene made it quite clear that she did not wish to remain anonymous so I have not changed her name.
3. In a recent survey I conducted of 397 GPs, out of the 125 that replied 57 per cent said they accepted ME and 81 per cent accepted CFS as a valid medical condition, whilst 35 per cent expressed supportive or sympathetic feelings towards such patients.
4. Because the methods used to estimate prevalence themselves are under debate it is difficult to quote any definitive studies that can be used to give evidence for this. However, most studies do show a much higher prevalence of the illness in women than men. Even as far back as 1959 Henderson, reviewing the scientific literature on the various outbreaks, noted that more women than men were affected by a ratio of at least 1.5 to 1, and that the severity of the disease had been considerably greater among females.
5. It has been noted both by sufferers themselves and by various researchers within the area that, whilst the more severely disabled do show physical signs of their disablement, such as severe weight loss or gain, dramatic hair loss in one or two cases, and even fingerprint loss in some, the less disabled ME sufferers show no physical signs of disease.
6. This term was first mentioned by Dr Kenneth Vickery in his foreword to the book *Chemical Victims* (Mackarness 1980):

   > to the weary sufferer these times must surely be felt as the age of psychosomatic presumption or the age of psychogenic dismissal, or simply the age of n.a.d. – nothing abnormal discovered . . . It is the sequel to n.a.d. which can be the really devastating part for many . . . when doctors try to dismiss their patients with the apologetic 'I don't for a moment think you are mentally ill or that you are imagining your symptoms, but I do think that if they persist a psychiatrist may be the only answer' . . . (Mackarness 1980: xi–xii)

   Vicky Rippere, editor of a clinical ecology newsletter, has taken up this term extensively in her journals.
7. Aesculapian authority was first named and defined by T. T. Paterson in 1957. He defined this authority as consisting of three types, sapiental, moral and charismatic.
8. In my survey of GPs' attitudes towards ME this was found to be the case. Several GPs and psychiatrists have also expressed their hostility to self-help groups in the lay and medical press.

References

Archard, L. (1992) Molecular virology of muscle disease: persistent virus infection of muscle in patients with postviral fatigue syndrome. In B. Hyde (ed) *The Clinical and Scientific Basis of ME/CFS*. Ottawa, Canada, Ottawa University Press.

Archard, L. C., Bowles, N. E., Behan, P. O., Bell, F. I. and Doyle, D. (1988) Postviral fatigue syndrome: persistence of enterovirus RNA in muscle and elevated creatine kinase, *Journal of the Royal Society of Medicine*, 81, 326–9.

Arksey, H. (1994) Expert and lay participation in the construction of medical knowledge, *Sociology of Health and Illness*, 16, 448–68.

Aronowitz, R. A. (1992) From myalgic encephalomyelitis to yuppie flu. In C. E. Rosenberg and J. Golden (eds) *Framing Disease*. New Jersey, Rutgers University Press.

Beetham, D. (1991) *The Legitimation of Power*. London, Macmillan.

Berger, P. and Luckman, T. (1967) *The Social Construction of Reality*. London, Allen Lane.

Calnan, M. (1988) Lay evaluation of medicine and medical practice: report of a pilot study, *International Journal of Health Services*, 18, 311–22.

Calnan, M. and Williams, S. (1996) Lay evaluation of scientific medicine and medical care. In S. Williams and M. Calnan (eds) *Modern Medicine: Lay Perspectives and Experiences*. London, UCL Press.

Chanfrault-Duchet, M.-F. (1991) Narrative structures, social models, symbolic representation in the life story. In S. B. Gluck and D. Patai (eds), *Women's Words: The Feminist Practice of Oral History*. London, Routledge.

Chronic Fatigue Syndrome, Report of joint working group of the Royal Colleges of Physicians, Psychiatrists and General Practitioners, October (1996). Published by Royal College of Physicians, London.

Costa, D. C. *et al.* (1992) Brain stem hypoperfusion in patients with ME/CFS, *European Journal of Nuclear Medicine*, 19, 733.

Demitrack, M. A. *et al.* (1991) Evidence of impaired activation of the hypothalamio-pituitary-adrenal axis in patients with chronic fatigue syndrome, *Journal of Clinical Endocrinological Metabolism*, 73, 1224–34.

Dinan, T. G. (1995) Neuroendocrinology of chronic fatigue syndrome. Paper given at First World Congress on Chronic Fatigue Syndrome and Related Disorders, Brussels, 9–11 November.

Habermas, J. (1970) Technology and science as ideology. In *Toward a Rational Society*. Boston, Beacon Press.

Habermas, J. (1975) *Legitimation Crisis*. Boston, Beacon Press.

Henderson, D. and Shelokov, A. (1959) Epidemic neuromyasthesia-clinical syndrome? *New England Journal of Medicine*, 260, 757–64.

Hilgers, A. and Frank, J. (1994) Immune dysfunction, the role of pathogens and toxic agents, and neurological and cardiac alterations in patients with Chronic Fatigue Syndrome. Paper presented to Dublin International Conference on CFS.

Hyde, B. (1992) *The Clinical and Scientific Basis of Myalgic Encephalomyelitis/Chronic Fatigue Syndrome*. Ottawa, Canada, The Nightingale Research Foundation.

Interaction (1993) *Journal of Action for Myalgic Encephalomyelitis*, no. 14.

Isle of Man Examiner (1995) *Doctors Accused*. 26 December.

Johnson, H. (1996) *Osler's Web*. New York, Crown Publishers.

Katon, W. and Walker, E. A. (1993) The relationship of chronic fatigue to psychiatric illness in community, primary care and tertiary care samples. In *Chronic Fatigue Syndrome*. Chichester, Wiley (Ciba Foundation Symposium 173).

Kelleher, D. (1994) Self-help groups and their relationship to medicine. In J. Gabe, D. Kelleher and G. Williams (eds) *Challenging Medicine*. London, Routledge.

Kleinman, A. (1980) *Patients and Healers in the Context of Culture*. London, University of California Press.

Lancet, editorial (1996) 12 October, 348, 971.

MacCormack, C. (1981) Health care and the concept of legitimacy, *Social Science and Medicine*, 15B, 423–8.

Mackarness, R. (1980) *Chemical Victims*. London, Pan Books.

Mishler, E. (1986) *Research Interviewing*. London, Harvard University Press.

Parsons, T. (1951) *The Social System*. London, Routledge.

Paterson, R. R. (1957) *Aesculapian Authority*. Unpublished manuscript.

Plummer, K. (1995) *Telling Sexual Stories*. London, Routledge.

Ray, C. (1992) Role of depression in chronic fatigue syndrome. In R. Jenkins and J. Mowbray (eds) *Post-viral Fatigue Syndrome*. Chichester, John Wiley and Sons.

Report from the National Task Force on Chronic Fatigue Syndrome, Post Viral Fatigue Syndrome, Myalgic Encephalomyelitis, (1994) Bristol, Westcare.

Rosenberg, C. E. (1992) *Framing Disease*. New Jersey, Rutgers University Press.

Scott, S., Deary, I. and Pelosi, A. J. (1995) General practitioners' attitudes to patients with a self diagnosis of myalgic encephalomyelitis, *British Medical Journal*, 310, 508.

Singer, A., Fitzgerald, M. and Von Legat (1984) Hypoglaecemia: a controversial illness in US society, *Medical Anthropology*, Winter.

Taerk, G. S. *et al.* (1987) Depression in patients with neuromyesthenia, *International Journal of Psychiatry in Medicine*, 17, 49.

Taussig, M. T. (1980) Reification and the consciousness of the patient, *Social Sciences and Medicine*, 14B, 1–33.

Ware, N. C. (1992) Suffering and the social construction of illness: the delegitimation of illness experience in CFS, *Medical Anthropology Quarterly*, 6, 347–61.

Weber, M. (1968) (ed) *Economy and Society*, vol. 3. New York, Bedminster Press.

Wessely, S. (1990) Chronic fatigue and myalgia syndromes. In N. Sartorius *et al.* (eds) *Psychological Disorders in General Medical Settings*. Hogrefe and Huber Toronto, Lewiston.

Wessely, S. (1994) Neurasthenia and chronic fatigue syndrome: theory and practice, *Transcultural Psychiatric Review*, 31, 173–209.

Wessely, S. and Powell (1989) The nature of fatigue: a comparison of chronic 'postviral' fatigue with neuromuscular and affective disorders, *Journal of Neurologies and Neuro-surgical Psychiatry*, 52, 940–8.

Williams, G. and Popay, J. (1994) Lay knowledge and the privilege of experience. In J. Gabe, D. Kelleher and G. Williams (eds) *Challenging Medicine*. London, Routledge.

Williams, S. and Calnan, M. (1996) Modern medicine and the lay populace. In S. Williams and M. Calnan (eds) *Modern Medicine: Lay Perspectives and Experiences*. London, UCL Press.

Willis, E. (1994) *Illness and Social Relations*. St Leonard's, Australia, Allen and Unwin.

Woodward, R. V., Broom, D. H. and Legge, D. G. (1994) Diagnosis in chronic illness: disabling or enabling – the case of chronic fatigue syndrome, *Journal for the Royal Society of Medicine*, 88, 325–9.

Woolgar, S. and Pawluch, D. (1985) Ontological gerrymandering: the anatomy of social problems explanation, *Social Problems*, 32, 214–27.

Young, A. (1981) The creation of medical knowledge: some problems in interpretation, *Social Science and Medicine*, 15B, 379–86.

Chapter 14

A Fortunate Man

John Berger

[Sassall] is acknowledged as a good doctor. The organization of his practice, the facilities he offers, his diagnostic and clinical skill are probably somewhat under-rated. His patients may not realize how lucky they are. But in a sense this is inevitable. Only the most self-conscious consider it lucky to have their elementary needs met. And it is on a very basic, elementary level that he is judged a good doctor.

They would say that he was straight, not afraid of work, easy to talk to, not stand-offish, kind, understanding, a good listener, always willing to come out when needed, very thorough. They would also say that he was moody, difficult to understand when on one of his theoretical subjects like sex, capable of doing things just to shock, unusual.

How he actually answers their needs as a doctor is far more complicated than any of these epithets imply. To understand this we must first consider the special character and depth of any doctor–patient relationship.

The primitive medicine-man, who was often also priest, sorcerer and judge, was the first specialist to be released from the obligation of procuring food for the tribe. The magnitude of this privilege and of the power which it gave him is a direct reflection of the importance of the needs he served. An awareness of illness is part of the price that man first paid and still pays for his self-consciousness. This awareness increases the pain or disability. But the self-consciousness of which it is the result is a social phenomenon and so with this self-consciousness arises the possibility of treatment, of medicine.[1]

We cannot imaginatively reconstruct the subjective attitude of a tribesman to his treatment. But within our culture today what is our own attitude? How to we acquire the necessary trust to submit ourselves to the doctor?

We give the doctor access to our bodies. Apart from the doctor, we only grant such access voluntarily to lovers – and many are frightened to do even this. Yet the doctor is a comparative stranger.

The degree of intimacy implied by the relationship is emphasized by the concern of all medical ethics (not only ours) to make an absolute distinction between the roles of doctor and lover. It is usually assumed that this is because the doctor can see women naked and can touch them where he likes and that this may sorely tempt him to make love to them. It is a crude assumption, lacking imagination. The conditions under which a doctor is likely to examine his patients are always sexually discouraging.

The emphasis in medical ethics on sexual correctness is not so much to restrict the doctor as to offer a promise to the patient: a promise which is far more than a reassurance that he or she will not be taken advantage of. It is a positive promise of physical intimacy without a sexual basis. Yet what can such intimacy mean? Surely it belongs to the experiences of childhood. We submit to the doctor by quoting to ourselves a state of childhood and simultaneously extending our sense of family to include him. We imagine him as an honorary member of the family.

In cases where the patient is fixated on a parent, the doctor may become a substitute for this parent. But in such a relationship the high degree of sexual content creates difficulties. In illness we ideally imagine the doctor as an elder brother or sister.

Something similar happens at death. The doctor is the familiar of death. When we call for a doctor, we are asking him to cure us and to relieve our suffering, but, if he cannot cure us, we are also asking him to witness our dying. The value of the witness is that he has seen so many others die. (This, rather than the prayers and last rites, was also the real value which the priest once had.) He is the living intermediary between us and the multitudinous dead. He belongs to us and he has belonged to them. And the hard but real comfort which they offer through him is still that of fraternity.

It would be a great mistake to 'normalize' what I have just said by concluding that quite naturally the patient wants a *friendly* doctor. His hopes and demands, however contradicted by previous experience, however protected they may be by scepticism, however undeclared even to himself, are much more profound and precise.

In illness many connexions are severed. Illness separates and encourages a distorted, fragmentated form of self-consciousness. The doctor, through his relationship with the invalid and by means of the special intimacy he is allowed, has to compensate for these broken connections and reaffirm the social content of the invalid's aggravated self-consciousness.

When I speak of a fraternal relationship – or rather of the patient's deep, unformulated expectation of fraternity – I do not of course mean that the doctor can or should behave like an actual brother. What is required of him is that he should recognize his patient with the certainty of an ideal brother. The function of fraternity is recognition.

This individual and closely intimate recognition is required on both a physical and psychological level. On the former it constitutes the art of diagnosis. Good general diagnosticians are rare, not because most doctors lack medical know-ledge, but because most are incapable of taking in all the possibly relevant facts – emotional, historical, environmental as well as physical. They are searching for specific conditions instead of the truth about a man which may then suggest various conditions. It may be that computers will soon diagnose better than doctors. But the facts fed to the computers will still have to be the result of intimate, individual recognition of the patient.

On the psychological level recognition means support. As soon as we are ill we fear that our illness is unique. We argue with ourselves and rationalize, but a ghost of the fear remains. And it remains for a very good reason. The illness, as an undefined force, is a potential threat to our very being and we are bound to be highly conscious of the uniqueness of that being. The illness, in other words, shares in our own uniqueness. By fearing its threat, we embrace it and make it specially our own. That is why patients are inordinately relieved when doctors give their complaint a name. The name may mean very little to them; they may understand nothing of what it signifies; but because it has a name, it has an independent existence from them. They can now struggle or complain *against* it. To have a complaint recognized, that is to say defined, limited and depersonalized, is to be made stronger.

The whole process, as it includes doctor and patient, is a dialectical one. The doctor in order to recognize the illness fully – I say fully because the recognition must be such as to indicate the specific treatment – must first recognize the patient as a person: but for the patient – provided that he trusts the doctor and that trust finally depends upon the efficacy of his treatment – the doctor's recognition of his illness is a help because it separates and depersonalizes that illness.[2]

So far we have discussed the problem at its simplest, assuming that illness is something which befalls the patient. We have ignored the role of unhappiness in illness, the factors of emotional or mental disturbance. Estimates among G.P.s of how many of their cases actually depend on such factors vary from five to thirty per cent: this is perhaps because there is no quick way of distinguishing between cause and effect and because in nearly *all* cases there is emotional stress present of one kind or another which has to be dealt with.

Most unhappiness is like illness in that it too exacerbates a sense of unique-ness. All frustration magnifies its own dissimilarity and so nourishes itself. Objec-tively speaking this is illogical since in our society frustration is far more usual than satisfaction, unhappiness far more common than contentment. But it is not a question of objective comparison. It is a question of failing to find any confirma-tion of oneself in the outside world. The lack of confirmation leads to a sense of futility. And this sense of futility is the essence of loneliness: for, despite the horrors of history, the existence of other men always promises the possibility of purpose. Any example offers hope. But the conviction of being unique destroys all examples.

An unhappy patient comes to a doctor to offer him an illness – in the hope that this part of him at least (the illness) may be recognizable. His proper self he believes to be unknowable. In the light of the world he is nobody: by his own lights the world is nothing. Clearly the task of the doctor – unless he merely accepts the illness on its face value and incidentally guarantees for himself a 'difficult' patient – is to recognize the man. If the man can begin to feel recognized

– and such recognition may well include aspects of his character which he has not yet recognized himself – the hopeless nature of his unhappiness will have been changed: he may even have the chance of being happy.

I am fully aware that I am here using the word Recognition to cover whole complicated techniques of psychotherapy, but essentially these techniques are precisely means for furthering the process of recognition. How does a doctor begin to make an unhappy man feel recognized?

A straightforward frontal greeting will achieve little. The patient's name has become meaningless: it has become a wall to hide what is happening, uniquely, behind it. Nor can his unhappiness be named – as is the case with an illness. What can the word 'depressed' mean to the depressed? It is no more than the echo of the patient's own voice.

The recognition has to be oblique. The unhappy man expects to be treated as though he were a nonentity with certain symptoms attached. The state of being a nonentity then paradoxically and bitterly confirms his uniqueness. It is necessary to break the circle. This can be achieved by the doctor presenting himself to the patient as a comparable man. It demands from the doctor a true imaginative effort and precise self-knowledge. The patient must be given the chance to recognize, despite his aggravated self-consciousness, aspects of himself in the doctor, but in such a way that the doctor seems to be Everyman. This chance is probably seldom the result of a single exchange, and it may come about more as the result of the general atmosphere than of any special words said. As the confidence of the patient increases, the process of recognition becomes more subtle. At a later stage of treatment, it is the doctor's acceptance of what the patient tells him and the accuracy of his appreciation as he suggests how different parts of his life may fit together, it is this which then persuades the patient that he and the doctor and other men are comparable because whatever he says of himself or his fears or his fantasies seems to be at least as familiar to the doctor as to him. He is no longer an exception. He can be recognized. And this is the prerequisite for cure or adaptation.

We can now return to our original question. How is it that Sassall is acknowledged as a good doctor? By his cures? This would seem to be the answer. But I doubt it. You have to be a startlingly bad doctor and make many mistakes before the results tell against you. In the eyes of the layman the results always tend to favour the doctor. No, he is acknowledged as a good doctor because he meets the deep but unformulated expectation of the sick for a sense of fraternity. He recognizes them. Sometimes he fails – often because he has missed a critical opportunity and the patient's suppressed resentment becomes too hard to break through – but there is about him the constant will of a man trying to recognize.

'The door opens,' he says, 'and sometimes I feel I'm in the valley of death. It's all right when once I'm working. I try to overcome this shyness because for the patient the first contact is extremely important. If he's put off and doesn't feel welcome, it may take a long time to win his confidence back and perhaps never. I try to give him a fully open greeting. All diffidence in my position is a fault. A form of negligence.'

It is as though when he talks or listens to a patient, he is also touching them with his hands so as to be less likely to misunderstand: and it is as though, when he is physically examining a patient, they were also conversing.

Sassall needs to work in this way. He cures others to cure himself. The phrase is usually no more than a cliché: a conclusion. But now in one particular case we can begin to understand the process.

Previously the sense of mastery which Sassall gained was the result of the skill with which he dealt with emergencies. The possible complications would all appear to develop within his own field: they were medical complications. He remained the central character.

Now the patient is the central character. He tries to recognize each patient and, having recognized him, he tries to set an example for him – not a morally improving example, but an example wherein the patient can recognize himself. One could simplify this – for now we are not dealing with the complexities of the average case but with Sassall's motives – by saying that he 'becomes' each patient in order to 'improve' that patient. He 'becomes' the patient by offering him his own example back. He 'improves' him by curing or at least alleviating his suffering. Yet patient succeeds patient whilst he remains the same person, and so the effect is cumulative. His sense of mastery is fed by the ideal of striving towards the *universal*.

The ideal of the universal man has a long history. It was the working ideal of Greek democracy – even though it depended on slavery. It was revived in the Renaissance and became for a number of men a reality. It was one of the principles of the eighteenth-century Enlightenment and after the French Revolution was maintained, at least as a vision, by Goethe, Marx, Hegel. The enemy of the universal man is the division of labour. By the mid nineteenth century the division of labour in capitalist society had not only destroyed the possibility of a man having many roles: it denied him even one role, and condemned him instead to being part of a part of a mechanical process. Little wonder that Conrad believed that 'the true place of God begins at any spot a thousand miles from the nearest land': there, men could fully prove themselves. Yet the ideal of the universal man persists. It could be the promise implicit in automation and its gift of long-term leisure.

Sassall's desire to be universal cannot therefore be dismissed as a purely personal form of megalomania. He has an appetite for experience which keeps pace with his imagination and which has not been suppressed. It is the knowledge of the impossibility of satisfying any such appetite for new experience which kills the imagination of most people over thirty in our society.

Sassall is a fortunate exception and it is this which makes him seem in spirit – though not in appearance – much younger than he is. There are superficial aspects of him which are still like a student. For example, he enjoys dressing up in 'uniforms' for different activities and wearing them with all the casualness of the third-year expert: a sweater and stocking cap for working on the land in winter: a deer-stalker and laced leather leggings for shooting with his dog:

an umbrella and homburg for funerals. When he has to read notes at a public meeting he *deliberately* looks over his glasses like a schoolmaster. If you met him outside his area, on neutral ground, and if he didn't begin talking, you might for one moment suppose that he was an actor.

He might have been one. In this way too he would have played many roles. The desire to proliferate the self into many selves may initially grow from a tendency to exhibitionism. But for Sassall as the doctor he is now, the motive is entirely transformed. There can be no audience. It is only he who can judge his own 'exhibition'. The motive now is knowledge: knowledge almost in the Faustian sense.

The passion for knowledge is described by Browning in his poem about Paracelsus – whose life story was one of the tributaries to the later Faust legend.

> I cannot feed on beauty for the sake
> Of beauty only, nor can drink in balm
> From lovely objects for their loveliness;
> My nature cannot lose her first imprint;
> I still must board and heap and class all truths
> With one ulterior purpose: I must know!
> Would God translate me to his throne, believe
> That I should only listen to his word
> To further my own aim!

Sassall, unlike Paracelsus, is neither a theosophist nor a *Magus*; he believes more in the science than in the art of medicine.

'When people talk about doctors being artists, it's nearly always due to the shortcomings of society. In a better society, in a juster one, the doctor would be much more of a pure scientist.'

Or:

'The essential tragedy of the human situation is not knowing. Not knowing what we are or why we are – for *certain*. But this doesn't lead me to religion. Religion doesn't answer it.'

Yet this difference of emphasis is mostly an historical one. At the time of Paracelsus sickness was thought of as the scourge of God: and yet was welcomed as a warning because it was finite whereas hell was eternal. Suffering was the condition of the earthly life: the only true relief was the life to come. There is a striking contrast in medieval art between the way animals and human beings are depicted. The animals are free to be themselves, sometimes horrific, sometimes beautiful. The human beings are restrained and anxious. The animals celebrate the present. The humans are all waiting – waiting for the judgement which will decide the nature of their immortality. At times it seems that some of the artists envied the animals their mortality: with that mortality went a freedom from the closed system which reduced life here and now to a metaphor. Medicine, such as it was, was also metaphorical. When autopsies were performed and actually revealed to the eye the false teachings of Galenic medicine, the evidence was dismissed as accidental or exceptional. Such was the strength of the system's metaphors – and the impossibility, the irrelevance of any medical science. Medicine was a branch of theology. Little wonder that Paracelsus who came from such a system and then challenged it in the name of independent observation resorted sometimes to mumbo-jumbo! Partly to give himself confidence, partly for protection.

I am not, of course, implying that Sassall is an historically comparable figure to Paracelsus. But I suspect that he is in the same vocational tradition. There are doctors who are craftsmen, who are politicians, who are laboratory researchers, who are ministers of mercy, who are businessmen, who are hypnotists, etc. But there are also doctors who – like certain Master Mariners – want to experience all that is possible, who are driven by curiosity. But 'curiosity' is too small a word and 'the spirit of enquiry' is too institutionalized. They are driven by the need to know. The patient is their material. Yet to them, more than to any doctor in any of the other categories, the patient, in his totality, is for that very reason sacred.

When patients are describing their conditions or worries to Sassall, instead of nodding his head or murmuring 'yes', he says again and again 'I know', 'I know'. He says it with genuine sympathy. Yet it is what he says whilst he is waiting to know more. He already knows what it is like to be this patient in a certain condition: but he does not yet know the full explanation of that condition, nor the extent of his own power.

In fact no answer to these open questions will ever satisfy him. Part of him is always waiting to know more – at every surgery, on every visit, every time the telephone rings. Like any Faust without the aid of the devil, he is a man who suffers frequently from a sense of anti-climax.

This is why he exaggerates when he tells stories about himself. In these stories he is nearly always in an absurd position: trying to take a film on deck when the waves break over him; getting lost in a city he doesn't know; letting a pneumatic drill run away with him. He stresses the disenchantment and deliberately makes himself a comic little man. Disguised in this way and forearmed against disappointment, he can then re-approach reality once more with the entirely un-comic purposes of mastering it, of understanding further. You can see this in the difference between his two eyes: his right eye knows what to expect – it can laugh, sympathize, be stern, mock itself, take aim: his left eye scarcely ever ceases considering the distant evidence and searching.

I say scarcely ever, but there is one exception. This is when he is occupied with some relatively minor surgical task. He may be setting a fracture in his surgery, or attending to one of his patients in the local hospital. On these occasions both eyes concentrate on the task in hand and a look of relief comes over his face. As soon as he takes his coat off, rolls up his sleeves, washes his hands, puts on gloves or a mask, this relief is apparent. It is as though his mind is wiped clean (hence the relief) in order to concentrate exclusively on the limited operation in hand. For a moment there is certainty. The job can be done well or badly: the distinction between the two is beyond dispute: and it must be done well.

I saw a similar expression on the face of a farmer who lives only a few miles from Sassall. This farmer is mad about flying and owns a six-cylinder open-cockpit Czech plane. His farm is not a large or particularly prosperous one. Nor is he part of the gentry. He lives by himself and likes speed. He keeps the plane under an oak-tree in one of his fields. When we had driven the sheep to the other end of the field, and I had turned the prop and he and Jean Mohr were settled and the engine was warm, he signalled to me to let go of the tip of the wing – I was holding it for the plane had no brakes – and at that moment, just before they took off, although there was a gusty wind blowing and the field was very rough and the take-off was liable to be quite tricky, I saw exactly the same look of relief pass over the farmer's unshaved, chunky, middle-aged face. The problems now were limited to aerodynamics and the functioning of a small internal-combustion engine: the problem of prices, mortgages, Monday's market, relations, reputation, would all in a moment be beneath them.

The difference between the farmer and Sassall is that the farmer would like to be able to spend all his life blithely flying and gliding – or anyway believes that he would; whereas Sassall needs his unsatisfied quest for certainty and his uneasy sense of unlimited responsibility.

So far I have tried to describe something of Sassall's relationship with his patients. I have tried to show why he is thought of as a good doctor, and how being 'a good doctor' answers some of his own needs. I have suggested something of the mechanism by which he cures others to cure himself. But all this has been on an individual basis. We must now consider his relationship to the local community as a whole. What do his patients expect of him publicly when they are not ill? And how does this relate to their barely formulated expectations of fraternity within the privacy of illness?

Sassall lives in one of the larger houses of the village. He is well dressed. He drives a Land Rover for his practice, and another car for his private use. His children go to the local grammar school. Without any doubt at all the part allotted him is that of *gentleman*.

The area as a whole is economically depressed. There are only a few large farms and no large-scale industries. Fewer than half the men work on the land. Most earn their living in small workshops, quarries, a wood-processing factory, a jam factory, a brickworks. They form neither a proletariat nor a traditional rural community. They belong to the Forest and in the surrounding districts they are invariably known as 'the foresters'. They are suspicious, independent, tough, poorly educated, low church. They have something of the character once associated with wandering traders like tinkers.

Sassall has done his best to modify the part of gentleman allotted him, and has partly succeeded. He leads almost no social life of his own – except in the village with the villagers. It is when he is talking with his few middle-class neighbours that one is most aware of his own class background. This is because they assume in conversation and attitude that he shares their prejudices. With the 'foresters' he seems like a foreigner who has become, by request, the clerk of their own records.

Let me try to explain what I mean by 'the clerk of the foresters' records'.

'Where you're different Doc is I know I can say Fuck You to your face if I want to.' Yet the speaker never has said Fuck You to Sassall.

'You're the laziest bitch I've ever come across,' says Sassall to the middle-aged woman draper whose day is now made. Yet only he can say this to her.

'What have you got on?' he asks about a menu at a factory canteen.

'Do you want to start at the top,' answers the girl at the counter pointing to her breasts, 'or at the bottom?' lifting her skirts up high. Yet she knows she is safe with the doctor.

Sassall has to a large extent liberated himself and the image of himself in the eyes of his patients from the conventions of social etiquette. He has done this by becoming unconventional. Yet the unconventional doctor is a traditional figure. Where Sassall perhaps is different is that traditionally the unconventionality has only allowed the doctor to swear at and shock his patients instead of vice versa. Sassall would like to think that anybody can say anything to him. But insofar as this is true, it confirms rather than denies his position of privilege. To your equals you cannot say anything: you learn very precisely the form and area of their tolerance. The theoretical freedom of address towards Sassall implies his authority, his special 'exemption', precisely because theoretically it is total. In practice anything unconventional which he says or which is said to him in public is a gesture – no more – against the idea that his authority is backed by the authority of society. It is the form of personal recognition he demands of his patients in exchange for the very different recognition he offers them.

In the village there is a medieval castle with a wide, deep moat round it. This moat was used as a kind of unofficial dump. It was overgrown with trees, bushes, weeds, and full of stones, old wood, muck, gravel. Five years ago Sassall had the idea of turning it into a garden for the village. Tens of thousands of man-hours of work would be involved. He formed a 'society' to occupy itself with the task and he was elected chairman. The work was to be done in the summer evenings and at week-ends whenever the men of the village were free. Farmers lent their machinery and tractors; a roadmaker brought his bull-dozer along; somebody borrowed a crane.

Sassall himself worked hard on the project. If he was not in the surgery and not out on a call, he could be found in the moat most summer evenings. Now the moat is a lawned garden with a fountain, roses, shrubs and seats to sit on.

'Nearly all the planning of the work in the moat,' says Sassall, 'was done by Ted, Harry, Stan, John, etc., etc. I don't mean they were better at doing the work, better with their hands – they were that – but they also had better ideas.'

Sassall was constantly involved in technical discussion of these ideas with the men of the village. The conversations over the weeks continued for hours. As a result a social – as distinct from medical – intimacy was established.

This might seem to be the obvious result of just getting on with a job together. But it is not as simple or as superficial as that. The job offers the possibility of talking together, and finally the talk transcends the job.

The inarticulateness of the English is the subject of many jokes and is often explained in terms of puritanism, shyness as a national characteristic, etc. This tends to obscure a more serious development. There are large sections of the

English working and middle class who are inarticulate as the result of wholesale cultural deprivation. They are deprived of the means of translating what they know into thoughts which they can think.[3] They have no examples to follow in which words clarify experience. Their spoken proverbial traditions have long been destroyed: and, although they are literate in the strictly technical sense, they have not had the opportunity of discovering the existence of a written cultural heritage.

Yet it is more than a question of literature. Any general culture acts as a mirror which enables the individual to recognize himself – or at least to recognize those parts of himself which are socially permissible. The culturally deprived have far fewer ways of recognizing themselves. A great deal of their experience – especially emotional and introspective experience – has to remain *unnamed* for them. Their chief means of self-expression is consequently through action: this is one of the reasons why the English have so many 'do-it-yourself' hobbies. The garden or the work bench becomes the nearest they have to a means of satisfactory introspection.

The easiest – and sometimes the only possible – form of conversation is that which concerns or describes action: that is to say action considered as technique or as procedure. It is then not the experience of the speakers which is discussed but the nature of an entirely exterior mechanism or event – a motor-car engine, a football match, a draining system or the workings of some committee. Such subjects, which preclude anything directly personal, supply the content of most of the conversations being carried on by men over twenty-five at any given moment in England today. (In the case of the young, the force of their own appetites saves them from such depersonalization.)

Yet there is warmth in such conversation and friendships can be made and sustained by it. The very intricacy of the subjects seems to bring the speakers close together. It is as though the speakers bend over the subject to examine it in precise detail, until, bending over it, their heads touch. Their shared expertise becomes a symbol of shared experience. When friends recall another friend who is dead or absent, they recall how he always maintained that a front-wheel drive was safer: and in their memory this now acquires the value of an intimacy.

The area in which Sassall practises is one of extreme cultural deprivation, even by English standards. And it was only by working with many of the men of the village and coming to understand something of their techniques that he could qualify for their conversation. They then came to share a language which was a metaphor for the rest of their common experience.

Sassall would like to believe that the metaphor implies that they talk as equals: the more so because within the range of the language the villagers mostly know far more than he. Yet they do not talk as equals.

Sassall is accepted by the villagers and foresters as a man who, in the full sense of the term, lives with them. Face to face with him, whatever the circumstances, there is no need for shame or complex explanations: he will understand even when their own community as a whole will not or cannot. (Most unmarried girls who become pregnant come to him straightway without any prevarication.)

Insofar as he is feared at all, it is by a few older patients in whom a little of the traditional fear of the doctor still persists. (This traditional fear, apart from being a rational fear of the consequences of illness, is also an irrational fear of the consequences of making their secret but outrageous and insistent demand for fraternity to doctors who always behave and are treated as their superiors.)

In general his patients think of Sassall as 'belonging' to their community. He represents no outside interest – in such an area any outside interest suggests exploitation. He is trusted. Yet this is not the same thing as saying that he is thought of or treated as an equal.

It is evident to everybody that he is privileged. This is accepted as a matter of course: nobody resents or questions it. It is part of his being the kind of doctor he is. The privilege does not concern his income, his car or his house: these are merely amenities which make it possible for him to do his job. And if through them he enjoys a little more comfort than the average, it is still not a question of privilege, for certainly he has earned a right to that comfort.

He is privileged because of the way he can think and can talk! If the estimate of his privilege was strictly logical, it would include the fact of his education and his medical training. But that was a long time ago, whereas the evidence of the way he thinks – not purely medically but in general – is there every time he is there. It is why the villagers talk to him, why they tell him the local news, why they listen, why they wonder whether his unusual views are right, why some say 'He's a wonderful doctor but not what you'd expect', and why some middle-class neighbours call him a crack-pot.

The villagers do not consider him privileged because they find his thinking so impressive. It is the style of his thinking which they immediately recognize as different from theirs. They depend upon common-sense and he does not.

It is generally thought that common-sense is practical. It is practical only in a short-term view. Common-sense declares that it is foolish to bite the hand that feeds you. But it is foolish only up to the moment when you realize that you might be fed very much better. In the long-term view common-sense is passive because it is based on the acceptance of an outdated view of the possible. The body of common-sense has to accrue too slowly. All its propositions have to be proved so many times before they can become unquestionable, i.e. traditional. When they become traditional they gain oracular authority. Hence the strong element of *superstition* always evident in 'practical' common-sense.

Common-sense is part of the home-made ideology of those who have been deprived of fundamental learning, of those who have been kept ignorant. This ideology is compounded from different sources: items that have survived from religion, items of empirical knowledge, items of protective scepticism, items culled for comfort from the superficial learning that *is* supplied. But the point is that common-sense can never teach itself, can never advance beyond its own limits, for as soon as the lack of fundamental learning has been made good, all items become questionable and the whole function of common-sense is destroyed. Common-sense can only exist as a category insofar as it can be distinguished from the spirit of enquiry, from philosophy.

Common-sense is essentially *static*. It belongs to the ideology, of those who are socially passive, never understanding what or who has made their situation as it is. But it represents only a part – and often a small part – of their character. These same people say or do many things which are an affront to their own common-sense. And when they justify something by saying 'It's only common-sense', this is frequently an apology for denying or betraying some of their deepest feelings or instincts.

Sassall accepts his innermost feelings and intuitions as clues. His own self is often his most promising starting-point. His aim is to find what may be hidden in others:

'I don't find it hard to express uncensored thoughts or sentiments but when I do, it keeps on occurring to me that this is a form of self-indulgence. That sounds somewhat pompous, but still. At least it makes me realize and understand why patients thank me so profusely for merely listening: they too are apologizing for what they think – wrongly – is their self-indulgence.'

Using his own mortality as another starting-point he needs to find references of hope or possibility in an almost unimaginable future.

'I'm encouraged by the fact that the molecules of this table and glass and plant are rearranged to make you or me, and that the bad things are perhaps badly arranged molecules and therefore capable maybe of reorganization one day.'

Yet however fanciful his speculations, he returns to measure them by the standards of actual knowledge to date. And then from this measurement begins to speculate again.

'You never know *for certain* about anything. This sounds falsely modest and trite, but it's the honest truth. Most of the time you are right and you do *appear* to know, but every now and then the rules seem to get broken and then you realize how lucky you have been on the occasions when *you think you have known* and have been proved correct.'

He never stops speculating, testing, comparing. The more open the question the more it interests him.

Such a way of thinking demands the right to be theoretical and to be concerned with generalizations. Yet theory and generalizations belong by their nature to the cities or the distant capital where the big general decisions are always made. Furthermore, to arrive at general decisions and theories one needs to travel in order to gain experience. Nobody travels from the Forest. So nobody in the Forest has either the power or the means to theorize. They are 'practical' people.

It may seem surprising to place so much emphasis on geographic isolation and distances when England is so small a country. Yet the subjective feeling of remoteness has little to do with mileage. It is a reaction to economic power. Monopoly – with its mounting tendency to centralization – has even turned what were once large, vital towns, like Bolton or Rochdale or Wigan, into remote backwaters. And in a country area, where the average level of political consciousness is very low, all decision-making which is not practical, all theory, seems to most of the local inhabitants to be the privilege and prerogative of distant policy-makers. The intellectual – and this is why they are so suspicious of him – seems to be part of the apparatus of the State which controls them. Sassall is trusted because he lives with them. But his way of thinking could only have been acquired elsewhere. All theory-makers have cast at least one eye on the seat of power. And that is a privilege the foresters have never known.

There is another reason why they sense that Sassall's way of thinking is a privilege, but as a reason it is less rational. Once it might have been considered magical. He confesses to fear without fear. He finds all impulses natural – or understandable. He remembers what it is like to be a child. He has no respect for any title as such. He can enter into other people's dreams or nightmares. He can lose his temper and then talk about the true reasons, as opposed to the excuse, for why he did so. His ability to do such things connects him with aspects of experience which have to be either ignored or denied by common-sense. Thus his 'licence' challenges the prisoner in every one of his listeners.

There is probably only one other man in the area whose mode of thinking is comparable. But this man is a writer and a recluse. Nobody around him is aware of how he thinks. There are clergymen and schoolmasters and engineers, but they all use the syntax of common-sense: it is only their vocabulary which is different because they need to refer to God, O-levels, or stresses in metal. Sassall's privilege seems locally unique.

The attitude of the villagers and foresters to Sassall's privilege is complex. He has got a good brain, they say, why, with a brain like this – and then, remembering that he belongs to them, they realize that his choice of their remote country practice again implies a kind of privilege: the privilege of his indifference to success. But now his privilege becomes to some extent their privilege. They are proud of him and at the same time protective about him: as though his choice suggested that a good brain can also be a kind of weakness. They often look at him quite anxiously. Yet they are not, I think, so proud of him as a doctor – they know he is a good doctor but they do not know how rare or common that is – rather, they are proud of his way of thinking, of his mind, which has mysteriously allowed him to choose to stay with them. Without being directly influenced by it, they make his way of thinking theirs by giving it a local function.

He does more than treat them when they are ill; he is the objective witness of their lives. They seldom refer to him as a witness. They only think of him when some practical circumstance brings them together. He is in no way a final arbiter. That is why I chose the rather humble word *clerk*: the clerk of their records.

He is qualified to be this precisely because of his privilege. If the records are to be as complete as possible – and who does not at times dream of the impossible ideal of being totally recorded? – the records must be related to the world at large, and they must include what is hidden, even what is hidden within the protagonists themselves.

Some may now assume that he has taken over the role of the parish priest or vicar. Yet this is not so. He is not the representative of an all-knowing, all-powerful being. He is their own representative. His records will never be offered to any higher judge. He keeps the records so that, from time to time, they can consult them themselves. The most frequent opening to a conversation with him, if it is not a professional consultation, are the words 'Do you remember when . . . ?' He represents them, becomes their objective (as opposed to subjective) memory, because he represents their lost possibility of understanding and relating to the outside world, and because he also represents some of what they know but cannot think.

This is what I meant by his being the requested clerk of their records. It is an honorary position. He is seldom called upon to officiate. But it has its exact if unstated meaning.

Notes

1. For the philosophical implication of early medicine see the first two volumes of Henry Sigerist's *History of Medicine*: vol. 1, *Primitive and Archaic Medicine* (New York: Oxford University Press, 1951); vol. 2, *Early Greek, Hindu, and Persian Medicine* (New York: Oxford University Press, 1961).
2. For a full study of the subject see Michael Balint's brilliant book *The Doctor, His Patient and The Illness* (London: Pitman, 1964).
3. My novel *Corker's Freedom* (London: Panther, 1966) attempts to illuminate this situation.

PART IV
Creating Sickness

CHAPTER 15

Creating Sickness

We used to heal ourselves when we were in the country. We hardly went to doctors and nurses. These days, they have taken over everything and Innu medicines are slowly disappearing. It is too bad this is happening. I think Innu medicines were better for the Innu.

Miste Shishin, elder of the nomadic Mushuau Innu, who were sedentarized in the community of Davis Inlet, Canada (Innu Nation, 1995)

Thus far, the readings in this book have discussed or exemplified a number of different kinds of health belief. In very broad terms, these beliefs can be grouped according to their orientation towards what causes illness. They congregate under two very broad headings: biomedical and psychological theories of illness. The first adopts a materialist philosophy, constituting the body as machine-like and radically separating an ethereal mind from a physical body. This almost universal approach was described by René Dubos (1960: 102) as 'unquestionably the most constructive force in medical research for almost a century . . . it . . . constitute[s] the bulk of modern medicine'. The second approach, the psychological, associates particular patterns of behaviour or personal character with illness. This model may also view non-material or external, possibly even spiritual, agents as operating through the mind or brain to produce sickness. In terms of treatment, biomedicine emphasizes interventions upon the body and technological methods of healing, concentrating on neutralizing a specific material pathogen. Psychological approaches, by contrast, view health and illness as determined by complex balances between the individual, their psyche, their physiology and their experience in the world. Healing focuses on a range of interventions used to alter conduct, change ways of thinking and facilitate health restoration through non-invasive means. These include psychotherapeutic techniques, alternative medicine and behaviourist therapies. But these two approaches overlap in complex ways. Just as biomedical practitioners would not always rule out psychological factors, those who promote a psychological understanding of illness would not necessarily deny the relevance of biological factors.

A third possibility, hinted at already in previous sections and exemplified by the readings in this section, is drawn from 'social medicine'. Broadly speaking, this approach advances the idea that large-scale social transformations *directly* cause sickness. Two broad forms of social change are specifically implicated: industrialism, both capitalist and socialist, and colonialism. The analysis of social medicine implies that radical reversals to or alterations of 'progress' are called for if destructive global patterns of illness are to be addressed. If health problems are to be confronted, the industrial and economic expansion that scientific activity has made possible, but which has been a virtually unquestioned ambition in both capitalist and socialist societies, will have to be restrained and its most toxic effects on specific populations recognized. Industrialization, often arriving with biomedicine in its wake, has followed colonial expansion, transforming whole ecologies, first by mechanized agriculture and then by factories. As has been well documented, perhaps the major consequence of this expansion has been disease and displacement for indigenous peoples around the world.[1] A further result of expansion has been the suppression and decline of indigenous medicines and healing systems. The nomadic Innu people, who only recently were forced to settle into villages in order that their land could be more easily industrialized, illustrate the sense of loss incurred by these processes, as shown in the quotation that began this chapter.

TUBERCULOSIS AND SOCIAL MEDICINE

If personality types are metaphors for particular kinds of illness, tuberculosis could be a metaphor for industrialism. In fact, tuberculosis is a most ironic metaphor, since it was originally used as a prime example of the doctrine of specific aetiology – the identification of a specific material cause of disease, so vital to the image of 'progress' in biomedical science. The doctrine itself was made possible by the nineteenth-century discoveries of Robert Koch and Louis Pasteur. With the invention of the microscope and the discovery of microorganisms, the effects of particular microbes and viruses on animal and human bodies could be ascertained through experimentation. Koch often injected himself in order to identify the effects of particular microbes.

In 1882 Koch isolated the tubercle bacillus, which is responsible for the infectious disease tuberculosis (TB), a major contributor to mortality in nineteenth-century Europe. Koch found the tubercle bacillus in all tubercle tissues that he studied and demonstrated how symptoms of tuberculosis could be produced by injecting it into guinea-pigs and other animals. Although social measures were taken to reduce the spread of the disease through quarantining patients in sanatoria, Koch's demonstration led to biomedical research emphasizing the neutralization of the tubercle bacillus. However, drugs such as streptomycin that were effective in countering the bacillus were not synthesized until the twentieth century, by which time the incidence of TB had declined markedly. Nonetheless, the efficacy of drugs such as streptomycin easily led to the perception that they were 'cures' for the disease. These simple lines of causation – from tubercle bacillus as cause to TB disease as effect and on to drugs as cure or neutralization

– draw out a clear, precise and self-contained biomedical health belief. The belief delineates a cause-and-effect relationship and proposes a medical intervention to remedy the undesired effect.

More than a century after these medical discoveries, one-third of the world's population is infected with TB, and the number of new cases in 1990 was 8 million, mostly in Asia (Brown, 1992). In India, where half the world's cases of TB occur, one person a minute dies of its effects (see Upleker and Rangan, 1996). If it were not for this, the virtual eradication of tuberculosis in many parts of the Western world could have been viewed as a clear demonstration of the success of biomedicine.[2]

However, this has not been the end of the story. Not only has TB persisted in the Third World, it has re-emerged in many Western cities. In 1990 the Centers for Disease Control in Atlanta 'warned that tuberculosis was not only reappearing but was out of control in the USA' (Perutz, 1994: 38). The recent wave of TB sufferers in the United States are disproportionately poor and from ethnic minority groups. Outbreaks of TB have occurred in homeless shelters and in prisons. A high proportion of the cases that are coming to the attention of physicians are classified as multi-drug-resistant because they do not respond to some or all of the drugs normally used to treat TB. An illuminating article in *New Scientist* discussed many of the puzzles that scientists and doctors are faced with in fighting it. It pointed out that TB remains largely a mystery to biologists, but without irony stated categorically that 'certainly we know that M. tuberculosis causes it, but the rest is a mess' (Brown, 1992: 34).

With tuberculosis, it could be argued that the bacillus is only one cause. What about 'the rest'? Although the microbe multiplies in the body, it rarely results in the symptoms of the disease. Who then 'gets' TB? This depends on both the internal physiology of the infected person and the external physical environment. If infected people also have HIV, which accounts for a sizeable proportion of the recent cases, their chances of developing TB are much greater, because the immune system is weaker.

We know that there is a social patterning to TB. It has been a disease, in terms of both those infected and those having the disease, historically and in the present, associated more with poverty and unhygienic environments than with affluence. In the recent epidemic in Western cities, it has spread rapidly among the poor, the homeless and the most disenfranchised sections of society (see Farmer, 1997). Because TB is transmitted from person to person in the air, and because the probability of this occurring is multiplied by stale air, overcrowding and a lack of sanitation, social conditions could just as well be elevated to the status of 'cause' of the disease as the tubercle bacillus. However, if these social factors were elevated to cause in this way, the treatment and policy agenda would have to alter radically. Duster (1990: 53–4) presents an analogous case for spina bifida, a disorder of the central nervous system. Although spina bifida is classified as a genetic disorder, the highest incidence in the world is in a small industrial town in Wales. Spina bifida 'on scientific grounds alone' could just as easily be classified as an industrial or environmental disorder. Instead of genome research and screening, this would call for steps to be taken to address the toxicity in the environment created by industry.

One of the most famous expositions of the social causation of illness or 'social medicine' in Britain lies in the writings of Thomas McKeown (1965, 1979, 1988). His general thesis, applied to other diseases in addition to TB, is that decreases in mortality since the nineteenth century in Britain, popularly attributed to medical technology and doctors' healing powers, are better explained by the social policies directed at alleviating poverty, the building of sanitation facilities in family dwellings, better nutrition, the advent of a safe water supply and, generally, the raised standards of living that occurred in the twentieth century. Streptomycin and other drugs, as McKeown (1979: 95) points out, came late in the history of the disease and contributed only a small amount to the decline in mortality from TB. McKeown (1979: 94) estimates that the contribution of medical therapy to the decline was only 3.2 per cent in England and Wales between 1848 and 1971. What is of paramount importance are the conditions under which people become exposed to the disease. Now that we know that we are not, as McKeown supposed two decades ago, 'late in the history of the disease', it is remarkable that the social factors which appeared to have produced the disease and the large-scale social and political measures attacking the conditions of poverty, which seemed to be crucial to controlling it, have been given so little priority. In the United States, the medical response to the current resurgence of TB emphasizes the allocation of funds for the provision of clinics and services for screening, drug therapy and surveillance of patients on drug therapy (see, for example, Nolan, 1997).

MARXISTS ON DISEASE AND DISEASE IN MARXIST SOCIETIES

One answer to this apparent paradox can be gleaned from Marxist writings in the area of health and social medicine. In our first reading in this section, a segment from **Friedrich Engels'** classic treatise *The Condition of the Working Class in England* (1845), the high incidences of TB or 'consumption' and other illnesses of the English working class was associated with the miserable social conditions in which Engels observed the industrial workforce to live. In this reading, we can notice many elements of what would come to be a 'Marxist' account of illness causation.[3] Marxists have emphasized that illness is the result of capitalist exploitation of the working class.

The broader context for this observation is the movement from stable, long-established agrarian economic structures to industrialized economies based less on skill, craft and paternal bonds and more on alienated, individualized and technology-driven labour. Chronicled most famously by Karl Marx, the massive dislocation of the peasantry which accompanied the shift from feudalism to capitalism heaped untold misery on the European masses. For Marx, the workforce moved from the exploited, but relatively stable environment of the feudal manor to the oppressive and unhealthy confines of factories. The automation of the labour process did not presage any decrease in physical exertion, but a shift towards cramped, indoor and repetitive rhythms of work. In the Marxist vision, the industrial worker was 'alienated'. This was conceived of both materially, in that the labourer was 'alienated' from the end-products of his or her work, and psychologically, in that the conditions of work precipitated a psychic or spiritual malaise in the worker. The conditions in factories, where workers were forced to sell their labour, reduced the worker to, in Marx's memorable phrase, 'an appendage to the machine'. Men, women and children under capitalism were forced to work for a subsistence wage, while the profit from their toils was creamed off by the owners of capital. By the end of the nineteenth century, time-and-motion studies had been inaugurated to rationalize the bodily efforts of the worker and to ensure that work was directed towards maximum productivity.

The poor health of manual workers in capitalist economies is, for Marxists, an end result of the degradation and dehumanization of work in industry and the perpetual economic insecurity of workers, who must endure the continual boom-and-bust cycles of the capitalist economy. Capitalism, in Marxist analyses, requires 'free labour' – that is, labour not tied to feudal systems of paternalism – as well as a 'reserve army' of unemployed and disenfranchised labourers to call on when need be. In these conditions of an oversupply of workers, the health of the workforce is irrelevant to capitalists, since the 'reserve army' can always be called upon. And for those incapable of work, Scull (1993: 35) has suggested that the growth of mental asylums in nineteenth-century Britain was a direct result of the capitalist need to separate the able-bodied from the non-able-bodied. Thus, the definition of mental abnormality was highly tied in with productivity within the capitalist economy, and the grounds for incarceration were connected to the necessity of participation in the wage economy.

The squalor and destitution in which the English industrial working classes lived has been vividly and amply documented by reformers such as Friedrich Engels, Charles Booth, Seebohm Rowntree, Henry Mayhew and George Orwell. The life they portray is a precarious one in which work is hard, brutal and perpetually insecure. The rewards for the vast bulk of workers barely covered subsistence. Orwell (1958: 95–6), writing in the 1930s, comments on the tendency of the unemployed and working poor to eat only the most unwholesome, processed foods – a trend that he identified as a product of degraded work and poverty. This trend has continued to the present, with a vast gulf still separating the diets of working- and middle-class Britons (see Calnan, 1990).

The Condition of the Working Class in England contains some of the most vivid and evocative observations of life among the newly urbanized working classes of nineteenth-century England. Engels' scathing indictment of an uncaring and even murderous capitalist society ruled by industrialists and the middle classes draws direct linkages between capitalist exploitation and the extremely poor health of the workers. In Marxist accounts, the vitality of the middle classes is directly a product of the infirmity of the workers. Rudolf Virchow, a German cellular pathologist of the nineteenth century who advanced what we might call a Marxist social medicine, remarked, 'may the rich remember during the winter, when they sit in front of their hot stoves and give Christmas apples to their little ones, that the shiphands who brought the coal and apples died of cholera' (quoted by Waitzkin, 1983: 73). Virchow attributes this to sheer back-breaking hard work combined with unsanitary living conditions and poor, often adulterated food. In the rush to industrialize, basic considerations regarding the freshness and safety of foods were often neglected. The milk supply, for example, was heavily infected throughout the nineteenth century (McKeown, 1965: 48). For the capitalists, the workers were mere animals, beasts of burden. In many places, Engels notes that their living quarters were unfit for human habitation. Workers were thrown together in appallingly decrepit structures: 'one can see how little space human beings need to move about in, how little air – and what air – they need to breathe in order to exist, and how few of the decencies of civilisation are really necessary in order to survive' (Engels, 1958 [1845]: 63–4). We could read Engels' view of industrialization, as distinct from the general tenor of the writings of Marx, who saw industry as a necessary and positive feature in the development of society, not as 'progress', but as catastrophe. There is little in Engels' description to suggest that industrial capitalism, economically dynamic as it was, was any improvement over the more socially stagnant feudal order.

The physical and social conditions Engels found in the living quarters of Manchester factory workers in the mid-nineteenth century are not dissimilar to those found in 'Third World' shanty towns and the slums, prisons and homeless shelters of New York and London. Yet, in the face of clear evidence that infectious diseases such as TB proliferate in particular types of landscape inhabited by the poor, medical science prioritizes high-technology remedies that focus upon the bacillus itself rather than the wider world in which this bacillus roams. Currently, TB research concentrates on the search for effective drugs that will be able to overpower the multi-drug-resistant strains and on manipulation of the genes of M. tuberculosis (Brown, 1992). This would seem to parallel Engels' statements in the reading classifying the feeble efforts of the middle classes to rectify the 'social murder' inflicted upon the workers as 'a few precautionary reforms of trifling significance'.

Marxism provides us with an explanation for the seeming paradox that the *social* contexts and factors involved in diseases like TB have been underestimated and neglected by both physicians and policy-makers. The medical profession is, for Marxists, part of the ideological state apparatus. As Waitzkin (1983: 57) puts it, 'medicine fosters an ideology that helps maintain and reproduce class structure and social domination.' The profession, along with educators, lawyers and other elements of the middle class, plays a key role in legitimating the capitalist state and the search for profit and capital accumulation upon which the economic and social system relies. By presenting illness and disease as an individual, rather than a social issue, physicians contribute to legitimating the social conditions which create illness as well as profit. However, on the other hand, Marxists are not suggesting that capitalism thrives on a sick population – only that when there is an excess of labourers over employment (as there has been at most times

since the nineteenth century), sickness like unemployment can be not only tolerated but approved, since its costs are predominantly borne by either individuals
or the state.

Both Marxism and social medicine posit a challenging position. While they
do not deny or reject the materialist underpinning of biomedicine that specific
material agents cause disease, the innovation of Marxism and social medicine
lies in broadening the definition of what is considered an aetiological factor.[4]
The causes of illness, in this view, should be sought out in a number of social and
political factors connected to the distribution of resources in society, economic
exploitation, class oppression, the physical conditions of life, the role of physicians and the changing natural environment.

For Marxists, capitalism in its drive to produce commodities and accumulate
capital contributes directly to the premature deaths of the working classes. Environmental toxins, back-breaking or mindless work, stress and poverty all contribute
to sickness among those in the West who suffer disproportionately from illness
and disease. Hence, in capitalist societies vast inequalities in health coexist with
the ideologies of progress, equality and liberalism. This has been documented
particularly well in contemporary Britain, where researchers have statistically
documented inequalities in health to suggest causal factors, policy implications
and potential preventive methods. Systematic and widespread differences have
been found in the occurrence of ill health, in the infant mortality rate and in
morbidity rates from almost all causes according to social class.

These differences were exposed in the 1980 Black Report and the 1987 follow-
up publication *The Health Divide*, both of which were suppressed by the Conservative government of the time. The Department of Health and Social Services
published the Black Report in a limited edition on a public holiday in 1980, and
the Health Education Authority published *The Health Divide* as a low-budget,
stapled pamphlet. It was the mass media and Penguin, which published both
reports as books, rather than the government that publicized the findings. A
more recent study in 1998 demonstrated that health inequalities in Britain have
continued to widen in tandem with increasing disparities in income. The report
recommends that all future health policies are evaluated in terms of their impact
on health inequalities, that women of childbearing age and children are prioritized
and that action to reduce income inequalities and improve living standards is
taken (Acheson, 1998).

The Black Report found that 'despite more than thirty years of a National
Health Service expressly committed to offering equal care for all, there remains a
marked class gradient in standards of health. Indeed, that gradient seems to be
more marked than in comparable countries . . . and in certain respects has been
becoming more marked' (Black et al., 1982: 15). Although the general health of
the British population had improved, that of the lowest social classes had actually deteriorated, and the gap between manual and non-manual groups in terms
of chronic sickness had considerably widened. A 1997 study revealed that 'for
major specific causes (such as ischaemic heart disease, cerebrovascular disease,
lung cancer, and accidents), the health gains to society as a whole have failed to

reach its less advantaged members' (Scott-Samuel, 1997: 753). The Acheson Report (1998: 2) concluded that 'the weight of scientific evidence supports a socioeconomic explanation of health inequalities. This traces the roots of ill health to such determinants as income, education and employment as well as to the material environment and lifestyle.'

While these reports are not styled as Marxist or social medicine texts, they broadly support the basic position that social and economic conditions are the main determinants of health problems. In their quest to improve the health of the working classes in Western societies, Marxists and socialists have attached a great deal of importance to the openness of access to health services, which are nearly always conceived as conventional biomedical facilities. Along with access, however, Marxists have stressed the need for preventive public health or social medicine policies through screening and other procedures. More broadly, they have advocated the reform of economic and social relations between workers and owners of capital and an overall increase in living standards. Because Marx and most Marxists subscribe to European Enlightenment notions of 'progress' and 'development', these have been thought to be best achieved through constantly expanding industrial productivity through scientific technology. This aspect of Marxism has been articulated well by Serge Latouche (1996: x) in his essay on Westernization:

> Marxist analysis blames most of the contradictions, injustices and dysfunctions of the contemporary world on the exploitative dynamics of capital accumulation and its consequences (exploitation etc.). In other words all the troubles come from the unbridled development of productive forces. These criticisms are very forceful and still remain largely convincing; but the only remedy suggested for the evil, after the revolution, is the reinforcement of this same accumulation of capital, in other words, development, perhaps at an even more frenetic development of the *same* productive forces.

These basic assumptions were evident in the former Soviet Union and Eastern bloc countries, as well as Cuba. Under the Bolsheviks, the USSR was transformed from an agrarian, feudal society into a superpower in a relatively short space of time. A consequence of this development was that there were fewer problems of access to the health services or 'polyclinics' than anywhere else in the world by 1940, and at the same time there were more doctors per capita in the USSR than in Britain and the USA (Nettl, 1967: 136).

Within these terms of development, Cuba can be seen as a successful model of Marxist health planning. In Cuba, medicine was always conceived to be part of a broader social transformation to end the legacy of colonialism and underdevelopment, along with the poverty, poor housing, discrimination and exploitation that were part of it. Doctors were recruited not from the upper middle classes, as they are in capitalist countries, but from blue-collar workers. The principles of equality of access, an integral approach to health and popular participation in health inform all Cuban health programmes (Feinsilver, 1993: 28). Currently,

Cuba has a lower infant mortality rate (IMR) than any of the old Warsaw Pact countries and all of Latin America, and its rate is only slightly higher than that of the United States. Cuba's IMR is only 1 point higher than the rate for all 'developed' countries, and 73 points lower than the average for the 'developing' countries (Feinsilver, 1993: 94).

However, in the Soviet Union, the cost of the achievements in access to health care has been high. The tremendous drive under state socialism for economic growth, military power and scientific achievement has led to immense environmental disaster, termed 'ecocide' by Feshbach and Friendly (1992). They argue that Chernobyl' is only the tip of the iceberg. The incidence of lung cancer, for example, doubled from 1970 to 1988 and is growing two times as fast as in the United States (Feshbach and Friendly, 1992: 189). There is extensive evidence of higher rates of illness and birth defects in most polluted areas, locations near industrial dumping grounds, metallurgical centres and oil refineries (p. 184). This is, of course, paralleled in other countries, but elsewhere environmental controls on industry were tighter and more likely to be enforced. The health of the Soviet population was subordinated to the goal of rapid industrialization of the state. Thus it is not simply capitalist societies that contain social conditions that create and perpetuate illness. Rather, what is implied is that it is the devotion to the idea of 'progress' which drives Western societies (socialist and capitalist) to equate industrialization with 'development' and improvement. It is significant that, since the fall of communism and the introduction of a market economy in Russia, the health of the population in general has deteriorated even more markedly. Tulchinsky and Varavikova (1996) report that life-expectancy has declined, maternal mortality has increased, infectious diseases, once under control, have reappeared, and mortality rates from cardiovascular disease are increasing.

COLONIALISM AND IMPERIALISM

Another important factor in the global creation and perpetuation of sickness is colonialism. Colonialism, as Marxists and sociologists of development have pointed out, exploited the natural and human resources appropriated in the colonies. These appropriations became the basis for the industrial take-off in Europe and created immense earnings for magnates. In their ruthless pursuit of wealth and profit around the world, Europeans wreaked havoc upon native societies, inflicting violence and spreading disease. European colonization of Africa, Asia and the New World contributed directly to the high rates of mortality among native peoples after conquest.

The diffusion of disease among native peoples was a potent force. Since contact, more indigenous people in North America died from European diseases that they had no immunity to (and which were not known to them) than from any other means. Among the diseases Europeans brought to native peoples were smallpox, measles, influenza, bubonic plague, diphtheria, typhus, cholera, scarlet fever, chicken pox, yellow fever and whooping cough. These diseases were responsible for massive depopulation and the extinction of whole societies of indigenous people. Pre-contact population estimates vary widely, but what is not in doubt is that the late nineteenth century witnessed a nadir in the population of Native Americans, which dropped to perhaps one-quarter of a million from over five million in 1492 (see Thornton, 1987). Much of the decline in native populations can be attributed to purposeful calculation on the part of Europeans, who spread disease and inflicted violent massacres. Even Jaffe (1992: 109), who argues for relatively low pre-contact numbers, suggests that diseases were used 'in lieu of Hitler's "modern" death factories to kill as many natives as possible'. In seventeenth-century New England, the mortality rates in the wake of English settlement were rarely less than 80 or 90 per cent (Cronon, 1983: 86). The same rates of population decline occurred over longer periods for other groups such as the Kayapo in Brazil and the Mandans of the Great Plains (McNeill, 1976: 181). In Australia, likewise, the Aboriginal population was devastated by disease and frontier violence within 150 years of European settlement. The native population declined swiftly, with as many as 90 per cent of the population dying in the 60 years from 1788 to 1848 (Saggers and Gray, 1991: 66). In various promontories of European expansion – Tasmania and Newfoundland, for example – native populations had been exterminated completely by the 1830s. This process is, of course, still contemporary and cannot be consigned to the status of an unfortunate incident in the European past. As Kraut (1994: 11–12) notes, while Euro-Americans were celebrating Columbus Day in 1992, the Yanomami people of the Amazon were being decimated by European-delivered diseases, especially malaria.

While colonizing forces were much less affected by disease contracted through contact with native peoples, illnesses suffered by colonizing armies and administrators proved to be a constant hindrance to the expansion of territories. Hence, the British established the London and Liverpool Schools of Tropical Medicine in 1899 to undertake research into the perils to health encountered in imperial pursuits (see Worboys, 1988). As **Megan Vaughan** puts it in the second of our readings in this section, 'the new medical science ... did not fail to feed off Africa as a diseased environment for its research'.

However, there was also a less definable, less visible process by which colonial powers imposed certain, largely racist and derogatory, representations of natives. These have remained in the European imagination and have informed a whole range of policies – educational, legal, medical and social – towards native peoples in colonized and settler states. The mortality from European diseases, for example, has often been written off in terms of the *inevitable* result of the collision between 'civilized' and 'savage' societies. In Darwinian terms, the 'dying off' of such populations follows from the 'fitter' constitutions of the Europeans (see Arnold, 1996: 85–91). The remedies proposed and implemented by Europeans in the colonial and postcolonial contexts have combined two basic processes: intense native assimilation into European ways of life and making Western medicine available to native populations in the hope of stemming the decline in their numbers.

In the process of colonization, Western medical centres were established to care for the health of both natives and colonizers. This served to transplant Western medicine and to undermine indigenous health and healing systems. Using close readings of colonial medical reports and jungle doctors' memoirs, Vaughan broadly argues that biomedicine played a role, not only directly as an agent of colonialism in Africa, but in helping to shape the 'African' as an object of medical and social knowledge. Biomedicine elaborated a classification system intrinsic to colonialism. Populations were not individualized by biomedicine, as in Europe, but aggregated and homogenized as members of a group or 'tribe' said to possess distinctive psychologies and bodies and to be susceptible to peculiar patterns of illness. Over the past two centuries, Vaughan argues, Africans have provided the raw material in medicine for the elaboration of colonial theories of difference. The 'primitiveness' of the Africans was thought to predispose them to certain diseases. Their psychology was believed to be either backward, inferior or pathological.

Perhaps the most important commentator on the psychological consequences of colonialism is Frantz Fanon, a psychiatrist and philosopher from Martinique. For Fanon, colonialism instigates a brute violence that is used to dominate and subjugate, but it also uses a more subtle violence to legitimate itself and to undermine indigenous culture and well-being. The colonial world that Fanon describes is suffused with simplistic dualisms – white–black, European–native, advanced–primitive, developed–undeveloped – which are constantly reinforced in the language and administration of conquest. Like Engels' observation about the transformation of workers into beasts of burden, colonial language, according to Fanon, dehumanizes natives, turning them into animals. The poverty, displacement and relocation which colonialism has brought for the mass of colonized peoples reduce natives to dependants who are forced to rely on colonizers for hand-outs of food and other necessities; this turns them against each other, because they must now compete for the favour of the colonial ruler. Hence, 'every colony tends to turn into a huge farmyard, where the only law is the knife' (Fanon, 1963: 308).

The colonized person is not just a dominated person, but a person being told that they are something other than what they thought they were. 'Colonialism forces the people it dominates to ask themselves the question constantly: in reality who am I?' (Fanon, 1963: 250). According to Fanon, this produces ontological uncertainty and with it an upsurge in mental pathology and criminality – more nervous breakdowns, more psychoses, more alcoholism, more violence. As can be seen among colonized peoples around the world, anger and aggression are directed not against the colonial powers, but against the self and one another. These tragedies must be considered not only in the context of colonial wars – in Fanon's case the Algerian war of liberation against France – but also in terms of the manipulation of personal identity which colonialism produces through its reckless efforts to dominate and assimilate others.

The residues of these illness-generating social processes are apparent in the native populations of European settler states such as the United States, Canada and Australia. In our third reading in this section, the Yup'ik writer **Harold Napoleon** uses the history of his own aboriginal people, in Alaska under US control, directly to confront the physical and psychological ills by which both he and his community have been affected. Napoleon focuses on alcoholism in particular. He considers this a disease, not because it has some physiological, genetic or material cause, but because 'the people who suffer from it do not volunteer to become infected'. Within living memory, European contact accompanied a number of epidemics – Napoleon's 'great death' – that cut a swathe through the Yup'ik population. The survivors, 'born into shock', were subject to the intense efforts of their colonizers to assimilate them into Euro-American ways. In a world of imposed Christianity and Western education, Napoleon's survivors turned in upon themselves through alcohol, self-neglect and suicide. Eventually the distinct Yup'ik ways of life were abandoned as the people reeled from what Napoleon describes as a process akin to Post-Traumatic Stress Disorder, common among Vietnam War veterans.

Contemporary Yup'ik children measure themselves against the impossible standards set by American television. By any yardstick of Euro-American culture, Napoleon argues, Yup'ik can see themselves to have failed. The Yup'ik situation, sketched out in harrowing detail here, approximates that of many other indigenous peoples. It fits a broader pattern of social breakdown, self-harm, violence, poor health and child abuse in indigenous communities throughout North America and elsewhere. Suicide, for instance, accounted for over a third of all deaths of aboriginal youth in Canada at the beginning of this decade (Kirmayer, 1994: 3) and is the second largest cause of death for Native American and Alaska Native adolescents in the United States (National Institute of Mental Health, 1990). In general, suicide is one of the leading causes of death of native North Americans (Bachman, 1992: 109). The mortality rate for alcohol-related health problems is about four times higher for Native Americans in the United States than for non-natives (Young, 1994: 201). The life-expectancy of US Native Americans is about 10 years lower than the national average (Kivisto, 1995), and in Australia Aborigines' life-expectancy can be up to 20 years lower than that of other Australians (Saggers and Gray, 1991: 102). Mortality rates from infections, neoplasm, endocrinal/nutritional/metabolic disorders, mental health problems, circulatory ailments and injuries/poisonings are higher for native Canadians than other Canadians (Young, 1994: 42). Similar patterns of excess morbidity have been extensively documented among Aboriginal people in Australia (Saggers and Gray, 1991: ch. 4).

One current example of the extreme suffering of Native Americans from physical illnesses, suicide and alcoholism in the context of colonial domination are the Ojibwa, who recently were relocated to Grassy Narrows, Ontario. In her book on the subject, Shkilnyk (1985: 175) states that,

> in the end, the system proved its extraordinary effectiveness in pursuing the objective of assimilation. In the span of only one generation after the relocation of Grassy Narrows, the central institutions of Ojibwa culture, the people's moral values and beliefs, customary social relationships, political organisation, and mode of production

– all were rendered impotent, useless, even superfluous under the imposed conditions of the new reserve.

The reserves, reservations and communities of aboriginal people throughout
Canada, the United States and Australasia bear witness to the extensiveness of
such catastrophic processes.

An important contribution to these patterns is undoubtedly the undermining
of the validity of native cosmologies, spirituality and ways of viewing the world.
To Europeans, as Napoleon mentions, natives were 'savages', steeped in superstition and hardly recognizable as humans. It cannot be merely accidental that
self-destructive tendencies are so pervasive in colonized and formerly colonized
populations. A common explanation in Australia for the drastic decline in the
Aboriginal population is that natives had lost the will to live (Saggers and Gray,
1991: 66). For Fanon, it was this manipulation of personal identity which was
the essential context for the tragedies he observed among the colonized peoples
in Algeria.

MODERNIZATION, HUNGER AND SICKNESS

At the time of colonization, European expansion was believed to bring the
benefits of 'civilization' and 'progress' to those who were brought into contact
with it. The seventeenth-century English philosopher John Locke provided a
strong rationale in colonial law for dispossession on the premise that North
American Indians did not have any fixed property, since this could only be claimed
through cultivation, 'improvement of the soil' and labour. They therefore had
no land rights as such and could only benefit from 'civilization', which would
teach them the virtues of labour and private property (see Tully, 1995: 71–8).
One of the prime advantages that colonized peoples were later supposed to gain
from this expansion was from European medical science.

Ivan Illich (1976) has argued quite stridently that the expansion of Western
medicine has been disastrous for those peoples who have had it imposed upon
them. He believes that this expansion is a form of 'cultural iatrogenesis'. That is,
it amounts to a form of physician-inflicted harm, not just at the level of the
individual, but for whole cultures. Western medical intervention, for Illich, robs
people of the autonomy to care for themselves. Its presence discourages the
cultivation of self-healing potentialities. Pain becomes not a natural or spiritual
process, but a demand for ever more effective drugs. Under colonialism, the
ailments that peoples had lived with for millennia suddenly became reduced to
physical bodily pain which individuals had to accept as outside their control.
Western medicine fosters a culture of passivity, but over the long term it 'attempts
to do for people what their cultural and genetic heritage formerly equipped them
to do for themselves' (Illich, 1976: 126). Equally important, Western Medicine
has derided and opposed virtually every indigenous healing system it has encountered. When native people have then been ravished by disease, violence and

sickness under colonialism, they have often had to face these tragedies either without their own views and methods of medical healing or while they were being eroded under Western domination.

For **Nancy Scheper-Hughes,** in the final reading of this book, as well as for Harold Napoleon, modernization and the intrusion of European technologies, medicine and views of the world is a deeply incapacitating process. Scheper-Hughes's detailed ethnographic study of the northeastern Brazilian shanty town of Bom Jesus has been a long-term project spanning the period from the mid-1960s to the late 1980s. During that time, she visited the community on numerous occasions, as both a professional anthropologist and a political activist, a *companheira* to the women of the Alto do Cruziero in Bom Jesus. Her concern here is with the transformation of the symptoms of poverty and oppression – the folk syndrome *nervoso* – into the anodyne and depoliticized language and epistemology of biomedicine. The poor, exploited and dispossessed of the Alto experience bodily distress from hunger that manifests itself in numerous ways, expressed graphically in the anatomical illustration in the reading. These symptoms are taken by the medical establishment, not as indicative of a 'social illness', rooted in hunger and degradation, but as a psychological illness that is treated with tonics and psychotropic medication. For Scheper-Hughes, the doctors are acting with profound 'bad faith' in their failure to recognize the political sources of the complaints of their patients. In the process, they convert what is a critique of society, a 'hungry body', into a 'sick body', which indicts no one.

Scheper-Hughes draws a parallel between what she has observed in Brazil with the medicalization of the complaints of the shanty-town-dwellers and the discourse on somatization in medical anthropology. Associated with the work of Arthur Kleinman and others – often anthropologists who are also physicians or psychiatrists – 'somatization' is used to describe a kind of false consciousness in the patient. What is 'really' a mental health problem is presented by the sufferer as a physical symptom. Kleinman (1980: 138) estimates that 70 per cent of the patients he interviewed at a clinic in Taipei with 'documented psychological disorders' complained of physical symptoms. Such patients, so the view goes, are suffering from stress, depression, anxiety and situational problems but complain of physical symptoms such as dizziness, non-specific pain, headaches and backaches.

In Britain, somatization is used extensively as an explanation for the low use of psychiatric services by people of Asian descent. This is articulated in what has become a 'textbook' used by psychiatrists dealing with ethnic minority patients – Philip Rack's (1983) *Race, Culture and Mental Disorder*. In a penetrating critique of the book and the concept, Watters (1996) points out that Asians are represented as having an inordinate tendency to somatize psychological distress. They do this, according to Rack, because they perceive the doctor's role as related to physical illness and therefore only mention these complaints. The somatic complaint, in this view, may be a metaphor used because Asian languages are not sufficiently rich to express emotional distress. In this context, Rack emphasizes the 'peasant origins' of Bengalis in Bradford in the north of England. As with *nervoso*, there is not even a hint from psychiatrists subscribing to the somatization thesis that the complaints of patients may be expressive of experiences of oppression rather than mental pathology. For Asian patients, such 'symptoms' may speak more loudly as to the displacement, racism, discrimination and poverty that they have experienced in Britain than anything else.

Somatization is sometimes seen by psychiatrists as a manifestation of a more 'primitive' culture. Another British 'transcultural' psychiatrist, Julian Leff (1986: 33), explains it in the following way;

> . . . over time there has been a shift in focus from the bodily expression of distress to its communication through language, with a progressive differentiation of the vocabulary of emotion. The historical process has occurred unevenly, so that in many cultures today emotional distress is *still* communicated through a rich variety of somatic symptoms. [Emphasis added]

Thus, for physicians such as Leff, the bodily expression of distress is a sign of primitiveness. Kleinman (1980: 138) also implies that those who somatize are somehow backward, arguing that, 'in the United States, such patients are . . . particularly members of ethnic minorities from lower class backgrounds with limited education, [and] *still* are to be found complaining of somatic symptoms in medical clinics' (emphasis added). For Scheper-Hughes, on the other hand, there is no advance signified by the framing of health problems in psychological or psychiatric terminology. The bodily, for her, is more immediate, more real and less tied to the psychological abstractions that the middle classes must continually rest on for the articulation of their ailments. Yet, she appears to be telling us, it is vital to recognize the sheer power of medical and other Eurocentric ascriptions on those who have become objects. 'How is it,' Scheper-Hughes asks, 'that the mortally tired cane cutters and washerwomen define themselves as weak rather than as exploited?' What occurs when people are vulnerable, as the residents of the Alto undoubtedly are, is that they become victims of a hegemonic process – perhaps, the charisma of medicine – which 'names' their complaint as something other than the shameful 'hunger', and thereby exculpates the catastrophic processes of 'modernization' that so afflict them.

Notes

1. A detailed account of this process in New England is presented by Cronon (1983). Arnold (1996) describes the ecological and biological impacts of European expansion more generally. The Australian case is analysed by Butlin (1983).
2. There were, of course, several major exceptions. A notable exception in North America has been the case of Native Americans. Although the rate of tuberculosis for native Canadians has declined, the incidence has remained as much as ten times higher than that for the general population of Canada (Young, 1994: 60).
3. Interestingly, the most prominent Marxist scholars of health and illness are themselves physicians. See Navarro (1976, 1978) and Waitzkin (1983).

4. As Turner (1995: 212) has observed, Marxism is silent on the phenomenology of sickness. Engels, and we could add the social medicine view of McKeown and subsequent Marxist writers, often approvingly quotes physicians and medical reports.

References

Acheson, Sir Donald (1998), *Independent Inquiry into Inequalities in Health Report*, London: HMSO.

Arnold, David (1996), *The Problem of Nature: Environment, Culture and European Expansion*, Oxford: Blackwell.

Bachman, Ronet (1992), *Death and Violence on the Reservation: Homicide, Family Violence and Suicide in American Indian Populations*, Westport, CT: Greenwood.

Black, Sir Douglas, *et al.* (1982), *Inequalities in Health: The Black Report*, London: Penguin.

Brown, Phyllida (1992), 'The Return of the Big Killer', *New Scientist*, 10 October, 30–7.

Butlin, N. G. (1983), *Our Original Aggression: Aboriginal Populations of South Eastern Australia 1789–1850*, Sydney: George Allen and Unwin.

Calnan, Michael (1990), 'Food and Health: A Comparison of Beliefs and Practices in Middle-Class and Working-Class Households', in Sarah Cunningham-Burley and Neil McKeganey (eds), *Readings in Medical Sociology*, London: Routledge, 9–36.

Cronon, William (1983), *Changes in the Land: Indians, Colonists and the Ecology of New England*, New York: Hill and Wang.

Dubos, René (1960), *The Mirage of Health*, London: George Allen and Unwin.

Duster, Troy (1990), *Backdoor to Eugenics*, New York: Routledge.

Engels, Friedrich (1958) [1845], *The Condition of the Working Class in England*, translated and edited by W. O. Henderson and W. H. Chaloner, Stanford, CA: Stanford University Press, 1958.

Fanon, Frantz (1963), *The Wretched of the Earth*, New York: Grove Press.

Farmer, Paul (1997), 'Social Scientists and the New Tuberculosis,' *Social Science and Medicine*, 44(3): 347–58.

Feinsilver, Julie (1993), *Healing the Masses: Cuban Health Politics at Home and Abroad*, Berkeley, CA: University of California Press.

Feshbach, Murray, and Alfred Friendly, Jr. (1992), *Ecocide in the USSR: Health and Nature under Siege*, London: Aurum Press.

Illich, Ivan (1976), *Medical Nemesis*, New York: Bantam.

Innu Nation (1995), *Gathering Voices: Finding Strength to Help Our Children*, Vancouver: Douglas and McIntyre.

Jaffe, A. J. (1992), *The First Immigrants from Asia: A Population History of North American Indians*, New York: Plenum.

Kirmayer, Laurence (1994), 'Suicide among Canadian Aboriginal Peoples', *Transcultural Psychiatric Research Review*, 31: 3–58.

Kivisto, P. (1995), *Americans All*, Belmont, CA: Wadsworth.

Kleinman, Arthur (1980), *Patients and Healers in the Context of Culture*, Berkeley, CA: University of California Press.

Kraut, Alan (1994), *Silent Travelers: Germs, Genes and the 'Immigrant Menace'*, New York: Basic Books.

Latouche, Serge (1996), *The Westernization of the World: The Significance, Scope and Limits of the Drive towards Global Uniformity*, translated by Rosemary Morris, Oxford: Polity.

Leff, Julian (1986), 'The Epidemiology of Mental Illness across Cultures', in John Cox (ed.), *Transcultural Psychiatry*, London: Croom Helm, 23–36.

McKeown, Thomas (1965), *Medicine in Modern Society*, London: George Allen and Unwin.

—— (1979), *The Role of Medicine: Dream, Mirage or Nemesis?*, Oxford: Basil Blackwell.

—— (1988), *The Origins of Human Disease*, Oxford: Blackwell.

McNeill, William (1976), *Plagues and Peoples*, New York: Anchor.

National Institute of Mental Health (1990), *Indian Adolescent Mental Health*, Washington, DC: Office of Technology Assessment.

Navarro, Vicente (1976), *Medicine under Capitalism*, New York: Prodist.

—— (1978), *Class Struggle, the State and Medicine: An Historical and Contemporary Analysis of the Medical Sector in Great Britain*, London: Martin Robinson.

Nettl, J. P. (1967), *The Soviet Achievement*, New York: Harcourt Brace Jovanovich.

Nolan, Charles (1997), 'Topics for Our Times: The Increasing Demand for Tuberculosis Services – A New Encumbrance on Tuberculosis Control Programs', *American Journal of Public Health*, 87(4): 551–3.

Orwell, George (1958) [1937], *The Road to Wigan Pier*, New York: Harvest.

Perutz, M. F. (1994), 'The White Plague', *New York Review of Books*, 26 May: 35–9.

Rack, Philip (1982), *Race, Culture and Mental Disorder*, London: Tavistock.

Saggers, Sherry, and Dennis Gray (1991), *Aboriginal Health and Society: The Traditional and Contemporary Aboriginal Struggle for Better Health*, North Sydney: Allen and Unwin.

Scott-Samuel, Alex (1997), 'Health Inequalities Recognised in UK', *The Lancet*, 350 (13 September): 753.

Scull, Andrew (1993), *The Most Solitary of Afflictions: Madness and Society in Britain, 1700–1900*, New Haven, CT: Yale University Press.

Shkilnyk, Anastasia (1985), *A Poison Stronger than Love: The Destruction of an Ojibwa Community*, New Haven, CT: Yale University Press.

Thornton, Russell (1987), *American Indian Holocaust and Survival: A Population History since 1492*, Norman, OK: University of Oklahoma Press.

Tulchinsky, Theodore, and Elena Varavikova (1996), 'Addressing the Epidemiologic Transition in the Former Soviet Union: Strategies for Health System and Public Health Reform in Russia', *American Journal of Public Health*, 86(3): 313–20.

Tully, James (1995), *Strange Multiplicity: Constitutionalism in the Age of Diversity*, Cambridge: Cambridge University Press.

Turner, Bryan (1995), *Medical Power and Social Knowledge*, 2nd edn, London: Sage.

Uplekar, Mukund, and Sheela Rangan (1996), *Tackling TB: The Search for Solutions*, Bombay: The Foundation for Research in Community Health.

Waitzkin, Howard (1983), *The Second Sickness: Contradictions of Capitalist Health Care*, New York: Free Press.

Watters, Charles (1996), 'The Representation of Asians in British Psychiatry', in Colin Samson and Nigel South (eds), *The Social Construction of Social Policy*, London: Macmillan, 88–105.

Worboys, Michael (1988), 'Manson, Ross and Colonial Medical Policy: Tropical Medicine in London and Liverpool, 1899–1914', in Roy MacLeod and Milton Lewis (eds), *Disease, Medicine and Empire: Perspectives on Western Medicine and the Experience of European Expansion*, London: Routledge, 21–37.

Young, T. Kue (1994), *The Health of Native Americans: Toward a Biocultural Epidemiology*, New York: Oxford University Press.

CHAPTER 16

Results of Industrialisation[1]

Friedrich Engels

... If one individual inflicts a bodily injury upon another which leads to the death of the person attacked we call it manslaughter; on the other hand, if the attacker knows beforehand that the blow will be fatal we call it murder. Murder has also been committed if society[2] places hundreds of workers in such a position that they inevitably come to premature and unnatural ends. Their death is as violent as if they had been stabbed or shot. Murder has been committed if thousands of workers have been deprived of the necessities of life or if they have been forced into a situation in which it is impossible for them to survive. Murder has been committed if the workers have been forced by the strong arm of the law to go on living under such conditions until death inevitably releases them. Murder has been committed if society knows perfectly well that thousands of workers cannot avoid being sacrificed so long as these conditions are allowed to continue. Murder of this sort is just as culpable as the murder committed by an individual. But if society murders a worker it is a treacherous stab in the back against which the worker cannot defend himself. At first sight it does not appear to be murder at all, because responsibility for the death of the victim cannot be pinned on any individual assailant. Everyone is responsible and yet no one is responsible, because it appears as if the victim has died from natural causes. If a worker dies no one places the responsibility for his death on society, though some would realise that society has failed to take steps to prevent the victim from dying. But it is murder all the same. I shall now have to prove that, every day and every hour, English society commits what the English workers' press rightly denounces as social murder. I shall now have to prove that English society has created for the workers an environment in which they cannot remain healthy or enjoy a normal expectation of life. I shall have to prove that English society gradually undermines the health of the workers and so brings them to an early grave. Moreover I shall also have to prove that English society *is fully aware* how dangerous is this environment to the health and life of the workers, and yet takes no action to reform the situation. I shall have proved my point if I can produce evidence concerning the deaths of workers from such unimpeachable sources as official documents, Parliamentary papers and Government reports. Evidence of this kind proves conclusively that society is aware of the fact that its policy results not in manslaughter but in murder.

It is self-evident that a social class which lives under the conditions that we have described and is so poorly supplied with the most indispensable necessities of existence can enjoy neither good health nor a normal expectation of life. Let us, however, review once more the various factors which have a detrimental effect upon the state of health of the English workers. The concentration of the population in great cities has, in itself, an extremely deleterious influence. The air of London is neither so pure nor so rich in oxygen as that of the countryside; two and a half million pairs of lungs and two hundred and fifty thousand coal fires concentrated in an area of three to four geographical square miles[3] use up an immense amount of oxygen, which can only be replaced with difficulty since the layout of English towns impedes ventilation. The carbon dioxide gas produced by people breathing and fires burning fails to rise from the streets because of its specific gravity and is not dispersed by the winds which blow over the rooftops. The inhabitants of the towns do not take in sufficient oxygen when they breathe and this leads to mental torpor and low physical vitality. Consequently the dwellers in great towns suffer from chronic ailments to a greater extent than country people who breathe a purer atmosphere.

On the other hand the town dweller is less exposed to acute attacks of inflammatory disorders. If life in the great towns is unhealthy, how much worse must it be for those who live in the unwholesome atmosphere of the working-class quarters where, as we have already seen, everything combines to pollute the air. In the country no harm may come from having a dung heap near a house, because it is more exposed to the fresh air. In the middle of a big town, on the other hand, it is quite a different matter to have dung heaps in alleys and courts in built up areas where there is no ventilation. Decaying animal and vegetable refuse produces gases which are injurious to health and if these gases are not blown away they pollute the atmosphere. The filth and the stagnant pools in the working class quarters of the great cities have the most deleterious effects upon the health of the inhabitants because they engender just those gases which give rise to disease. The same effect follows from the miasma exuded by foul streams. But that is not the whole story by any means. The way in which the vast mass of the poor are treated by modern society is truly scandalous. They are herded into great cities where they breathe a fouler air than in the countryside which they have left. They are housed in the worst ventilated districts of the towns; they are deprived of all means of keeping clean. They are deprived of water because this is only brought to their houses if someone is prepared to defray the cost of laying the pipes. River water is so dirty as to be useless for cleansing purposes. The poor are forced to throw into the streets all their sweepings, garbage, dirty water, and frequently even disgusting filth and excrement. The poor are deprived of all proper means of refuse disposal and so they are forced to pollute the very districts they inhabit. And this is by no means all. There is no end to the sufferings

which are heaped on the heads of the poor. It is notorious that general overcrowding is a characteristic feature of the great towns, but in the working-class
quarters people are packed together in an exceptionally small area. Not satisfied
with permitting the pollution of the air in the streets, society crams as many as a
dozen workers into a single room, so that at night the air becomes so foul that
they are nearly suffocated. The workers have to live in damp dwellings. When
they live in cellars the water seeps through the floor and when they live in attics
the rain comes through the roof. The workers' houses are so badly built that the
foul air cannot escape from them. The workers have to wear poor and ragged
garments and they have to eat food which is bad, indigestible and adulterated.
Their mental state is threatened by being subjected alternately to extremes of
hope and fear. They are goaded like wild beasts and never have a chance of
enjoying a quiet life. They are deprived of all pleasures except sexual indulgence
and intoxicating liquors. Every day they have to work until they are physically
and mentally exhausted. This forces them to excessive indulgence in the only
two pleasures remaining to them. If the workers manage to survive this sort of
treatment it is only to fall victims to starvation when a slump occurs and they are
deprived of the little that they once had.

How is it possible that the poorer classes can remain healthy and have a
reasonable expectation of life under such conditions? What can one expect but
that they should suffer from continual outbreaks of epidemics and an excessively
low expectation of life? The physical condition of the workers shows a progressive
deterioration. Let us examine the facts concerning the health of the workers.

There is ample proof that the dwellings of the workers who live in the slums,
combined with other adverse factors, give rise to many illnesses. The article in
the *Artizan*[4] which we have already quoted is perfectly right in stating that lung
diseases must inevitably follow in such living conditions and are in fact particularly rife among the workers.[5] The flushed appearance of many of the passers-by
in the streets of London indicates to what an extent the polluted atmosphere of
the capital, particularly in the workers' quarters, fosters the prevalence of consumption. If one goes into the streets of London, when people are on their way to
work, it is astonishing to note how many of them appear to be suffering to a
greater or lesser degree from consumption. Even in Manchester one does not see
these pale, emaciated, narrow-chested and hollow-eyed ghosts who are to be met
with in such large numbers every minute in London. From their appearance one
would judge them to be weak, flabby, and lacking in all energy. But, of course,
large numbers of people also die every year of consumption in the factory towns
of the North. In addition to consumption the workers suffer from other lung
infections, to say nothing of scarlet fever. Above all typhus is the illness which is
most deadly as far as the workers are concerned. The official report on the health
of the working classes[6] states that this widespread scourge is due to bad living
conditions, in particular to bad ventilation, damp and dirt. This report was
written by some of the leading doctors in England on the basis of information
supplied by other medical men. These experts state that any badly ventilated court
or undrained cul-de-sac—particularly if grossly overcrowded and if organic refuse

is allowed to decay there—may well engender fever and does in fact nearly always do so. This fever is nearly always of the same type and practically always develops into definite cases of typhus. The disease is to be found in the working-class quarters not only of all the great cities, but even in isolated groups of slum dwellings in smaller places, where its effects are naturally felt most severely, but, of course, there are occasional cases of typhus in better class quarters. In London it has been endemic for some time; and the violent epidemic of 1837 gave rise to the report to which reference has already been made. Dr. Southwood Smith, in the annual report on the London Fever Hospital for 1843 stated that 1,462 patients were admitted in that year, which represented an increase of 418 over any previous year. Typhus raged in the damp, dirty slums of East, North and South London. Many of the patients [in the London Fever Hospital] were migrants from the provinces who had endured dire privations both on the way to London and on their arrival in the capital. Unable to find work, they suffered from lack of food and had to sleep in the streets with insufficient clothing to cover them. It was in these circumstances that they caught fever. They were in such a weak condition when taken to hospital that unusually large quantities of stimulant such as wine, brandy and ammonia had to be administered to them. Deaths among those admitted amounted to 16.5 per cent.[7] This malignant fever is also to be found in Manchester. It has never been wholly stamped out in such bad slums as those of the Old Town, Ancoats and Little Ireland, though it must be admitted that here, as in other English provincial towns, typhus has not spread so much as one would expect. In Scotland and Ireland, on the other hand, typhus rages with a violence which is difficult to credit. In Edinburgh and Glasgow there were violent epidemics of typhus in 1817, after the famine, and both in 1826 and 1827, after the commercial crises. On each of these occasions the epidemic lasted for about three years before there was any appreciable decline in its incidence. In Edinburgh there were 6,000 cases of typhus in 1827 and 10,000 in 1837. Each new epidemic was characterised by an increase in the number of cases, the violence of the disease, and the mortality rate.[8] But the violence of the typhus in earlier times seems to have been mere child's play compared with what happened after the commercial crisis of 1842. One-sixth of all the poor in Scotland were laid low by fever. The disease was spread with extreme rapidity by beggars tramping the country. In two months there were more cases of fever than in the whole of the previous twelve years. In Glasgow in 1843 there were 32,000 cases of fever and this represented 12 per cent of the population. Nearly one-third (32 per cent) of those stricken by the disease died. In Manchester and Liverpool, on the other hand, the mortality from typhus is usually only 8 per cent of those affected. The disease reaches its crisis on the seventh and fifteenth days. The patient usually assumes a yellow hue on the fifteenth day and Dr. Alison suggests that this shows that the disease is not purely physical in origin but is due to excitement and anxiety.[9] In Ireland, too, fever is endemic. In 21 months of 1817–18, 39,000 cases were admitted to the Dublin hospitals.[10] Sheriff A. Alison, in the second volume of his *Principles of Population*,[11] says there were actually 60,000 admissions in a subsequent year. In Cork the fever hospital admitted [a number

of patients exceeding] one-seventh of the population of the town in the two years
1817–18; at Limerick at the same period a quarter of the population was laid
low by the disease, while nineteen-twentieths of the inhabitants of the slums of
Waterford were attacked by the disease.[12]

In view of all the circumstances it is indeed surprising that so infectious a
disease as this fever is not more widespread. Consider how the workers live; how
tightly packed are the dwellings of the poor; how every corner is crammed with
human beings; how sick and healthy sleep together in one room and even in one
bed. Consider how little medical care is available for those who fall ill; how
many of them are ignorant of the commonest rules of diet to be observed by fever
patients. In view of these facts the mortality from fever is by no means excessive.
Dr. Alison, who has much experience of this disease, ascribed it to the low
standard of living and general wretched conditions of the poor. The report to
which reference has already been made stresses the same points.[13] Dr. Alison
asserts that privation and insufficient food, clothing and shelter make the poor
incapable of resisting the ravages of the disease. This is the reason why fever
epidemics spread with such rapidity. Dr. Alison explains that in Scotland and
Ireland a period of depression—a commercial crisis or harvest failure—always
leads to the appearance of a typhus epidemic, and that its full fury is felt almost
exclusively by the working classes. Dr. Alison draws attention to a striking feature
of the epidemics: the majority of the typhus victims are the fathers of families and
are therefore those who can least be spared by their families. The Irish doctors
quoted by Alison also draw attention to this aspect of the epidemics.[14]

Other diseases are due less to the poor dwellings than to the poor food of the
workers. The food commonly consumed by the working classes is difficult for
adults to digest and is quite unsuitable for the diet of young children. The workers
have neither the time nor the money to procure proper food for their children. In
addition reference should be made to the widespread custom of giving children
brandy, even opium. Poor diets, combined with the generally unsatisfactory environment in which the children of the poor grow up, are the cause of various
stomach disorders which affect the children for the rest of their lives. Nearly all
workers suffer from weak stomachs, but nevertheless they are forced to continue
on the very diet which originally caused the complaint. They are ignorant of the
cause of their illness; even if they knew what was wrong with them, how could
they procure more suitable food unless they adopted a different way of life and
enjoyed a better education? These digestive troubles lead to new illnesses even in
childhood. Scrofula is an almost universal complaint among the working classes.
Scrofulous parents have scrofulous children, especially if the original cause of
the illness continues to operate in full force upon the inherited tendency of the
children. Rickets[15] is another consequence of insufficient nourishment in the early
years of growth and is consequently very common among the children of the
workers. The hardening of the bones is delayed and the development of bodily
structure is stunted; so that in addition to the usual effects of rickets it is quite
common to find that the victims of the disease suffer from deformities of the
spine and legs. It is obvious that these diseases are aggravated by the fact that the

workers suffer so much from fluctuations in trade. At times of industrial crisis their wages are reduced and they must go short of food. Practically every worker at some time in his life has had to go short of food and this naturally aggravates conditions caused by long periods of living on an unsuitable (though not inadequate) diet. Children who do not get enough to eat at the very time when they most require adequate nourishment, inevitably fall victims to digestive troubles, scrofula and rickets. Very many suffer in this way during periods of bad trade and even at times of comparative prosperity. Common observation shows how the sufferings of childhood are indelibly stamped on the adults. The vast mass of the workers' children are neglected; this leaves traces which are never wholly removed and leads to the weakening of a whole generation of workers. Moreover the workers wear unsuitable clothing which does not give them adequate protection from catching cold. They are forced to work as long as they possibly can when they fall ill, because they know that if they are unable to work their families will suffer. When the poor are ill they very seldom have any medical attention. All these unfavourable circumstances inevitably have a deleterious effect on the health of the English working classes. I do not propose to discuss, at this stage, the occupational diseases to which workers in particular branches of industry are liable.

There are still other factors which have an adverse effect on the health of the workers. Of these, drink is the most important. The worker is under every possible temptation to take to drink. Spirits are virtually his sole form of pleasure and they are very readily available. The worker comes home tired and exhausted from his labours. He finds that his comfortless and unattractive dwelling is both damp and dirty. He urgently needs some stimulant; he must have something to recompense him for his labours during the day and enable him to face the prospect of the next day's dreary toil. He is out of sorts; his nerves are on edge and he feels thoroughly depressed. This state of mind arises originally from his poor state of health, particularly his indigestion. It is greatly aggravated by the circumstances in which he finds himself—the uncertainty of his job, his lack of resources to fall back on, his state of insecurity, his complete inability to do anything to make his position more secure, make him think that life is unbearable. His physique is poor and his health has been undermined by bad air and poor food. So the worker urgently feels the need of some stimulant. Moreover, his need for company can be satisfied only in the public house, for there is nowhere else where he can meet his friends.

In these circumstances the worker is obviously subject to the strongest temptation to drink to excess, and it is hardly surprising that he often succumbs. Given these conditions, it is in fact inevitable that a large number of workers should have neither the moral nor the physical stamina to resist the temptation. Quite apart from the influences, which are mainly of a physical nature, driving the worker to drink, it should be remembered that many other factors of a different nature contribute to this result. These include the desire to follow the crowd; the neglected education of the workers; the impossibility of shielding young people from the temptation to drink; the frequent example of hard-drinking parents who actually give spirits to their children; and the certainty that drink will, at any rate for a few hours, enable the worker to forget the hard and miserable life that he leads. These and a hundred other influences are so powerful that no one could really blame the workers for their excessive addiction to spirits. In view of the general environment of the industrial workers, drunkenness ceases to be a vice for which the drunkard must accept responsibility. It becomes a phenomenon which must be accepted as the inevitable consequence of bringing certain influences to bear upon workers, who in this matter cannot be expected to have sufficient will-power to enable them to act otherwise. The responsibility lies with those who turned the factory hand into a soulless factor of production and have thus deprived him of his humanity. If it is inevitable that many workers should be driven to drink, it is equally inevitable that they should suffer physically and morally from over-indulgence. All the diseases to which the workers are liable because of the way in which they live and work are aggravated by drink. The ravages of lung diseases, of abdominal complaints and of typhus are immensely increased by gross intemperance.

Another reason for the poor state of health of the working classes is to be found in the impossibility of securing skilled medical attention in the event of illness. It is true that there are a number of charitable institutions which try to meet this need. The Manchester Infirmary, for example, deals with 22,000 patients a year; some of these are treated in the hospital; others are out-patients who are given medicine and advice—but what does that amount to in a city in which, according to Gaskell, three-quarters of the inhabitants need medical attention every year?[16] English doctors charge high fees which the workers are unable to pay. The workers either do without medical advice, or they are forced to patronise charlatans and make use of quack remedies which, in the long run, do more harm than good. A very large number of quack doctors ply their trade in all the towns of England. By means of advertisements, posters and other publicity stunts they recruit their clients from the poorer classes. In addition large numbers of patent medicines are sold as cures for all sorts of actual and imaginary complaints. Morrison's Pills, Parr's Life Pills, Dr. Mainwaring's Pills and thousands of other pills, medicines and ointments which are all capable of curing all the illnesses under the sun. While these medicaments seldom contain substances which are actually harmful, they often have injurious effects if taken frequently or in too large quantities. Since the ignorant workers are told in all the advertisements that no one can ever consume too much of these medicines, it is not surprising that they continually consume quantities far in excess of their needs. It is by no means unusual for the manufacturers of Parr's Life Pills to sell between 20,000 and 25,000 boxes of these wonderful nostrums in a week. They are taken to relieve an astonishing variety of different complaints—constipation as well as diarrhoea, fever as well as lassitude. Just as peasants in Germany go to be bled or cupped at certain seasons of the year, so the English workers now gulp down their patent medicines, injuring themselves while filling the pockets of the proprietors. One of the most harmful of these patent medicines is a preparation of opiates, particularly laudanum, which is sold under the name of Godfrey's

Cordial.[17] Women who work at home and have to look after their own and other people's children dose them with this medicine, not only to keep them quiet, but because of a widely prevalent notion that it strengthens the child. Many women give the children this medicine while they are new-born infants, and go on dosing them without realising the harmful consequences of this method of 'strengthening the heart' until the children die. When the child's system develops a greater resistance to the effects of opium, the dose is gradually increased. When Godfrey's Cordial is no longer effective it is replaced by pure laudanum and doses of from fifteen to twenty drops at a time are given. In evidence before a Parliamentary enquiry[18] the Nottingham coroner stated that one druggist had admitted using 13 cwt of treacle in a year in the manufacture of Godfrey's Cordial.[19] The effects on the children dosed in this way can easily be imagined. They become pale, stunted and weak, generally dying before they are two years old. The use of this medicine is widespread in all the great cities and industrial towns of the country.[20]

All these adverse factors combine to undermine the health of the workers. Very few strong, well-built, healthy people are to be found among them—at any rate in the industrial towns, where they generally work indoors. And it is with the factory workers that we are concerned here. They are for the most part, weak, thin and pale. The bone structure is prominent but gives no evidence of strength. All their muscles are flabby, except for those which may have been abnormally developed because of the nature of their work. Nearly all suffer from digestive troubles, and consequently they suffer from more or less permanent mental depression and general irritability, so that their outlook on life is a gloomy one. Their weakened bodies are in no condition to withstand illness and whenever infection is abroad they fall victims to it. Consequently they age prematurely, and die young. This is proved by the available statistics of death rates.

The Report of Mr. G. Graham, the Registrar General, states that the annual death rate for England and Wales is a little under 2¼ per cent, i.e., one in every 45 persons[21] die every year. This was the average for the registration year 1839–40. The following year (1840–1) the death rate declined somewhat and only amounted to one in 46. In the big cities, however, the situation is quite different. Official statistics printed in the *Manchester Guardian* of July 31st, 1844,[22] which is now lying before me, include the following data concerning the death rates in some of the great towns. In Manchester, including Salford and Chorlton, the death rate was 1 in 32.72, and excluding Salford and Chorlton, 1 in 30.75. In Liverpool, including the suburb of West Derby, the death rate is 1 in 31.9, and excluding West Derby, 29.9. On the other hand, in all those parts of Cheshire, Lancashire and Yorkshire included in this return—and these include many rural and semi-rural districts—the average death rate in a population of 2,172,506 persons is 1 in 39.8. How unfavourably situated the urban worker is from this point of view may be seen from the mortality of Prescot in Lancashire. This is a colliery town and since coalmining is a relatively unhealthy occupation the health of the town falls somewhat below the standard of that in an agricultural community. But the workers in Prescot live in the countryside and the death rate is 1 in 47.54, which is better by nearly 2½ than the national average of 1 in 45.

Table 16.1

Class of streets	Class of houses	Rate of mortality
1st	1st	1 in 51
	2nd	1 in 45
	3rd	1 in 36
2nd	1st	1 in 55
	2nd	1 in 38
	3rd	1 in 35
3rd	1st	Not given
	2nd	1 in 35
	3rd	1 in 25

The figures which have been quoted from the *Manchester Guardian* of July 31st, 1844, all refer to the year 1843. The death rate in Scottish towns is higher still—in Edinburgh in 1838–39 it was 1 in 29 and in 1831 it was actually 1 in 22 in the Old Town. Dr. [Robert] Cowan in his paper 'Vital Statistics of Glasgow [illustrating the sanitary condition of the population]' states that since 1830 the average death rate in that city has been 1 in 30, and in certain years between 1 in 22 and 1 in 24.[23] There is overwhelming evidence that this drastic reduction in the average span of life falls mainly on the working classes. Indeed the death rate among the workers is obviously somewhat higher than the average for the whole country, since the members of the upper and middle classes live longer than the workers. Among the most recent evidence available is that collected by Mr. P. H. Holland [surgeon], of Manchester. He undertook an official survey of the Manchester suburb of Chorlton-on-Medlock.[24] He classified both the houses and streets into three categories and found the differences in the death rates [shown in Table 16.1].[25]

From the evidence supplied by Mr. Holland in several other tables it is clear that the death rate in *streets* of the second class is 18 per cent higher than in those of the first class. The death rate in *streets* of the third class is 68 per cent higher than in those of the first class. The death rate in *houses* of the second class is 22 per cent higher than in those of the first class and the death rate in houses of the third class is 78 per cent higher than in those of the first class. Mr. Holland also showed that in slum streets which had been improved the death rate had declined by 25 per cent. He concludes his report with a comment which is unusually frank for a member of the English middle classes:

> When we find the rate of mortality four times as high in some streets as in others, and twice as high in whole classes of streets as in other classes, and further find that it is all but *invariably* high in those streets, which are in bad condition, and almost as invariably low in those whose condition is good, we cannot resist the conclusion that multitudes of our fellow-creatures, *hundreds of our immediate neighbours*, are annually destroyed for want of the most evident precautions.[26]

The *Report on the Sanitary Condition of the Labouring Population* contains corroborative evidence of this. In 1840 in Liverpool the average age at death of the 'gentry and professional persons' was 35 years, of 'tradesmen and their families' 22 years and 'labourers, mechanics and servants' was actually only 15 years.[27] The same parliamentary report contains many statistics of a similar nature.[28]

The main reason for the high death rate is the heavy mortality among infants and small children. A child's constitution is normally so weak that it is least able to withstand the harmful effects of a low standard of living. If both parents go out to work for their living, or if either parent is dead, the child is so neglected that its health inevitably suffers. In the circumstances it is not surprising to learn from the report that we have just cited that in Manchester, for example, nearly 54 per cent[29] of the workers' children die before attaining their fifth birthday. On the other hand only 20 per cent of the children of the middle classes die before they are five. In the rural districts rather less than 32 per cent of all children die before they are five.[30]

The article in the *Artizan*[31] to which we have already frequently referred gives more detailed information concerning infantile mortality in England. The article lists the proportion of deaths due to various diseases in both urban and rural districts. These tables prove that epidemics in Manchester and Liverpool generally kill three times as many children as in rural districts;[32] that diseases of the nervous system are five times more fatal in the towns than in the country; that diseases of the digestive organs kill more than twice as many children in the towns than in the rural districts, while diseases of the respiratory organs are two and a half times as deadly in the towns as in the country. Fatal cases of smallpox, measles, whooping cough and scarlet fever carry off four times as many infants in the cities as in the rural districts. Similarly deaths from water on the brain are three times and convulsions ten times more deadly in urban than in rural districts.

Another acknowledged authority may be quoted on this subject. This is Dr. Wade, who has written a *History of the Middle and Working Classes* (London, 1835, 3rd edition). In this work Dr. Wade abstracts [Table 16.2] from the Report of Sadler's Committee.[33]

The very high mortality among infants and small children is caused not only by various diseases, which are the inevitable consequence of the neglect and oppression of the poorer classes, but also by other factors which must be taken into account. In many families the wife leaves home to go to work as well as the husband, and this results in the utter neglect of the children, who are either locked in the house or handed over to somebody else's care. No wonder that hundreds of such children lose their lives owing to all kinds of mishaps. Nowhere are so many children drowned or burnt to death as in the great cities of England. Deaths from burns or from being scalded by boiling water are very common. In Manchester and in London at least one case of this kind occurs ever week in the winter months. It is rare, however, for these cases to be reported in the press. I have by me, however, a copy of the *Weekly Dispatch* for December 15th, 1844, which reports six such incidents [in London] alone during the week ending

Table 16.2 Comparative duration of life in every 10,000 persons in manufacturing and agricultural districts

	Under 5 years	5–19	20–39	40–59	60–69	70–79	80–89	90–99	100 and upwd.
Rutland, healthy county	2,865	891	1,275	1,299	1,189	1,428	938	112	3
Essex, marshy	3,159	1,110	1,526	1,413	953	1,019	630	77[a]	3
Carlisle, 1779–1787, before manufactories	4,408	911[b]	1,006	1,201	940	826	533	153	22
Carlisle, now partly manufacturing and spinning	4,738	930	1,261	1,134	677	727	452	80	1
Preston, factories, cotton spinning	4,947	1,136	1,379	1,114	553	532	298	38	3
Leeds, factories, woollen, flax, silk	5,286	927	1,228	1,198	593	512	225	29	2

[a] [Engels wrongly gave 177 instead of 77.]
[b] [Engels wrongly gave 921 instead of 911.]

December 7th.[34] These unfortunate children, who come to such a shocking end, are simply the victims of our extremely defective social arrangements, which are perpetuated in the interests of the property-owning classes. It may well be that this frightful and painful death is a blessing in disguise for the children, since it spares them from a long life of toil and wretchedness, rich in suffering and poor in enjoyment. This is actually the position in England to-day. The middle classes read these things every day in the newspapers, and do nothing at all about it. But they have no grounds for complaint if I accuse them of social murder and support my charge by producing the official and unofficial witnesses I have already cited, of whose evidence they cannot possible be ignorant. The middle classes should either put an end to this scandalous state of affairs, or they should hand over to the working classes the power to make regulations for the common good. The bourgeoisie have no desire to surrender their powers and—so long as they are blinded by their middle-class prejudices—they are powerless to set matters right. After hundreds of thousands have fallen victim to neglect the middle classes have at last embarked upon a few precautionary reforms of trifling significance. The Metropolitan Buildings Act [1844] has been passed which restricts to some extent the more blatant cramming of working-class dwellings on to a limited space. The middle classes pride themselves upon measures which barely touch the fringe of the problem, which in no way approach the root of the matter, and even fail to satisfy the minimum requirements of any self-respecting health authority. Such measures in no way absolve the middle classes from the accusations I have made. The only choice before the English bourgeoisie is this—either to plead guilty to the irrefutable charge of [social] murder and to keep power in spite of such an admission, or to abdicate its authority in favour of the working classes. So far the bourgeoisie has chosen the first alternative.

Notes

1. [Engels's rather bald title for this chapter consisted of the single word 'Resultate'.]
2. Here and elsewhere I speak of society as a responsible entity which has its rights and duties. But by 'society' I do not mean the whole population, but only that social class which at this moment actually wields political and social authority. It is this class which is responsible for the position of those members of society who are excluded from exercising any political or social authority. In England, as in other civilised countries, this position as the ruling class is held by the middle classes. As this book is being written for German readers there is no need for me to approve the proposition that society as a whole, and in particular the middle classes—which wield social power—have the duty of at least protecting the lives of all individual citizens and must take measures to prevent anybody from starving. If I were writing for the English middle classes I would have to explain this in greater detail [*Note by Engels to first edition.*] *Engels added to the English translation of* 1887: And so it is now in Germany. Our German capitalists are fully up to the English level in this respect at least, in the year of grace, 1886. *Engels added a further note to the German edition of* 1892: How things have changed in the last fifty years. To-day there are members of the English middle classes who recognise that society has duties to the individual citizen—but as for the German middle classes?!?
3. The German geographical mile is 7.42 kilometres or 4.64 English miles.
4. [Engels prints this as *Artisan.*]
5. [*The Artizan*, October 1843, p. 229, col. 1. This passage is a summary of a paragraph on p. 406 of the report on Leeds in the *Journal of the Statistical Society of London*, Vol. 2 (1839–40)].
6. [Engels is presumably referring either to Dr. T. Southwood Smith's two reports to the Poor Law Commissioners on sanitary conditions in Bethnal Green and Whitechapel in 1838 and on the prevalence of fever in twenty metropolitan areas in 1839, or to Edwin Chadwick's *Report on the Sanitary Condition of the Labouring Population of Great Britain* (1842).]
7. [This passage appears to be a summary of the following paragraph in the *Northern Star*, no. 328, February 24th, 1844, p. 7, col. 3:

RECORD OF DESTITUTION

FRIGHTFUL SPREAD OF FEVER FROM DESTITUTION

Dr. Southwood Smith has just given his annual report upon the state of the London Fever Hospital during the past year, from which it appears that the admissions during the period were 1,462, being an excess of 418 above that of any preceding year. Fever raged most violently in the Central, Northern, and Southern Districts, which was attributable to the undrained, close, and filthy condition of these localities. A large proportion of the inmates were agricultural labourers or provincial mechanics, who had come to London in search of employment, and who were seized with the malady either on the road or soon after their arrival, evincing the close connexion between fever and destitution. These poor creatures ascribed their illness—some of them to sleeping by the sides of hedges, and others to a want of clothing, many being without stockings, shirts, shoes, or any apparel capable of defending them from the inclemency of the weather; while the larger number attributed it to want of food, being driven by hunger to *eat raw vegetables, turnips, and rotten apples*. Their disease was attended with such extreme prostration as generally to require the administration of an unusually large proportion of wine, brandy, and ammonia, and other stimulants. The gross mortality was 16½ per cent. An unprecedented number of nurses and other servants of the hospital were attacked with fever, namely twenty-nine, of whom six died.]

8. Dr. W. P. Alison, *Management of the Poor in Scotland* (1840) [pp. 12–3 (Edinburgh and Glasgow)].

9. Dr. W. P. Alison's paper to the British Association for the Advancement of Science read at York in October 1844. [See *Journal of the Statistical Society of London*, Vol. 7 (1844), pp. 316–8: 'Notes on the Report of the Royal Commissioners on the operation of the Poor Laws in Scotland'.]

10. Dr. W. P. Alison, *Management of the Poor in Scotland* (1840), p. 16.

11. [Sir Archibald Alison, *Principles of Population* (1840), Vol. 2, p. 80.]

12. [Dr. W. P. Alison, *Observations on the Management of the Poor in Scotland* (1840), pp. 16–7, quoting Drs. F. Barker and J. Cheyne, *An Account of the Rise, Progress and Decline of the Fever lately epidemical in Ireland . . .* , Vol. 2 (1821), pp. 16, 26, 40.]

13. [Presumably Dr. Southwood Smith's report on the work of the London Fever Hospital for 1843, quoted in the *Northern Star*, no. 328, Feb. 24th, 1844, p. 7, col. 3—'Frightful Spread of Fever from Destitution'.]

14. Dr. W. P. Alison, *Management of the Poor in Scotland* (1840), pp. 16–7, 18–32.

15. Engels adds: 'Die englische Krankheit ("The English disease"): knotty protuberances on the joints'.

16. P. Gaskell, *The Manufacturing Population of England* (1833), chapter 8. [Gaskell gave the number of patients admitted to the Manchester Royal Infirmary in 1831 as 21,196—see p. 230. The figures for patients treated in the Manchester Royal Infirmary (for the twelve months ending June 24th, in each case) are as follows: 1827–8: 16,680; 1828–9: 18,002; 1829–30: 16,237; 1830–1: 19,628; 1831–2: 21,349; 1832–3: 21,232 (compiled from the official annual reports of the Manchester Royal Infirmary).]

17. [Godfrey's Cordial consisted of a mixture of tincture of opium (laudanum) and treacle.]

18. *Report of Commission of Inquiry into the Employment of Children and Young Persons in Mines and Manufactories. . . .* This report is usually referred to as the 'Children's Employment Commission's Report'. It is one of the best official reports of its kind and contains an immense quantity of evidence which is both valuable and horrifying. The first report was issued in 1842 and the second in 1843. [See *Appendix to 2nd Report* (Trades and Manufactures) Part 1, Reports and Evidence from Sub-commissioners (1842) F 10–11, f 60–2.]

19. [In the 1887 American edition the translator amended this sentence to read: 'used thirteen hundredweight of *laudanum* in one year in the preparation of Godfrey's Cordial', and this mistake was approved by Engels.]

20. [For the widespread use of Godfrey's Cordial in Wolverhampton see Children's Employment Commission, *Appendix to 2nd Report* (1842), Part 2, Q 30.]

21. *5th Annual Report* of the Registrar-General of Births, Deaths and Marriages [(1843), p. iii].

22. [*Manchester Guardian*, July 31st, 1844, p. 6, cols. 4–5: article on 'Quarterly Table of Morality' in 115 registrars' districts for the quarter ending June 30th, 1844. Engels's figures for the death rates appear to have been calculated from a table in

this article giving the population of certain towns in 1841 and the deaths registered therein in 1843.]

23. [*Journal of the Statistical Society of London*, Vol. 3, 1840, p. 265. Cowan's table of the mortality in Glasgow was: 1831: 1 in 33.845; 1832: 1 in 21.672; 1833: 1 in 35.776; 1834: 1 in 36.312; 1835: 1 in 32.647; 1836: 1 in 28.906; 1837: 1 in 24.634; 1838: 1 in 37.939; 1839: 1 in 36.146.]

24. *Report of the Commission of Enquiry into the State of large Towns and Populous Districts*, 1st Report, 1844, Appendix [pp. 202–17].

25. [Engels may have taken these figures from the article on 'Sanitary Condition of Large Towns' in the *Manchester Guardian* of July 31st, 1844, p. 6, cols. 3–4.]

26. [*Manchester Guardian*, July 31st, 1844, p. 6, col. 4.]

27. [E. Chadwick, *Report on the Sanitary Condition of the Labouring Population* (1842), p. 159, octavo edition.]

28. [See 'Tabular views of the ages at which deaths have occurred in different classes of society', *ibid.*, pp. 162–3.]

29. [Engels wrote 'over 57 per cent'.]

30. [This information appears to have been extracted partly from the Second Report of the Factories Enquiry Commission (1833), D3, p. 5—medical reports by Dr. Bisset Hawkins, who in turn relied on information supplied by Mr. J. Roberton, described as 'the chief statistical authority of Manchester'. Engels's statement that 'only 20 per cent of the children of the middle classes die before they are five' was taken from Edwin Chadwick's *Report on the Sanitary Condition of the Labouring Population of Great Britain* (1842), p. 162. Chadwick arrived at his figure by taking an average of the mortality of children under 5 born to 'Gentry and Professional Persons' in nine localities (Manchester, Leeds, Liverpool, Bath, Bethnal Green and the poor law unions of the Strand, Kendal, Wiltshire and Rutland).]

31. [October 1843, pp. 228 *et seq.*]

32. [See 'Comparative Table of Mortality from various classes of disease in England and Wales . . .': *Artizan*, Oct. 1843, p. 228.]

33. [Engels based this table on that printed on p. 560 of Dr. John Wade's *History of the Middle and Working Classes*, 1st edn., 1833. Wade, in turn, abstracted it from pp. 608–612 of the Report from the Select Committee on the Bill to regulate the labour of children in the mills and factories of the United Kingdom: *Parliamentary Papers*, Session 1831–2, Vol. 15, no. 706.]

34. [*Weekly Dispatch*, no. 2251, p. 598, col. 3—'Mortality in the Metropolis'. The news item states: 'Among the violent deaths are six cases. The unfortunate victims, with one exception being very young children, were burnt to death from their clothes taking fire'.]

CHAPTER 17

Rats' Tails and Trypanosomes: Nature and Culture in Early Colonial Medicine

Megan Vaughan

On Sunday 18 September 1910, Dr Hugh Stannus, Medical Officer in Zomba, Nyasaland, sat down to write his regular letter to his sister in England. He wrote of his work:

> As usual I am torn in different directions with many ideas being never content with any one thing. My native hospital is one of my chief delights and my notes on Native Diseases take a lot of time. I am always running about to catch some abnormality or removing something to be pickled or getting a photo of some oddity though my anthropological measurements and notes are getting rather left alone. Now there is some doubt whether we have the same sleeping sickness Trepanosome as in Uganda and I want in the next few weeks to get some work done on the rats to help settle the point though I am so handicapped I am afraid it will come to nothing.[1]

Enclosed in the letter was the timetable of work he had followed that day:

Sunday 18th September
7.45 three notes
7.50 breakfast
8.15 to office for daily reports
8.25 Native Hospital. Operate on big abscess of leg. Saw 20 other cases. Reported on a prisoner from an out-station, took photo of a deformity.
9.00 segregation hospital – took blood of sleeping sickness case.
9.15 European hospital
9.45 Dr Hearsey and a lady patient
10.00 a man with a dog – took its blood and microscoped it.
10.15–12.15 microscoped blood various
12.30 ordered my boy to produce 3 rats

12.45 lunch
1.45 rats produced
2–4 microscoped bloods – cow, rats, sleeping sickness etc.
4.00 tea
5.00 inoculated rat from sleeping sickness patient
5.30–6.00 reading room
6.00 fed rats
6.15 visited European people
6.45–7.30 developed photographs
7.30 dinner
8.00 I look at a pile of literature and wonder when it will get read.
Cigarette.

This somewhat extraordinary document inscribes the practices and concerns of 'tropical medicine' in Africa at the beginning of this century. Like many of his colleagues, Stannus had first arrived in Africa as a military doctor. From 1905 to 1910 he was medical officer to the King's African Rifles and based at Fort Johnston on Lake Nyasa. During these early years he spent his time 'investigating the endemic diseases of man and animals in the area, but also engaged in ethnological studies'.

His letters of this period reveal a wide range of interests and activities. In April 1906, for example, he had been placed under orders to go and investigate the 'causes of mortality among cattles two days from here'. In August 1906 he wrote of his efforts to grow strawberries, the presence of a predatory lion, and of nursing a European blackwater fever patient. In December 1906 he wrote at length about his hunting exploits. In June 1907 he was examining prospective labour migrants, and in July he was investigating sleeping sickness and thinking of buying a mule which he had had in quarantine for the 'tsetse fly-disease'.

What we might think of as straightforwardly 'medical' activities did not feature prominently in Stannus's work. He was obliged to minister to the British population of Fort Johnston at a time when European mortality rates were still very high in this part of Africa, but spent more of his time engaged in research. Some of this research, such as that into the 'tsetse-fly disease' was carried out on the direct instructions of the colonial administration, but the rest was motivated by Stannus's own curiosity and interests.

From the perspective of late-twentieth-century medicine with all its specialisms, Stannus's publication list from this period, like his Sunday timetable, is extraordinarily all-encompassing.

In 1910 he published a paper on 'Native Paintings in Nyasaland', another (in the anthropological journal, *Man*) on 'Alphabet Boards', and another entitled 'Notes on British Central Africa Natives'. In the same year he published a paper on 'Piroplasmesis in Cattle', and continued to produce a 'Sleeping Sickness Diary'. During this time he had also been investigating the problem of pellagra which he had identified amongst prisoners in Zomba prison. He published a paper on this in 1911, and another in 1913, both in the *Transactions of the Royal Society for Tropical Medicine and Hygiene*. In 1911 he also published a paper on 'Human

Trypanosomiasis in Nyasaland', another on 'Ovarian Cysts in an African women', and another (in the *Journal de la Salpetrière*) on 'Micromelio'. In the same period up to the First World War, he wrote on yaws, 'jigger disease', on 'Pre-Bantu Inhabitants of Central Africa', on 'Tribal Tattoos in Nyasaland', on 'Angoni Smelting Furnaces', on 'Blackwater Fever Suppression', on the 'Life Span of Negroes', on the 'Causes of Hypertrophy of the Lower Limbs', on 'Congenital Anomalies in Africans', and on 'Anomalies of Pigmentation – Albinism'. In 1922, as an outcome of this pre-war work, he published his major ethnological piece, 'The Wayao'.

Stannus was a great enthusiast for the modern aid to research – photography – and his photograph albums from this period also capture the breadth of his interests. One is the common tropical medic's catalogue of horrors, from ele-phantiasis of the scrotum to advanced cases of leprosy and yaws. Another fea-tures photographs of cases of albinism, another shows women with lip plugs and others with 'tribal tattoos'. Yet another is a collection of full-frontal photographs of naked or near naked Africans, many of them young and with what (in view of Stannus's ethnological interests) at first look like more 'tribal tattoos' but which, on closer inspection, reveal themselves to be chalk markings indicating the posi-tion and size of the spleen. In addition there are more naturalistically posed photographs of village scenes and activities.

Though interpreting these visual images is hazardous, there are a few things which can be said about Stannus's photograph albums. Firstly, they expose the relentless empiricism of the early tropical doctor. Everything that Stannus saw or touched in his time in Nyasaland was photographed, catalogued and labelled, in the belief that scientific knowledge would thereby be advanced. Secondly, the Africans of Nyasaland are presented in these photographs as objects of study and classification, like any other feature of the 'natural' environment – head shapes, hair styles, and length of torso are all documented here.

The picture that emerges of Stannus's work and views is a complex one. The scientific objectification of the African subject is clear, as are the evolutionist premises of his work. Stannus was a product of a specific intellectual environment, and his attention to anthropometry is indicative of the concern with 'racial' origins and development which underpinned the biology and anthropology of the turn of the century.[2] But 'race', for Stannus, was inseparable from 'environ-ment'. His interest in the 'racial' characteristics of Africans, then, was underpinned by Darwinian assumptions about adaptation.

The end of the nineteenth century saw a 'revolution' in biological science and medicine shaped by the discoveries of Pasteur and Koch. The discovery by bac-teriologists of specific causal external agents of disease is widely regarded as a watershed in medical science. Germ theory focused the medical and biological gaze on the individual, on individual pathology and the behaviour of specific micro-organisms. As many writers have pointed out, the role accorded to the environment in this new theory of disease causation diminished as the focus on individual pathology increased. The discipline of epidemiology blossomed, but its unit of study was not the society but the individual, epidemics being described in terms of aggregations of individual pathologies. Meredith Turshen, in her work on the political ecology of health in Tanzania, sees the late-nineteenth-century bacteriological revolution as the source of many of the ills of colonial and post-colonial Tanzania and reflects radical critiques of western medical science more generally.[3] The failures, inadequacies and neglect of public health policies are attributed to the biological blinkers of the medical establishment. Epidemiologists may possess large amounts of information and analyse it using sophisticated statistical techniques but, say the critics, so long as they continue to view society as an 'aggregation of self-contained individuals', and to neglect completely the realm of social and economic relations, then epidemiology will always fail to address the real causes of much ill-health. The 'natural history of disease' in Africa is, argues Turshen, profoundly 'unnatural'; disease patterns of the twentieth century cannot be abstracted from the changes wrought by capitalism and colonialism in the modes of production and social reproduction.

The new medical science, whilst ill-equipped conceptually to deal with the social reality of twentieth-century Africa, did not fail to feed off Africa as a diseased environment for its research. 'Discovery' was what this science was about and the reputations of a new group of professionals – the tropical medical men – were at stake. Africa was a prime site for investigation of those insect-borne diseases which were misleadingly thought to be typically 'tropical', and great expectations were invested in the great medical expeditions of the turn of the century.[4] The new specialism of tropical medicine was, as Michael Worboys has shown, closer to being a branch of biology than a branch of medicine.[5] Tropical medicine was a postgraduate specialism at the turn of the century, and an attractive one for ambitious scientific medics. According to Worboys, an astonishing 20 per cent of British medical graduates then went on to practise in tropical and sub-tropical climates, most of them with the armed forces. Success in this new field depended as much on a knowledge of and interest in ecology and taxonomy as it did in human pathology. It was the triad of agent/host/environment which was seen to hold the key to the understanding of the diseases of Africa sleeping sickness, malaria, yellow fever. This emphasis on understanding the environment gave some of the early tropical medics the all-encompassing interests seen in the person and career of Stannus and implies something of a qualification to the general characterization of post-1890s medicine as being obsessed with individual pathology. If the biological model was, as Turshen argues, a profoundly individualistic one, then this model was never fully applied to the medical problems of Africa and Africans.

To begin with, a pre-Pasteurian, holistic and sanitarian view of disease was not completely or immediately eliminated by the more reductionist, curative and laboratory-based school.[6] Worboys sees the triumph of the latter over the former in the field of tropical medicine as being epitomized by the differences and disputes between two famous 'pioneers' of tropical medicine, Manson and Ross. Though both were equally involved in the very individualistic pursuit of pathogens and the fame resulting from their discovery, their policy prescriptions were very different. Ross was a sanitarian at heart, with a strong belief in public health measures. This was, as we now know from the work of McKeown and others, a well-founded belief, for the sanitary measures of the early to mid nineteenth century had lowered mortality rates in industrial Britain (and amongst Europeans on the west coast of Africa) long before germ theory was proclaimed and the microscopes got to work.[7]

Notions of the environment and its control, born in late-eighteenth-century Europe, continued to exert an influence over the late-nineteenth and early-twentieth-century European mind. This view of the environment has been characterized by Ludmilla Jordanova:

> a cluster of variables which acted upon organisms and were responsible for many of their characteristics. An understanding of human beings in sickness and in health was to be based on a large number of powerful environmental factors; climate, diet, housing, work, family situation, geography and atmosphere. This notion of environment could be split into two. First there were variables such as custom and government which were human creations and were, at least in principle, amenable to change. Second, there were parameters such as climate, meteorology in general, geographical features such as rivers and mountains, which were in the province of immutable natural laws and proved more challenging to human power. In the first case environment denoted culture, in the second, nature.[8]

It was the tension and perceived struggle between 'nature' and 'culture' which, Jordanova tells us, dominated much medical discussion of the late eighteenth and nineteenth centuries. In the course of this period the notion of culture had undergone a marked change and had begun to denote a state of civilization, identified in particular with science, technology and the capacity for abstract thought. Jordanova traces the effects of this shift on stereotypes of women. Nature and culture become opposing forces in this ideological schema, and they are gendered concepts, women being identified with nature, men with culture.

In the observations of early colonial medics like Stannus, however, there are strong elements of the early tradition of perceptions of the environment, in which the separation of 'nature' and 'culture' was less marked, and of an earlier tradition of medical science. By the end of the First World War, the vestiges of this tradition had been eroded by two developments. In the first place, the holistic view of the sanitarian had been marginalized and its place taken by the medical research 'campaign' and the relentless pursuit of the pathogen. Secondly, 'culture' and the notion of cultural difference had become reified, separated from 'nature' and conceived of as a causal factor in disease. Medical research and practice in colonial Africa drew on and investigated 'nature' in the form of the pathogen, and 'culture' in the form of African cultural practices.

Stannus viewed African cultures as integral to a larger environment. Both the physical and cultural attributes of the Africans of Nyasaland were, for Stannus, features of a larger landscape. He approached the study of hair styles, lip plugs and basket-making in much the same way as he approached the study of yaws, pellagra and sleeping sickness. The effect of his classifications, measurements and photographs was, of course, to objectify, but this was objectification without explicit reference to any supposed inferiority on the part of his objects of study. Africans, in Stannus's view, were 'different', but this difference was to be explained by the nature of the environment they lived in, and could be investigated empirically as part of a wider study of that environment.

Stannus's holistic perception of disease and its causation did not bear much direct relation to medical practice in this early colonial period. Most early colonial doctors were attached either to Christian missions or to the military. The practices of mission medicine were to some extent distinct . . . The military doctors and a handful of government medical officers mostly treated the European sick in their stations, and performed very few curative services for Africans. Stannus's enthusiasm for his 'native hospital' and his attempts to provide some curative services for Africans were unusual at this time. When not treating European military and civilian patients, most doctors were involved in 'campaigns' of various sorts.

There were two sorts of early colonial medical 'campaign'. One was the large research expedition such as those which were conducted in pursuit of the cause of sleeping sickness; the other was the more direct attempt to prevent the spread of epidemic disease such as smallpox and plague.[9]

A contemporary of Stannus's in Nyasaland was Dr J. B. Davey, who had, as a young doctor, participated in the first type of 'campaign', the pursuit of the pathogen.[10] Trained at the Middlesex Hospital, he had served as a Civil Surgeon in the South African War of 1901–2, and had in 1902 been appointed by the Foreign Office as a medical officer in British Central Africa (later Nyasaland). During 1910–11 he worked with the Royal Society's Sleeping Sickness Commission, led by David Bruce. This, like many other sleeping sickness research expeditions in Africa, was a fraught affair, torn apart by the personal ambitions of its participants. Bruce, one of the many tropical medical men of this period to feel cheated of the recognition he felt he had earned, behaved imperiously, fought with his collaborators, and regularly flogged his African assistants.[11] Davey was a very junior member of the expedition and his desultory diary entries reveal that he spent most of this period catching, or more often not catching, tsetse flies on the shores of Lake Nyasa. Sleeping sickness research for Davey meant spending many hours scouring the lake shore with a net, aided by African assistants.

Of 15 January 1910 Davey wrote: 'After lunch I wandered about amongst the palms near the village. Thinking I heard tsetse I got the net and a boy and spent about an hour and a half catching only one G. fusca . . .' A similarly frustrating day was 18 January: 'Alifeya (houseboy and fly catcher) went around the village looking for Glossina. A boatman was however bitten on the hand by a G. fusca which he caught right amongst the huts as he was passing water against some bushes. This was about 4 pm. I then spent some time trying to find more without success.' Amongst his seniors in the world of tropical medicine, there was real excitement in the cut-throat pursuit of the 'secret' of sleeping sickness. For

Davey, the only relief from the frustrating task of fly-catching was in a more conventional chase: 'After tea went out with man from village to dambo country to north-east of the village and got a male waterbuck brought down with one shot too.'[12]

The structure of these research expeditions was rigidly hierarchical and their focus narrow. At this stage in sleeping sickness research the complex interaction of people, animals, pathogen and environment which John Ford later found to characterize the disease[13] was obscured by a narrowly biologistic focus on identification of the pathogen, a focus just broadened sufficiently to take into view the insect vector. To this extent the sleeping sickness enquiries conformed to the picture painted by Turshen and others of medical science and its inability to address the larger 'political ecology' of disease. Though insects feature heavily in Davey's diaries, the human inhabitants of the shores of Lake Nyasa feature only as the 'boys' who are treated like extensions of the nets which they carry.

Sleeping sickness research represented the very biologistic end of 'tropical medicine' as described by Worboys, its leading figures being closer in their interests to parasitology and taxonomy than to medicine as more generally conceived and practised at this time. Tropical medical research of the Manson school was, as Worboys says, mission-oriented, and pathogen-obsessed. Africa was a laboratory in which the possibilities of the new bacteriology could be explored in a challenging way.[14] Africa was a place in which scientific reputations could be made. In the glamour of the early century research 'chase' in tropical Africa, the sanitarians like Ross lost out, as did the eighteenth-century holistic view of the environment, as held by Stannus and others like him. But we should not exaggerate the success and influence of the biologists, or imagine that public health issues were completely drowned out, for the other side of tropical medicine was represented by the 'great campaigns' against epidemic disease.

In the first half of the twentieth century any contact which the majority of Africans had with colonial medicine was likely to have been in the form of a 'great campaign'. Epidemics of smallpox, of meningitis, of plague, and sleeping sickness posed a constant threat to the economic (and political) viability of the early colonial state. The rise of tropical medical research was an outcome not merely of the elevation of germ theory, but of the continuing threat posed by epidemic disease to the entire colonial enterprise. As in India, so in Africa, early medical provision was entirely oriented towards protecting the lives of the continent's new European inhabitants, particularly soldiers.[15] Philip Curtin has shown how deeply the nineteenth-century European perception of the west coast of Africa, and of the people of West Africa, was moulded by the experience of very high European mortality.[16] The representation of Africa as a place of disease, danger and death was one which survived the reductions in European mortality effected by sanitarian policies of the mid-century, and later advances in curative medicine.

In late-nineteenth- and early-twentieth-century East and Central Africa Europeans still perceived of themselves as grappling with a wild and uncontrolled environment, of which Africans were an integral part. In part this was an outcome of the extension of the separation of 'nature' and 'culture' described by Jordanova as characterizing the development of nineteenth-century European thought. The 'wild', whether in the form of the moorland, 'woman', or African wildlife was simultaneously romanticized and feared in European culture of the late nineteenth century. Recent work on colonial ecological history, and on the imperial hunting cult, has emphasized the process by which European male colonialists perceived and constructed 'Africa' and the African environment through this peculiar cultural lens, and has pointed to the European obsession with control.[17] The human and animal diseases of Africa were, of course, seen as integral to this environment waiting to be conquered and controlled, and the observations of early colonial medical men contributed to this larger European perception of Africa as a continent waiting to be tamed.

But early colonial concerns over epidemic disease were not simply the product of the nineteenth-century hunting mentality which sought to capture and control, for it now appears that the early twentieth century in much of East and Central Africa was a peculiarly unhealthy time. The extent to which this unhealthiness marked a radical break from the period immediately preceding colonial rule is still a matter for debate, as are the demographic consequences of disease patterns of the late nineteenth and early twentieth centuries.[18] In some areas the mid to late nineteenth century had taken, through the war and social disruption accompanying the slave trade, and the spread of epidemic disease, a great toll on the health of African communities. In other places this pattern was less marked. But, in either case, colonial conquest facilitated the spread of epidemic diseases in a number of related ways.

In the first place, the mobility of the population increased enormously. Colonial states relied heavily on armies of human porters to move goods from one place to another. In some territories the movement of men as labour migrants began early in the colonial period. Some migrated to the industrial centres of southern Africa, bringing back with them the new diseases of industrialization, including tuberculosis and venereally transmitted syphilis, and facilitating the spread of other diseases. Secondly, the political and social disruption of the colonial conquest contributed, in some places, to the disruption of a complex set of beliefs and practices which had constituted a 'public health' system in pre-colonial African societies.[19] Thirdly, the colonial intrusion brought about the introduction of diseases which were new to most African societies. New diseases, such as measles, could sweep through whole regions, causing high mortality. Not only was there no immunity to these diseases but as new diseases their transmission was little understood and indigenous mechanisms of control were therefore lacking.

Early colonial administrations in this region therefore frequently faced a major epidemic of one sort or another. Most often the fear was that European populations would be affected. Africans were regarded as a 'reservoir' of disease and, as Maynard Swanson has demonstrated for the case of plague in South Africa, this often provided a medical rationale for racial segregation.[20] Settler economies were, of course, much more prone to this particular formulation than were the peasant-based economies of Uganda and Tanganyika, where the economic consequences of depletion of the African producing population was a focus of another kind of concern. In either case, there were only scant resources at the disposal of the colonial state to deal with the problem of epidemic disease. This was not, at this stage, because of the triumph of the 'individual pathology' model of disease and a resulting bias towards curative medicine. Rather it was because the early colonial state was generally impoverished, and in any case did not conceive of its role as providing health (or education) services on any scale, except to white minorities. The problem of epidemic disease threw this issue into relief for, though epidemics affected the poor most severely, they also showed an alarming tendency to cross race and class barriers. If one was going to protect the health of the European population, then the health status of Africans would have to be addressed, at least in a minimal way.

Far from being obsessed with curative medicine, the early colonial medical departments were taken up with prevention – more particularly with preventing the spread of disease from the African to the European. This did not mean that any enlightened and widespread public health system was instituted in British East and Central Africa. Rather, the public health of these territories was addressed piecemeal, through sporadic, militaristic 'campaigns' to prevent or treat one epidemic disease or another. In these 'campaigns' Africans were conceived of as an undifferentiated mass, part of a dangerous environment which needed to be controlled and contained. Prior to the elevation of the idea of 'cultural difference' in the inter-war period, there was a heavy strand of environmentalism, and even of 'political economy' in the medical discourse on African disease problems, and this was evident in the practice of some of the 'great campaigns' against epidemic disease of this period.

C. J. Baker was one of those early colonial doctors who had first arrived on African soil as a Civil Surgeon to the British forces during the Boer War, and then worked his way north.[21] In 1908 he supervised the running of a sleeping sickness camp in the West Nile district of Uganda, and by 1912 he was in Kampala and expressing concern over lack of sanitation in the town. In 1920 a serious epidemic of plague broke out in Kampala and Baker was in charge of an investigation into its causes, as well as directing measures for its control. His research uncovered a complex interaction of economic and social factors in the causation of the epidemic.

He began by investigating the rat population of Uganda and questioned local people about the species of rat to be found there. There were three species well known locally, and a fourth which people said was a new species in the area and which they associated with the rise of the cotton industry and the erection of ginneries. Baker became convinced that the spread of rats and of the plague had some connection with the cotton industry. He found the connection in the world market for cotton: 'The recent slump in the cotton trade caused the natives to store their cotton in their houses for months in the hope of obtaining a rise in the market price, and this cotton proved a great attraction to the rats . . .' This was not the whole story, however, for the differential incidence of the disease in different parts of Uganda could not simply be explained by the cotton industry – previous attempts to eradicate local rats had left some areas less protected than others: 'If the highly susceptible black rat invades such an area it will rapidly multiply, as it will have no competition to contend with, and eventually pick up the dormant infection from the surviving local rats and thus start epizootic plague.'[22] The causes of the epizootic were several, then. Firstly, a new species of rat had been introduced to Uganda, it was thought from the coast and via the railway. This species possessed little immunity to the disease, which was carried by rat fleas. Secondly, this susceptible rat species had multiplied rapidly in some areas owing to previous public health drives which had reduced the populations of indigenous, and more disease-resistant, rats. Thirdly, the cotton industry, and the economic slump, had combined to create conditions favourable for the breeding of these rats.

Understanding the epizootic was one thing, controlling the human epidemic quite another. At this time Baker was in correspondence with Andrew Balfour, Director of the Wellcome Bureau for Scientific Research and a great campaigner on tropical 'hygiene'. On hearing from Baker of the plague epidemic in Uganda, Balfour complained that this was yet another result of the colonial neglect of the 'sanitation' issue. He had been 'hammering away' for years, he wrote, at the need to appoint more British-trained sanitary inspectors in the colonies, but 'the Treasury seems always to be a stumbling block'.

In fact, as Baker has shown, the causes of the epidemic could only be called 'sanitary' in the wide, nineteenth-century sense of the word. The rest of their correspondence on the subject was highly technical, including recipes for rat varnish, and advice on the 'bird lime' method of rat destruction.

If Baker's understanding of the disease was sophisticated, the methods at his disposal for dealing with the immediate crisis were crude. He listed the following as preventive measures: the burning of infected houses (or disinfection in the case of brick-built houses in towns), the isolation of the sick, the segregation of contacts, inoculation of the population with Haffkine's prophylactic, distribution of information in the vernacular, and rat destruction.

Baker was apprehensive about enforcing what he feared would be unpopular measures on the African population. Inoculation proved popular, however, and a total of 57,016 inoculations were performed during the epidemic. The wholesale movememt of people and the destruction of their houses, however, were, as Baker knew, likely to be viewed as highly provocative measures.

In Kamuli Baker held a conference with the District Commissioner and chiefs and urged them to organize a rat destruction campaign. But when he returned three weeks later he found that the epidemic had taken a firm hold over an area 25 miles in diameter, and that the death rate was increasing steadily. Segregating the infected population seemed to Baker to be totally impracticable, and it was impossible to keep control over contacts. The only remedy appeared to be total evacuation, 'but at first I hesitated to advocate such a drastic measure because I anticipated opposition from the inhabitants (in which I was wrong) and because if the people were removed to a distance famine might complicate matters'.

Despite fears of opposition, Baker did manage to remove people from the most heavily infected group of houses. The results of this evacuation were, apparently, very quickly seen in a fall in the death rate, such that 'it was possible to demonstrate to the Chiefs and people the necessity of applying the measure to the whole infected area'.

Meanwhile 'war' was waged on the rats. The rat destruction campaigns of early colonial Africa presented a bizarre spectacle. In Kampala Baker addressed the European population on the necessity for organizing rat destruction campaigns. If the right words had to be found to persuade chiefs that their people should be moved, their houses destroyed and funerals suspended, so the right words had also to be found to persuade the European inhabitants of Kampala that rat destruction was not only necessary, but could also be fun. Baker appealed to the imperial hunting instincts of the male European population. Rat destruction drives could, he suggested, be organized like hunting parties, with a sweepstake thrown in. They would also be organized in such a way as would express the hierarchies of colonial rule:

> I suggest that we should get up a rat-catching sweep – I leave the details to you –
> whereby each European should write up say Rs5/-, take charge of a fixed number of
> men as rat hounds (if he can employ dogs as well so much the better) and see how
> many rats he can bring to me in a week, the winner of course to take the pool . . .
> You will find it is not as exciting as Big game but not bad fun all the same and you
> will certainly be doing good to the community at large.

Snapshots of the Kampala rat destruction campaign show Baker and other officials proudly surveying piles of rat tails arranged to form the letters RATS.

Rat destruction was a feature of anti-plague measures elsewhere in colonial Africa. James Brown has described the anti-plague measures undertaken in Zongo, Ashanti during the 1920s.[23] In Zongo large numbers of rat traps were set every day, and twopence offered for every rat brought to the authorities. Slogans with the message 'Kill Rats and Stop Plague' were whitewashed on buildings throughout the town. During the 1919 outbreak of plague in the north of Nyasaland, payment was also made to Africans for the destruction of rats. This made the campaign relatively popular amongst local people, or at least amongst small boys, who found it surprisingly profitable, as one medical officer reported:

> It is not, I think, realised how easily money paid for dead rats is earned by natives
> . . . Trapping is carried out by small boys, and to some extent by women, who day
> after day troop in with their catches and at the end of the month must reap a
> reward exceeding far their wildest dreams of wealth. When payments were made in
> October for a period extending over three months it was a common sight to see a
> small boy of about 10 years of age receiving as much as 16/- to 25/-, the rate of pay
> of an ordinary labourer in this district being 4/- to 6/- per month.[24]

Here, as elsewhere, the plague epidemic highlighted the absence of any real public health system, and the need for an improvement in living conditions if epidemic disease was to be controlled.[25]

Many officials, both medical and administrative, understood that the real causes of epidemics lay in the major economic changes taking place in rural Africa. In northern Nyasaland the epidemic was most widespread in areas where people had grown a surplus of food for sale which was inadequately stored in houses and grain-bins, attracting large numbers of rats. Medics like Baker were not obsessively 'bacteriological' in their outlook. Rather they were aware of the complexity of the production of the epidemics they had to deal with. Neither were they, like many of their successors, prone to attributing blame by alluding to predisposing 'cultural' factors. Rather, they regarded the problems of public health in colonial Africa to be much the same as those experienced in Victorian Britain and amenable to the same 'sanitary' solutions.

When it came to practice, however, the military type of campaign was the only model available, and in the colonial context such campaigns were liable to be read as aggressive expressions of colonial power. Public health measures were, by definition, administrative as much as medical in their presentation. In colonial Africa what this meant in practice was that the medical officer became indistinguishable from the administrator in the eyes of the African community. There could be no convincing pretence of neutrality and, as Baker and others knew, this made the job of persuading people that it was in their interest to have their houses burnt and their crops destroyed all the more difficult. This was particularly so in many areas where the early colonial period was marked by the periodic raiding and burning of villages in tax-collecting drives and it may have been enhanced by the experience of the First World War when again the colonial state drafted thousands of Africans into its employ as porters and soldiers.

This was not always a straightforward encounter between the colonizer and the colonized, however. The agents of public health encountered by most villagers were not the white medical officers (of whom there were very few), or even the white administrators (though these did make an appearance when a crisis occurred) but rather African agents of the colonial sanitary state.

In early colonial Nyasaland 'smallpox police' were employed to tour the villages and enforce vaccination. They did not have an easy task in persuading people that vaccination was beneficial, or that it was more effective than their own systems of variolation. During the 1919 epidemic, the entire system of compulsory vaccination was called into question by the smallpox police themselves, who were finding it impossible to prevent widespread evasion. Smallpox cases were not reported, and women hid their babies and children when the smallpox police were in their area. The task of these vaccinators was not helped by the fact that the vaccine with which they were provided was frequently inert by the time they came to administer it, and this had been particularly the case during the First World War. In general it was a mild form of smallpox which affected Nyasaland, and mortality was usually low. Vaccination, on the other hand, was often inexpertly administered and painful, and people complained that they could not hoe their fields for weeks afterwards.[26]

Most administrators felt that it would be easier, and less provocative, to use village headmen to control smallpox epidemics – a system which was to be further elaborated with Indirect Rule in the 1930s. The Resident at Chinteche, for instance, wrote that smallpox police had never been employed in that district, and argued, in the strange language of public health, that 'these people are quite capable of running a smallpox epidemic and looking after it well'.[27] The British colonial system of 'running epidemics' was characterized by this devolution of responsibility on to village headmen and chiefs, and the employment of African vaccinators. To a large extent control over these measures fell into the hands of the administrators, to whom the village headmen reported directly, rather than to the medical department and its officials. One District Commissioner in Northern Nyasaland in the 1930s made a point of vaccinating people himself.[28] One can only speculate as to how people received this direct exercise of colonial 'bio-power', and the association between political and medical control which it implied.

Medical officers in Nyasaland recognized that many of the real difficulties of controlling smallpox lay in the mobility of the population, and in the inefficacy of vaccination. In the 1929 epidemic, Sub-Assistant Surgeon Chetan Dev reported that in Dowa less than 10 per cent of the vaccinations performed had been successful. Arm to arm vaccination was almost universally a failure, and, as this was a tsetse area, there was no possibility of cultivating lymph in cows.[29] Here, as in Kasungu district, the Sub-Assistant Surgeon reported that labour migrants, making their way on foot from Southern Rhodesia through Mozambique, were spreading the disease:

> patients have been discovered walking with active smallpox from Kalindawulu's section in Portuguese East Africa to their respective villages in Kasungu district following the Fort Johnston–Kasungu road . . . the immigrants are mostly from the Southern Rhodesia mines . . . While suffering themselves they had not reported to the headmen or other authority but managed to work their way on to their villages until discovered concealing the disease by following unfrequented ways during the day and calling in for food during the night.

The long-distance mobility of the male population probably meant that the scale of smallpox epidemics increased at this time, and made control all the more difficult.[30] Medical officers were aware that the problem was not likely to have a strictly medical solution, and their inability to deal effectively with smallpox was still evident in the late 1940s when an epidemic of a severe strain of the disease claimed thousands of lives.[31]

Smallpox, like plague, achieved epidemic proportions through changes in the political economy of this period. Though some control was effected through medical technique – inoculation against plague, for example, was an important feature of control of the disease – in general such means were bound to be ineffective without massive investment, and maybe not even then. The increased mobility of African people and the poor conditions in which they worked were, of course, the real problems to be grappled with. Unable to address the underlying problems of ill-health and susceptibility to epidemic disease, medical departments continued to respond to sporadic crisis through sporadic campaign. One can only feel sympathy for medical orderlies and vaccinators like Mr Sichimata who were sent to the 'front line' of the public health 'battle' inadequately equipped:

> I came alone to one village of Nyasaland [he wrote in 1936], I give them vaccination, 19 men and 15 women, and therefore I arrives at Dambo village, Northern Rhodesia, and asked him if they the Nyasaland people they infection for smallpox here and Dambo answer me said here my village have no smallpox and I say better bring all peoples nearby to me I want to see them how they are, and to give vaccination to their arms, and he say, We do not want your medicine because the medicine makes sores suffer much and again he said some year ago we was done that medicine and smallpox had comes in 1932 it was touched all of us and some of us has been death from smallpox, therefore we do not want again you better go off. Surely I left that Dambo village, I getting Mutelewa village . . . My heart have been change the mind and I live in the village with the people of Nyasaland is very good peoples much willing the medicine not the Northern Rhodesian peoples and myself had been suffering from headache, and coughing and the pump of bicycle has been lost . . .[32]

By the 1930s, however, the whole place of public health in the colonial medical system, and the theories of health which underlay it, were quite substantially changed from Stannus's time. A number of elements combined to produce this shift. Firstly, with advances in curative medicine, more of the (gradually increasing) colonial government resources for health were being spent on curative services.[33] Until the post-war period access to such state-run services remained largely limited to urban dwellers, but mission-sponsored medical services had created a demand amongst rural Africans. In particular the spectacular success of chemical treatments for yaws created a vocal demand for 'injections' of all sorts. This increasing use and popularity of the technical, curative end of western medicine was combined, however, with a shift in the colonial medical discourse away from the wide environmentalist public health theories of those like Stannus, towards a reification of the idea of cultural difference. This was, of course, part of a much wider shift in colonial discourse which incorporated a shift from emphasis on 'racial' difference to a 'liberal' cultural relativist position. Stannus's concern with physical 'types' and their relationship to environment was replaced with a concern with cultural difference. This focus displaced attention from the larger environmental and economic causes of disease and towards the idea that Africans were differentially susceptible to certain diseases on account of their cultural practices. It tended towards the attribution of blame. In Britain this shift in medical discourse had taken place at the beginning of the century and was largely focused on individual pathology and individual responsibility.[34] In colonial Africa it took a different form, focusing not on the individual but on the 'tribal' collectivity. Susceptibility to disease in Africans, then, was defined not through an analysis of the conditions under which they lived and worked, or through notions of individual lifestyle and responsibility (though missionary medicine stressed exactly this), but rather through the idea that the cultural practices of different ethnic groups disposed them to various disease patterns.

This was not a uniform process, nor was it a complete break with the early colonial period. An emphasis on cultural rather than 'racial' difference had, of course, been around in anthropology since early in the century: it did not suddenly appear in the 1930s.[35] There were continuities between the concern of someone like Stannus to document not only physical 'types' but differences in material culture, and the later concerns of cultural anthropology which found their way into medical discourse. But a shift is nevertheless clear, and it had an impact on medical practice in colonial Africa. This now became much more biologistic in orientation and began, at this period, to approximate to the picture of western medicine offered by critics such as Turshen. But the increasingly technical appearance of biomedicine went hand in hand with an elevation of the notion of cultural difference, replacing 'race' and environment as a central determinant of disease patterns. Colonial biomedicine was never without its cultural and social preoccupations and premises.

As part of this development public health, as many writers have noted, was downgraded and kicked to the side. Tropical medical research remained important, and medical campaigns continued but these became more and more narrowly curative and less preventive in orientation. Preventive public health was not a fashionable area to be in for medics and in some cases was completely taken out of the hands of Medical Departments into separate Sanitary Departments.

Notes

1. Hugh Stannus papers, Mss. Afr.s.476, Rhodes House, Oxford (hereafter Stannus papers). Stannus to Ethel, 18.9.1910.
2. Russett (1989).
3. Turshen (1984).
4. MacLeod and Lewis, eds (1988); Arnold, ed. (1988).
5. Worboys (1988a).
6. See, for example, the survival of climatic theories of health and disease in Australia in Helen Woolcock's account of attitudes to health in colonial Queensland: Woolcock (1988).
7. McKeown (1979); Curtin (1961).
8. Jordanova (1989), p. 46.
9. For the history of sleeping sickness research in colonial Africa see the work of Maryinez Lyons on northern Zaire: Lyons (1987); Ford (1979); McKelvey (1973).
10. J. B. Davey papers, Mss. Afr.s.97, Rhodes House, Oxford.
11. Davey papers, Diary entries, 1910–11.
12. For the significance of hunting in colonial ideology see John MacKenzie's work: MacKenzie (1988).
13. Ford (1971).
14. Worboys (1988a).
15. For India see Ramasubban (1988); Arnold (1988); Catanach (1988).
16. Curtin (1961).
17. MacKenzie (1988); Beinart (1989).
18. Iliffe (1987); Kjekshus (1977).
19. Feierman (1985).

20. Swanson (1977).
21. C. J. Baker papers, Mss. Afr.s.1091, Rhodes House, Oxford.
22. Baker papers, Box 3, File 2, 1921.
23. Brown (1978). The medical department in Lagos produced a health education film in 1937 entitled *Anti-Plague Operations in Lagos*. This film shows European officials supervising the trapping of rats in a poor African housing area, and the subsequent redevelopment of the area into a 'model township' (National Film Archives, London). See Chapter 8.
24. Malawi National Archives (hereafter MNA): S1/326/19: Bubonic Plague, 1919, Lambourn to Provincial Medical Officer, 1.2.19.
25. MNA: S1/326/19: John Abraham to Acting Chief Secretary, 31.8.20.
26. MNA: S1/1243/19: Smallpox, 1919–20.
27. MNA: S1/1243/19: Resident Chintechi to Chief Secretary, 21.11.21.
28. MNA: M2/5/16: Smallpox: General, 1929–32, Extract from Report of the District Commissioner, Mzimba, for quarter ended 30.9.30.
29. MNA: M2/5/16: Sub-Assistant Surgeon, Chetan Dev, to Director of Medical and Sanitary Services, 12.12.29.
30. Marc Dawson has argued this in his study of smallpox epidemics in early colonial Kenya: Dawson (1979).
31. MNA: M2/5/49: Smallpox, 1946–8.
32. MNA: M2/5/15: Medical Orderly Thomas Sichimata: Report on smallpox at Mwenya village, 17.8.36.
33. This paragraph draws on a survey of the annual medical reports on Nyasaland, Northern Rhodesia, Southern Rhodesia, Kenya and Tanganyika.
34. This is clear from the history of medical approaches to tuberculosis, for instance: Linda Bryder's work on the history of tuberculosis in twentieth-century Britain: Bryder (1988).
35. Harris (1968); Stocking (1969).

References

Arnold, David, ed. (1988), *Imperial Medicine and Indigenous Societies*, Manchester.
Beinart, William (1989), 'Introduction: the Politics of Colonial Conservation', *Journal of Southern African Studies*, vol. 15, pp. 143–62.
Brown, James W. (1978), 'Increased Communication and Epidemic Disease in early Colonial Ashanti', in Gerald W. Hartwig and K. David Patterson, eds, *Disease in African History: an Introductory Survey and Case Studies*, Durham, N.C., pp. 180–207.
Bryder, Linda (1988), *Below the Magic Mountain: a Social History of Tuberculosis in Twentieth Century Britain*, Oxford.
Catanach, I. J. (1988), 'Plague and the Tensions of Empire: India, 1896–1918', in Arnold, ed. (1988), pp. 149–72.
Curtin, Philip (1961), ' "The White Man's Grave": Image and Reality', *Journal of British Studies*, vol. 1, pp. 94–110.
Dawson, Marc (1979), 'Smallpox in Kenya, 1880–1920', *Social Science and Medicine*, vol. 13B, pp. 245–51.
Feierman, Steven (1985), 'Struggles for Control: the Social Roots of Health and Healing in Modern Africa', *African Studies Review*, vol. 28, pp. 73–147.
Ford, John (1971), *The Role of Trypanosomiasis in African Ecology*, Oxford.

Ford, John (1979), 'Ideas which have Influenced Attempts to Solve the Problem of African Trypanosomiasis', *Social Science and Medicine*, vol. 13B, pp. 269–75.

Harris, Marvin (1968), *The Rise of Anthropological Theory*, New York.

Iliffe, John (1987), *The African Poor: a History*, Cambridge.

Jordanova, Ludmilla (1989), *Sexual Visions*, Hemel Hempstead.

Kjekshus, Helge (1977), *Ecology Control and Economic Development in East African History*, London.

Lyons, Maryinez (1987), 'The Colonial Disease: Sleeping Sickness in the Social History of Northern Zaire, 1903–1930', PhD. thesis, University of California.

McKelvey, J. J. (1973), *Man Against Tsetse: Struggle for Africa*, Ithaca, N.Y.

MacKenzie, John (1988), *Empire of Nature*, Manchester.

McKeown, T. (1979), *The Role of Medicine: Dream, Mirage or Nemesis?*, Oxford.

MacLeod, Roy and Milton Lewis, eds (1988), *Disease, Medicine and Empire: Perspectives on Western Medicine and the Experience of European Expansion*, London and New York.

Ramasubban, Radhika (1988), 'Imperial Health in British India, 1857–1900', in MacLeod and Lewis, eds (1988), pp. 38–61.

Russett, Cynthia Eagle (1989), *Sexual Science: the Victorian Construction of Womanhood*, Cambridge, Mass.

Stocking, George W. (1969), *Race, Culture and Evolution*, New York.

Swanson, Maynard (1977), 'The Sanitation Syndrome: Bubonic Plague and Urban Native Policy in the Cape Colony, 1900–1909', *Journal of African History*, vol. 18, pp. 387–410.

Turshen, Meredith (1984), *The Political Ecology of Disease in Tanzania*, New Brunswick.

Woolcock, Helen (1988), '"Our Salubrious Climate": Attitudes to Health in Colonial Queensland', in MacLeod and Lewis, eds (1988), pp. 176–94.

Worboys, Michael (1988a), 'Manson, Ross and Colonial Medical Policy: Tropical Medicine in London and Liverpool, 1899–1914', in MacLeod and Lewis, eds (1988), pp. 21–38.

CHAPTER 18

Yuuyaraq: The Way of the Human Being

Harold Napoleon

INTRODUCTION

For the past four years I have repeatedly tried to write letters and papers address-ing the problem of alcoholism and alcohol abuse among Alaska's Native people. Each time I have stopped or thrown the paper away because the picture was never complete. There was always something missing. My efforts were like an incomplete sentence.

Since the death of my son, due directly to my own abuse of and addiction to alcohol, understanding the causes of this disease has occupied much of my time here at the Fairbanks Correctional Center. This prison has been like a laboratory to me; there is no shortage of subjects to be studied, namely, Alaska Natives from all parts of the state whose own abuse of alcohol also brought them here.

From my own family and village history and the histories and backgrounds of the hundreds of young Native people I have met, I have a profile of the Native addict or abuser. While the subjects may be from different villages and tribes, in almost every case the background remains the same. So now it is possible to make fairly accurate statements as to the cause or causes of this disease which yearly takes so many lives through suicide, homicide, accidental death, disease, and heartbreak. It also helps us understand the hopelessness, the frustration, the anger, the prejudice so many people have, which tragically erupts in violence under the influence of alcohol.

The theory that Native people are somehow biologically susceptible to alcohol abuse and alcoholism may have some credence, but I have discounted it as being almost insignificant. Through my own studies of the history of Alaska Native people and the history of the abusers and alcoholics I have met here and by listening to elders, I have come to the conclusion that the primary cause of alcoholism is not physical but spiritual. And to carry this one step further, since the disease is not physical or caused by physical or biological factors, then the cure must also be of the spirit.

As to my credentials, I do not hold a master's or a doctorate, but I am a Yup'ik Eskimo and I was born into a world which no longer exists. My education began in my village of Hooper Bay. I did not begin to learn English until I went to school at six years of age. I then was sent at age twelve to Copper Valley School, supposedly because the school in my village could not teach me what I needed to know.

I love to read. From the first day that I learned the alphabet and acquired a dictionary, I have read everything I could get my hands on. I ruined my eyes reading. The whole world opened up to me and I drank it in thirstily. I do not wish to boast, but I think I know the English language as well as if not better than most English speakers. I learned it from books. I am also fluent in and think in my Native tongue.

I graduated from St. Mary's High School in May 1968 and was valedictorian of my class. Thereafter I went to Great Falls, Montana, for my first year to university where I chose to study history. From there I transferred to the University of Alaska where I also studied history. In 1972 I became executive director of the Association of Village Council Presidents and in that capacity got to know more intimately my own Yup'ik people. All I had to offer them was ideas and I never tired of presenting these. The germ of freedom and self-government was introduced to them then and, happily, today they still seek independence and self-government. I was 22, I was tireless, and I fell in love with them. Soon their problems became mine. Naively, I thought I could solve them all, but needless to say, I did not.

I helped house them, clothe them, feed them, educate them, and protect their rights. I lobbied on their behalf and fought tooth and nail for them. But I now see I failed to look to the most critical part of our existence—our spiritual well being.

When I first started to work for our villages I did not drink; I did not like to drink—I didn't even like the taste. But after five years of countless meetings in Anchorage, Juneau and Washington, being with others for whom drinking was a part of their lives, like so many other Native people, I soon became addicted. But I did not know this; it just became a part of my life.

Perhaps I took myself and my responsibility too seriously, but it was what I perceived to be my failures and the subsequent frustration and anger that led to my becoming an alcoholic. I was too young, too inexperienced, and I took everything to heart. But something in my soul, in my background, my family's and village's history, had preconditioned me to internalize and personalize every perceived defeat.

This is not to say I did no good. Certainly I must have, because in many ways, I left our people in better shape than when they gave me so much responsibility at age twenty-two. I gave them my best, and so did my family. We sacrificed a great deal for them. I was hardly home but my children had to stay home waiting for me. Yes, I gave my best and my children gave me, their father, to others.

My whole adult life has been spent working for our Yup'ik people; I have had no other employer but them. I have been their executive director, vice-president,

president and vice-chairman. This is my history until June of 1984 when my world, as I knew it then, ended with the death of my son.

I am now 39 years of age at the writing of this paper. The first 21 years of my life I was in school, and the next 13 years I spent working for our Yup'ik people. The last five years I have spent in prison as a direct result of my alcoholism. These last five years I have spent grieving, not only for my son, but for all the others who have died in this long night of our alcohol-induced suffering. I have also spent that time looking into my own soul and the souls of my fellow Native people who have become afflicted with this disease.

It is a disease because the people who suffer from it do not volunteer to become infected. No one volunteers to live a life of misery, sorrow, disappointment, and hopelessness. No one in his right mind chooses to lose a loved one, to break his family's heart, to go to prison. It is a disease because no one will beat his wife, molest his children, or give them little rest, because he wants to. No man dreams of this. Yet sadly, this is what is happening too often in our villages and in our homes, and we have to stop it. We have to arrest this disease, this unhappiness, this suffering, and the good news is that we can.

This paper tries to deal with the causes of alcoholism and alcohol abuse among this generation of Alaska Native people. It is a not intended to be a history or a study of the cultures of the various tribes. But because of the nature of the subject, pertinent aspects of the old Yup'ik culture will be briefly discussed so as to give the reader some background and a better understanding of the subject. Things don't just happen; there are causes and reasons, and if we try to understand these causes and reasons, then conceivably we will know how to better deal with the problem.

Although I am an Alaska Native, I am first a Yup'ik, and it is from this perspective that I think and write. However, I have found so many similarities among the important cultural aspects of the various tribes that it would be safe to say that we are, in fact, one tribe of many families.

YUUYARAQ

Prior to the arrival of Western people, the Yup'ik were alone in their riverine and Bering Sea homeland—they and the spirit beings that made things the way they were. Within this homeland they were free and secure. They were ruled by the customs, traditions, and spiritual beliefs of their people, and shaped by these and their environment: the tundra, the river and the Bering Sea.

Their world was complete; it was a very old world. They called it *Yuuyaraq*, "the way of being a human being." Although unwritten, this way can be compared to Mosaic law because it governed all aspects of a human being's life. It defined the correct behavior between parents and children, grandparents and grandchildren, mothers-in-law and daughters and sons-in-law. It defined the correct behavior between cousins (there were many cousins living together in a village). It determined which members of the community could talk with each other and which members could tease each other. It defined acceptable behavior for all members of the community. It outlined the protocol for every and any situation that human beings might find themselves in.

Yuuyaraq defined the correct way of thinking and speaking about all living things, especially the great sea and land mammals on which the Yup'ik relied for food, clothing, shelter, tools, kayaks, and other essentials. These great creatures were sensitive; they were able to understand human conversations, and they demanded and received respect. *Yuuyaraq* prescribed the correct method of hunting and fishing and the correct way of handling all fish and game caught by the hunter in order to honor and appease their spirits and maintain a harmonious relationship with them.

Yuuyaraq encompassed the spirit world in which the Yup'ik lived. It outlined the way of living in harmony within this spirit world and with the spirit beings that inhabited this world. To the Yup'ik, the land, the rivers, the heavens, the seas, and all that dwelled within them were spirit, and therefore sacred. They were born not only to the physical world of the Bering Sea, the Yukon, and the Kuskokwim rivers, but into a spirit world as well. Their arts, tools, weapons, kayaks and umiaks, songs and dances, customs and traditions, thoughts and actions—all bore the imprint of the spirit world and the spirit beings.

When the Yup'ik walked out into the tundra or launched their kayaks into the river or the Bering Sea, they entered into the spiritual realm. They lived in deference to this spiritual universe, of which they were, perhaps, the weakest members. *Yuuyaraq* outlined for the Yup'ik the way of living in this spiritual universe. It was the law by which they lived.

THE SPIRIT WORLD

To the Western explorers, whalers, traders, and missionaries who first met them, the Yup'ik were considered backward savages steeped in superstition. Their villages were small and hard to find because they were a part of the earth. Grass grew on their houses, making it hard to see the village. Only when the warriors came out in their kayaks and umiaks did the newcomers see them and then they were surprised that humans would already be in this part of the world.

The river banks were red with fish drying on racks, along with seal, walrus, and whale meat. Women and children were everywhere, curious and afraid. The old men were curious but unafraid, their interest piqued by these white men who came on winged wooden ships.

They could not communicate by tongue so they tried to converse by signs. The white men gave the Eskimo scouts small gifts. The Yup'ik soon saw that these whites seemed friendly so they allowed them into their villages although the newcomers did not want to eat when offered food. The visitors saw the semi-subterranean sod houses with underground entrances and they smelled the stench from within. They saw the oily, unwashed faces and the tangled hair. They saw the worn skin clothes and smelled the seal oil. They saw the labrets, the nose bones, the beauty marks on the women, and the fierce, proud faces of the men. Then they were invited to a night of dancing. There they saw the wooden masks worn by the men during their dances. They felt the beating of the drums and were carried away by the singers, drummers, and dancers.

To the explorer or missionary witnessing the dancing in a dimly lit, crowded, stiflingly hot *qasgiq* (men's house), the men, stripped of their clothing, and the women, dancing naked to the waist, must have seemed like heathen savages. The *kass'aqs* (white men) thought they were witnessing a form of devil worship and might even have been frightened by it. The white men did not understand what they were seeing. They did not know that for a brief time they had entered the spirit world of the Yup'ik Eskimo.

To the Yupiit, the world visible to the eye and available to the senses showed only one aspect of being. Unseen was the spirit world, a world just as important as the visible, if not more so. In fact, Yup'ik life was lived in deference to this world and the spirit beings that inhabited it.

What the white men saw was not worship of the devil, but a people paying attention—being mindful of the spirit beings of their world with whom they had to live in harmony. They knew that the temporal and the spiritual were intertwined and they needed to maintain a balance between the two. The Westerners had witnessed the physical representation of that spirit world as presented by dance, song, and mask. But they did not understand what they were seeing; they were strangers in the spirit world of the Bering Sea Eskimo.

IINRUQ

The Yup'ik word for spirit is *iinruq*. The Yup'ik believed that all things, animate and inanimate, had *iinruq*. *Iinruq* was the essence, the soul, of the object or being. Hence, a caribou was a caribou only because it possessed a caribou *iinruq*, a caribou spirit.

Iinruq were indestructible, unlike the bodies in which they resided. And in the case of men, fish, and game, death was the spirit leaving the body. This is why the Yup'ik prescribed respectful ways of treating even dead animals. They believed the *iinruq* would, in time, take another body and come back, and if it had been treated with respect, it would be happy to give itself to the hunter again. For a people solely dependent on sea and land mammals, fish, and waterfowl for subsistence, it was imperative that all members of the community treat all animals with respect or face starvation as a result of an offended spirit. For this reason, annual feasts were held to celebrate and appease the spirits of the animals the village had caught during that year. Some white men witnessed such feasts.

The Russian naval officer L. A. Zagoskin and the American ethnographer Edward W. Nelson witnessed the Bladder Feast. They called it that because the center of attention seemed to be the bladders of sea mammals hanging in the center of the *qasgiq*. Hanging with the bladders were spears, throwing darts, bows and arrows—all the hunting implements of the hunters. Both observers were moved by the dancing, the oratory they did not understand, and the ritual. But what they did not understand was the unseen—the spirits represented by the bladders.

Not only the animals possessed *iinruq*, humans also possessed them. But human spirits were not called *iinruq*. In the Hooper Bay dialect, they are called *anerneq*—literally, "breath"—and as in animals, a human being could not live without its breath. Death came when the *anerneq* left the body due to injury, illness, or by the will of the person. The human spirit was a very powerful spirit and, like the spirits of other living creatures, was reborn when its name was given to a newborn. These spirits were appeased and celebrated through the Great Feast of the Dead, as Nelson called it.

Even so, animal and human spirits wandered the earth, as did monsters and creatures of the deep and the underground, good spirits and evil spirits (*alangrut*) that either helped or caused havoc, even death, for humans and animals alike. Every physical manifestation—plenty of food or famine, good weather or bad, good luck or bad, health or illness—had a spiritual cause. This is why the shamans, the *angalkuq*, were the most important men and women in the village.

The *angalkuq* were the village historians, physicians, judges, arbitrators, and interpreters of *Yuuyaraq*. They also understood the spirit world and at times entered into it to commune with the spirit beings in fulfillment of their responsibility as intermediaries between humans and the spiritual realm. *Angalkuq* are said to have gone to the moon, to the bottom of the sea, and to the bowels of the earth in their search for understanding and solutions to problems which faced their people, such as famine, bad weather, and illness.

In the old Yup'ik world, the *angalkuq* were powerful and indispensable forces because they represented, protected, and upheld *Yuuyaraq*, even against the spiritual realm, of which they were members. They were the guardians of an ancient culture that had become brittle with age, a culture whose underpinnings the rest of the world would never understand, a culture that was about to crumble as a result of temporal forces from the one direction the *angalkuq* were not looking—the physical world.

ILLNESS AND DISEASE

Not knowing of microbes, bacteria, or viruses, the old Yup'ik attributed illness to the invasion of the body by evil spirits. They knew that certain plants and spoiled food caused death and they strictly forbade the eating of them. But illness unattributed to the ingestion of poisons through the mouth was attributed to evil spirits. Such illness was treated by the *angalkuq* in their role as medicine men and women.

Certain herbs, plants, and even animal parts provided commonly known remedies for many ailments suffered by the Yup'ik. They also had home remedies for small burns and cuts, sore backs, sprains, and other minor ailments. The *angalkuq* were not called in unless the illness was deemed to be serious and of an unknown nature, probably caused by an evil spirit and thus requiring a spiritual remedy.

The *angalkuq* must have known that some of the ailments were, by nature, physical. Their knowledge of the human anatomy was probably as good as that of their Western counterparts at that time. Some *angalkuq* were even said to have performed surgeries, amputations, and autopsies. They had names for all major bones, muscles, arteries, veins, and organs, and knew roughly the function of each. But their remedies for unknown disease were different from their Western counterparts who used bromides and elixirs, while the *angalkuq* used songs, dances, and chants.

The important thing to remember is that the old Yupiit believed that illnesses unattributed to the ingestion of poisons or injury were caused by the invasion of the body by evil spirits. With the arrival of Western man, the Yupiit (and *Yuuyaraq*) would be accosted by diseases from which they would never recover. The old Yup'ik culture, the spirit world and its guardian, the *angalkuq*, were about to receive a fatal wounding.

The World Goes Upside Down

When the first white men arrived in the Yup'ik villages, the people did not immediately abandon their old ways. It is historical fact that they resisted Russian efforts to colonize them. They did not abandon their spirit world or their beliefs upon first hearing the Christian message of the priests. That the missionaries met resistance is clear from the derogatory and antagonistic references they made about the *angalkuq* in their diaries. They called them rascals, tricksters, even agents of the devil.

The Yupiit saw missionaries as curiosities, as they saw all white men. The Yupiit said of them, *yuunritut*,—"they are not human beings." Obviously they were not impressed by the white men, even though they quickly adopted their technology and goods. But resistance to Western rule would crumble, *Yuuyaraq* would be abandoned, and the spirit world would be displaced by Christianity.

The change was brought about as a result of the introduction of diseases that had been born in the slums of Europe during the dark and middle ages, diseases carried by the traders, the whalers and the missionaries. To these diseases the Yup'ik and other Native tribes had no immunity, and to these they would lose up to 60 percent of their people. As a result of epidemics, the Yup'ik world would go upside down; it would end.

This period of Yup'ik history is vague. There is no oral or written record of their reaction to this experience, but we can and must attempt in our minds to recreate what happened because this cataclysm of mass death changed the persona, the lifeview, the world view, of the Yup'ik people.

The Great Death

As a child I heard references to *yuut tuqurpallratni*—"when a great many died," or The Great Death. I never understood when it happened, nor was I told in detail what it was. But I learned that it was a time-mark for our Yup'ik people and that it was caused by disease.

I heard references to *yuut tuqurpallratni* from three men, my granduncles, all of whom are now dead. Their white man-given names were Joe Seton, Frank Smart, and Sam Hill, but of course we did not call them that. To me they were my *Apakcuaq*, my *Apaiyaq*, and my *Angakalaq*. In almost every reference to the experience, they used the word *naklurluq*, or "poor," referring both to the dead and to the survivors, but they never went into detail. It was almost as if they had an aversion to it.

From looking at the various epidemics which decimated the Native people, I at first thought of them collectively as the Great Death, but I am now convinced that the Great Death referred to the 1900 influenza epidemic which originated in Nome. From there it spread like a wildfire to all corners of Alaska, killing up to 60 percent of the Eskimo and Athabascan people with the least exposure to the white man. (Details are reported by Robert Fortuine in his book, *Chills and Fever*). This epidemic killed whole families and wiped out whole villages. It gave birth to a generation of orphans—our current grandparents and great-grandparents.

The suffering, the despair, the heartbreak, the desperation, and confusion these survivors lived through is unimaginable. People watched helplessly as their mothers, fathers, brothers, and sisters grew ill, the efforts of the *angalkuq* failing. First one family fell ill, then another, then another. The people grew desperate, the *angalkuq* along with them. Then the death started, with people wailing morning, noon, and night. Soon whole families were dead, some leaving only a boy or girl. Babies tried to suckle on the breasts of dead mothers, soon to die themselves. Even the medicine men grew ill and died in despair with their people, and with them died a great part of *Yuuyaraq*, the ancient spirit world of the Eskimo.

THE SURVIVORS

Whether the survivors knew or understood, they had witnessed the fatal wounding of *Yuuyaraq* and the old Yup'ik culture. Compared to the span of life of a culture, the Great Death was instantaneous. The Yup'ik world was turned upside down, literally overnight. Out of the suffering, confusion, desperation, heartbreak, and trauma was born a new generation of Yup'ik people. They were born into shock. They woke to a world in shambles, many of their people and their beliefs strewn around them, dead. In their minds they had been overcome by evil. Their medicines and their medicine men and women had proven useless. Everything they had believed in had failed. Their ancient world had collapsed.

From their innocence and from their inability to understand and dispel the disease, guilt was born into them. They had witnessed mass death—evil—in unimaginable and unacceptable terms. These were the men and women orphaned by the sudden and traumatic death of the culture that had given them birth. They would become the first generation of modern-day Yup'ik.

THE SURVIVORS' WORLD

The world the survivors woke to was without anchor. The *angalkuq*, their medicines, and their beliefs, had all passed away overnight. They woke up in shock, listless, confused, bewildered, heartbroken, and afraid. Like soldiers on an especially gruesome battlefield, they were shell shocked.

Too weak to bury all the dead, many survivors abandoned the old villages, some caving in their houses with the dead still in them. Their homeland—the tundra, the Bering Sea coast, the riverbanks—had become a dying field for the Yup'ik people: families, leaders, artists, medicine men and women—and *Yuuyaraq*. But it would not end there.

Famine, starvation, and disease resulting from the epidemic continued to plague them through the 1950s, and many more perished. These were the people whom the missionaries would call wretched, lazy, even listless. Gone were the people whom Nelson so admired for their "arts, ingenuity, perseverance and virtuosity," the people whom Henry B. Collins claimed had reached the "peak" of modern Eskimo art. Disease had wiped them out. The long night of suffering had begun for the survivors of the Great Death and their descendants.

THE END OF THE OLD CULTURE

The Yup'ik people of today are not culturally the same as their forebears. They are, however, linked to the old through the experience of the Great Death. One was wiped out by it, the other was born out of it and was shaped by it. It is from this context that we have to see the modern Yup'ik Eskimo. It is only from this context that we can begin to understand them.

Like any victim or witness of evil, whether it be murder, suicide, rape, war or mass death, the Yup'ik survivors were in shock. But unlike today's trauma victims, they received no physical or psychological help. They experienced the Great Death alone in the isolation of their tundra and riverine homeland. There was no Red Cross, no relief effort. The survivors of the Great Death had to face it alone.

They were quiet and kept things to themselves. They rarely showed their sorrows, fears, heartbreak, anger, or grief. Unable to relive in their conscious minds the horror they had experienced, they did not talk about it with anyone. The survivors seem to have agreed, without discussing it, that they would not talk about it. It was too painful and the implications were too great. Discussing it would have let loose emotions they may not have been able to control. It was better not to talk about it, to act as if it had never happened, to *nallunguaq*. To this day *nallunguaq* remains a way of dealing with problems or unpleasant occurrences in Yup'ik life. Young people are advised by elders to *nallunguarluku*, "to pretend it didn't happen." They had a lot to pretend not to know. After all, it was not only that their loved ones had died, they also had seen their world collapse.

Everything they had lived and believed had been found wanting. They were afraid to admit that the things they had believed in might not have been true.

Traumatized, leaderless, confused, and afraid, the survivors readily followed the white missionaries and school teachers, who quickly attained a status once held only by the *angalkuq*. The survivors embraced Christianity, abandoned *Yuuyaraq*, discarded their spirit world and their ceremonies, and buried their old culture in the silence of denial.

Having silently abandoned their own beliefs, the survivors were reinforced in their decision not to talk about them by the missionaries who told them their old beliefs were evil and from the *tuunraq*, "the devil." They learned to sternly tell their grandchildren not to ask them questions about the *angalkuq*, the old symbol of Yup'ik spiritualism, as if they were ashamed of them and of their old beliefs. They would become good Christians—humble, compliant, obedient, deferential, repentant, and quiet.

The survivors were fatalists. They were not sure about the future or even the next day. They told their children to always be prepared to die because they might not even wake up in the morning. They cautioned against making long-range plans. From their own experience they knew how fleeting life was, and from the missionaries they knew how terrible the wrath of the Christian God could be. As new Christians, they learned about hell, the place where the missionaries told them most of their ancestors probably went. They feared hell. They understood fear and they understood hell.

The survivors also turned over the education and instruction of their children to the missionaries and the school teachers. They taught them very little about *Yuuyaraq*. They allowed the missionaries and the school teachers to inflict physical punishment on their children; for example, washing their children's mouths with soap if they spoke Yup'ik in school or church. Their children were forbidden, on pain of "serving in hell," from dancing or following the old ways. The parents—the survivors—allowed this. They did not protest. The children were, therefore, led to believe that the ways of their fathers and forefathers were of no value and were evil. The survivors allowed this.

The survivors taught almost nothing about the old culture to their children. It was as if they were ashamed of it, and this shame they passed on to their children by their silence and by allowing cultural atrocities to be committed against their children. The survivors also gave up all governing power of the villages to the missionaries and school teachers, whoever was most aggressive. There was no one to contest them. In some villages the priest had displaced the *angalkuq*. In some villages there was theocracy under the benevolent dictatorship of a missionary. The old guardians of *Yuuyaraq* on the other hand, the *angalkuq*, if they were still alive, had fallen into disgrace. They had become a source of shame to the village, not only because their medicine and *Yuuyaraq* had failed, but also because the missionaries now openly accused them of being agents of the devil himself and of having led their people into disaster.

In their heart of hearts the survivors wept, but they did not talk to anyone, not even their fellow survivors. It hurt too much. They felt angry, bewildered, ashamed, and guilty, but all this they kept within themselves. These survivors became the forebears of the Yup'ik people and other Alaska Native tribes of today. Their experiences before, during, and after the Great Death explain in great part the persona of their children, grandchildren, and great-grandchildren who are alive today.

POSTTRAUMATIC STRESS DISORDER: AN ILLNESS OF THE SOUL

In light of recent cases of Vietnam veterans who witnessed or participated in war-related events repugnant to them, and who have subsequently been diagnosed to suffer from a psychological illness called posttraumatic stress disorder (PTSD), it is apparent to me that some of the survivors of the Great Death suffered from the same disorder.

The syndrome is born of the attempted suppression in the mind of events perceived as repugnant or evil to the individual who has witnessed or participated in these events. These events were often traumatic to the individual because they involved violence, death, and mayhem by which he was repelled and for which he felt guilt and shame. Not all veterans became infected by this illness. It was mainly the veterans who tried to suppress and ignore their experiences and the resultant feelings of guilt and shame who became ill.

Posttraumatic stress disorder can cripple a person. The act of suppressing the traumatic event, instead of expunging it from the mind through confession, serves to drive it further into the psyche or soul, where it festers and begins to color all aspects of the person's life. The person who suppresses that which is unbearable to the conscious mind is trying to ignore it, trying to pretend it isn't there. In time, and without treatment, it will destroy the person, just as any illness left untreated will in time cripple and kill the body.

Because of his guilt, the person suffering from PTSD does not like himself. He is ashamed of himself, ashamed of what he saw or participated in, and is haunted by the memory, even in sleep. He becomes withdrawn, hypervigilant, hypersensitive, and is constantly living in stress. Soon he is unable to speak truthfully with other people about himself or his feelings and becomes unable to carry on close interpersonal relationships. Living under a great deal of stress in his soul, he becomes less and less able to deal with even the minor difficulties of everyday life.

To such a person, escape from self becomes a necessity because even in sleep he finds no peace. He becomes a runner, running from his memory and from himself. He gets tired and begins to despair. In this day and age, alcohol and drugs become a readily available escape from the illness. For a time, these numb the mind and soul. Without treatment, many veterans and others who suffer from PTSD become alcohol and drug abusers. Many become addicted, and as a result lost friends, wives, families, and become isolated, exacerbating an already bad situation. Being unable to hold jobs, some become dependent on others for support. Some become criminals, further isolating themselves and further depressing an already depressed soul.

Tragically, under the influence of alcohol and drugs, the pent-up anger, guilt, shame, sorrow, frustration, and hopelessness often is vented through outbursts of violence to self and others. Such acts, which are difficult for others and even for the sufferer to understand, drive him further into the deadly vortex of guilt and shame. Family and friends who knew him before be became ill swear that he is not the same person and that they do not know him anymore.

Posttaumatic stress disorder is not a physical illness, but an infection of the soul, of the spirit. I use the word infection because the person suffering from PTSD does not volunteer to become ill and does not choose the life of unhappiness which results from it. I refer to PTSD as an infection of the soul because the disease attacks the core of the person, the spirit. The disease is born out of evil or of events perceived as evil by the person. And the nature of evil is such that it infects even the innocent, dirtying their minds and souls. Because it is infectious, it requires cleansing of the soul through confession. If PTSD sufferers do not get help, they will in time destroy themselves, leaving in their wake even more trauma and heartbreak.

Posttraumatic Stress Disorder in the Survivors of the Great Death

Not all the survivors of the Great Death suffered from posttraumatic stress disorder, but a great many did. This may explain the great thirst for liquor that whalers and other Westerners found in the Eskimos along the Bering Sea and the Arctic. It was reported by whalers and the officers of the early revenue cutters that the Eskimos craved the liquor, trading all they had for it and almost starving themselves as long as they had molasses with which to make rum.

Like the Vietnam veteran or victims and witnesses of other violent and traumatic events, these Eskimos found in liquor a narcotic which numbed their troubled minds. The reports of the whalers, the revenue cutters, and other observers confirm that the Eskimos quickly became addicted to alcohol.

The only explanation for this type of behavior is that for some reason these Eskimos were psychologically predisposed to seek relief through the narcotic effects of alcohol. And although in the case of the St. Lawrence Islanders this behavior was reported in the mid-nineteenth century, it must be remembered that they had already begun to see their world crumbling as a result of interaction with Western sailors and diseases much earlier than the Yup'ik, Inupiaq, and Athabascan people who were located farther away from established sea lanes. The St. Lawrence story was only a precursor for the tragedy that would unfold on the mainland at the turn of the century.

Judging from the abrupt changes the Yup'ik and other Native people accepted at the turn of the century, literally without a fight, one can assume that they were not themselves. No people anywhere will voluntarily discard their culture, beliefs, customs, and traditions unless they are under a great deal of stress, physically, psychologically, or spiritually. Yet for some reason, the Yup'ik people did exactly that, overnight in the span of their cultural history. There may have been pockets of resistance, but they were insignificant.

With the Yup'ik people and most Alaska Native tribes, the case can be made that resistance collapsed because of mass death, resulting from famine, illness, and the trauma that accompanied these. The case can also be made that many of the survivors of the Great Death suffered from posttraumatic stress disorder, and that it was in this condition that they surrendered and allowed their old cultures to pass away.

The survivors had been beaten by an unseen great evil (mass death) that had been unleashed in their villages, killing over half the men, women, and little children. They had witnessed the violent collapse of their world, of *Yuuyaraq*. Having barely escaped the grip of death, the survivors were shaken to the core. They staggered, dazed, confused, brutalized, and scarred, into the new world, refugees in their own land, a remnant of an ancient and proud people. The world looked the same, yet everything had changed. But the memories would remain, memories of the spirit world, the way life used to be, and memories of the horrors they had witnessed and lived through.

We who are alive today cannot begin to imagine the fear, the horror, the confusion and the desperation that gripped the villages of our forebears following the Great Death. But we have learned, through the experience of Vietnam veterans infected by PTSD, that the cries of horror and despair do not end unless they are expunged from the soul. Yes, the Yup'ik survivors cried, they wailed, and they fought with all they had, but they were not heard. They had been alone in a collapsed and dying world and many of them carried the memory, the heartbreak, the guilt, and the shame, silently with them into the grave.

But we hear them today. They cry in the hearts of their children, their grandchildren, and great-grandchildren. They cry in the hearts of the children who have inherited the symptoms of their disease of silent despairing loneliness, heartbreak, confusion, and guilt. And tragically, because the children do not understand why they feel this way, they blame themselves for this legacy from their grandparents, the survivors of the Great Death who suffered from what we now call posttraumatic stress disorder.

THE CHILDREN AND GRANDCHILDREN OF THE SURVIVORS

At the time of the Great Death, there were white people in some of the villages, mostly missionaries and traders, but they were few in number. They witnessed the Great Death, and in many cases they did the best they could to help the Native people. Yet it would be these same people who would take advantage of the demoralized condition of the survivors to change them, to civilize them, to attempt to remake them. They, and the men and women who would follow them, had no understanding of or respect for the old cultures. They considered them satanic, and made it their mission from God to wipe them out. They considered the survivors savages and used derogatory adjectives in describing them in their letters and diaries. And because of what they had just lived through, and because of their disoriented and weakened condition, the survivors allowed these newcomers to take over their lives.

What followed was an attempt at cultural genocide. The priests and missionaries impressed on the survivors that their spirit world was of the devil and was evil. They heaped scorn on the medicine men and women and told the people they were servants of the devil. They told the survivors that their feasts, songs, dances, and masks were evil and had to be abandoned on pain of condemnation and hellfire. Many villages followed these edicts. The dances and feasts disappeared.

The priests and missionaries forbade parents from teaching their children about *Yuuyaraq* and about the spirit world. They forbade the parents and children from practicing old customs and rituals based on *Yuuyaraq*, calling them taboo. Again, the survivors obeyed and their children grew up ignorant about themselves and about their history. If the children asked about the old culture, they were told by their parents not to ask such questions, as if they were ashamed or hiding something. From listening to the priest and observing the behavior of their parents, the children would come to believe that there was something wrong with their people, some dark secret to be ashamed of.

In the schoolhouse, the children were forbidden to speak in Yup'ik. The survivors did not protest even when it was learned that the schoolteachers were washing the mouths of their children with soap for speaking their mother tongue. In the schoolhouse, the children came to believe that to be Yup'ik was shameful and that to become like white people was not only desirable but essential. The children began to look down at their own people and began to see the observances of their people as quaint, shameful, and funny. That the survivors allowed all this is testimony to the degree of their individual and collective depression, especially in regard to the treatment of their children. Had Nelson made similar decrees during the time he was visiting these same villages (1870–1875), he would have been killed. Yet after the Great Death, some villages were ruled autocratically by a single priest.

The survivors were stoic and seemed able to live under the most miserable and unbearable of conditions. They were quiet, even deferential. They did not discuss personal problems with others. If they were hurt, they kept it to themselves. If they were angry, they kept it to themselves. They were lauded as being so respectful that they avoided eye-to-eye contact with others. They were passive. Very few exhibited their emotions or discussed them.

The survivors did as they were told. They were not fighters or protesters. They almost lost everything: their cultures, their languages, their spiritual beliefs, their songs, their dances, their feasts, their lands, their independence, their pride—all their inheritances. This was their way of coping with life after the cataclysm of the Great Death. The survivors had gone into themselves and receded with their tattered lives and unbearable emotions into a deep silence. It was in this condition that they raised their children, who then learned to be like their parents—passive, silent, not expressing emotions, keeping things to themselves, and not asking too many questions.

The survivors told their children about kindness, forgiveness, and sharing, yet they were unwilling to face and discuss the problems and unpleasantness in the family or the village. They did not teach their children about *Yuuyaraq*, the spirit world, or about the old culture because it was too painful to do so. Besides, the priest said it was wrong. Those who told stories told only the harmless ones. This would become part of the persona of the survivors and their descendants. Without meaning to, the survivors drove the experience of the Great Death and the resultant trauma and emotions deep into the souls of their children, who became psychologically and emotionally handicapped and who passed these symptoms on to their children and grandchildren.

The survivors' children are the grandparents of the present day Eskimo, Indian, and Aleut. It is these traits, these symptoms of posttraumatic stress disorder, which are handicapping the present generation of Alaska Native people. Several generations of suppressed emotions, confusion, and feelings of inferiority and powerlessness now permeate even the very young.

AN ANOMALY

Since the early 1960s, Native people have seen their material lives improve. They are no longer hungry, they are well clothed, and they now live in comparatively warm, comfortable homes. This has largely been achieved by the anti-poverty programs which were instituted in the years before and after the Great Society. Being by and large unemployed in the cash economy, Native people benefited greatly from the civil rights and anti-poverty programs of the 1960s and 1970s.

Yet, as their physical lives have improved, the quality of their lives has deteriorated (see Figure 18.1). Since the 1960s there has been a dramatic rise in alcohol abuse, alcoholism, and associated violent behaviors, which have upset family and village life and resulted in physical and psychological injury, death, and imprisonment. Something self-destructive, violent, frustrated, and angry has been set loose from within the Alaska Native people. And it is the young that are dying, going to prison, and maiming themselves. Their families, their friends, their villages say they cannot understand why. Every suicide leaves a stunned family and village. Every violent crime and every alcohol-related death elicits the same reaction. The alcohol-related nightmare has now become an epidemic. No one seems to know why.

One thing we do know—the primary cause of the epidemic is not physical deprivation. Native people have never had it so good in terms of food, clothing, and shelter. We can also state that it isn't because the federal and state governments have ignored the problem. Hundreds of millions of dollars have been spent on Alaska Natives to improve their lives, their health, and their education. Hundreds of millions have been spent just trying to combat alcoholism and alcohol abuse among them. Local option laws have been passed that prohibit the importation, the sale, and even the possession of alcohol. Yet the carnage goes on.

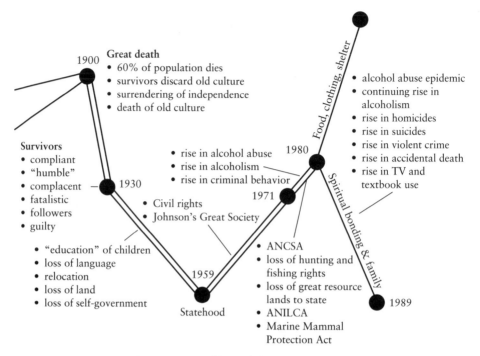

Figure 18.1 Lifeline of the Yup'ik people

The numbers are shocking. According to Matthew Berman,

> From 1977 to 1988, the last year for which complete data are available, 1,789 Native Americans died violently in Alaska. These figures include 394 deaths by suicides, 257 by homicides, and 1,138 by accident out of a total population of only 64,000 (1980 Census), representing a claim of about 3 percent of the native population over a twelve-year period (Berman 1991).

The numbers of incidents of domestic violence, imprisonments, alcohol affected children, and deaths from disease attributable to alcohol are equally shocking. Yet the numbers are misleading because they do not measure the true extent of the damage being done to the Native people. The numbers cannot quantify the heartbreak, discouragement, confusion, hopelessness, and grief. The numbers cannot measure the trauma. It is like repeating the Great Death all over again, and like then, the Alaska Natives blame themselves and do not know or understand why. And like the first Great Death, a whole generation of Alaska Natives is being born into trauma, just like their grandparents and parents. It is history repeating itself in a tragic, heartbreaking way. It is a deadly cycle that began in the changing of the times for the Yupiit and the other tribes of Alaska Natives.

WHY?

We now know that our ancestors were besieged by ship-borne diseases like small-pox, measles, chicken pox, and colds that culminated in the Great Death, the influenza epidemic at the turn of the century. Not knowing of microbes, they attributed these diseases to evil spirits and to their own weaknesses. They blamed themselves and their way of life, and abandoned themselves and their way of life as a result. But that did not end the suffering. Famine, poverty, confusion, polio, tuberculosis, and spiritual depression followed, ending in the death of the old cultures around the 1950s.

The present epidemic is a little harder to explain, but certainly it was born out of the Great Death itself, and the disease is one of the soul and the psyche of this present generation of Alaska Native people. It is an inherited disease, passed from parent to child. But it has been passed down unintentionally, unknowingly, and innocently. Nevertheless, it is deadly and unless treated, it will give birth to another generation of infected souls.

The cry of the survivors of the Great Death was why. That same cry is now heard from the confused, shocked, and heartbroken hearts of today's Alaska Native people.

A GENERATION TURNS ON ITSELF

Many of today's generation of Alaska Natives have turned on themselves. They blame themselves for being unemployed, for being second-class citizens, for not being successful as success is portrayed to them by the world they live in. They measure themselves by the standards of the television America and the textbook America, and they have failed. For this they blame themselves. There is no one to tell them that they are not to blame, that there is nothing wrong with them, that they are loved. Sometimes they don't even know who they are, or what they are.

This, of course, does not describe all young Alaska Native people. But it de-scribes the suicides, the alcohol abusers, the ones in prison, the ones with nothing to do in the villages. These are the numbers we hear in reports. They are living human beings—Eskimos, Aleuts, and Indians—the ones we pay no attention to until they become numbers. Chances are that their parents also were alcohol abusers, if not alcoholics. Chances are that they were disappointed, emotionally hurt, heartbroken children. Chances are they saw physical, verbal, and psycho-logical violence in the home. Chances are that they were not given enough atten-tion and thought themselves unloved and unwanted. Chances are they were hungry, were dirty, were tired, and were unsuccessful in school. Chances are they yearned for happiness and a normal home but were denied it. And now, chances are they no longer communicate with others—not their parents, not their relatives, not their friends, or anyone else.

By the time such children are grown, they are deeply depressed in their souls. They have become demoralized, discouraged, and do not think very much of themselves. Deep in their hearts they are hurt, angry, frustrated and confused. They never talk. They have turned inward.

These are the ones who, when they drink alcohol, quickly become addicted to it, psychologically first, and then physically. When under the influence, they begin to vent their anger, hurt, frustration, and confusion, seemingly out of the clear blue sky. And sadly, their outbursts are directed at themselves and those closest to them: their parents, their brothers and sisters, their friends, and members of their villages. The most tragic events are those involving a blacked-out male Eskimo, Aleut, or Indian, who, while completely out of control, vents his deadly emotions in violence and mad acts resulting in dismemberment and death, thereby leaving even more traumatized victims and witnesses.

So what causes this? Is it the young man's or young woman's fault? Or is it the fault of parents who may have been abusers and alcoholics? Or is it the fault of grandparents who did not raise their children right because they themselves were traumatized by the Great Death and felt guilty about the subsequent loss of culture, language, and independence? Whose fault is it?

Certainly the dead will be buried, the suicides buried, the assaulter and abuser jailed and charged with the appropriate crime and put away in prison for a few years or a lifetime. But there are only so many prison cells. Can we seriously be thinking of putting everyone into prison? And do we keep burying the other victims of the Great Death until not a one is left? Is this to be our way of life until the end, burying the victims of the victims?

When will all this end? How will it end? How can we end it? When can we end it? Or do we even want to end it? Have we become so callous, so hard-hearted, our spiritual senses so dulled, that we are no longer moved by all this? Is it to be as Darwin put it, the survival of the fittest? My answer at least is this: We who are also the survivors of the Great Death must end it. We must activate all our energies and resources to end it. And we must do it soon because as time goes by it will become harder and harder.

Every human life is sacred. Every Yup'ik, Inupiaq, Athabascan, Aleut, Eyak, Chugiak, Tlingit, Haida, Koniag, and Tshimsian life is sacred. We are not so many that we can endlessly absorb the trauma each tragic death inflicts on our physical and psychic body. We are too few. The question is how to stop the epidemic.

BEGINNINGS

If we were to look at the experience of the various tribes as the experience of individuals, and if they were exhibiting the symptoms we have described and which are now so well documented, we would have to spend some time just talking to them. We would have them truthfully tell their life stories, leaving nothing out, to see what was causing these disturbances in their lives. So it is in this way that we must begin to treat this particular syndrome of the various Alaska Native villages, beginning at the personal and familial levels.

The living elders must tell all they know, tell their experiences, because theirs are the experiences of the whole village, whether the whole village is aware of them or not. The very oldest are the most important because they will be able to tell their remembrances to the whole village. They must relate the old beliefs of their people, no matter the subject. They must also relate the experiences of the epidemics, no matter how painful, because these haunt not only them, but their children and grandchildren as well. They must tell why they gave everything up, why they discarded the old ways, the old beliefs, why they allowed the culture to die. They must explain how and why they gave up governing themselves, why they allowed school teachers to wash their children's mouths with soap, why they gave up so much land. The elders must speak of all that hurts them and haunts them. They owe this to their children and to their children's children because without knowing why the descendants feel the same as their elders do.

The one fear I have is that the first survivors of the Great Death—the ones who lived in the old world, were nurtured by it, and who loved it—are now almost all gone. They are the ones in whom was born the disease that afflicts Alaska Natives today. They are the ones who felt the full brunt of the fatal wounding of their world. They are the ones who saw it, were horrified by it, and whose hearts were broken. Hearing them, we will recognize the emotions in our hearts, emotions we have long attributed to a weakness within ourselves. We would at least mourn with them, mourn together the passing of our old world. Then they and we would not be alone any more.

The children of these survivors must also speak. They are now grandparents, even great-grandparents. They must speak of their childhoods, their world, what they saw, what they perceived, what they thought, how they felt. They too must share with us their life stories, leaving nothing out, the good and the bad, because their experiences are ours, and we are their seed. We also love them.

Then the parents of this new generation must speak together, as a group, to the rest of the villages. They too must relate their life stories, their experiences, their sorrows. They must turn their hearts to their children who so love them, who so long to know them. Their experiences are ours. We are shaped by them. Then we, their children, must speak to our parents, to our grandparents if we still have them, and to our own children. We, too, must tell our story to our people, because our experience is theirs too. We must tell our feelings, our anger, our frustrations, and ask questions of our parents.

We must do this because we don't know each other anymore; we have become like strangers to each other. The old do not know or understand the young, and the young do not know or understand the old. Parents do not know their children, and the children do not know their parents. As a result of this silence, a gulf has grown between those who love and care for each other the most. It is so very sad. I have been in homes where members of the same household do not even speak to each other. I wondered how they could even stand to be in the same house together like this.

And out of this will grow more hurt, misunderstanding, and unfulfilled love. Even in the family, while surrounded by those one loves the most, a person can become isolated, a stranger even to those who love him and are closest to him. Needless to say, there will be tension, stress, and frayed nerves.

Only communication, honest communication from the heart, will break this down, because inability to share one's heart and feelings is the most deadly legacy of the Great Death. It was born out of the survivors' inability to face and speak about what they had seen and lived through. The memory was too painful, the reality too hard, the results too hard to hear.

Without knowing it, the survivors began to deal with the difficulties of life by trying to ignore them, by denying them, by not talking about them. This is the way they raised their children and their children raised us the same way. Holding things in has become a trait among our families and our people. The results have been tragic.

Over the many years of suppressed emotions, of not communicating from the heart, Native people and Native families grew apart. Somewhere along the line, something had to give. The body of the Alaska Native family, village, and tribe, being unable to withstand the stresses built up from within, began breaking down.

We have seen this breakdown since the latter 1960s. Alcohol abuse has become rampant. Violence directed at self and at others in the home has erupted. The intensity and the level of self-destruction of the Alaska Native are appalling. The only way it will end is if the built-up stresses, misunderstandings, and questions are released and satisfied by truthful dialogue from the heart. It is only through this heart-to-heart dialogue, no matter how painful or embarrassing the subject, that the deadly stresses born of trauma on top of trauma can be released. Then slowly, we can all go home again, be alone and lonesome no more, be a family and a village again.

It is time we bury the old culture, mourn those who died with it, mourn with those who survived it. It is time we buried our many dead who have died in this long night of our suffering, then go forward, lost no more. We have been wandering in a daze for the last 100 years, rocked by a succession of traumatic changes and inundations. Now we have to stop, look at ourselves, and as the New Alaska Natives we are, press on together—not alone—free of the past that haunted and disabled us, free of the ghosts that haunted our hearts, free to become what we were intended to be by God.

NEW ALASKA NATIVES

Several first steps should be taken to the road to health and to freedom long lost. First on the village level, those whose hearts are with their people should institute Talking Circles, where elders, parents and the young can come together to share themselves, and where the truth can be spoken about all things communal, familial, and personal.

The circle would not be a place for debate or argument, but a place to share oneself, and one's experiences, feelings, and thoughts with the rest of the village. Patience and a love for one another is a requirement for a circle. Once a circle begins, it will grow and it will strengthen those within it. It is not only a place to get things off one's chest, but a place to reestablish bonds between family members and the rest of the village. If the circle goes well, some mothers will see their sons for the first time, some sons see their fathers for the first time, and they will love them even as understanding grows.

The circle has to be open to all members of the village. No one should ever be excluded. In fact everyone must not only be invited, but welcomed and openly received by the circle. If all goes well, the bonds between family members and village members will grow. Hopefully it will enable all members of the village family to go home again. The chasm of suffering and pain that the Great Death brought to our people will close. If this should happen, then all the suffering and those who gave their lives in this long night will not have been in vain.

Another first step is the establishment of Talking Circles specifically for members of the village who have become addicted to alcohol and other drugs. Like the circle for the village in general, this circle would help the alcoholics to understand better why they became addicted and, with the help of recovering addicts, get on the road to recovery and health. To this circle should come elders, parents, and friends who love them—to hear them, to see them, to reassure them, to receive them.

In addition to the circles, the village council should sponsor, on a regular basis, activities for the whole village that require no money but would serve to entertain and allow the families to come together as one big family, which the village is. These might be weekly potlucks with singing and dancing, perhaps even dancing classes for the bigger feasts. The village council should also reinstitute the various potlatches where the whole village can come together to celebrate their lives and the gifts they have received from their Creator.

There are a lot of things the village councils and their people can do for one another to help themselves, to bring themselves together. Even the young women could give all the mothers a night or day off by taking care of the children for one day or night so the mothers can come together as a group. There is no end to what good people in the villages can do for one another, no end to the kindnesses and small considerations they can give to each other. The important first step is for the families and the village to come together as a family. Their health and happiness depend on each other.

On Public Policies

The United States Congress has recently enacted legislation creating a commission to study the problem we have been discussing. And certainly this is one of the things Congress can do to help Native people on their road to recovery. However, it is a mistake to think that Congress or any other group can bring the Alaska Native people back to health. Money, programs, or loans, no matter how well intentioned, cannot end the unhappiness, dissatisfaction, anger, frustration, and sorrow that is now leading so many Alaska Natives to alcohol abuse,

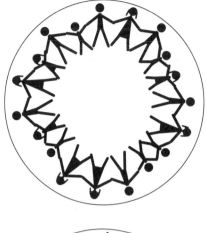

- A healthy village is a circle whose people are safe within its fold.

- Love, understanding, kindness, culture, history, goals, and truth make the circle strong and protect the village, the family, and the individual.

- A healthy village is a gift of the Creator to His children.

- For many Alaska Natives the circle was broken by the trauma of mass death through epidemics.

- Families and villages lost communication and grew apart.

- A circle broken is incomplete. It hemorrhages, and life flows out of it. It breeds unhappiness. Unless the circle is repaired in time, it will die.

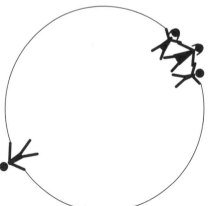

- The circle can only be made whole again by those who live in it, its people.

- The circle, being spirit, can only be repaired by love, understanding, kindness, forgiveness, and patience, with the help of the Creator who established the circle. It can only be done by its people coming together in truth.

Figure 18.2

alcoholism, and tragedy. Only Alaska Natives can do this. To look elsewhere for solutions is illusory.

However, Congress can take some concrete steps to assist the Native villages in reestablishing themselves. First, Congress can affirm, by law, what is now reality: that Alaska Native people are legally Indians, and as such fall under the special protections of the U.S. Constitution and Federal Indian Law. Congress can reaffirm Alaska Natives' inherent right to self-government under whatever democratic form that government may take. It can reaffirm their right to establish tribal courts and ordinances and the power to enforce these.

Congress can reaffirm the right of Alaska Native people in the villages to hunt and fish for subsistence and give them priority rights to the economic utilization of fish and game resources so their dependence on federal welfare programs may decrease and hopefully in time, disappear. It makes no sense at all that presently many Native people are unable to hunt and fish on their lands and waters for commercial purposes while others, even foreigners, are allowed to do so, and this in an economically depressed village where there is 80 percent unemployment and where 90 percent of the families are on various welfare programs.

Congress should use some of the oil lease money it earns from lands and waters adjacent to the villages to fund scholarships for Alaska Native students studying at universities worldwide. As it is now, the benefits received by Alaska Natives come in the form of welfare payments and other grants-for-the-needy programs for which they are eligible.

Congress should also establish correctional facilities for Alaska Native offenders that would be run by Alaska Natives themselves. This would be in recognition of the fact that the village offender is not the same as the black or white offender, and that his rehabilitation can only be brought about through culturally relevant programs. These facilities should have a span of twenty years and then close at the end of that period. Congress should also appropriate funds for the establishment of substance abuse programs designed and run by Alaska Natives themselves. As with the correctional facilities, these should also have a life span of twenty years, to be closed at the end of that period.

Yes, the Congress of the United States can help the Native people on their road to recovery from the various traumas they have lived through in the past hundred years. But that help cannot come in the form of more welfare programs or programs conceived anywhere else but in the villages and by Natives themselves. The Congress of the United States is supposed to be the protector of Alaska's Native people, but for the past hundred years it has neglected them, failed to protect them, and instead has become a party to elements which would completely disenfranchise them as a people.

Yes, the Congress and the American people can help the Eskimos, Aleuts, and Indians to become free, self-supporting Americans, but they must realize that Native people can only do this in their own way, as Eskimos, Aleuts, and Indians. To continue to assimilate them, to continue to keep them as pets unable to care for themselves, to continue to attempt to remake them into anything else but what they are, is to commit slow cultural genocide.

As for the state of Alaska, it must realize that Native people are not its enemies, seeking to undermine it; they are in fact the state's first citizens who never went to war against the immigrants who later settled here but rather accepted them with open arms. Neither are the resources of the state threatened by Alaska Natives who to this day have managed to conserve those natural resources. The state must, by constitutional amendment, accept the existence of Eskimos, Aleuts, and Indians and accept the fact that their needs are not the same as the needs of immigrants from other states and countries.

Relations are sad between the state and its first citizens who gave up much so that they could exist together. Certainly this can change. The state must play a role in helping its first citizens back to health.

THE ALASKA FEDERATION OF NATIVES

The Alaska Federation of Natives (AFN) was established to halt the loss of Native land to federal, state, and private parties, and to acquire title to lands owned by Native people on the basis of aboriginal land rights. Now the AFN must turn to seeking redress for other equally important inheritances of Native people, inheritances that were lost because the basis for holding them was slowly eroded by detrimental laws and adverse decisions in federal and state courts.

The AFN must realize that Native people have given up all they can give up; there is nothing left to give up in compromise any more. The federation must halt any further erosion of the inherited rights of village people. In fact they must begin again to seek redress and the reinstatement of rights already lost.

Specifically, AFN must return to Congress, not to amend the land settlement it successfully fought for, but rather to settle the other equally important claims of their people:

1. the right to self government,
2. the right to establish ordinances,
3. the right to enforce the ordinances,
4. the right to establish courts,
5. the right to hunt and fish for subsistence without interference by state law,
6. the right to use subsistence resources like salmon and other game on their lands and waters for commercial purposes so as to end economic dependence on state and federal welfare programs, and
7. the right to tax exemptions on their properties and holdings which are exemptions now enjoyed by other Native peoples of this country.

These rights are inherent to Alaska's Native people and they were never voluntarily given up by them. In fact, they were taken away without their knowledge and without their approval. They were stolen. The tribes which together comprise the federation, for the good of their people, for their very survival, must now turn in earnest to recovering their rights. They must do this now while the elders who survived the Great Death and their children are still with us.

To argue their case for redress they do not need lawyers. Their case is simple and compelling. They would not be asking for more money or more programs. Neither would they be asking for something which they did not need, or something that someone else could give them or do for them. They would only be asking to be themselves again, to run their own lives again, to pick up the struggle for life again.

Since the turn of the century, they have been ruled by others, trustingly, patiently, quietly. Because of the trauma of disease and the collapse of their world, they have quietly allowed this to happen. And, for a time, it may have been good that there was someone there to help them replace the system that had collapsed around them. But that time has gone on too long. It is time for the survivors of the Old World to pick up the struggle for life again. The system they are living in now is killing them, the way they are living now is killing them, further depressing an already depressed soul.

Alaska Native villages and people are indeed depressed. Not only are we suffering spiritually as a result of seemingly forgotten assaults to our psyche, but this psychological depression is exacerbated by the possibility of total dependence on handouts from federal and state governments. From birth to death many Alaska Natives are cared for by government. Many of us hold high-school diplomas but are unemployed. Our families, living on government dole, do not need each other for support. Too often, we feel useless and have nothing to do.

This almost total dependence on others further undermines the already depressed spirit of many Native people. And the only way it can end is if we take back the responsibility of feeding, clothing, and housing our people; indeed, take back responsibility for all aspects of our physical and spiritual lives. Only then can we pick up once again the struggles of life.

This opportunity to pick up the struggles of life is what the AFN and its member villages must fight for. To some, the seven rights we have to regain mean sovereignty. To the Alaska Natives in the villages, these rights mean life, real life, with hard work, sweat, and no time to feel sorry for ourselves.

Native villages and Native people who seek to regain the seven rights are not asking for something new, something we never held before. We seek the opportunity to live not only the way our forebears lived, but to regain responsibilities now held by federal and state governments. These responsibilities belong to us. We want to be normal again. The way many of us live now is abnormal, like caged animals. We are fed, housed, watered, cared for, but we are not free, and it is killing us.

This is what the Alaska Federation of Natives can and should do. The time of giving up things is over. There is nothing left to give away. There is nothing left with which to negotiate. The AFN and its village people are against the wall. There is no more room for retreat. If the AFN wishes to help its village people back to health, it has to finish the job that only started with the Alaska Native Claims Settlement Act. We must secure the seven rights that are basic to the continued survival and soul of Alaska Native people, rights that mass death through disease and trauma took away from us.

Alaska Native people are ready to reassume these rights and responsibilities; without them, we will cease to exist as a people. It is not a matter of semantics or politics; it is a matter of survival.

CLOSING

I do not know if anyone will understand or agree with what I have written. Nor do I know that if it is understood, the recommendations will be followed. But I am convinced that what I have written is the truth and will be supported by facts. What I have written is the summary of five years' work, sometimes frustrating and anguishing work, but work nonetheless. It did not come to me in one flash, rather it came in bits and pieces. But finally the pieces fit, so I wrote them down for others to read.

Certainly there are others more qualified and more respected than I who could probably compose a more perfect letter. But this letter is from the heart and is born out of my own suffering and imprisonment. In suffering and imprisonment, I have found, life becomes starkly clearer, shed of the noise and the static of the world.

Yet I did not withdraw from the only world I have ever known, the world of my childhood and the world in which I struggled with seemingly insignificant results. No, while I might have been five years in prison, I have never left my village, nor my own Yup'ik people. In fact I return to them in spirit. While missing out on the seemingly good aspects of the life of my village and people, I certainly have not been spared their sorrows and their own suffering. These I have shared with them fully, sorrowing with them, seeking all the harder in our collective soul for answers.

At times I have felt like giving up. Sometimes things look hopeless. But from the Apostle Paul I have been trying to learn to be content in whatever state I am in. I now see those things that brought me—and still bring so many of my brothers and sisters—to alcohol abuse and alcoholism. So now, when I see them, their suffering, their unhappiness, I see my old self and try all the harder to lead them to the truth, the truth that freed me even as I sat in this prison, the same truth that can free all Native people who have become prisoners of the unhappiness born of the evil of the Great Death and the subsequent trauma which it fathered.

This little that I have written is a part of that truth, the truth which was hidden from me by my previous life, by my own stubbornness, pride, unvented emotions, and my addiction to alcohol, which momentarily eased the suffering these bring.

This letter is not from a wise man, because were I wise I would not be where I am. This letter is from a man who learned only from suffering, the lessons literally beaten into his soul. But for this I am grateful, for now I have finally seen what was before my very eyes from the time I was a child. So I share what I have learned—been taught—in hope that the tragedy which engulfed my life and that of my family and villages may never happen again.

I will close by saying that I, once the most hopeless of men, no longer am without hope. I now live in hope. I also have faith that The One who started this good work in us by creating us will complete it.

CHAPTER 19

Nervoso: Medicine, Sickness, and Human Needs

Nancy Scheper-Hughes

There are few vigorous, well-built, healthy persons among the workers.... They are almost all weakly, of angular but not powerful build, lean [and] pale.... Nearly all suffer from indigestion, and consequently from a more or less hypochondriacal melancholy, irritable, nervous condition.

Friedrich Engels ([1845] 1958: 118)

My sickness is both physical and moral.

Carolina Maria de Jesus (1962: 83)

Nervous Hunger

In Bom Jesus one's ear is at first jarred by the frequent juxtapositions of the idioms *fome* and *nervos*, "hunger" and "nervousness," in the everyday conversation of the people of the Alto. Later, the expressions lose their special poignancy, and they come to seem natural, ordinary. A mother stops you on her way up the Alto to say that things aren't well, that her *meninos estão tão nervosos porque não têm nada para comer* (her children are nervous because they are hungry). Biu, on returning from *feira*, says, as she drops heavily into a chair and removes the food basket from her head, that she became dizzy and disoriented, made "nervous" by the high cost of meat. She was so *aperreada* (harassed), she says, that she almost lost her way coming home from the market.

I stop in to visit Auxiliadora, whose body is now wasted by the final stages of schistosomiasis, to find her shaking and crying. Her "nervous attack" (*ataque de nervos*) was prompted, she says, by uncovering the plate of food her favorite son, Biu, has sent her.[1] There in the midst of her beans was a fatty piece of salted *charque* (beef jerky). It will offend her "destroyed" liver. But to eat her beans *simples*, without any meat at all, makes her angry-nervous. And so she explains the "childish" tears of frustration that course freely down her cheeks.

Descending the hill I stop, as always, at the home of Terezinha. She says that Manoel came home from work *doente* (sick), his knees shaking, his legs caving in, so "weak and tired" that he could hardly swallow a few spoonfuls of dinner. She says that her husband suffers from these "nervous crises" (*crises de nervos*) often, especially toward the end of the week when everyone is nervous because there is nothing left in the house to eat. But Manoel will recover, she adds, after he gets a glucose injection at Feliciano's pharmacy.

The theme of nervous hunger and nervous sickness is universal among the people of the Alto do Cruzeiro. It appears, for example, in the stories and vignettes told by youngsters in response to the Thematic Apperception Test (TAT) that I administered to a dozen Alto youths between the ages of nine and fifteen.[2] Their stories had a pressured, almost obsessive quality to them, overdetermined by a free-floating and intrusive hunger anxiety. There was little variety in the themes; the stories all seemed alike, and I soon gave up the exercise. Terezinha describes her fifteen-year-old son as "weak and useless" as well as "emotional and oversensitive," in short, *nervoso*. "He cries for no reason at all," she complains. The source of the boy's fatigue, emotional fragility, and chronic nervousness is made clear in his TAT stories:

> *Card 1* (boy sitting next to a violin): "This boy is thinking about his life. . . . He wants to be able to give things to his children when he grows up. He is going to see to it that they always have something to eat."
> *Card 3BM* (kneeling figure next to a small object): "The boy is crying. . . . He is all alone in the world and he's hungry."
> *Card 3GF* (a young woman with bowed head standing next to a door): "This woman is thinking about what she is going to put on the table when her husband comes home from work. The *feira* basket is empty, and she wishes she could run away. Her husband will be very angry with her."
> *Card 12M* (a man leaning over a boy who is lying down): "This man found this boy on the street and brought him home, and he's trying to revive him. ["What was wrong with him?"] He collapsed from weakness."
> *Card 13BG* (a barefoot boy in front of a log cabin): "This boy is very poor, and his mother and father leave the house every day to look for money and food for the family. Their situation is serious. He is the oldest son, and he stays at home to take care of the others, his brothers and sisters. Now he is crying about what might happen to them. ["What's that?"] Some of them could die."

There was hardly a card that did not elicit from Severino or the other Alto youths questioned a theme of deprivation, sickness, hunger, death, all of them laced with the characteristic symptoms of *nervoso*. This was the case even with pictures meant to evoke themes of sexuality, relaxation, or play. Pedro, an occasional street child whose mother's boyfriend often chased him out of the house, looked for a long time at the card with several men in overalls lying in the grass, supposedly "taking it easy" (card 9BM), before answering, "These men are 'drunk' from overwork. They are lying down in the sugarcane because the sun is so hot. This one here is too weak to get up again. ["Then what?" Pedro shook his head with a troubled expression on his twelve-year-old face.] He's not going to get hired next time. He's completely finished; he's washed up."

Hunger and deprivation have set the people of the Alto do Cruzeiro on edge, have made them lean, irritable, and nervous. Their lives are marked by a free-floating, ontological, existential insecurity. There is not enough, and it is almost inconceivable that there could ever be enough to satisfy basic needs. Perhaps this is what George Foster (1965) meant to imply in his model of "the limited good."[3] It is a worldview that conforms to the reproduction of scarcity in the conflict among *casa*, *rua*, and *mata*, plantation, town, and forest. Those who suffer chronic deprivations are, not surprisingly, nervous and insecure. Reflecting on their social condition, the foresters refer to themselves as "weak," "shaky," "irritable," "off balance," and paralyzed, as if without a leg to stand on. These metaphors used so often in the everyday conversations of Alto people mimic the physiological symptoms of hunger. There is an exchange of meanings, images representations, between the body personal and the collective and symbolic body social.

If food and sex are idioms through which the people of the Alto reflect on their social condition as *os pobres*, nerves and nervousness provide an idiom through which they reflect on their hunger and hunger anxiety. The consequences are at once unintended and far-reaching. The prototypical limited good on the Alto do Cruzeiro is food, and nervous hunger is the prototypical form of *nervoso* or *doença de nervos* (nervous sickness), an expansive and polysemic folk syndrome. Here I explore the process through which a population, only recently incorporated into the biomedical health care system, becomes prey to the medicalization of their needs. *Nervos*, a rich folk conceptual scheme for describing relations among mind, body, and social body, is appropriated by medicine and transformed into something other: a biomedical disease that alienates mind from body and that conceals the social relations of sickness. The madness, the *delírio de fome*, once understood as a terrifying end point in the experience of angry and collective starvation, is transformed into a personal and "psychological" problem, one that requires medication. In this way hunger is isolated and denied, and an individualized discourse on sickness comes to replace a more radical and socialized discourse on hunger.

The medical appropriation of the folk syndrome *nervoso*, the failure of those in power to recognize in the diffuse symptoms of *nervos* the signs of nervous hunger, and their willingness to treat "it" with tranquilizers, vitamins, sleeping pills, and elixirs are glaring examples of bad faith and of the misuse of medical knowledge. They are also an oblique but powerful defense strategy of the state. The irritable hunger of the squatters exists as a standing critique of, and therefore a threat to, the social order, itself at this transformative juncture shaky, nervous, and irritable. Hence, the "nervous system," a notion I have borrowed from Taussig (1989a) but with a different interpretive slant so as to link the three bodies: the existential body self, the representational social body, and the body politic, all of them "nervous." The medicalization of hunger and childhood malnutrition in the clinics, pharmacies, and political chambers of Bom Jesus da Mata represents a macabre performance of distorted institutional and political relations.

Gradually the hungry people of Bom Jesus da Mata have come to believe that they desperately need what is readily given to them, and they have forgotten that what they need most is what is cleverly denied. But there is more to the story than bad faith and false consciousness, for both obscure the symbolic uses of *nervoso*, its expression of the refusal of Alto men (in particular) to accept at face value the logic and terms of their abuse at the "foot" of the sugarcane. And so my analysis must be taken as incomplete and contradictory, like reality itself.

CRITICAL CONSCIOUSNESS: THE METHOD OF PAULO FREIRE

> The aspect of things that are most important for us are hidden because of their simplicity and familiarity. (One is unable to notice something because it is always right before one's eyes.) Ludwig Wittgenstein (cited in Sacks 1985: 42)

Insofar as I am engaged here in an ongoing work of praxis—theory derived in the context of political practice—the themes I am addressing did not arise in a social vacuum. Rather, they emerged within open and often chaotic discussions of the weekly *assembléia geral* of UPAC, the squatters' association, since 1982 also the ecclesiastical base community of the Alto do Cruzeiro.[4]

The "method" of the Brazilian base community movement is derived from Paulo Freire's (1970, 1973) *conscientização*, meaning action based on critical reflection. The method begins at the "base," ground level, with the immediately perceived and the "practically" true, that is, the given, experiential world. This reality is then subjected to a relentless form of deconstruction and to critical, oppositional, and "negative" questioning. What is revealed and what is concealed in our commonsense perceptions of reality? Paradoxes are proposed. Whose interests are being served? Whose needs are being ignored? The Freire method is open and dialogic. Any member of the community can suggest "key words" or generative themes for critical reflection, discussion, and clarification, including such words as *fome*, *nervos*, *susto* (fright), *à míngua de* (for lack of, scarcity of), or *jeito* (a knack, way, means, solution). And so part of this analysis was derived in this public and contested manner at UPAC meetings with the residents of the Alto. Out of the dialogue, at least in theory, emerges a critical form of practice.

The essential insight, derived from European critical theory (see Geuss 1981: 1–3), is that commonsense reality may be false, illusory, and oppressive. It is an insight shared with all contemporary critical epistemologies, including modern psychoanalysis, feminism, and Marxism. All variants of modern critical theory work at the essential task of stripping away the surface forms of reality to expose concealed and buried truths. Their aim then, is to "speak truth" to power and domination, in individuals and in submerged social groups or classes. These are reflexive, rather than objective, epistemologies. Theory is regarded as a tool for illumination and for praxis. Action without reflection is wrongheaded; reflection without action is self-indulgent.

At the heart of all critical theories and methods is a critique of ideology and power. Ideologies (whether political, economic, or religious) can mystify reality, obscure relations of power and domination, and prevent people from grasping their situation in the world. Specific forms of consciousness may be called "ideological" whenever they are invoked to sustain, legitimate, or stabilize particular institutions or social practices. When these institutional arrangements and practices reproduce inequality, domination, and human suffering, the aims of critical theory are emancipatory. The process of "liberation" is complicated, however, by the unreflexive complicity and psychological identification of people with the very ideologies and practices that are their own undoing. Here, Antonio Gramsci's notion of hegemony is useful. Gramsci (1971: chap. 1) recognized that the dominant classes exercised their power both directly through the state and indirectly through a merging with civil society and identification of their interests with broad cultural ideas and aims. It is through this blend of instrumental force and the expressive, contradictory (but also consensual) common sense of everyday culture that hegemony operates as a hybrid of coercion and consensus. The role of "traditional" intellectuals, the bourgeois agents of the social consensus, is pivotal in maintaining hegemonic ideas and practices.

Increasingly in modern bureaucratic states, technicians and professionals come to play the role of traditional intellectuals in sustaining commonsense definitions of reality through their highly specialized and validating forms of discourse. Gramsci anticipated Foucault, both in terms of understanding the capillary nature of diffuse power circuits in modern states and in terms of identifying the crucial role of "expert" forms of power/knowledge in sustaining the commonsense order of things. In the context of this discussion, doctors occupy the pivotal role of "traditional" intellectuals whose function, in part, is to misidentify, to fail to see the secret indignation of the sick poor expressed in the inchoate folk idiom *nervos*.

But anthropologists, too, can play the role of the "traditional" intellectual. The specific issues dealt with here, the concealment of hunger in the folk (ethnomedical), and later in the biomedical, discourse on *nervos*, concern the way that people can come not only to acquiesce but even to participate in their own undoing. For anthropologists to deny, because it implies a privileged position (i.e., the power of the outsider to name an ill or a wrong) and because it is not pretty, the extent to which dominated people come to play the role, finally, of their own executioners is to collaborate with the relations of power and silence that allow the destruction to continue.

Hence, my analysis is addressed to multiple audiences. First, it is offered to my *companheiros* in UPAC as a tool for discussion, reflection, and clarification and as a challenge to collective action. Second, it is addressed to my colleagues in anthropology. As social scientists (not social revolutionaries) critical practice implies for us not so much a practical as an epistemological struggle. Here the contested domain is anthropology itself. It concerns the way in which knowledge is generated, the interests it serves, and the challenge to make our discipline more relevant and nonoppressive to the people we study. And so the "bad faith" community to which I refer in this chapter has analogues in the applied anthropological community. What prevents *us* from developing a radical discourse on the suffering of those populations that, to use Taussig's (1978) apt turn of phrase, provide us with our livelihood? What prevents us from becoming "organic" intellectuals, willing to cast our lots with, and cleave to, the oppressed in the small, hopefully not totally meaningless ways that we can? Finally, this analysis is addressed to physician-practitioners as a challenge to participate in Brazil with the new Church in putting their resources and loyalties squarely on the side of suffering humanity . . . and letting the political chips and consequences fall where they may.

NERVOS AND *FRAQUEZA*: METAPHORS TO DIE BY

> Excuse me doctor, but you left out something very important in those questions. You never asked me anything about mental problems. . . . The patient then proceeded to talk about nervousness, *nervoso*, and he said that the biggest problem that Brazilians had was hunger. He said that he himself was extremely nervous and shaky and that he suffered from palpitations in the head, that he'd gone to many doctors, had many X-rays taken, but that he continued to be very nervous.
> *Do Relatório Sobre o Nervoso* (cited in Duarte 1986: 143)

Nervos, *nervoso*, or *doença de nervos* is a large and expansive folk diagnostic category of distress. It is, along with such related conditions as *fraqueza* (weakness) and *loucura* (madness), seething with meanings (some of them contradictory) that have to be unraveled and decoded for what the terms reveal as well as conceal. In fact, *nervos* is a common complaint among poor and marginalized people in many parts of the world, but especially in the Mediterranean and in Latin America. The phenomenon has been the subject of extensive inquiries by anthropologists, who have tended (as with the analysis of hunger) toward symbolic and psychological interpretations. *Nervos* has generally been understood as a flexible folk idiom of distress having its probable origins in Greek humoral pathology. Often *nervos* is described as the somatization of emotional stress originating in domestic or work relations. Gender conflicts (D. Davis 1983), status deprivation (Low 1981), and marital tensions and suppressed rage (Lock & Dunk 1987) have been suspected in the etymology of *nervos* (or *nervios*, *nevra*, or "bad nerves," depending on locality). In all, *nervos* is a broad folk syndrome (hardly culturally specific) under which can sometimes fall other common folk afflictions such as *pasmo* (nervous paralysis) or *susto* (magical fright), *mau olhado* (evil eye), and "falling out" syndrome among poor black Americans.

What all of these ills have in common is a core set of symptoms. All are "wasting" sicknesses, gravely debilitating, sometimes chronic, that leave the victim weak, shaky, dizzy and disoriented, tired and confused, sad and depressed, and alternately elated or enraged. It is curious that in the vast and for the most part uninspiring literature on *nervos*, there is no mention of the correspondence between the symptoms of *nervos* and the physiological effects of hunger. I would not want to make the mistake of simply equating the two (conceptually and symbolically, at least, *nervos* and *fome* are quite distinct in the minds of the people of the Alto) or suggest that in stripping away the cultural layers that surround a diagnosis of *nervos*, one will *always* find the primary, existential, subjective experience of hunger, the *delírio de fome*, at its base. Nonetheless, it does *not* seem likely that the situation I am describing here is completely unique to Northeast Brazil.

On the Alto do Cruzeiro today *nervos* has become the primary idiom through which both hunger and hunger anxiety (as well as many other ills and afflictions) are expressed. People are more likely today to describe their misery in terms of *nervos* than in terms of hunger. They will say, "I couldn't sleep all night, and I woke up crying and shaking with *nervos*" before they will say, "I went to bed hungry, and then I woke up shaking, nervous, and angry," although the latter is often implied in the former. Sleeping disorders are not surprising in a population raised from early childhood with the mandate to go to bed early when they are hungry. People on the Alto sleep off hunger the way we tend to sleep off a bad drunk.

Closely related to *nervos* is the idiom of *fraqueza*; a person who "suffers from nerves" is understood to be both sick and weak, lacking in strength, stamina, and resistance. And weakness has physical, social, and moral dimensions. Tired, overworked, and chronically malnourished squatters see themselves and their children as innately sick and weak, constitutionally nervous, and in need of medications and doctoring.

But this was not always so. There was a time, even at the start of the politically repressive years of the mid-1960s, when the people of the Alto spoke freely of fainting from hunger. Today one hears of people fainting from "weakness" or nerves, a presumed personal deficiency. There was a time not long ago when people of the Alto understood nervousness (and rage) as a primary symptom of hunger, as the *delírio de fome*. Today hunger (like racism) is a disallowed discourse in the shantytowns of Bom Jesus da Mata, and the rage and the dangerous madness of hunger have been metaphorized. "It doesn't help [*não adianta*] to complain of hunger," offers Manoel. Consequently, today the only "madness" of hunger is the delirium that allows hungry people to see in their wasted and tremulous limbs a chronic feebleness of body and mind.

The transition from a popular discourse on hunger to one on sickness is subtle but essential in the perception of the body and its needs. A hungry body needs food. A sick and "nervous" body needs medications. A hungry body exists as a potent critique of the society in which it exists. A sick body implicates no one. Such is the special privilege of sickness as a *neutral* social role, its exemptive status. In sickness there is (ideally) no blame, no guilt, no responsibility. Sickness falls into the moral category of bad things that "just happen" to people. Not only the sick person but society and its "sickening" social relations (see Illich 1976) are gotten off the hook. Although the abuses of the sickness exemption by "malingering" patients are well known to clinicians as well as to medical sociologists (see Parsons & Fox 1952), here I wish to explore a "malingering" social system.

DIALOGUES AND DECONSTRUCTIONS:
DECODING POPULAR CULTURE

I told [the director of a city school] that I was nervous and that there were times
I actually thought of killing myself. She told me that I should try to be calmer.
And I told her that there were days when I had nothing to feed my children.
Carolina Maria de Jesus (1962: 92)

Here is the voice of Carolina Maria de Jesus, certainly one of the most passionate
and literate voices to have come from the Brazilian *favela*—and one of the most
critically self-reflexive as well. The clarity of Carolina's vision stands apart; she is
one of Gramsci's "organic intellectuals" speaking out eloquently on behalf of her
class.[5] Most individuals trapped by their poverty in a cycle of sickness, worry,
and despair are less aware, less critically reflective about their lives, lives that are,
as one woman of the Alto put it, "too painful to think about." It is not surprising, then, that attempts to elicit discussions about *nervos*, *fraqueza*, and *fome* so
often resulted in popular interpretations that were fuzzy, inconsistent, and not
infrequently contradictory. It is usual for the anthropologist to impose an order
on her subject matter, to overlook the inconsistencies in the ways in which people
make sense of the world in which they live. Here, an analysis of "epistemic
murk" and contradiction is the task at hand.

We begin with the following conversation, which took place one afternoon on
the doorstep of Black Irene's house, where several neighbors were gathered during the quiet part of the day after lunch. One can note the juxtaposition of folk
and biomedical idioms and the considerable ambiguity and confusion that allow
for the medicalization of hunger and hunger anxiety. Everything from anger, sadness, discontent, and hunger through parasitic infections is understood in terms
of the folk ailment. *Nervos* functions as a "master illness" or a master explanatory model that is similar to the folk concept of "stress" as it is invoked by
distressed middle-class North Americans.

Sebastiana initiated the discussion with a sigh: "As for me, I'm always sick; I
have weak nerves."

"What are your symptoms?"

"Trembling, a chill in my bones. Sometimes I shake until I fall down."

Maria Teresa interjected, "There are many kinds of nerves: anger nerves, fear
nerves, worrier's nerves, falling down nerves, overwork nerves, and sufferers"
nerves."

"What are anger nerves about?"

Black Irene said, "That's like when your *patroa* says something that really
ticks you off but because she's your boss you can't say anything, but inside you
are so angry that you could kill her. The next day you are likely to wake up
trembling with anger nerves."

"And fear nerves?"

Terezinha explained that her fifteen-year-old son, Severino, had suffered from
nervos de medo, "fear nerves," ever since the night Black Irene's mother died:

"Irene gave out such a blood-curdling yell in the middle of the night that we all woke with a great *susto*. Severino leapt from his hammock and ran to see what had happened. When he came back from Irene's house, he was so shook up that he collapsed on the floor clutching his heart in an *agonia* of *nervos*. Ever since that night he has suffered from *nervos*."

"But as for me," Beatrice broke in, "I suffer only from overwork nerves. I've washed clothes all my life, for almost sixty years, and now my body is as beaten down and worn out as Dona Dora's bed sheets [a slur against her miserly *patroa*]. When I come home from the river with that heavy basin of wet laundry on my head, my knees begin to shake, and sometimes I lose my balance and fall right on my face. What humiliation!"

"Is there a cure for overwork nerves?"

"Sometimes I take tonics and vitamin A."

"Others take nerve pills and tranquilizers."

"Don't forget about sleeping pills."

"Why sleeping pills?"

"At night when everything is still," explained Sebastiana, "so dark, and so *esquisito* [strange], time passes by slowly. The night is long. I almost go mad with nerves at times like that. I think of so many things; so many sad and bitter thoughts cross my mind: memories of my childhood and how hard I was made to work at the foot of the cane and on an empty stomach. Then the tremors begin, and I have to get out of bed. It's no use, I won't sleep anymore that night. *A minha doença e minha vida mesmo*; my illness is really just my own life."

Terezinha added, "*E os aperreios da família*, and the worries and aggravations of family life."

"But you can get *nervos* from worms and parasites, too," broke in Black Irene, putting a new twist on the discussion. "I almost died from it. Twice they carried me in an ambulance to the hospital in Recife. The first time I was in crisis with pains and shaking. My mouth was full of blood. It was my liver; the worms had gotten to it. They were getting fat on me! The next time it was a crisis from amoebas. I had to take so many pills, every kind, but in the end it was useless. Amoebas never die. They leave eggs inside you and the pills can't kill them. So they just keep on growing and growing until they take up all the room inside you. Sometimes they're quiet, but when they wake up and start attacking you, that's when you have a *crise de nervos*."

Terezinha interjected, tapping on her own bloated belly, "*Tá vendo*? When I have an attack of amoebas I can feel them, tum, tum, tum, drumming on the inside of my belly. There's an army of the nasty things inside there. Sometimes I'll go for a whole week without defecating. What miserable things they are! Then, when I finally lie down at night, I can hear brr, brr, brr, *fervendo* [boiling] inside me. What are they doing now? I ask the doctor for pills to attack the amoebas, but he gives me nerve pills so that they won't keep me awake at night."

It is clear that *nervos* is a polysemic phenomenon, an explanation for tiredness, weakness, irritability, the shakes, headaches, angers and resentments, grief, parasitic infections ... *and* hunger. What I wish to explore are the correspondences between *nervos* and hunger. I am not arguing, however, that *nervos* can be reduced to hunger alone or that *nervoso* is an exclusively poor or working-class phenomenon. *Nervos* is an elastic category, an all-purpose complaint, one that can be invoked by a frustrated middle class to express its dashed expectations in the wake of the decanonized economic miracle, by the urban working class to express its condition of relative powerlessness (see Duarte 1986; Cardoso 1987) *and* by an impoverished class of displaced sugarcane cutters and their families to express their hunger.

In this particular context, the relevant question to be asked is, How have these people come to see themselves primarily as nervous and only secondarily as hungry? How is it that the mortally tired cane cutters and washerwomen define themselves as weak rather than as exploited? Worse, when overwork and exploitation *are* recognized, how in the world do these get reinterpreted as an illness, *nervos de trabalhar muito*, for which the appropriate cure is a tonic, vitamin A, or a sugar injection? Finally, how does it happen that chronically hungry people "eat" medicines while going without food? As one woman commented on the choice between buying food or purchasing a tranquilizer for a nervous family member: "*Ou se come ou se faz outra coisa*—Either you can eat or you can do something else [with the money you have]." That something is, more often than not, a trip to the pharmacy, of which there are more than a dozen in the small town of Bom Jesus.

So I decided finally to challenge my friends on their *nervos* and *fraqueza*. During a small UPAC meeting with the leaders and several activist women of the Alto present, I launched the suggestion "Why don't we do some *conscientização* about *nervos*? People say they are nervous and weak, but a lot of what is called *nervos* looks like hunger to me. It's the *nervousness* of hunger."

The women laughed and shook their heads. "No, you're confused," they offered. "*Nervos* is one thing, and *fome* is another." Beatrice tried to explain: "*Fome* is like this: a person arrives at *feira* almost crazy, with a stomachache, shaking and nervous, and then she sees spots and bright lights in front of her eyes and hears a buzzing in her ears. The next thing she faints from hunger. *Nervos* is something else. It comes from weakness or from worries and perturbations in the head. You can't sleep, your heart pounds, your hands begin to shake and then your legs. You can have a headache. Finally, your legs get soft. They can't hold you up anymore, and so you fall over; you pass out."

"And the weakness, where does that come from?"

"That's because we are just like that, poor and weak."

"And hungry?"

"Yes, we are hungry, too . . . and sick."

"So weakness, hunger, and *nervos* are sometimes the same thing?"

"No, they are very different."

"You'll have to explain it better then."

Irene rushed in to rescue Beatrice: "*Fome* starts in your belly, and it rises up to your head and makes you dizzy and disoriented, without balance. If you eat something, you feel better right away. The trembling stops. *Nervos* begins in your head, and it can travel anywhere in the body—to your heart or to your liver or to your legs."

Biu interjected, "When I suffer a *crise de nervos*, it gives me an *agonia* in my heart. It can give a person a fit. It can paralyze you so you can't walk."

"Yes, *nervos* can even kill you," continued Beatrice.

"Do men suffer from *nervos*?"

Zefinha replied, "Here on the Alto a lot of men suffer from nerves. They have heart palpitations, headaches, no appetite, and tiredness, Poor things, some even have trouble walking up the Alto. Some get agitated and wild and try to beat their wife or children. Others have such pain that you can hear them screaming in the night."

"What's the difference between weakness and nerves?"

Biu answered, "*Fraqueza* comes from inside a person, from their own organism. Some people are born weak like that. They can't take much in life. Everything affects them strongly because their body isn't well organized. Every little thing that happens makes them sick. Then there is the weakness that comes from anemia in the blood or from parasites or from amoebas or from tired lungs."

"Is there a treatment for *fraqueza*?"

Zefinha replied, "You can drink a strong *vitamina caseira* [a homemade vitamin tonic] made from Nescau [a Nestlé's powdered-milk fortifier], pineapple, apples, beets, carrots, and oranges. If you drink that once a day, it will strengthen the blood."

"So then hunger *weakens* the blood?" I forged on.

"If you have weak blood," an elderly woman remarked, "you will suffer weakness in the head as well. The veins of the body are connected everywhere and so are the nerves. The nerves in our hands and feet are the same ones in our head. If you eat poorly, you can't be strong; it will affect the blood and the whole organism. Not enough food leads to *fraqueza*, naturally! Your head becomes weak because of a lack of food in the stomach and in the intestines. Weak food leads to weak blood, and weak blood will give you *nervos* because you will have no resistance to anything, and soon you are completely good for nothing."

"But *comadre* Conceição," broke in Teresa, "you can also get *nervos* because of worry. The thought begins in the head, and it starts to build up pressure and give you a headache; and then it spills over, and it can move from the head right to the heart of a person. Then the person can have an *ataque de nervos* with a terrible *agonia* in the chest. Isn't it the head that rules over the body? So bad thoughts can reach the heart and destroy a person because the heart sends bad blood [*sangue ruim*] everywhere in the body and to all the nerves."

Later, João Mariano, the political *orientador* of UPAC, who had been puzzling over the riddle of *nervos*, *fome*, and *fraqueza* since the foregoing meeting, suggested that I visit two men of the Alto, Seu Tomás and Severino Francisco, both of whom were cane cutters until they fell sick and weak from *nervos*. "I think maybe it is nervous hunger, as you say," my friend offered.

Severino Francisco, the proud owner of the tiny Barbearia Unisex (The Unisex Barber and Shave Shop, much to my amusement) on the Rua da Cruz of the Alto do Cruzeiro, looked considerably older than his thirty-five years. He invited me to step inside his shop, although there was barely room for the barber and his client seated on a sturdy kitchen chair in front of a fragment of what was once a much larger mirror. He had been expecting me, and he conducted the "interview" via the mirror so that he could observe his work and have eye contact with me simultaneously. He apologized for the "weak" condition of his business and mused about the expansion he could effect once he had purchased a "proper" barber's chair. He had been cutting hair for seven years, ever since he had been cut down by his illness. Yes, it was *nervos*, he assured me, although he added, "But the doctors here don't understand anything about this illness. All they know is how to write prescriptions."

Until the age of twenty Severino was a man "of health and of strength" on the Alto do Cruzeiro. He began cutting cane with his father when he was a boy of eight. His only schooling was a year of alphabetization in the local grade school. He worked in the cane without stop until his illness began with stomachaches, tiredness, and general malaise. He lost his appetite, and with his empty stomach, he suffered from the dry heaves. He lost his "taste" for food, and he now lived on coffee. Gradually his legs became weak and soft; they "collapsed" under him. He thought perhaps he might have burst a vein. Or maybe he had become sick from working in the cold rain while his body was heated up from the exertion of his labor. Or perhaps he had hurt himself by lifting too many stalks of cut cane. In any event, it had gotten so bad that he had had to quit working in the fields, and then he had begun his frustrating search for a true cure.

"What have the doctors told you?" I asked, knowing already from João Mariano that Severino had been to every clinic in Bom Jesus as well as to hospitals in Recife.

"They don't know anything. They never told me what was wrong. They never operated on me. They just kept sending me home with *remédios* for my heart, for my blood, for my liver, for my nerves. Believe me, *só vivo de remédios* [I live on medications]."

Once, during a *crise de nervos*, he began to vomit blood, and he was carried by ambulance to a hospital in Recife, where he "really started going down hill." The nurses told his wife that there was no hope for him, and so she returned to Bom Jesus. The next day she sent for his body with a rented funeral car. But when the car arrived, the nurses exclaimed. "He got lucky; he escaped [death]!"

"But to tell you the truth, I don't know if I was lucky or not," Severino continued, "because I never did get better. Even today only a part of me is alive. I have no strength; my legs have no 'force' in them. All I have left are my hands [and he waved them gracefully in the air over the head of his young client]. My hands are as strong and as steady as a rock; the miserable *nervos* never got to them!

"At first I had no way of making a living. What does a cane cutter know besides his machete and his *foice* [sharp hoe]? I'm a donkey; I can't even read the sign outside my shop! And without my disability papers signed by the doctors, I can't get any benefits. Those bastards denied me what I had coming to me after all those years in the cane! So here I am today, a cane cutter cutting hair instead. Bah! As if this were any kind of work for a real man [*homem mesmo*].

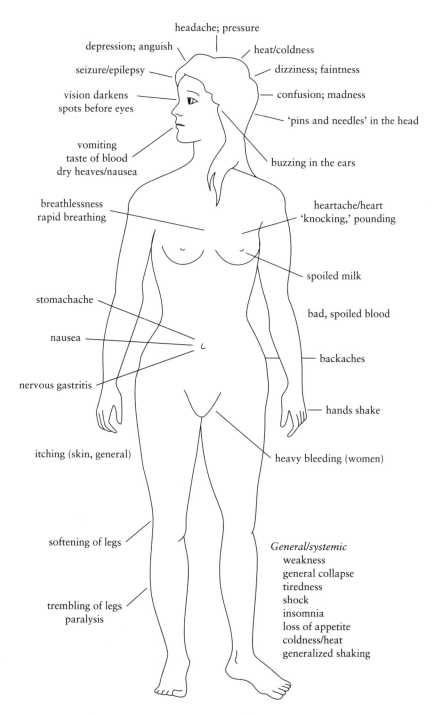

Figure 19.1 Common sites and symptoms of *nervos*

This job is a *besteira* [a bit of nonsense]. Men today are worse than women [and he fairly glowered in his mirror at the nervous young man captive in his chair]. They want me to make them into little dolls with curls and waves and streaks in their hair. Tsk! The men today are all *veados* [queer]! And with all this, I barely make enough to feed my wife and children. The *caçula* [the last born] cries for milk all the time, but I have to deny her because out of the little *besteira* that I earn I have to put something aside every week for my medicines. The pharmacy won't let me buy them on credit. And like I told you, I live on medications. Would you call this a life?"

A group of men, unemployed and sitting in front of a little candy stand at the top of the Alto, directed me to the home of Seu Tomás. "Yes, his situation is truly *péssimo* [miserable]," they assured me and perhaps themselves as well. (It is always consoling to find one whose condition is even worse than one's own.) Seu Tomás and his wife were both thirty-two. Tomás apologized for not getting up from his hammock because he was "very weak." There was no place for me to sit down; even the earthen floor was muddy from the last rain. It was a miserable hut crowded with crying babies. "A poor house but rich in children," Seu Tomás joked, with a hint of sarcasm in his tremulous voice. He and his wife, Jane Antônia, had been married for nine years. They had seven children, of whom only one had died, thanks in part (he added) to the Franciscan nun, Sister Juliana, who had brought them a basket of food every week for the previous two years. Seu Tomás had been unemployed for those two years, unable to work in the sugarcane that had been his life since the age of nine.

"What is your problem?"

"A weakness in my lungs and tiredness," he replied, adding that the doctors could find no sign of tuberculosis.

"Anything else?"

"A coldness in my head, pains in my stomach, and a paralysis in my legs. There are days when my legs start to tremble and they can't hold up my body. I also have dizziness and fainting spells."

"Do you eat regular meals?"

"In this house it's a case of eat when you can, and when you can't, you try to sleep until the next day."

"What treatments have you received?"

At this Seu Tomás pulled himself with some difficulty out of his hammock and shuffled over to a small table in the corner. I noted that, like Severino Francisco, Tomás was able to walk but that his movements were stiff and awkward. Later, I asked to palpate his legs, which, although thin, were flexible and responsive to touch. I suspected that the "paralysis" of which Tomás and so many other Alto residents complained was part physical (hunger weakness) and part metaphorical or symbolic. Standing and walking concerned a good deal more than the "simple" acts of locomotion.

Men like Tomás are paralyzed within a stagnant semifeudal plantation economy that treats them as superfluous and dependent. The weakness of which these men complain is as much social structural as physical. They are trapped in a "weak" position. A healthy, vigorous person does not give a thought to the acts of breathing, seeing, walking. These come without thinking, and they go without saying. But these men (and women) have been made exquisitely aware and self-conscious of "automatic" bodily functions. They describe themselves as breathless, wobbly, disoriented, embarrassed, and unsure of their gait. How has this come about? We can begin by asking what it means—symbolically, existentially—to stand upright, to face the world squarely, standing on one's own two feet.

The psychiatrist Erwin Strauss provides us with a clue. Some years ago he wrote about patients in his practice who could "no longer master the seemingly banal arts of standing and walking. They [were] not paralyzed, but under certain conditions, they could not, or felt as if they could not, keep themselves upright. They tremble and quiver. Incomprehensible terror takes away their strength" (1966: 137). Strauss analyzed his patients' existential dilemmas in terms of language. He noted that the expression *to be upright* carries two connotations. It means to be mobile, independent, free. It also means to be honest and just and to "stand by" one's deepest convictions. His patients had been morally compromised in some way. In the Brazilian instance I point to another connotation of "upright posture" in asking what the difference is between "standing up" to someone or something and "lying down," sinking, yielding, succumbing, giving up. In the cases of Severino Francisco and Seu Tomás, the language of the body is the language of defeat. It is as if they have had the wind knocked out of them or their chairs pulled out from under their legs. They have lost their balance. Yet one does not blame these men for their "succumbing" to the overwhelming forces of domination that have stolen their manhood. Their "failure of nerve" is understandable. The cards have been unfairly stacked against them. And yet one wishes, one hopes, one wants to hold out, for more than a chemical solution to their problems in living, indeed their very problem in "being" at all.

Among Tomás's collection of half-used medicines were the usual assortment of antibiotics, painkillers, worm medications, sleeping pills, and vitamins found in most Alto homes. Less common, however, was Tomás's antidepressant.

"Which of these are you taking now?"

Tomás picked up the antibiotic. "This was effective at first. The doctor gave it to me for my lungs. But then it began to offend me. Often I had to swallow the pills on a empty stomach, and they made my stomach pains worse."

"Why are you treating your nerves and not your hunger?"

He laughed. "Who ever heard, Dona Nancí, of a treatment for hunger? Food is the only cure for that."

"Which is worse—hunger or *nervos*?"

"Hunger is worse. When you are sick, like me, it takes a long time for you to die. When you are hungry, you can't be without food for more than a day. You *have* to get something to eat."

"Then why buy medicine rather than food?"

"With medicine you have to pay cash. Sometimes we can get food on credit."

"And yet you say that you and your children often go without food. Why is that?"

"It's easier to get help with *remédios*. You can show up at the *prefeitura* with a prescription, and if it is in stock, Seu Félix will give it to you, or he will contribute something to the cost. But you can't go to the mayor and beg for food!"

"Why not?"

"Why not? Because it's not done. He will tell you to go out and work."

"But you are hungry because you are sick. Isn't that why he's giving you the *remédios*? If you are sick enough to be taking all these drugs, how can you possibly be well enough to work?"

"I'm a *matuto*, Dona Nancí; I have no head to answer a question like that." And so there the dialogue rested, but not before Seu Tomás struck up a pose, leaning and not quite "upright," in front of his table of not-so-magical medicines.

EMBODIED LIVES, SOMATIC CULTURE

How are we to make sense of *nervos*? Are the *Nordestino* cane cutters suffering, in addition to everything else, from a kind of metaphorical delirium that clouds and obscures their vision? Is false consciousness sufficiently explanatory? Or can we best understand *nervos* as an alternative form of embodiment, or body praxis?

Embodiment concerns the ways that people come to "inhabit" their bodies so that these become in every sense of the term "habituated." This is a play on Marcel Mauss's (1950: 97–119) original meaning of "habitus" (a term later appropriated by Pierre Bourdieu) by which Mauss meant all the acquired habits and somatic tactics that represent the "cultural arts" of using and being in the body and in the world. From the phenomenological perspective, all the mundane activities of working, eating, grooming, resting and sleeping, having sex, and getting sick and getting well are forms of body praxis and expressive of dynamic social, cultural, and political relations.

It is easy to overlook the simple observation that people who live by and through their bodies in manual and wage labor—who live by their wits and by their guts—inhabit those bodies and experience them in ways very different from our own. I am suggesting that the structure of individual and collective sentiments down to the feel of one's body is a function of one's position and role in the technical and productive order. Nonetheless, the tendency in biomedicine, psychiatry, and conventional medical anthropology is to standardize our own socially constructed and culturally prescribed mind/body tactics and to understand and label the somatic tactics of others as deviant, pathological, irrational, or inadequate. Here I am referring to the exhaustive and generally unenlightening literature in medical anthropology on "somatization." Arthur and Joan Kleinman (1986), for example, understood "somatization" as a generally maladaptive and fairly primitive defense mechanism involving the deployment of the body in the production or exaggeration of symptoms as a way of expressing negative or hostile feelings. Here I am trying to recuperate and politicize the uses of the body and the secret language of the organs that play such a large part in the lives of many anthropological "subjects."

When I refer to the "somatic culture" of the displaced and marginalized sugar-cane workers of the Alto do Cruzeiro, I mean to imply that theirs is a social class and culture that privilege the body and that instruct them in a close attention to the physical senses and symptoms. Here I am following the lead of the French phenomenologist Luc Boltanski (1984), who in his brilliant monograph translated into Portuguese as *As Classes Sociais e O Corpo* argued that somatic thinking and practice are commonly found among the working and popular classes that extract their basic subsistence from physical labor. He noted the tendency of the poor and working classes in France to communicate with and through the body so that, by contrast, the body praxis of the bourgeois and technical classes may appear alienated and impoverished. In the middle classes personal and social distress is expressed psychologically rather than physically, and the language of the body is silenced and denied. This, incidentally, is viewed as the norm in biomedicine and psychiatry and has consequently affected anthropological thinking as well.

Among the agricultural wage laborers living on the hillside shantytown of Alto do Cruzeiro, who sell their labor for as little as one dollar a day, socioeconomic and political contradictions often take shape in the "natural" contradictions of sick and afflicted bodies. In addition to the expectable epidemics of parasitic and other infectious diseases, there are the more unpredictable explosions of chaotic and unruly symptoms, whose causes do not readily materialize under the microscope. I am referring to symptoms like those associated with *nervos*, the trembling, fainting, seizures, and paralysis of limbs, symptoms that disrespect and breech mind and body, the individual and social bodies. In the exchange of meanings between the body personal and the social body, the nervous-hungry, nervous-weak body of the cane cutter offers itself both as metaphor and metonym for the socio-political system and for the weak position of the rural worker in the current economic order. In "lying down" on the job, in refusing to return to the work that has overdetermined most of their child and adult lives, the workers are employing a body language that can be seen as a form of surrender and as a language of defeat. But one can also see a drama of mockery and refusal. For if the folk ailment *nervos* attacks the legs, it leaves the arms and hands unparalyzed and free for less physically ruinous work, such as cutting hair. And so young men suffering from nervous paralysis can and do press their legitimate claims as "sick men" on their political bosses and patrons to find them alternative, "sitting down" work. In this context *nervos* may be seen as a version of the work slowdown or sickout, the so-called Italian strike.

But *nervos* is an expansive and polysemic folk concept. Women, too, suffer from *nervos*, both the *nervos de trabalhar muito* (the overwork nerves from which male cane cutters also suffer) and the *nervos de sofrer muito* (sufferers' nerves). Sufferers' nerves attack those who have endured a recent, especially a violent, shock or tragedy. Widows and the mothers of husbands and sons who have been murdered in violent altercations in the shantytown or abducted and "disappeared" by the active local death squads . . . are especially prone to the mute, enraged, white-knuckled shaking of sufferers' nerves. In these instances

Taussig's (1989a) notion of the "nervous system" as a generative metaphor linking the tensions of the anatomical nervous system with the chaos and irritability of an unstable social system is useful. And so one could read the current nervousness of the people of the Alto—expressed in an epidemic of *nervoso* —as a collective and embodied response to the nervous political system just now emerging after nearly a quarter century of repressive military rule but with many vestiges of the authoritarian police state still in place. On the Alto do Cruzeiro the military presence is most often felt in the late-night knock on the door, followed by the scuffle and abduction of a loved one—father, husband, or adolescent son.

The "epidemic" of sufferers' nerves, *sustos*, and *pasmos* signifies a general state of alarm, of panic. It is a way of expressing the state of things when one must move back and forth between an acceptance of the given situation as "normal," "expectable," and routine—as "normal" and predictable as one's hunger—and a partial awareness of the real "state of emergency" into which the community has been plunged (see Taussig 1989b: 4). And so the rural workers and moradores of the Alto are thrown from time to time into a state of disequilibrium, nervous agitation, shock, crisis, *nervos*, especially following incidents of violence and police brutality in the shantytown. To raise one's voice in active political protest is impossible and wildly dangerous. To be totally silenced, however, is intolerable. One is a man or a woman, after all. Into "impossible" situations such as these, the nervous, shaking, agitated, angry body may be enlisted to keep alive the perception that a real "state of emergency" exists. In this instance nervous sickness "publicizes" the danger, the fright, the "abnormality of the normal." Black Elena, who has lost both her husband and eldest son to the local death squads, has been struck mute. She *cannot* speak. But she sits outside her hut near the top of the Cruzeiro, dressed in white, and she shakes and trembles and raises her clenched fists in a paroxysm of anger nerves. Who can reduce this complex, somatic, and political idiom to an insipid discourse on patient somatization?

THE BODY AS BATTLEGROUND: THE MADNESS OF *NERVOS*

But there still remain the "negative" expressions of this somatic culture in the tendency of these same exploited and exhausted workers to blame their situation, their daily problems of basic survival, on bodies (their own) that have seemingly collapsed, given way on them. Insofar as they describe the body in terms of its immediate "use" value, they call it "good and strong" or "worthless." A man slaps at his wasted limbs (as though they were detachable appendages from the self) and says that they are now completely "useless." A woman pulls at her breasts or a man clutches his genitals and declares them "finished," "used up," "sucked dry." They describe organs that are "full of water" or "full of pus" and others that are *apodrecem por dentro*, "rotting away from within." "Here," says Dona Irene, "put your ear to my belly. Can you hear that nasty army of critters, those amoebas, chomping away at my liver-loaf?"

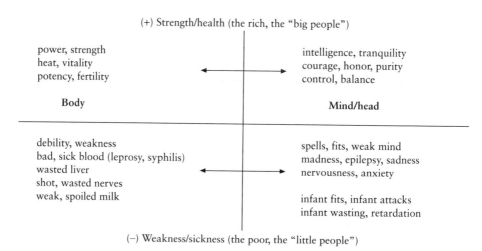

Figure 19.2   The phenomenology of *nervos*

In the folk system *nervos* may be understood as the zero point from which radiates a set of core conceptual oppositions: those between *força/fraqueza* (strength/weakness), *corpo/cabeça* (body/head, mind, morality), and *ricos/pobres* (rich/poor), as illustrated in Figure 19.2. Underlying and uniting these core oppositions is a single, unifying metaphor that gives shape and meaning to people's day-to-day realities. It is the driving and compelling image of "life as a *luta*," as a series of uphill "struggles" along the *caminho*, the "path" of life. One cannot escape this generative metaphor; it crops up everywhere as an all-purpose explanation of the meaning of human existence. The *Nordestino* metaphor of the *luta* portrays life as a veritable battleground between strong and weak, powerful and powerless, young and old, male and female, and, above all, rich and poor. The *luta* requires strength, intelligence, cunning, courage, and know-how (*jeito*). But these physical, psychological, and moral qualities are seen as inequitably distributed, thereby putting the poor, the young, and the female in a relatively disadvantaged and "disgraced" position, making them particularly vulnerable to sickness, suffering, and death. Above all, it is *força*, an elusive, almost animistic constellation of strength, grace, beauty, and power, that triumphs. The folk concept of *força* is similar to what Max Weber (1944: 358–386) meant by charisma. *Força* is the ultimate *jeito*, the real "knack" for survival. The rich and males have *força*; the poor and females have *fraqueza*.

These perceived class and gender differences emerge at birth. Alto women comment on the natural beauty of the infants of the rich, born fat, strong, fair, unblemished, pure, whereas their own infants are born weak, skinny, ugly, already blemished with marks and spots. Some poor infants are born weak and "wasted" before their lives have even begun, and they are labeled with the folk pediatric disorder *gasto* (spent), a quality of incurable *nervoso infantil*. Similarly, adolescent girls are prone to sickness at puberty, a time when the *força de mulher*—the female principle, sexual heat, and vitality—comes rushing from the girl's loins in her *regras*, her periodic menses, the "rules," the discipline of life. The softer among the girls sicken at this time, and some even die.

The rich fare better over all and at all stages of life, just as men fare better than women. The rich are "exempted" from the struggle that is life and appear to lead enchanted lives. Their days and nights are given to erotic pleasures (*sacanagem*) and to indulgence in rich and fatty foods; yet rarely do their bodies show the telltale signs of moral dissipation and wretched excess: bad blood and wasted livers. The poor, who can hardly afford to *brincar* (have fun, also used with reference to sex play) at all, are like "walking corpses" with their *sangue ruim*, *sangue fraco*, *sangue sujo* (bad, weak, dirty blood); their ruined and wasted livers (*fígado estragado*); and their dirty and pus-filled skin eruptions, leprosy, yaws, and syphilis. These illnesses come from "inside", and they are not sent from God but come from man, the wages of extravagance, sin, and wretched excess. The body reflects the interior moral life; it is a template for the soul and the spirit.

Within this ethno-anatomical system there are key sites that serve as conduits and filters for the body, trapping the many impurities that can attack the body from without and weaken it. The liver, the blood, and mother's milk are three such filters, and the very negative evaluation of this organ and these fluids by the people of the Alto reveals a profoundly damaged body image. The filter metaphor is particularly appropriate, however, to people accustomed to worrying about their contaminated water supply and who, in clearing the porous candle that traps filth and slime from their own water supply, often wonder aloud whether their own body "filters" may not be just as filthy.

One falls sick with tuberculosis, venereal disease, leprosy, liver disease, and heart disease because of the way one has lived: an agitated, nervous life given to excess. Bad blood or sick blood is the result of bad living, and people with these nervous diseases are said to be *estragado*, "wasted" by drugs, alcohol, or sex. If unchecked, these afflictions brought on by dissipation and excess lead to *loucura*, the most acute and dangerous form of *nervos*.

Dona Célia, once a powerful and feared old *mãe de santos* (a priestess in the Afro-Brazilian possession religion, Xangô), fell sick after Easter in 1987. Within a few months her already lean body became even more wasted, an *esqueleto* (skeleton), she commented sadly, and she lacked the strength to pull herself out of her hammock. A stay at the local hospital resolved nothing, and she was discharged without a diagnosis or any treatment beyond intravenous *soro* (sugar, salt, potassium, water). "So many ways of being sick," mused Célia, "and yet only one treatment for all the *pobres*." Her illness, she said, was *nervos*. Her nerves were frayed and jumpy and brought on wild flutterings in her chest, so that her heart seemed like a wild, caged bird beating its wings to escape. There were other symptoms as well, but it was an infernal itching that was driving her mad.

When I visited her, Célia was straddling her tattered old hammock, busily casting a spell to bring about the return from São Paulo of an errant husband who had abandoned his young wife, leaving her both very lonely and very pregnant.

I waited respectfully until the long incantation was completed and the candle at her feet was almost extinguished.

"That will 'burn' his ears all right," Célia reassured the tearful young client with a roguish smile on her face. The Franciscan sister, Juliana, passing by the open door, shook her head and said disapprovingly, "Can a reunion brought about by magic be worth anything?"

"Oh, it's worth something, Sister," replied Célia. "I work with the spirit messengers of the saints, not with the devil!"

"How are you doing, *comadre* Célia?" I inquired.

"Poorly, *comadre*," she replied. "I no longer sleep, and the vexation [*vexame*] in my chest never leaves me. I can't eat and every day I grow weaker. I have a terrible *frieza* [coldness] in my head, and it's difficult for me to concentrate. I can't even remember my spells, I'm becoming so forgetful. But it's the strange itch, the *coceira esquisita*, that I can't stand. It gives me such agony, I fear that I am going to lose my mind.'

Célia's neighbors were divided on the diagnosis. Most accepted that Célia's illness was *nervos*, but they disagreed on its origins, whether it came *por dentro* or *por fora* (from inside Célia or from outside) and whether it was a "natural" disease that came from God or an evil disease that came from man (through witchcraft). Those who were friendly to the old woman said that Célia was simply "wasted" from years of hard fieldwork. In other words, hers was simply a case of *nervos de trabalhar muito*. But those who were fearful of the old woman, resented her, or accused her of witchcraft dismissed *nervos* as secondary to her "true" illness: *lepra* (leprosy) resulting from her "sick" and "dirty" blood, the wages of the old sorceress's extravagance. They pointed to Célia's many moral infractions: her ritualized use of marijuana and other drugs in the practice of Xangô, her casting of spells both for good and evil, her many lovers over the years—in short, her generally independent and irreverent attitude toward the dominant Catholic mores of the community.

I stood helplessly by as Célia gradually began to slip away, daily growing more thin and haggard from her ordeal. It was painful to see a once strong and powerfully built woman so physically reduced and humbled. Although I was able to reassure Célia that she was suffering from a bad case of scabies, not from the dreaded *lepra*, I could do nothing to alleviate her nervous symptoms: her weakness, her melancholy, the *agonia* in her heart, and her adamant refusal to eat the small bits of food offered to her by her loyal friends and her few compassionate neighbors. Everything filled her with "nausea," she said. It was no use; she would never eat again.

As a going away present I brought Célia a hand-carved black *figa* (a wooden fetish, in the shape of a clenched fist with a thumb clasped between the fore and middle fingers, used to ward off evil) that I had purchased in Bahia, where Afro-Brazilian religion is practiced with greater acceptance and with more openness than in rural Pernambuco. Célia was so weak that she could barely speak, but she grabbed onto the holy object with a passion that startled me. After implanting a forceful kiss on the *figa*, with it she made a sweeping sign of the cross over her own withered body, and then she blessed me with it as well. I have been blessed many times in my life as a Catholic, but never did I feel as protected and enclosed as in that moment, or as humble.

Less than a week later (but after I had already left Bom Jesus), a few friends gathered to carry Célia in a municipal coffin to her pauper's grave in the local cemetery. There would be no marker and no inscription to honor the remains of the devout sorceress, so I could not visit the grave on my return. Célia's sullen and blasphemous daughter, Ninha, cursed her dead mother and tossed her magical apparatus in the place where pigs forage and garbage is burned on the Alto do Cruzeiro. "She'll pay for that," said Nita Maravilhosa, Nita the Marvelous, who was the old sorceress's apprentice on the Alto do Cruzeiro.

What prevented Célia from eating was, in part, her fear of an impending descent into total madness, *loucura*, the final stage and end point of *nervoso*. "Do you think I am losing my mind?" she would ask me fearfully, and I would try to reassure her, but without success. During this same period, at the time of Célia's rapid decline and anorexia, there were several cases of *loucura*, and the Alto was astir with the scandalous behavior of Vera-Lúcia, the *doida*, the "wild woman" of the Rua dos Índios. Here, the madness of hunger and the hunger of madness merged once and for all in a case of *nervoso* that would not soon be forgotten.

"Vera-Lúcia would never do that," her fifty-two-year-old mother said without looking up from the floor, where she sat busily weaving a large basket of rushes. "She would never kill her own child." I had come to the slippery cliff called the second crossway of the Rua dos Índios in search of a woman named Vera-Lúcia who had registered the deaths of three small children during a period of eighteen months. The last to die, a two-year-old named Maria das Graças, was treated in the local hospital, and her death certificate listed the cause of death as *pancada na cabeça*, "a blow to the head."

"The baby was pushed down the ravine by the crazy deaf-mute daughter of Maria Santos," offered Vera's mother. "The other two died of *gasto*." As we spoke, Vera-Lúcia, her belly huge with another child, sat rocking in a corner with a slightly bemused, absorbed, and distant expression, When I walked over and gently ran my hand over her abdomen, Vera lashed out, "Take care of your own belly; mine is full of shit." Her mother then dropped all pretense to explain how impossible it was for a poor widow to care for a daughter who was both crazy and violent.

"When Vera-Lúcia is having a fit, an *ataque de nervos*," she began, "there is no one who can control her. She is totally fierce. You have to tie her down, or else she will break everything in the house. It's a *quebradeira mesmo*: glass breaking, plates flying, chairs overturned, name calling, bad words, even cursing Jesus and the saints. Sometimes she is so raving that she foams like a wild dog. But without the right connections, I can't even have her taken away to the asylum in Recife. I wonder whether living with a *doida* can make you crazy as well."

"Even as a baby Vera was always sick. She had weak nerves, and she suffered from *pereba* [infected sores] in her mouth and on her head. She couldn't eat anything except *papa d'água*, and she was as skinny as a stick. Once she came so close to dying that I carried her to church with the candle in her hand. It was a pity that God didn't take her then. But she survived, and now look what I have! A weak family can't support a person so *nervoso* and *fraca de juízo* as this. Once she woke up in a fit. It was during the full moon, and she began to bang her head against the wall, shaking and trembling all over with foam coming from her mouth. I washed a piece of raw meat around her mouth and threw it to a stray dog hoping that the *raiva* [madness] might pass into the animal and leave my daughter alone, but it was not to be. The wretched dog lived! I'll tell you something: with these nervous attacks there are no cures. If doctors knew how to cure this disease, the hospitals for the *doidos* in Recife wouldn't be so crowded. One has to accept what God wants. I only wish that God had wanted to take her when she was a baby."

"How long has she been ill this time?"

"Since Holy Week; since the night of Holy Thursday up until this day I have had no peace. On Good Friday I got on my knees and started praying, 'Blood of Christ, you have the power. Remove this nervous attack from my daughter; make her well.' But Vera heard me praying, and she yelled from the next room, 'I'd like to see this wretched blood of Christ spilled on the floor!' I shuddered at her blasphemies. I can only think that she has been bewitched by a sorcerer. Only Jesus can heal her, but I am afraid to bring her to church.

"Once I gave her a little statue of Cristo Redentor [a replica of the famous Christ Redeemer, the patron saint of Rio, who stands with arms outstretched at the top of Corcovado], and she became agitated. She smashed it to bits, saying, 'Once you were Cristo Redentor [Christ the Redeemer], but now you are Cristo Rebentado [Christ the Destroyed]!' And she laughed so that it froze my blood. On the night of Good Friday I walked her to the top of the Alto, and when we reached the crucifix, she became wild again. She flung herself at the cross, saying, 'Jesus, come down from there; I want to kill you myself!' But she didn't mean it because the next night she ran out of the house, and I found her at the foot of the cross where she was hitting herself with a *foice*. 'Just let me die here,' she was saying. I embraced her and she was shivering; there had been a terrible downpour. She began to cry, and finally she was able to pray, 'If you are Jesus, come down from your cross.' They say that even the devil can quote the Bible, but what she said didn't come from the devil, Nancí. Vera said to the Cristo, 'Feed your lambs; feed your sheep.'"

Such is the madness of *nervos* and the hunger of madness on the Alto do Cruzeiro. But despite her prayers, Vera-Lúcia didn't get better, and her new baby daughter survived only a few weeks. "It was a blessing," her mother told me when I returned in 1988 during the celebrations of *carnaval*. Vera-Lúcia was putting on her makeup and costume to join a local *bloco* of "Gypsies" who would be dancing in the streets below the Alto. A diagonal smear of very red lipstick traversed her lips to her chin. She flashed me a wild-eyed grin.

Nervos is a social illness. It speaks to the ruptures, fault lines, and glaring social contradictions in *Nordestino* society. It is a commentary on the precarious conditions of Alto life. *Doença de nervos* announces a general crisis or general collapse of the body as well as a disorganization of social relations. What, after all, does it mean to say, as did Sebastiana, "My sickness is really just my life," my nervous, agitated, threatened life? *Fraqueza* is as much a statement of social as of individual "weakness," for the people of the Alto are accustomed to referring to their home, work, food, or marketplace (as well as their own bodies) as *fraco*. The metaphor of the *luta* and its accompanying moral economy of the body, expressed through the idioms of nervousness and weakness, are a microcosm of the moral economy of the plantation society in which strength, force, and power always win. *Nervos* and *fraqueza* are poignant reminders of the miserable conditions of Alto life, where individuals must often compete for precious little.

Rather than a torrent of indiscriminate sensations and symptoms, *nervos* is a somewhat inchoate, oblique, but nonetheless critical reflection by the poor on their bodies and on the work that has sapped their force and their vitality, leaving them dizzy, unbalanced, and, as it were, without "a leg to stand on" (cf. Sacks 1984). But *nervos* is also the "double," the second and "social" illness that has gathered around the primary experience of chronic hunger, a hunger that has made them irritable, depressed, angry, and tired and has paralyzed them so that they sense their legs giving way beneath the weight of their affliction.

On the one hand, *nervos* speaks to a profound sort of mind/body alienation, a collective delusion such that the sick-poor of the Alto can, like Seu Manoel, fall into a mood of self-blaming that is painful to witness, angrily calling himself a worthless *rato de mato* (forest rat) who is *inutilizado*, "useless," a zero. On the other hand, the discourse on *nervos* speaks obliquely to the structural "weaknesses" of the social, economic, and moral order. The idiom of *nervos* also allows hungry, irritable, and angry *Nordestinos* a "safe" way to express and register their anger and discontent. The recent history of the persecution of the Peasant Leagues and the rural labor movement in Pernambuco has impressed on rural workers the political reality in which they live. If it is dangerous to engage in political protest, and if it is, as Biu suggests, pointless to *reclamar com Deus*, to "complain to, or argue with, God" (and it would seem so), hungry and frustrated people are left with the possibility of transforming angry and nervous hunger into an illness, covertly expressing their disallowed feelings and sensations through the idiom of *nervos*, now cast as a "mental" problem. When they do so, the health care system, the pharmaceutical industry, commerce, and the political machinery of the community are fully prepared to back them up in their unhappy and anything but free "choice" of symptoms.

Notes

1. Biu is a common nickname for both men and women among the dozens of Severinas and Severinos of the Alto, including several couples whose members are both named Biu.
2. The TAT consists of a series of standardized pictures that reflect everyday characters in a variety of poses, situations, and moods. The individual is asked to make up a story

for each picture and to tell what each character in the picture is thinking and feeling. The TAT is a straightforward projective test, relatively free of cultural bias and requires no depth-psychological analysis. One can read the responses to the pictures for their manifest content; themes, dilemmas, and emotions emerge right on the surface.

3. Foster's much maligned model of the "limited good" worldview of Mexican peasants who acted *as if* all material and psychological "goods" were in short supply so that one man or woman's gain was seen as another's loss is deficient only in its failure to analyze the social relations of production that make this worldview an accurate assessment of the social reality in which most contemporary peasants live. More important, however, is the precapitalist orientation to "goods" valued for use and not for surplus that is encoded in this peasant philosophy, a philosophy that is antagonistic to capitalist relations of work and production. Limited good thinking can be seen as a healthy antidote to the industrial capitalist fantasy of "unlimited goods." It is only a negative view if one sees the world through the lens of the Protestant work ethic and all that it entails.

4. In 1968 in Medellín the Catholic bishops of Latin America recommended the formation of ecclesiastical base communities through which a new "popular church" dedicated to a "preferential option for the poor" could be put into direct practice. These base communities are usually neighborhood organizations where people gather to reflect on the scriptures in light of their everyday practical problems in living. The Brazilian theologian of liberation, Clodovis Boff (1978), called for a grounded, down-to-earth theology, a *teologia-pé-no-chão* in which priests would serve as Gramscian organic intellectuals directly connected with popular struggles for liberation.

5. "All men are intellectuals," wrote Gramsci, "but all men do not have the function of intellectuals in society" (1957: 121). "Organic" intellectuals are those who arise out of, and are clearly identified with, a specific class. An impoverished or a working class is as capable of producing its own intellectuals as is the bourgeoisie.

References

Boff, Clodovis. 1978. *Teologia Pé-no-Chão*. Petrópolis: Vozes.
Boltanski, Luc. 1984. *As Classes Sociais e o Corpo*. Rio de Janeiro: Graal.
Cardoso, Marina D. 1987. "Médicos e Clientela: Sobre a Assistência Psiquiátrica a Coletividade." Masters thesis, Universidade Federal de Rio de Janeiro, Museu Nacional.
Davis, Dona. 1983. *Blood and Nerves*. St. John's Institute of Social and Economic Research, Memorial University of Newfoundland.
De Jesus, Carolina Maria. 1962. *Child of the Dark*. New York: Dutton. (Translation of 1960. *Quarto de Despejo*. Rio de Janeiro: Livraria Francisco Alves.)
Duarte, Luíz Fernando. 1986. *Da Vida Nervosa*. Rio de Janeiro: Vozes.
Engels, Friedrich. [1845] 1958. *The Condition of the Working Class in England*. Stanford, Calif.: Stanford University Press.
Foster, George M. 1965. "Peasant Society and the Image of the Limited Good." *American Anthropologist* 67 (2):293–315.
Freire, Paulo. 1970. *Pedagogy of the Oppressed*. New York: Seabury.
—— 1973. *Education for Critical Consciousness*. New York: Seabury.
Geuss, Raymond. 1981. *The Idea of Critical Theory*. Cambridge: Cambridge University Press.
Gramsci, Antonio. 1957. *The Modern Prince and Other Writings*. New York: International Publishers.

—— 1971. *Selections from the Prison Notebooks of Antonio Gramsci*, ed. Q. Hoare and G. N. Smith. New York: International Publishers.

Illich, Ivan. 1976. *Medical Nemesis*. New York: Pantheon.

Kleinman, Arthur, and Joan Kleinman. 1986. "Somatization: The Interconnections Among Culture, Depressive Experience, and Meanings of Pain." In *Culture and Depression*, ed. Arthur Kleinman and Bryon J. Good, 429–490. Berkeley and Los Angeles: University of California Press.

Lock, Margaret, and Pamela Dunk. 1987. "My Nerves Are Broken: The Communication of Suffering in a Greek Canadian Community." In *Health in Canadian Society*, ed. D. Coburn *et al.*, 295–313. Toronto: Fitzhenry and Whiteside.

Low, Setha. 1981. "The Meaning of Nervios." *Culture, Medicine, and Psychiatry* 5:350–357.

Mauss, Marcel. 1950. "The Notion of Body Techniques." In *Sociology and Psychology: Essays*, 97–119. London: Routledge and Kegan Paul.

Parsons, Talcott, and Renée Fox. 1952. "Illness, Therapy, and the Modern Urban American Family." *Journal of Social Issues* 8:31–44.

Sacks, Oliver. 1984. *A Leg to Stand On*. New York: Summit.

—— 1985. *The Man Who Mistook His Wife for a Hat*. New York: Simon and Schuster.

Strauss, Erwin. 1966. "Upright Posture." In *Phenomenological Psychology: The Selected Papers of Erwin W. Strauss*, 137–165. New York: Basic Books.

Taussig, Michael. 1978. "Nutrition, Development, and Foreign Aid." *International Journal of Health Services* 8 (1):101–121.

—— 1989a. "The Nervous System, Part I: Homesickness and Data." *Kroeber Anthropological Society Papers*, nos. 69–70:32–61.

—— 1989b. "Terror as Usual." *Social Text* (Fall–Winter):3–20.

Weber, Max. 1944. "Charismatic Authority" and "Routinization of Charisma." In *Max Weber: The Theory of Social and Economic Organization*, ed. A. M. Henderson and Talcott Parsons, 358–386. New York: Oxford University Press.

INDEX